THE PENGUIN CLASSICS

FOUNDER EDITOR (1944–64): E. V. RIEU

EDITOR: *Betty Radice*

EURIPIDES was an Athenian born in 484 B.C. A member of a family of considerable rank, he disliked performing the public duties expected of him, preferring a life of introspection. Such a man was likely to win only grudging admiration and little popularity, and during fifty years' writing of plays for the festivals of Dionysus he was awarded the prize only four or five times. His unpopularity seems to have come to a head towards the end of his life in some way unknown to us, and he went into voluntary exile at the court of Archelaus, king of Macedon; it was during these last months that he wrote what many consider his greatest work, *The Bacchae*. When news of his death reached Athens in 407 Sophocles appeared publicly in mourning for him. Euripides is thought to have written about ninety-two plays, of which seventeen known to be his survive. All of these are now available in the Penguin Classics.

PHILIP VELLACOTT is the translator of seven volumes for the Penguin Classics; these are works by Aeschylus, Euripides, Menander and Theophrastus. He was educated at St Paul's School and Magdalene College, Cambridge, and for twenty-five years he taught classics (and drama for twelve years) at Dulwich College. He has lectured on Greek drama on two tours in the U.S.A. and from 1967 to 1968 he was Visiting Lecturer at the University of California at Santa Cruz. Philip Vellacott, who is married, is also the author of several plays, mostly on Greek subjects, and *Ordinary Latin* (1962), a somewhat revolutionary teaching text-book.

EURIPIDES

ORESTES

AND OTHER
PLAYS

THE CHILDREN OF HERACLES
ANDROMACHE
THE SUPPLIANT WOMEN
THE PHOENICIAN WOMEN
ORESTES
IPHIGENIA IN AULIS

*

TRANSLATED
WITH AN INTRODUCTION BY
PHILIP VELLACOTT

PENGUIN BOOKS

Penguin Books Ltd, Harmondsworth, Middlesex, England
Penguin Books, 625 Madison Avenue, New York, New York 10022, U.S.A.
Penguin Books Australia Ltd, Ringwood, Victoria, Australia
Penguin Books Canada Ltd, 2801 John Street, Markham, Ontario, Canada L3R 1B4
Penguin Books (N.Z.) Ltd, 182–190 Wairau Road, Auckland 10, New Zealand

—

This translation first published 1972
Reprinted 1980
Copyright © Philip Vellacott, 1972
All rights reserved

—

Made and printed in Great Britain
by Hazell Watson & Viney Ltd,
Aylesbury, Bucks
Set in Monotype Perpetua

—

The terms for the performance of these plays
may be obtained from the League of Dramatists,
84 Drayton Gardens, London SW10,
to whom all applications for permission should be made

CONTENTS

INTRODUCTION

THE six plays in this volume span the last twenty-four years of Euripides' career, from the age of fifty to his death. They are all tragic in tone, though none of them corresponds to any definition of tragedy such as would include more 'orthodox' tragedies like *Medea*, *Hippolytus*, and *The Bacchae*. In the accounts offered of these plays it will be suggested that the legendary situations and characters described are in many cases analogous to contemporary Athenian politics. This is not to contend that the whole purpose of these plays was political; for a large part of the audience their prime interest was that of dramatic entertainment. The political and moral significances were there for those who would to observe and consider; and to us their truth may well appear timeless. Above all, in every play there is the universal quality of a comment on human life presented as a work of art. In some plays it can be called the art of tragedy, in others not; but the line is difficult to draw. The universal aspect of these plays is something that each reader will be able, in the degree appropriate to himself, to perceive and evaluate; it does not need to be always pointed out. The particular relation of each play to issues of the time needs some exposition; but the attention given to this aspect should not induce the reader to think it more important than the universal aspect, which is concerned with the artistic statement of philosophic truths. A play can be both a tract and a tragedy, and everyone who goes to a theatre has the right to say what he finds there. Some of these six have strong melodramatic elements; but merely to class them as melodramas says nothing about them worth saying. All are based on the traditional cycles of heroic legend. They differ widely in both form and content; interpretation of them has also been varied. They contain some of Euripides' finest poetic and dramatic writing. They have in common one dominant concern, one pervading method, and one persistent message.

The dominant concern is the war between the Athenians and the Spartans which began in 431 B.C. and ended in 404 with the total defeat of Athens and the demolition of her defences. The plays appear here in their chronological order, and the first three belong to the first decade of the war, when Athenian confidence remained high. From 421 to 418 there was a partial and uneasy peace which gave both sides time to recover their energy before beginning again. In 416 the Athenians annihilated the small island state of Melos, killing all the men and selling the women and children as slaves; this ferocious act (and it was not the first such act of which Athens had been guilty) inspired Euripides to write *The Women of Troy*, which he produced the following spring when a large Athenian army and fleet was about to set sail against Syracuse. This Sicilian expedition, the greatest ever undertaken by any Greek state, ended in 413 with the destruction of the entire Athenian army and fleet; a blow from which Athens never recovered. The last three plays in this book were produced in 409, 408, and 405; and they are overshadowed by the prospect of the final defeat of Athens which grew steadily more certain.

From the beginning there was in Athens a political faction opposed to the war. The Athenian constitution safeguarded free speech; and this right was no formal pretence, as is evident from the outspoken ridicule which Aristophanes poured, at the public expense, upon leading politicians and generals. But the position of the tragic dramatist was, if he cared to use it, one of special power. In Aristophanes' *Frogs* Dionysus makes it clear that Athenians looked to the poets for wise guidance on matters affecting the welfare of the city; they came to the theatre, not merely for entertainment or for intellectual and emotional stimulus, but for instruction; and having received it, if they did not like it, they might well be hostile to the man who offered it. Euripides knew that the war was a constant preoccupation with most of his audience, and increasingly so as the years passed. In the first three plays in this book he examines the ethics of war, studies the effects of war upon public and private life, pictures the attitudes – some heroic and others contemptible – which war encourages; he scrutinizes the ideologies which foster and excuse war; and insists that war does not alter the truth that revenge is wrong and mercy is compatible with military valour. In the last three plays he is addressing citizens who do not remember how or why the war began, who are still fighting because they cannot stop, and who in despair have lost both reason and morality. The dramatist, like his fellow-citizens, has the right of free speech; but to exercise it is for him more dangerous. He must find a method which will not provoke his hearers to silence him out of hand.

The pervading method which Euripides used in these plays was irony. Of course the speeches and actions were taken at their face-value by a large part of his audience; they have been so taken by many students of Euripides in modern times, and perhaps that is one reason why these six ironical plays all find themselves together in the last volume. The tragic poet had a duty to this large group of his fellow-citizens, as to the rest; but his truer thought was for those who expected from him a prophetic message, a statement of unpalatable truth, a reminder of moral principle. To these spectators he offered a mirror of the city of Athens with its varied types of citizen: the fire-eating patriot, the doctrinaire democrat, the broad-minded legalist, the young and the old each blaming the other. Comparisons are not laboured, and in the heat of performance will often be missed. Characters such as Peleus and Achilles are offered without overt comment, so that listener or reader may judge them for himself.

Irony is saying one thing and meaning something else. Since in drama the author speaks through the mouths of others, an indirectness of address to his audience is a necessary quality of his language. To understand meaning we must note not only what is said, but who says it, and to whom. Both Aeschylus and Sophocles used such irony on occasion; though for neither of them was it so essential to his main purpose as it was to Euripides. For example, why has it so seldom been perceived* that in *Agamemnon* Aeschylus presented the expedition against Troy as a wilful act of wickedness on a huge scale? Because in 458 B.C. it was natural for an Athenian audience to identify Troy with Persia the national enemy, and condemnation of Agamemnon was therefore not acceptable and had to be suggested subtly. So Euripides too has to address both the subtle and the dull. Irony is the filter which separates the various messages for their appropriate recipients; yet among the subtle there will be those who welcome what they hear and those who resent it. A fine example of Euripides' irony is found in *Orestes* 1131 ff., where Pylades addresses the audience in a shameless justification of his plan to murder Helen; here the dramatist points a finger at the ordinary citizen and says, 'This is the sort of speech to which you respond with your applause and your vote.' It was the hidden power of such irony that made ordinary citizens ready to hate Euripides; they were never sure when he was using irony and when he was not; when it was safer to applaud, to laugh, or to be indignant.

The persistent message was twofold. Its first clause was: Revenge is always folly. Thucydides the historian noted early in his work that this war was remarkable for the enormity of the revenges taken by men and cities upon their fellow-Greeks. Every one of these plays includes revenge in its pattern. Ever since Homeric times Greeks had been cruel, deceitful, aggressive, and treacherous; and yet had never lost their passionate sense of justice. To abandon revenge when one had been wronged was to deny one's own sense of justice and to encourage further injustice, as well as to lose face. Euripides insisted on trying to teach this hardest of all lessons to men who knew

* Until Kitto made the point clear in *Form and Meaning in Drama*, Chapter 1.

that they needed to learn it and were still determined not to learn; he was a conscience whose voice they wanted to hear, could not ignore, and would not obey.

By the time we reach the second group of plays the poet's message has a second clause. Not only is all revenge folly, but this particular war is a raging insanity which corrupts men and is destroying both Athens and her enemies. In the earlier plays we saw battles fought and won for just causes; in *Andromache* there is ironical reflection both on war and on what men say about war. But twelve years later the tone has changed to utter condemnation. In *The Phoenician Women* there is the eloquent second Stasimon beginning 'O Ares, bringer of agonized exhaustion . . .', and much else equally powerful; in *Orestes* the 'hero' in his insanity is a symbol of the whole fighting population of Hellas and of Athens in particular, and the theme of the play is that this insanity is incurable and infectious; while in *Iphigenia in Aulis* the theme of madness is repeated, but reinforced at many points by an unholy alliance of corruption, cowardice, stupidity, selfishness and mob-hysteria to oppress innocence at Aulis and extinguish a nation at Troy; and the whole expedition is presented as a pageant of bungling and brutal deception quite unconnected with its professed aims, suspect in its motives and barbarous in its objectives. The words and actions of heroes like Agamemnon and Achilles prompt the Chorus to a despairing question:

> Where now can the clear face of goodness,
> Where can virtue itself live by its own strength? –
> When ruthless disregard holds power,
> When men, forgetting they are mortal,
> Tread down goodness and ignore it,
> When lawlessness overrules law,
> When the terror of God no longer draws men together
> Trembling at the reward of wickedness?

This method and this message, then, were presented to those few whose ears were alert for every subtlety, men for whom

Euripides voiced their most passionate beliefs, their most pro-
found despair; of them we can only surmise that they received
in these performances a more complete and articulate message
from their spiritual prophet than our most imaginative interpretation can suggest. A message conveyed in a work of art
makes the profounder impact because the receiver must work
it out for himself; the ironical method leaves the wording to the
listener, and is an economical method of putting into two lines
what will take a page to interpret. For example: Why must
helpless and usually innocent people always suffer for the insane follies of men? – a question echoing from century to
century since wars began. Orestes offers – by the use of the
dramatic mirror – a clue to the answer, when, with his fine
gesture of heroic resolve, he says (*Orestes* 1167 ff.),

> I am the son of Agamemnon . . . whom I will not shame
> By a slave's death, but breathe my last like a free man . . .

and the noble act of freedom he is about to undertake, to win
his revenge, is the pointless cold-blooded murder of a helpless
woman.

One other theme calls for general notice before we proceed
to the particular study of each play. Ancient Greek myth contained many stories of father and son – Achilles and Neoptolemus, Oedipus and Eteocles, Agamemnon and Orestes. It is
clear that Greeks of the fifth century were vividly aware of the
actions and character of recent generations; and it is natural
that a contrast between a father and son of the heroic age
should be used in the theatre to illustrate a contrast between
two generations of the contemporary scene. In the earliest of
these plays, *The Children of Heracles*, a central figure is Demophon, son of the great Theseus. Theseus is dead, but his generation of Athenians is represented by a Chorus of Elders. They
could well have been Elders of Athens, but in fact they belong
to a rather remote townlet of Attica called Marathon. That
name has only one meaning for this audience; it recalls the

year 490 B.C. and the defeat of the first great Persian invasion
by a small Athenian army, in the glowing days of the infant
democracy. So in this play, produced near the beginning of the
Peloponnesian War, the past heroic age to which men look back
is the period of Athens' early greatness in the years of Marathon
and Salamis; and the second-rate Demophon stands for the
present-day Athenian. (The probability that most of Euripides'
audience did not realize he was second-rate is supported by the
curious fact that many modern students, suspending not only
disbelief but also disapproval, have not realized it either.)
Twenty years later, in the passage from *Orestes* quoted above,
the dead Agamemnon is spoken of by his degenerate son in
terms which suggest a reference to Pericles, who died of the
plague in 429. In the last stage of the war the bankruptcy of
conscience and the loss of hope made men look back with envy
to the confidence and the still respectable democratic principle
on which the enterprises of twenty years before had been
based; and the present generation is represented by a young
man – sick, enfeebled, guilty, and going mad. A still more
pessimistic picture of the succession of generations is found in
the final scene of *The Suppliant Women*; here the fathers are the
dead chiefs whose bodies Theseus has recovered from the
battlefield near Thebes, and their young sons form a kind of
second Chorus. After a clear distinction has been established
between a justified war and an unjustified one, after the folly of
revenge has been exposed and punished, and the needless
suffering caused has been shown in its most poignant aspect, the
new generation of aspirant soldiers arrives, still too young to
hold a sword, but already full of ardent desire for the time
when they too will be old enough to win glory by committing,
for the sake of revenge, every folly, wickedness, and cruelty
which the successive scenes of the play have condemned.

The interpretation of analogy in a dramatic work is full of
hazards. Modern dramatists are apt to disconcert enthusiastic
expounders by denying that their play was written to convey

any message at all; and in the study of Greek drama, though commentators often find references to a particular event or person (e.g., to Alcibiades in *The Suppliant Women* 190–91), they are much more cautious in recognizing symbols of some general situation or moral attitude belonging to the period when the play was written. Of these two kinds of reference, the latter is certainly the more valuable, if correctly perceived; and this caution, though right in principle, may well have been exaggerated. Everyone who has read any Plato knows how often, and to our minds how unconvincingly, Socrates uses the argument from analogy. Oracles from Delphi or elsewhere would, more often than not, be expressed in symbolic terms, like the oracle given to Adrastus (*The Suppliant Women*). In intellectual discourse among the ancient Greeks analogy and symbol seem to have held a natural and constant place. So in these plays, when we contemplate a king undertaking a just war but refusing mere revenge; a king embarrassed by refugees; a king using people as pawns in political intrigue; a city besieged by a ring of enemies; an ancient royal house collapsing to extinction as its surviving members, made desperate by their own crimes, sink to murderous insanity; and in several plays a clearly noted decline from an heroic age to one of unprincipled expediency and ignominious failure; how are we to believe that the author's theme was not, first and last, for those who would understand him, the city of Athens and the war which absorbed her energies and her thought throughout this period? Viewed in this light, these plays become a moral and political statement unique in the ancient world, and prophetically relevant in our own.

THE CHILDREN OF HERACLES

Some important parts of this play are missing; and the design of the whole can perhaps not now be re-discovered. At a superficial glance we observe, as in some other plays, a second half of the action apparently bearing only a partial relation to the first half; Demophon and Macaria forgotten, Iolaus laughed off; Alcmene (after a pointless appearance in the first half) holding the centre of the stage, while Hyllus, of whose movements and exploits we have been kept informed, never appears after all. There is no hero or heroine, no fateful choice, no unfolding of past mystery, no progress from cause to effect. The theme is war, and what is said about it is addressed to the people of Athens. The loss of lines (or possibly of a whole scene or more) is more serious in this case than in either *Iphigenia in Aulis* or *The Suppliant Women*. Some important questions remain unanswered, e.g., Was Macaria mentioned again, and was she in fact killed? Did Demophon reappear, and what did he say? Was Eurystheus put to death? Did Hyllus have a part? Did Heracles speak *ex machina*? To possess the full text would clarify for us the dramatic principles whose use Euripides was exploring here; but what our incomplete text tells us about his meaning, his 'lesson' ('the dramatic poet is the teacher of the citizens', says Aristophanes in *The Frogs*), is both clear and valuable enough to give this play a worthy place among the poet's surviving works.

The matter of the play as we have it comprises five main elements. First, the moral question of the obligations of a city towards refugees from other cities who come to seek asylum. Secondly, the moral question of the treatment of prisoners of war. The phrase 'the common laws of Hellas' occurs in 1010, and in the second fragment, and by implication in 458–60; and it clearly refers to these two issues, and perhaps to others as well. Thirdly, the concept of sacrifice in relation to war. Fourthly, the question of a city's obedience to a *chrésmos*, oracle. This is a matter which Euripides dealt with more emphatically a few years later in *The Suppliant Women*; here the 'lesson' is left for the intelligent to perceive. Fifthly, we have the theme of the unwisdom and unworthiness of revenge as a motive for action — again a theme treated more fully and specifically in *The Suppliant Women*.

Euripides was a patriot; he longed for Athens to be true to her own best ideals and to provide for the rest of Hellas an example of just and reasonable behaviour. No doubt he wished also that Athens might win the war against Sparta, or at least conclude an honourable peace. But in all his eight surviving plays on the theme of war, his message to his fellow-citizens is: Look at yourselves as you are, see your motives and your aims as they are; do not lose sight of peace as the end for which war is undertaken. This play, like the last three plays in this volume, is a mirror held up to the political life of wartime Athens. It shows the degeneration of the war-spirit. It begins with a leader (Demophon) who accepts a challenge, and a woman who makes a heroic sacrifice; the background is the tradition of Marathon. As events proceed, dramatic interest is transferred from moral issues to the prospect of revenge; the integrity of the leader falls under doubt as superstition corrupts principle; the heroic sacrifice is entirely forgotten and may even have proved unnecessary; while the tradition of Marathon, though it upholds principle through most of the action, seems to succumb finally to the insistence of mere revenge. The method Euripides uses for pointing out the character of this degeneration reminds us of a pattern used in *Alcestis*, where as the music of the funeral procession dies away it is mingled with the drunken singing of Heracles, and a scene of comedy follows; here the solemnity of Macaria's departure is separated only by a short Ode from the comedy of the jocular servant, the deaf old virago, and the senile warrior. The pattern is similar to that of *Alcestis*, but here its purpose is more serious and more urgently topical. This play is addressed to a nation already in danger of losing its soul in a war which after three agonizing years is beginning to take over the national life and remould it in its own shape.

The date of production is generally thought to have been not later than 427 B.C., four years after the beginning of the war with Sparta. Among the many exciting and distressing experiences of those years was one series of events which, to judge by the feeling, and the fullness, with which Thucydides describes them in the second and third books of his History, made a deep impression on the minds of Athenians; this was the fate of the small city of Plataea. Plataea, always afraid of domination by the powerful state of Thebes, an uncomfortably near neighbour, had been a close ally of Athens since 520 B.C.; and at the time of Marathon their entire fighting force of a thousand men had come, alone among the Greek states, to share with the Athenians the danger and the glory of facing the Persian invaders. The story of how the whole war began in 431 with a Theban attempt to take over Plataea; of the cold-blooded slaughter by the Plataeans of 180 Theban prisoners; of Plataean loyalty to the Athenian alliance, and the failure of Athens to do anything to help Plataea; of the long and desperate siege, the escape of half the garrison, the final surrender of the others, the mockery of a trial, and the cold-blooded slaughter of the 200 Plataean prisoners who were the last remnant of a city-state – all this must be read in Thucydides, who ends his account in these words, surely pregnant with the guilt felt by honourable Athenians: 'Such was the end of Plataea, in the ninety-third year after she became the ally of Athens.' (III, 68 fin.) At the beginning of hostilities all the women and children of Plataea had been sent for safety to Athens, in anticipation of a hard siege; and the appeals for help made by the Plataeans, which came repeatedly before the Athenian Assembly, must have been emotionally reinforced not only by the memory of Marathon, but also by the presence in the city of this numerous and pathetic crowd of refugees, whose numbers were subsequently increased by the arrival of some 200 men who had escaped from the besieged city.

When we see that at least three out of the five main elements in this play provide analogies to the situation existing between

Athens and Plataea at the time when this play was being written, it is reasonable to surmise that here Euripides is offering,
to those who will accept it, a poet's comment on contemporary
politics as acutely critical as the specific comment made by the
historian. The similarity of tone, which can be felt in the
speech of the Argive Herald (134–78), to that of the speeches
of the Corcyrean and the Corinthian envoys in Athens in 432
B.C. (Thucydides I, 32–44), further strengthens our impression
that in this play the poet is using an ancient legend to present a
contemporary scene full of pains and dilemmas all too familiar.
The atmosphere is that of the fifth century rather than the
thirteenth – as the treatment of Iolaus' miracle later confirms.
Into this modern atmosphere the dramatist intrudes elements
from the heroic tradition of the distant or legendary past – the
human sacrifice, the memories of Heracles and of Theseus, the
miraculous rejuvenation; and of the recent past – the tradition
of Marathon as embodied in the Elders; by these contrasts the
reality of the degenerate present, and the criticism of it implied
in the action, are made the more vivid. The Peloponnesian War
was, in many of its manifestations, a civil war dividing town
after town into mutually murderous factions; so it was not only
in Athens that groups of refugees were to be heard urging one
request, 'Not to be handed over' (97), and not only Plataeans
or Spartans who could massacre prisoners.

  The only person in the play who is a 'character' in the usual
theatrical sense is, as far as our text shows us, Demophon; and
the fact that we know nothing of his appearance (if any) after
the battle is a serious hindrance to our understanding of the
whole play. Certain things, however, are clear about him. He
is the son and heir of the hero Theseus; and we are directed to
compare him critically with his father, by his pronouncement
of the Hellenic code (130–31), and his assumption of the
heroic role (236–52); but particularly by Iolaus' words
(324–28):

You're no less
A man than Theseus! It's a rare thing nowadays
When quality begets its like; you'd hardly find
One in a score who's not a worse man than his father.

Demophon, having decided to meet Argos in the field, goes off
to mobilize his army. Part of the routine preparation for battle
was the strict performance of conventional sacrifice; but
Demophon does more. He 'assembled all the chanters of
oracles, and questioned them about ancient predictions'. Why
did he do this? Does Euripides indicate to us any possible
motive? It is certain that research into ancient predictions
could be relied upon to produce, if required, strong reasons for
not doing almost anything. Demophon was, as he himself
assures us, 'most anxious, as you see, to help . . .' (410); but
one is not one's own master. Only five lines later he mentions
'angry gatherings' of citizens; in 473 he says, 'These oracles
terrify me'; in 421-2 he lists the three equal considerations
which must govern his decision: 'your lives, this country, and
my good name'. The trend of all this is not yet quite clear,
though it leaves an unfortunate impression. One question needs
to be determined: How does Euripides intend us to react to
Demophon's report about these 'oracles'? Are we to call them
'savage superstition to be rejected by any Hellene'? or 'an
inscrutable expression of divine will'?

The answer is offered subtly in the latter part of Demophon's
speech, 410–24, where the tone of a weak man feeling his way
towards the breaking of a promise is painfully recognizable.
When he speaks of 'angry gatherings', the irony is that the
citizens direct their anger, not against the folly of heeding
'ancient predictions', but to the issue of the treatment of
suppliants, on which matter there ought to be no dispute, since
there is a clear and accepted 'common law of Hellas'. What
indeed is the function of a king such as Demophon, if not to
make a firm decision when some of his subjects want to break
the Hellenic code because of risks involved, and are ready to

resort to civil war to get their own way? To throw the decision back to the refugees is hardly less than shameful; though we to-day know as well as Euripides knew, that it is the most familiar of all official reactions. Demophon has already referred (130) to the difference between Greek and barbarian standards of be-haviour; and his second allusion (423-4) shows that the kind of democracy which abandons all claim to authority is no better than monarchy: 'I shall receive fair treatment if I give it' – a statement which may be suspected of meaning, 'I shall be obeyed so long as I please everybody'. Demophon does not once question the validity of the oracles upon which he proposes to act.

The Elders of Marathon, however, question it indignantly. 'Does a god really forbid this city to help refugees when it is eager to do so?' A question to be asked; but Iolaus, seeing that Demophon does not intend to ask or to answer it, realistically accepts the situation. 'We shall die, children; yes, we shall be handed over.' A little later (494), in speaking to Macaria, he says plainly that the king of Athens is screening his shameful decision behind words which obscure their meaning. It is natural for us, if we take the hint from Iolaus, to wonder whether Demophon began searching into 'ancient predictions' only when 'angry gatherings' had shown that it would be diffi-cult to carry the citizens with him in his decision to help the refugees. The Elders, after listening to Iolaus, beg him not to blame Athens, in words which surely imply that the king alone is to blame; and add that the mere suggestion – even though false – that Athens could hand over the suppliants is a disgrace.

In this play, then, the folly of heeding 'chanters of oracles' is attacked with subtlety. A more direct attack was made a few years later in *The Suppliant Women* (see pages 197-8), where we find the propriety of observing conventional sacrifices before a battle contrasted with the folly of trying to interpret an enig-matic oracle. But the clearest indication of what Euripides intended us to think about Demophon's 'oracles' is simply their content: the ritual murder of a human being. The most celebrated instance of this particular crime had already been dealt with by Aeschylus; the *Oresteia*, without trying to account for the oracle produced by Calchas, shows the sacrifice of Iphigenia as a criminal pollution which made the death of Agamemnon inevitable. The plays of Euripides express the same total condemnation in the case of Iphigenia (*Iphigenia in Tauris, Iphigenia in Aulis*) and of Polyxena (*Hecabe, Women of Troy*). Both were cases of an 'oracle' gaining authority by appeal to the superstition of an army which its commanders were afraid to command. Fifteen years after Euripides wrote this play, the Athenian army in Sicily lost its last hope of escape through a superstitious belief about the new moon – the issue was a live one. In the cases of Iphigenia and Polyxena the oracle named the required victim and promised specific benefits in return for the sacrifice; in *The Children of Heracles* the oracles quoted as authority by Demophon were 'ancient predictions' (405) having no reference to the present need, and demanding vaguely 'the maiden daughter of a noble father'. When Iolaus recognizes at once that this is simply Demophon's way of withdrawing from his promise, it is natural to suppose that Euripides intended at least some of his audience to draw the same conclusion.

In every war sacrifices are demanded from, and sometimes freely offered by, those who cannot make any contribution to the operations of force. Such sacrifices are accepted with emotional terms of praise; their moral value may indeed be appreciated at the time; but, whether or not they afterwards prove to have been necessary, or profitable, they are apt to be forgotten even by those who praise them most. We may perhaps acquit Demophon (since he, after all, belongs to the fifth century; it was his father Theseus who belonged to the heroic thirteenth) of any notion that a girl would in fact be selected and killed; what he wanted was to avoid fighting the Argives against the wishes of his citizens. Macaria, who at fifteen is an

experienced refugee, sees the situation as clearly as Iolaus: here
is a vacillating king who must be made to fight, if Heracles'
family is to survive. Her immediate response calls his bluff. He
is given thirty-one lines of silence, during which he can recover
composure and turn his shame into resolution. Macaria speaks
to Iolaus and to her brothers; not a word to Demophon.

Macaria's departure is followed by a short choral ode in
which the Elders speak of the power of destiny and the glory of
an heroic death; Demophon is not mentioned. The following
scene introduces a new character, a Servant of Hyllus; and an
entirely new note, that of ironic comedy, which persists until
the end of the episode and tends to recur in subsequent scenes
when the Servant is on stage. The next episode, 784–891, is
mainly occupied with the report of the battle; and the last
episode of our text is devoted to Alcmene and the captured
Eurystheus, and to the question whether it is right to kill
prisoners of war. In the play as we have it, after Macaria's departure neither she nor Demophon is mentioned again. It is
generally assumed that after the end of the second Stasimon,
629, a long passage has been lost, containing some account of
the sacrifice of Macaria and a lyrical *kommos*, or mourning anti-
phony, between Alcmene and the Chorus; and in so far as the
analogy with other plays is a sound argument, this seems likely.
On the other hand, when the MS resumes at 630, the Servant
enters with the news that 'Hyllus has returned'; Iolaus speaks
of the 'anguished suspense' with which Alcmene had been
awaiting him; and the Servant adds that Hyllus has brought 'a
strong force' to fight on the side of Athens. Will Hyllus stand
and see his sister's throat cut in obedience to vague 'ancient
predictions'? The sacrifice was demanded ostensibly to strengthen the chances of Athens in battle against Argos (491); and
now Hyllus brings a strong force to aid Athens, and later is
himself prominent in the battle (843). Logic, then, would suggest that perhaps Macaria was not killed after all; that instead
of an account of her death, the missing passage told how Hyllus,

hearing of the proposed sacrifice, had arrived in time to stop it, and had promised to bring an army to aid Athens in the battle. This would explain some of the Servant's dialogue first with Iolaus and then with Alcmene, would account for the absence of reference to Macaria's death, and would supply a neat end to the argument about the validity of out-of-date oracles; further, this supposition would make it easier to accept the farcical nature of the Servant–Iolaus dialogue, and would also make it possible – later in the play, in another lost passage – for Demophon to reappear, not as the murderer of Macaria but as her deliverer. Since an incomplete play can hardly be discussed at all without some speculation, this outline seems at least as plausible as any other.

An interesting feature of this play is the example it provides of Euripides' originality in the use of character as a part of dramatic structure. The drama is written to make an urgent comment on current affairs; it is addressed to the poet's fellow-citizens, who are inheritors of an heroic tradition. The only real 'character' is Demophon, the heir of the traditional hero Theseus; and the other persons are of interest chiefly as they relate to him and to the city he represents. Iolaus is merely a type, the hero in decay. In himself he is a bore (e.g., 'I too have been irked by excessive praise', 203–4), and capable of insensitive foolishness (543–5); he condemns the oracle as wicked, but thinks it necessary to obey. His function is to recall Heracles and the glories of the heroic age, and to cast a clear light on the degeneracy of Demophon. When he has done that, he first begins his abdication by declining to stand beside Macaria at the altar, and then is allowed, as Kitto says (*Greek Tragedy*, p. 254), to ride 'clean out of the play into fairyland'. Macaria too has only one function, to take Demophon at his word and suggest that the heroic spirit is not dead among civilian populations caught in the ruthless processes of the Peloponnesian War; she comes from nowhere, makes her swift decision, and vanishes. The Herald is a mouthpiece (with a much thinner part than his opposite number in *The Suppliant Women*); the Servant is a refreshing stooge. Alcmene (so far as her part has survived) is little more than a spirit of revenge, disowned by the Elders of Marathon. Eurystheus is the guilty victim, brought on stage to deny that guilt justifies the ultimate reprisal (the Plataeans whom the Spartans massacred were guilty of the same crime). All these persons simply fulfil their functions and are given no chance to divert our attention from the one person whose character and destiny must be affected by their decisions and actions.

Demophon in his first scene shows a dignity and courageous justice fully worthy of Theseus, and Iolaus praises him as the equal of his father. The next scene shows him without authority, or resolution, or pride, admitting that in face of the oracles he 'does not know what to do and is full of fear'. It is cruelly plain that here is 'a worse man than his father' (328). The Elders are taken aback; Iolaus is without illusion, and so is Macaria. One virtue left to Demophon is that he is deeply moved by Macaria's response; the other is that he will, after all (whether with or without the sacrifice, we do not know), fight bravely and win the battle. But will he also win back his integrity? Unhappily we have lost the last appearance of the one character for whose sake the play is written.

For Demophon is the poet's Athens, as she was in 427 B.C.; and the play is about Athens, and what is happening to her after the first few years of war and plague. To nerve her for the supreme military effort she was now making, the idealist tradition of Marathon had, we cannot doubt, been strenuously and incessantly invoked. This tradition is represented by the Chorus; and the poet confronts it with two challenges: the treatment of refugees and the treatment of prisoners. The Elders are meticulous in small points – they remonstrate against violence to a herald even when used to prevent the violation of an altar. They respect nobility of descent (235), and believe in judicial fairness (180). But they are also clear on the main issues. They tell Copreus that Justice is holy and will not allow suppliants to be dragged from an altar. They hold it the duty of Athenians 'to help the helpless' (329–30). Their sound instinct protests at Demophon's oracle because its content is against their tradition. They tell Alcmene bluntly that she is not to kill the prisoner. They love Athens both for her virtue and for her beauty (first Stasimon). They give an indirect but clear rebuke to Demophon (461–3) for retracting his promise. In the end they accept the fact that Macaria has honoured her father and Demophon has not honoured his; and since they belong to a less cynical generation they bid Iolaus 'endure the will of heaven'. They urge Athenians to find their destiny in 'the path of fairness' (901), warn them against 'a relentless nature, obsessive hatred' (926–7), and argue firmly against Alcmene's determination to kill Eurystheus. It seems most unlikely that the vagueness of 1053, 'I hold the same opinion', is in fact the Chorus finally agreeing with Alcmene. These Elders everywhere else represent Athens as she has been and still may be, the champion of the Hellenic code of *sōphrosyne*, controlled behaviour. Athens as she actually was after four years of war and two of plague, is represented in part by Alcmene – the heroic tradition turned sour and harsh, in part by the Servant – the unreflecting common man, and in part by Demophon – the energy of youth weakened by want of principle. Alcmene is at first clearly comedic (her conversation with Iolaus suggests that she is hard of hearing), and later sinister in her bloodthirsty persistence. Demophon is at first admirable, later lamentable; loss of his third appearance hides from us perhaps the most important thing that Euripides had to express in this play. But it is at least possible that the king's final scene reflected some degree of hope for the moral integrity of the Athenian state; it was, after all, early in the war.

Two of the fragments refer to the virtue of reverencing one's parents. The two parents involved in the play, through their sons, are Theseus and Heracles (Alcmene hardly qualifies for reverence). The second fragment also mentions 'the common laws of Hellas'; the lines might well be spoken *ex machina* by Heracles to Hyllus near the end of the play; but there is too little evidence for speculation to be interesting.

ANDROMACHE

The exact date of this play is uncertain; it is generally agreed to lie between 430 and 424 B.C.; 427 or 426 is a reasonable guess, and consonant with one important passage in the text. The question, What is the play about? is of special interest, because hitherto no satisfactory answer has been generally accepted.

The statement, frequently met, that this play is primarily an expression of patriotic indignation against the Spartans, can hardly be regarded as tenable. To begin with, it is strange that anyone familiar with the general thought of Euripides could believe, without cogent evidence, that he would write a play designed to voice a simplified wartime emotion of this kind; since other plays, and other parts of this play, demonstrate specifically that such emotions are no more simple than the situations which give rise to them. The inveterate and destructive Greek pastime of 'laying the blame' is satirized here as it is in other plays; while the judgement of people by categories and nationalities is an attitude condemned by almost every extant play of this author. Secondly, of the two Spartan characters, Menelaus and Hermione, though the one is certainly a villain, the other is no less certainly a victim both of Menelaus and of Orestes; while if Menelaus and Orestes divide between them the villainy of the piece, probably the heavier share goes to Orestes, who belongs not to Sparta but to Argos. Thirdly, there are two broadside attacks on the Spartan character, one by Andromache at the end of the second episode, and one by Peleus in the third. Of these, the former is evidently a serious

statement, and we shall consider its possible reference presently; the latter is ironical comedy designed to ridicule the fire-
eating patriot to whom any fatuity is a good enough weapon
for abusing the national enemy, and to ridicule no less the
ordinary member of the Athenian Assembly who would listen
without protest to this kind of nonsense. If Euripides had
wanted to write a play to work up war-fever against the
Spartans (and a play was not needed to do that) he would have
pursued his purpose more efficiently.

What, then, is the theme of *Andromache*? It combines two of
this poet's life-long preoccupations. The one great tragedy
extant from his pre-war work, *Medea*, gives us an intense treatment of the position of woman in a purely man-made society;
the last three plays in this book are examples of his ultimate
condemnation of the war in which Athens was engaged. In
Andromache, written when the war had run one fifth of its
course, we have the position of women in Greek society presented against the background of war, and shown in its exact
relation to war, as one of war's most unworthy and destructive
results.

The first sentence of the play introduces the economic aspect
of the problem: Andromache came to Hector of Troy with a
large dowry. Hermione's opening lines illuminate the same
aspect from another angle. (Medea in her first scene had drawn
the picture in realistic detail; Hippolytus had described it from
the point of view of the exasperated male.) Both Andromache
and Menelaus in their opposed speeches contribute to the
statement of the problem; so, from time to time, do the Chorus, as upholders of traditional values. The callous treatment of
Hermione by her father (which shatters her, but which she
hardly condemns at all), and her terror of her husband's anger,
provide further colour and background; while her pathetic
picture of the poisoned malice which this inhuman treatment
produces in an average group of wives chatting together, com-
pletes the dramatist's presentation of what his civilized

Hellenic cities do to one half of their free population. After we have seen Hermione hysterically threatening to kill Andromache, our condemnation of her is cancelled when we next see her – used as a pawn by her father, afraid that her husband will kill her, and finally blackmailed into total and willing submission by the terrifying Orestes, in his exit speech. The immortal Thetis could withdraw at will both from marriage with Peleus (which must have included its *longueurs*) and from social contact with the wretchedness of mortal women who were her neighbours; thus in the Epilogue her comfort is as cold as her charity, and fortunately neither woman is there to receive it. For Peleus the comfort is even colder; but romantic memory blindfolds him, and his devotion to accepted values makes him, in his last few lines, show his ultimately superficial nature (a thing not incongruous with physical valour) by reverting to the theme with which the Prologue opened – the economic aspect of marriage, the view of a wife as bringer of material advantage or disadvantage to her husband. This is the primary theme which constitutes the unity of a play usually criticized for lack of unity.

The secondary theme is war. The world which assigns to women such a degraded position derives its harsh and unjust character from the fact that the men who build and dominate it regard warfare and mutual slaughter as their paramount function. For some eighteen years the lives of four of the five main characters have been overshadowed by war. The women have been, in the one case, lonely and deprived, in the other, bereaved, brutally abused, and enslaved. The men have been demoralized and dehumanized and are unfit for any ordered society. Orestes was not old enough to fight at Troy; but war has nothing further to teach him, he is war's embodiment without any romantic trappings. As the first Stasimon shows, a quarrel between goddesses led to the war; and a world at war sets its female victims at war with each other. Once the unifying theme of the play is recognized, the close texture of its working-out from scene to scene cannot be missed.

Gilbert Murray, in the Preface to his Oxford Text of Euripides, says (in Latin): 'In my opinion Euripides needs more interpretation than emendation.' One theme in Euripides which needs constant interpretation is the theme of revenge, the question why Greeks were, and had been for as long as they could remember, obsessed with getting their own back, and more, for every injury.* *Andromache* is full of this theme: it was for revenge that Achilles killed Andromache's husband, that Menelaus burnt Troy, that Orestes killed Neoptolemus, and that Hermione wanted to have Andromache killed. The Messenger in his closing lines appeals to the audience to agree with him that 'to remember an ancient grievance' is the mark of an evil-hearted man, and no doubt most of them did agree, until the next time they became angry. The whole play shows, as the end-result of the tyrannous convention of revenge, an empty palace, and an 'old man's tears for his dead sons'. A corollary of the devotion to revenge is that the revenger must always find someone to blame for his sufferings; and a significant part of Euripides' attack on revengefulness is his satire on the search for a scapegoat. This line of satire is found in many plays, but this play contains the first appearance of the most notable instance of it. Andromache, in her elegiac song at the end of the Prologue, names Helen as the original cause of the Trojan War. Her speech replying to Hermione ends with a vicious insult involving Helen as Hermione's mother; and the repetition of this allusion in 248 is the line which seems most hurtful to Hermione. Andromache uses the same weapon yet again to put the finishing touch to her long speech to Menelaus (362). But Andromache's barbed allusions are mild beside the vituperations of Peleus (594 etc.) on the subject of Helen's

* Some of the answer is given in the stimulating chapter called 'Shame-Culture and Guilt-Culture', in *The Greeks and the Irrational*, by Professor E. R. Dodds.

wickedness. Several reflections follow from this curious harping on Helen, which seems out of place in this drama unless it is a part of the pattern which shows the sterility of hatred and condemnation. First, the Chorus in the first Stasimon find it just as reasonable (and a reflective listener may find it just as irrelevant) to blame Paris for the war and wish that he had been slaughtered in infancy. Next, the honourable attack on Sparta made by Andromache, and the ridiculous one made by Peleus, suggest that blaming Sparta for everything is as foolish as blaming Helen; cruelty and treachery are human diseases, and are found, and are to be condemned, in individuals like Menelaus and Orestes, whether from Sparta, Argos, or anywhere else. In several other plays, notably *The Women of Troy* (as a part of the action) and *Iphigenia in Tauris* (in a particularly vicious utterance by the Chorus), we find Euripides presenting without comment what was notoriously a popular commonplace, the notion that Helen was the prime cause of the suffering consequent on the war; and the climax to this series of ironies is found in *Orestes* (see pp. 70–1). If Euripides' constant repetitions of this vindictive theme are to be taken as seriously meant, they are banal and tedious, and the work of this author is less worthy of attention than is usually thought. If they are to be taken as an ironical comment on the tediousness of people who take such recriminations seriously, and on the foolishness of finding a scapegoat on whom hatred can be heaped, then these passages fill an appropriate place in the array of weapons with which Euripides conducts his persistent war on behalf of *sōphrosyne*, of forbearance and understanding.

The structure of *Andromache* is unique in one respect. In each successive scene from Prologue to Epilogue the interest of the audience, and the concern of every character, is constantly directed to the name and figure of a person who never appears, Neoptolemus. The story of the early death of Achilles' son was not perhaps among the best known of the ancient legends, but there is no reason to suppose that it was not known to a fair proportion of the audience. Those who knew it were likely to know also that he was said to have been murdered by Orestes at Delphi. So when in the Prologue we are told that Neoptolemus is already away at Delphi and that his return is urgently awaited, the thought that he may already be dead is at hand to lend dramatic colour to every phrase that voices reliance on his help. When Andromache points out to Menelaus the illogical absurdity of his plan to defend Hermione's marital position by killing Neoptolemus' son, and Menelaus, though full of shrewd self-interest, still pursues his illogical course, the quick-witted in the audience must surely suspect, not only that Neoptolemus is dead, but that Menelaus knows it. Anything said by Menelaus or by Orestes may be dismissed as evidence of what they are supposed to know about the facts; nothing is more obvious than that each of them is playing a secret game in which lies and deception are the essential method. On the other hand it is also clear that the naïve and superficial view of the plot accepted by most modern readers was similarly acceptable, first, to the large popular element in the first audience, and in the next few centuries to generations of scholars whose comments on many ancient plays still survive to show how rapidly and completely the understanding of fifth-century drama vanished away.

This particular matter is neatly settled by the dramatist in a few lines at the beginning of the Messenger's speech, where no one would have time to reflect on it while the play was in progress; but those of the audience whose response Euripides most desired perhaps worked it out on the way home. Neoptolemus and his party, says the Messenger, spent their first three days in Delphi sight-seeing, and on the fourth day Neoptolemus was murdered. The journey from Phthia to Delphi would take three to four days. Lines 75–6, and other passages, suggest that when the play opens Neoptolemus could be expected back any day, so that he has been away at least eight or nine days; when his body is brought back we can reckon that it was probably about eleven days since he left home. But if we take at its face-value Orestes' statement (995 ff.) that he is about to go to Delphi to kill Neoptolemus, then Neoptolemus must have spent not three days but at least fourteen days seeing the sights of Delphi; which seems unlikely – and why then should the Messenger say three days? His story implies that Orestes reached Delphi at about the same time as Neoptolemus, or perhaps rather sooner; the usual assumption of a long time-lapse during the fourth Stasimon makes him arrive there eleven days *later*. In any case, the simple arithmetic offered by the text of the play makes it certain that, for those who were concerned to think carefully, the action opens with the murder already done, and with Orestes approaching Phthia a few miles ahead of the party bearing the dead body, and already in close and secret touch with Menelaus. This supposition, the only one which makes coherent sense of the whole play, will be further examined in connection with later scenes; for the present we return to the Prologue.

Andromache's opening speech gives the necessary facts, and secures the sympathy of the audience, who will certainly dismiss the talk of witchcraft as nonsense and recognize that the adjustment of claims between the two women is exclusively the concern of the absent Neoptolemus. The function of the Female Slave is to strengthen the sympathy with Andromache, to anticipate the appearance of Peleus, and to indicate that he is in any case too old to give any help. Andromache's position is one familiar enough to the audience; the Peloponnesian War has been in progress for four or five years, and all over Hellas there are prisoners, refugees, enslaved foreigners, women whose men are away, helpless children. When the Chorus arrive, they express the ordinary person's common-sense attitude to such a plight – a carefully limited and unimaginative sympathy advocating unheroic acceptance.

Hermione, after beginning with an affected arrogance, finds she cannot keep it up; it is too thin a cover for the burning jealousy which weakens her and puts her at her slave's mercy. To understand Andromache's reply, and the attitude which she develops in the subsequent dialogue, we may compare her with Medea, whose jealousy Euripides made the theme of his famous tragedy five years earlier. That play, like this one, presents timeless emotions in terms appropriate to the fifth century B.C.; but Medea remains heroic, while we see Andromache – admittedly with every excuse – going half-way to meet on the same level the angry, helpless pugnacity of the younger woman; ending her contemptuous, wounding lecture with a nasty gibe at Hermione's mother, and using this weapon a second time a little later, because she knows it is the one which will reduce her rival to tears. All this is, of course, justified if one's life is being threatened; but though it has enough power to bring Hermione to a state almost beyond control, it is certainly not on the heroic plane. If the scene is played according to the text, its end should leave the impression of two unhappy women both equally the victims, partly of woman's nature, but still more victims of a social order which leaves both stripped of the dignity of freedom, utterly dependent on the man whose journey to Delphi has abandoned them to their fates and to the scheming of Menelaus.

A quarrel between jealous females may be no laughing matter; and the choral Ode which begins at this point with the Judgement of Paris between rival goddesses continues with the death of Troy which had enslaved Andromache, with Cassandra's entreaty to 'Kill that child', with a reminder for the audience of the suffering which four years of war have brought to their homes; and ends with 'old men's tears for their dead sons' – a forecast of the dramatic pattern now about to unfold.

When Menelaus enters he presents himself in a few sentences as a stagey villain engaged in a murderous and irreligious crime whose effect must surely be the opposite of its professed intention of safeguarding Hermione's position as Neoptolemus' wife. He has left his home and his responsibilities as a ruler, to make a journey of twelve days each way (at least 160 miles on land, much of it over devious mountain tracks; and a crossing of the Corinthian Gulf), for the purpose of interfering between his daughter and her husband in a way which can only be offensive in the extreme to Neoptolemus. Andromache finds Menelaus' behaviour inexplicable; and so should the audience, unless they are resolved to accept unquestioningly any improbability they are presented with – which is not the way to understand Euripides. But this is not the first time that Andromache has been faced with inexplicable follies which have none the less had power to kill; and now she has no visible reason for doubting that her life and her son's are indeed in danger. Even so, her contempt for Menelaus, and her incredulity about his expressed intentions, are so strong that she ends her speech with a gibe little calculated to sweeten his temper.

The rest of this scene offers an unusual theatrical experience. Menelaus, in a smooth, business-like manner devoid of humane feeling, pursues a project which he has evidently thought out beforehand, whose ostensible purpose is so perverse that it would seem there must be an ulterior reason for it. This intriguing puzzle is balanced by the pathos of Andromache – a very different pathos from that which she was to display a dozen years later in The Women of Troy. There her anguish is universal, being a familiar personal result of the timeless and impersonal operations of war. Here she is the victim, not of an almost cosmic machine, but apparently of the whim of one inhuman monster. An instinct will tell the more sensitive members of the audience that this situation, not being universal, can have no reality in a valid dramatic pattern; therefore if an able actor (or actress) provokes tears for this Andromache, the empathy will still be provisional; Andromache's own bewilderment will affect the acute spectator strongly enough to introduce doubt and prevent despair from being final. However, though despair is suspended, this is the moment which demands indignation; and here we meet Andromache's eloquent outburst against Spartan treachery and inhumanity, lines 445 ff.

If this passionate utterance is not the centre and *raison d'être* of the whole piece, what is it? There can, of course, be no certain answer; but a possible answer is to be found in the same series of events as that which has already been considered as the background of *The Children of Heracles*, the siege and annihilation of Plataea (see page 17). If that play was produced in 427, and written in 428, its two themes – the obligations to suppliants, and the treatment of prisoners of war – had already been provided by the presence of the Plataean refugees and the massacre by the Plataeans of 180 Theban prisoners on the first day of hostilities. The final capitulation came in 427, when a similar number of Plataeans and twenty-five Athenians surrendered on promise of a fair trial; the 'trial' was a formal mockery, and they were all slaughtered by the Spartans. This horrible outcome, impinging upon the bad conscience which already troubled decent Athenians for their failure to send help, must have produced exactly that access of fury which is voiced in this famous speech of Andromache. It is perhaps a relevant consideration that a good deal of emphasis is laid on Andromache's right to be formally 'tried' by Menelaus and Hermione on the charge of witchcraft, and the fact that no 'trial' was held, but a death-sentence arbitrarily imposed. In the circumstances of the play this seems artificial; but if the scene was written in 427 just after the news came from Plataea, when the streets of Athens were full of refugee widows and orphans, everything falls into place. Since the matter had been dealt with in *The Children of Heracles* while Plataea was still under siege, a single brief reference was all that was called for in a play produced in 426; but brevity had to be matched by clarity and passion, and that is what we find in *Andromache*.

When the speech is over, the bewilderment already induced by Menelaus' inexplicable behaviour combines with the intense emotion of Andromache's exit to make fully appropriate the surprisingly detached tone of the second Stasimon. The ladies of Phthia are not devoid of humane feeling, for at the end of their Ode they express a proper indignation at Menelaus' cruelty; but the coolly intellectual, and academically rhythmical, essay on duality which occupies most of the Ode belongs to an atmosphere where emotion is, perhaps, on the alert, but not engaged. At first they do not side either with Hermione or with Andromache; by implication they blame Neoptolemus, but their statements are kept general and innocuous. They don't understand what is going on any more than Andromache does; but they 'have their foot outside of trouble', and can analyse a situation and adduce telling analogies. Only at the end do they admit that the talk of killing may after all, however absurd it sounds, be more than talk; and then the two victims enter bound and accompanied, doubtless, by a grim henchman or two, with an unpleasant display of swords.

What is Menelaus going to do? What has he been doing? The answer to these puzzles will begin to be clear after he has departed at the end of the Episode, when we shall suddenly realize that he had after all no intention of killing anyone. (In 730–31 he is in fact telling the truth; in any case a play is not meant to give room for reflection at the time, and in the third Stasimon the Chorus keep our attention directed to Peleus.) In the lyric passage before Peleus' first entry Menelaus, having ascertained* that Peleus is already at the gates, is preparing for him the scene which he intends him to discover. Since he had intercepted the slave who was taking Molossus away to safety, he could certainly have arrested the old woman who went to fetch Peleus; but in fact Menelaus wanted Peleus to come, so Peleus comes.

The entertaining scene which follows ought surely to be

---

* A surely justifiable assumption. See lines 312–13, where Menelaus himself warns us that today's events are not happening by accident. Compare also the role of Menelaus in *Iphigenia in Aulis*; see page 87 of Introduction.

transparent; but in the most recently published book on Euripides (Conacher, *Euripidean Drama*, 1967) it is still assumed that by some means or magic which does not appear on the stage, the aged valour of Peleus 'routs' Menelaus. There is as yet no mention of armed force available on either side; Peleus speaks of it in 759–60 only after Menelaus has gone. The battle is purely one of words; and in this battle Peleus' fury robs him of all balance and coherence, while Menelaus is bland, coolly argumentative, and relaxed. In the course of Peleus' second speech the moment comes which Menelaus' intrigue has been designed to induce: Peleus shouts, 'Take yourself and your barren daughter out of this house, and quickly!' Once this has been said before witnesses, Menelaus can go; and he does so, with explanations as meaningless as the whole charade. Whatever may be the reason for his sudden abandonment of murderous intentions, it is certainly not a loss of nerve in the presence of Peleus. Such a loss of nerve may have been accepted (may have been meant to be accepted) by the rank and file of the first audience; but to accept it as the sum of the dramatist's intention for that part of the audience which included many men of comparable intelligence to his own, would appear to tax Euripides with a lack of sophistication and wit surprising, to say the least, in the author of *Alcestis* and *Hippolytus*. Menelaus might perhaps have made his terror before the majesty of Peleus rather more convincing; but, his object once gained, why should he bother? His final speech is that of a man who has successfully achieved what he came to do. What he has achieved is to make Hermione desperately afraid of her husband and anxious to leave him, and to make Peleus order her out of the house.

Ten minutes later we are going to discover that the twelve-day journey (it could well be longer) from the middle of the Peloponnese has been made at almost exactly the same time by another man, who by the strangest of coincidences is Menelaus' nephew Orestes; but before we pass to the next scene we must consider the third choral Ode. It is a curiously muddled statement, and seems to reflect the self-contradictory attitudes of ordinary people to the successes and failures of the great. When the women of Phthia say, 'Help can always be found if you are of noble blood', are they thinking of Andromache? If so, the 'great man' whose 'virtue is a beacon over his grave' would be Hector; but if, as is much more likely, the 'great man' is Achilles, then their earlier remarks in fact apply only to Molossus and not to Andromache. This relaxed combination of confused reasoning with easy platitudes is part of the character of this Chorus, which (like the Chorus, for example, of *Orestes*) is made to reflect the views and reactions of ordinary citizens. The second stanza is clearer; it condemns the cynicism of Menelaus and praises the humanity of Peleus. But the third stanza presents the eternal dilemma: humanity seems to be sadly out of date. Peleus has been a visible illustration of this; and his earlier history, full of mythical improbabilities, reaches back to a misty period when it was still a glorious exploit to 'stretch a girdle of blood about the walls of Troy' – a view already denied in the first Stasimon, and to be bitterly contradicted in the fourth. In short, this Ode suggests that the victory which has been gained with the departure of Menelaus is an equivocal one, and that the rejoicing which follows it is based on an unreal past. Even as the Ode closes, shrieks of despair are heard from inside the palace.

The new scene brings a series of surprises. First, it would appear (had we not attended closely to the earlier scenes) that Menelaus, in his eagerness to obey the formidable Peleus and be on his way back to Sparta, has forgotten all about the daughter whom he came to champion. This makes nonsense of Menelaus – unless his sudden absconding is deliberately intended to reduce Hermione to a state in which she will be ready to take the desperate step of deserting her husband. In that case Menelaus will need, as accomplice, someone to arrive at the height of Hermione's panic and offer himself as an eligible escort. Enter Orestes. He and Menelaus have apparently reached Phthia within a day or so of each other. For both the route would naturally lie through Delphi, where the absent Neoptolemus is supposed to be. Orestes' opening gambit dovetails so neatly into our dawning apprehension of Menelaus' game, that we need not credit the elite of Euripides' audience with any phenomenal acuteness, in supposing them immediately to see Menelaus and Orestes as collaborators in a carefully organized scheme. The purpose of this scheme was to bring to an end a marriage which had proved unsatisfactory and replace it by a marriage which both men regarded as likely to be more satisfactory to themselves. It is easy to see why each of them should desire the change. Menelaus, now that Orestes appeared to have shaken off the Furies, and to be ready to settle down as king of Argos, naturally wanted a strong alliance with a relative and near neighbour; he regarded Phthia as an impoverished and unimportant place (this is Hermione's attitude, 209 ff.) whose king Neoptolemus had become unpopular with the powerful Delphians; such an alliance, and at such a distance, was an encumbrance to be shed as conveniently as possible. A personal expedition occupying the best part of a month was hardly worth while if its purpose was merely to interfere in a conjugal disagreement, but was well worth while in order to effect such a desirable change of alliance. Orestes, as he says himself (974–5), was not finding it easy to get the sort of wife he wanted to join him in refounding the royal dynasty of Argos; if Menelaus could help him get Hermione, he would be a firm ally of Menelaus.

A slight and subtle point should be noted here, partly as illuminating the figure of Hermione, partly for consideration in the study of Euripides' method. Andromache in the Prologue says, 'Hermione desires my death; in this her accomplice is Menelaus'. A little later the old Slave speaks of 'some vicious plot'. The only thing in the play which can be called a 'plot' is Menelaus' promise to spare the child's life if his mother

abandons sanctuary, after which he explains that the promise
was only a ruse. Hermione knew that this ruse was going to be
employed (262 ff.), and may even have suggested it to Menelaus, though he clearly needed no prompting. The execution of
the plot, and the proposed murders, were entirely in Menelaus'
hands. He appears throughout as a cool and bland strategist
fully in charge of the situation; Hermione is consistently weak,
lacks confidence and self-control, and shows signs of hysteria in
both her scenes. But in the second half of the play this 'plot'
is repeatedly referred to, by the Nurse, by Hermione herself,
by the Chorus, and by Peleus, as being purely Hermione's plot,
in which her father was only her abettor. Who was the more to
blame, Hermione or Menelaus? Euripides, true to his principle, will not pursue the question, but leaves it to whatever
subtlety of inference his audience may care to exercise.

The speech of Orestes which ends the scene is of prime
importance. It begins as an address to Hermione. It is possible
that (as some have conjectured) after two lines of it he turns to
a group of the Chorus, who listen to his specific undertaking to
kill Neoptolemus, while Hermione is engaged elsewhere on the
stage; but to suppose this is surely to miss a climactic moment
in the drama. Hermione's hysterical fear has given Orestes already a strong advantage; and this open assertion that he is going to kill her husband – a statement made at a moment when
all her normal consciousness (there is no need to see her as an
abnormal or wicked young woman) is reeling with guilt and
bewilderment, dramatically and visibly clinches Orestes' hold
over her, as she tries to summon courage to protest but, faced
with Orestes' menacing eye, cannot. If Orestes had told her, 'I
have already killed Neoptolemus', she might have found the
courage to abhor and defy him. She may even guess the truth,
but can say nothing; and by saying nothing she doubles both her
own sense of guilt and the ascendancy of Orestes. This is one of
the most powerful scene-endings in Euripides' extant plays.

Is it possible to conceive that, after this speech, when

Orestes, dragging Hermione by the wrist, has gone off in the direction from which he came, to join Menelaus a little way along the southward road – is it now possible to conceive that a dramatist could coolly ask us to imagine that an interval of ten days elapses during the performance of the fourth choral Ode? Could Peleus, after ten days, come and say that a 'confused rumour' had only just reached him? In any audience, ancient or modern, there are those who accept everything as it comes, with little reflection; for the others, close attention to the dialogue up to this point, with an assumption that the author's method is a challenge to exact response, should reveal the closely-knit pattern of uninterrupted action which I have outlined.*

When Orestes has gone, the Chorus complete the pattern of their comment on the action with a passionate and moving elegy for the destruction and suffering caused by the war between Hellas and Troy. The emotional force and topical relevance of this poem, in contrast to the lighter tone of the first three Odes, puts the theme of the whole drama into focus. The unjust position of helpless women in a world organized by men has been shown as inevitable when men's lives and thoughts are dominated by war. The opening address ostensibly lays the blame for it all upon Apollo – and this is suitable since Apollo was in part responsible for the murder of Neoptolemus which is about to be revealed, as well as for Orestes' matricide; but Euripides is consistently cynical about the human – and particularly Greek – habit of laying the blame for every crime on someone other than the criminal. To the cry, 'O Phoebus, how can I believe?' the answer is, 'Concerning Phoebus you need believe neither good nor evil; look at Menelaus and Orestes, who need no oracle to inspire them – and wait for the Messenger's speech.' There are tears for Troy, tears for the

* Substantially this view of the play was put forward some sixty years ago by A. W. Verrall in *Four Plays of Euripides*. Because some of Verrall's work was marred by uncritical speculation, his more valuable perceptions, such as his insight into this play, have been largely ignored.

House of Atreus, tears for every home in Hellas; and the cause of tears is the war and the men who made it. The audience – whether in Athens or elsewhere – to whom this play is presented are as yet only in the fifth year of the Peloponnesian War, and the time has not yet come for the equation of war with insanity which first appears in *The Suppliant Women*, and is developed in the last three plays in this volume; but tears, and the plague (1044), are already familiar.

The beginning of the Messenger's speech confirms the impression already given by Orestes that he came to Phthia straight from the murder of Neoptolemus at Delphi. The story of three days spent by Neoptolemus and his party in sight-seeing neatly combines a motive for the anger of the Delphians with a further reason why we should not suppose all this to have happened while we were listening to the fourth Stasimon. In the account of the murder the part of Orestes as organizer and leader is made clear; he was present, but is not said to have confronted Neoptolemus or struck the final blow. The part played by Apollo is equivocally stated; what, or whose, was the voice which cried 'from the temple's inmost shrine'? Yet the Messenger in his last words lays the blame squarely on Apollo, not on Orestes. What are we to make of this? When we come to study *Orestes*, written about eighteen years later, we shall find Pylades addressing to the audience a speech whose import plainly is, 'This is the kind of disgraceful speech you Athenians are ready to applaud.' It is possible that in *Andromache* the end of the Messenger's speech carries the ironical implication, 'This is the way you habitually impute to the gods responsibility which you know belongs to men. It would pass in Agamemnon's day, but it is inexcusable now.' It is even more difficult for us than it was for the generations which followed Euripides, to say when he is being ironical and when he is not. It is relevant to remember that when he wrote this play he was over fifty, and the ironical habit so evident in his later work is likely to have been already well established.

In the last scene, with villains and victims departed, we find the light of tragedy focussed unexpectedly on Peleus, as in *Hippolytus* it falls upon Theseus, and in *The Bacchae* upon Cadmus. As the whole play has been vested in irony, the time allowed for heartfelt tears is short; then Thetis stirs, and irony resumes control. 'My first advice to you, Peleus, is: Do not let today's calamities cause you undue distress.' Immortals are impervious to human grief; and no divinity in a machine ever demonstrated this more fully than the charming Thetis, to whom the conferring of immortality on the aged Peleus appears as full compensation for every loss. 'Sit down . . . and wait until I come.' This doubtful instruction so overjoys Peleus that he does not heed the words which follow to snatch away the gift just bestowed: 'Death is a debt which every man must pay.' The mockery does not reach him. The trite, banal lesson which he draws from his experience of life is irrelevant to anything that has passed on the stage. He has endured grievous affliction; but he has found a way of dealing with it suitable to his credulous and unintelligent nature; and why should he not?

All Greek tragedies are unorthodox, and it is possible to say that this one is more unorthodox than most. The total disappearance of Andromache, the want of any tragic hero or heroine in the accepted sense, the apparent break in continuity after the departure of Menelaus (though the interpretation here offered partly disposes of this) – all these things make it difficult to describe a tidy structure for the piece. But why should we? Greek drama, even though Aeschylus had been thirty years dead, was still in the making; and who had the best right to create new designs? Today a vigorous performance of *Andromache*, giving the necessary scope to irony, will grip an audience for an unbroken hour and a half, and send them home arguing; and the actors will enjoy it no less.

THE SUPPLIANT WOMEN

This strangely compelling play, first produced about 421 B.C. (the tenth year of the Peloponnesian War), is unlikely to catch the interest of anyone today who is looking for something new and convincing to produce on a stage. Its style is formal, its drama symbolic or schematic; its use of plot so abstract, especially towards the end, as to suggest the structure of a ballet. It is, however, a play packed with positive meaning, with the poet's own individual message. The message is direct- ed towards problems which arose from the unchanging central tragedy of man; from the fact that, the greater his capacity becomes, the more resolutely he uses it for self-destruction. It is conveyed partly with a subtle irony, partly with a pathetic directness; and this contrast is accompanied by a series of other contrasts, which are static rather than dramatic: democracy, ideal and practical; war, moral and immoral; the communal and the private aspects of folly and of suffering; the logical revolt of maturity against war, and the subservience of the young to primitive emotion. Through this pattern of con- trasts Euripides gives us in remarkable completeness his critic- ism of the folly of war. The theme later developed in *The Women of Troy* and *Iphigenia in Aulis* had already been clearly thought out while the struggle with Sparta was still in its first phase. Comment on the play must here be limited* to two main themes: the criticism of war, and the character of Theseus; and two curiosities: Adrastus' funeral speech, and the scene devoted to Evadne and Iphis.

The recognition that war can be an honourable and glorious undertaking is voiced in Aethra's speech, in Theseus' reply,

* Kitto, *Greek Tragedy*, pp. 223 ff., gives an admirable general account of this play; in particular, his interpretation of the last 250 lines is convincing, and important for the understanding of Euripides' whole work and method.

and in the gratified comment of the Chorus. It is easy to see the difference between Adrastus' rash and ambitious attack on Thebes and the Athenian expedition to recover the bodies of the dead. But now comes a new note, in the speech of the Theban Herald. Ostensibly he delivers a shameless and defiant warning from the Theban monarchy to the Athenian democracy, not to vote for war; but in fact this speech goes far beyond his warrant, and aims straight at the sore point of contemporary politics:

> If Death stood there in full view while men cast their votes,
> Hellas would not be dying from war-mania.

This implies that democracies have the power, if they will but vote imaginatively, to bring the slaughter to an end. The statement that 'we know what good, what evil is' comes more strikingly from an enemy than it would from the virtuous Theseus. The Herald says not one word to justify his master Creon in refusing burial to the seven chiefs; their death, he says, was a punishment justly awarded by Zeus – which no one has disputed. Further, his moving and poetic praise of peace is uttered in terms which seem to forget the cause he has come to defend, and all other 'causes', and to appeal simply to the common reason and moral sense of all men. Theseus in replying maintains that war in a just cause is honourable; men should not shrink from battle. To deny burial is the ultimate impiety, and a hurt to the whole Hellene race. As he sets out for the battle he forbids Adrastus to accompany him. Adrastus' fortune is tarnished with aggression and defeat; that of Theseus is fresh and innocent.

Next comes the Messenger's factual account of the fight, and of Theseus' refusal to enter Thebes. In reply to this, Adrastus draws the moral from two sins of *hybris*, his own first, and now Creon's; and he adds to the legend a detail not mentioned elsewhere and evidently invented by Euripides for his own purpose. 'When Eteocles offered us peace on fair conditions, we refused, and then we were defeated.' Every Athenian knew that in 425 B.C. the Spartans had offered peace. This reference, in the mouth of the successful Theseus, would have been tedious moralizing; spoken by the chastised Adrastus it compels reflection. Adrastus condemns the folly of individuals and of states, in learning nothing from friendly counsel, but choosing the ordeal of blood; and before the end of the scene he appeals yet again to all mortal men to end war, to 'live quiet with quiet neighbours, and preserve your towns'.

So far, then, the play has clearly established the difference between a just and an unjust war. A war undertaken through lust for power or for revenge is wicked folly likely to bring its own punishment; a war strictly limited to the defence of a pious principle is honourable. Then at the end of the play come the sons of the dead chiefs, carrying the urns which contain their fathers' ashes; and they announce their intention of marching with an army, as soon as they are grown up, to avenge their fathers' death by sacking Thebes. The Chorus utter a few words of despairing protest – 'Is this evil not yet laid to rest?' – but no one takes any notice of them. When Athena arrives she urges the boys to 'lose no time' in carrying out their useless and barbarous intention; while Theseus, having pointed the moral clearly in the earlier part of the play, and being now ignored by the new generation and snubbed by Athena, has nothing further to say.

Euripides had already made some comment on war in *Andromache* and in *Hecabe*; but *The Suppliant Women* is a reflective judgement and an artistically complete statement. Its deep pessimism echoes the thought of Thucydides, and is evidently based on the poet's experience of the first ten years of war – especially the refusal of Athens to respond to Spartan offers of peace. Eight years later in *The Women of Troy* Euripides made his audience look at war through the eyes of helpless victims of conquest, to observe themselves in the role of conquerors; and nine years after that, in *Iphigenia in Aulis*, he showed the corruption and demoralization which war produces in those who make it, and glorified the trappings of military enterprise only to lift them and show the shabbiness underneath.

We come now to our second topic: what did Euripides mean us to make of his leading character, Theseus? It has sometimes been said that the so-called 'debate on democracy' which dominates his second scene (403 ff.) was irrelevantly patched on to the plot because this was a 'patriotic piece' designed to bolster the Athenians' pride in their city. Such an explanation of a great writer's work should be accepted only as a last resort. I would say rather that the theme here developed, the contrast of ideal and actual democracy, is a main concern of the play; that the concept of ideal democracy which Theseus outlines in the debate is closely attached to the *persona* of Theseus himself; and that this *persona* is in the course of the play subjected to some ironical questioning, and is not offered for acceptance simply as embodying everything that the Athenian citizen or leader ought to be. Similarly Athena seems to represent Athens as she actually is – traditional, confident, unreflecting; while it may not be extravagant to see in the broken and humbled Adrastus a warning picture of what Athens may become if she will not learn wisdom in time.

The somewhat stately eloquence of Aethra's opening speech is continued, after a passionate Ode by the Chorus, in the tone of Theseus' words. The long *stichomythia* between secure king and defeated suppliant elicits from Adrastus a frank confession of follies – reliance on a very obscure oracle, neglect of prophetic warning, and subservience to rash young citizens. There is a schoolmasterly priggishness in some of Theseus' remarks; but Adrastus accepts it all with dignity, and can without offence include in his replies one hint of warning: 'How should they know what suffering is? They are secure.' In reply to his final appeal Theseus delivers a sermon as impressive – and as equivocal – as that of Teiresias in *The Bacchae* – though on a different text: 'The good in life outweighs the ill'. Since the gods fill man's life with blessings, he says, Adrastus in trying to increase his power by making war on Thebes was obviously guilty of *hybris*. But this sermon has a certain uneasy quality. It is a theme for the successful; but its poetic eloquence is addressed to an audience who have endured ten years of war, two years of plague, seven summers of siege, and as many defeats as victories, with still no prospect of peace. This pious enumeration of the blessings heaven imparts would not make an obvious appeal to farmers who had barely raised one crop in the last decade. The Nurse in *Hippolytus* (produced seven years before this play) invited no contradiction when she told Phaedra the exact opposite – that for most people the ill in life outweighs the good. Is Theseus' piety perhaps out of touch with facts? His statement that war cannot be private, but involves guilty and innocent alike (226–8) is admirable; but it is followed by an elaborate attack on 'young men' who lead a city to ruin – the more surprising this, first because Theseus himself (as both Adrastus and the Chorus have pointed out) is a young man, and secondly because in the next scene Theseus tells the Theban Herald that a city's young men are its 'great resource', to be preciously preserved. Finally Theseus starts out on a new theme about 'three orders of citizens', of which 'the middle order is the city's life and health'. This diversion is a pity; because it breaks the thread of the argument, so that at 246 the speaker has to perform a noticeable side-step to reach his conclusion. Besides this, two further things detract from the effectiveness of a speech which began brilliantly. One is that the censorious complacency has now become almost unacceptable in a hero whose concern ought to be to preserve modesty and avoid nemesis. The other is the firm dignity of Adrastus' reply. The fact that soon after, in response to Aethra's arguments, Theseus with equal dignity changes his mind and shows himself not only a hero but a model democrat removes, for the present, any qualms about his status as the hero of this play; but these qualms will return when Athena – with less politeness than

Aethra – tells him just where he is wrong. Euripides, in fact, seems to be setting before us a variety of attitudes to the war which at this time were finding voice in the Assembly and in the Agora. Aethra, Theseus, the Chorus, the Theban Herald, the Sons, and finally Athena, reflect the multifarious sides of the daily debate on right and wrong, expedience and caution, the pious and the practical, in which every citizen was a voter and a decision-maker. On some issues the poet states his clear opinion; others he leaves to the judgement of his audience.

The next scene is a debate undisguised. Theseus in his first words to the Theban Herald challenges him with an assertion of the democratic ideal: this is 'a free city; the king here is the people'. It was only eight years since the death of Pericles, the man above all others whose career had exemplified, and whose mind and tongue had been capable of formulating, that ideal position of leadership in a democratic organism which Theseus claims in this play. There must have been many among Euripides' contemporaries for whom the kind of phrase familiar to us from the Funeral Speech in the second book of Thucydides expressed a reality still perceptible amidst the turmoil of everyday political and social life. It is equally certain that the ever-increasing strains of war roused more and more voices to disparage this ideal and to advocate the open-eyed acceptance of expediency and power as replacing moral principles in external affairs, and at home the supersession of popular democracy by expert authority. Theseus' short speech presents the democratic ideal broadside-on and unprotected to the salvo with which the Theban Herald promptly replies.

A man who is good at ploughing, says the Herald – as Socrates was saying every day – is not likely to be equally good at politics, which is a no less specialized craft. An Assembly gives power to the deceptive cleverness of unscrupulous orators, and a popular judicial system opens the door to corruption. All this is not simply an attack on Athens by an unenlightened foreigner; Athenian writers leave no doubt that such criticisms were everyday talk in the Agora. Greek democracy depended entirely on the assumption of a recognized moral standard among citizens; and no one who has read Thucydides' account (in Book III, 82–3) of the general demoralization of politics throughout Hellas by 427 B.C. – six years before this play was produced – can doubt that the dispute here formalized was raging openly in Athens. How does Theseus reply?

His speech is a good deal less forceful than the Herald's. He finds three things to say. First, he states the broad theory on which democracy was based: that liberty and equality are assured by free speech and the vote, and guarded by a written legal code. But this is not an answer to the Herald, who attacked practice rather than theory; indeed, his attack is un-answerable, except by pointing out the corresponding disad-vantages of any alternative system. Next, Theseus refers to 'the young men' of a city as its 'great resource', which only a democracy knows how to value. This wakes a curiously contra-dictory echo from Theseus' long lecture to Adrastus (232–7); there he gives a different picture of the role of young men in a state, and his tone there suggests strongly that his words con-tain a direct reference to contemporary politics. The third point made by Theseus is the weakest of all: 'A tyrant rapes the daughters of the citizens.' Doubtless many instances of this could be quoted; but in the cities of Greece tyrants can have accounted for only a very small proportion of enforced mar-riages. As an argument offered to sophisticated men, this must be classed with other wartime slogans mocked by Euripides, such as Agamemnon's declaration in *Iphigenia in Aulis* that 'Hellene wives must be saved from rape', or Peleus' tirade in *Andromache* against Spartan immodesty – 'A Spartan girl could not be chaste even if she wanted to.' Theseus concludes, 'Thus much in answer to the points you aimed at me'; and doubtless many in the audience were content to assume – having listened only to the tone, not to the words – that he had indeed answered the Herald's clearly-made points. It is no less certain that those who knew what to listen for in a play by Euripides observed that not a single one of the Herald's damaging indictments had received a word of direct answer.

The Herald now proceeds to give his message. Its content, its style, its arguments, its illustrations and generalities, remind one strongly of the speeches in Thucydides, Book I, which define the respective positions of the Corcyreans, Corinthians, and Athenians at the beginning of the war. It contains, in the two lines already quoted, the most cogent plea for peace to be found in the play – embedded in a fabric of threats, but none the less cogent; and the Herald goes on to speak of 'peace, the chief friend and cherisher of the Muses; peace, the enemy of revenge . . .' It is for each listener or reader to make what he will of such words spoken by a man who stands there to defend impious outrage against dead bodies; the fact is that the poet has inserted into a fictional dispute a statement of actual truth which momentarily drags each hearer out of the mythic past to look squarely at the tragic present.

This vision can only be momentary. Theseus' next speech quickly re-establishes the dramatic sequence, and re-establishes Theseus as hero by his moving assertion of the rights of the dead, and of the principle of nature on which those rights are based:

> For we have in our own bodies
> But a life-tenancy, not lasting ownership.

Thus before the end of the scene irony has been forgotten; and past and present, the play and the people watching it, are united in considering that ultimate issue of piety against impiety, for which Athens had once risked everything. The urgency of this issue is enforced in the next scene, when the Messenger, reporting the victory of Theseus and the recovery of the bodies, describes how the king with his own hands lifted and cared for the putrid remains of the corpses. Gilbert Murray (*Euripides and his Age*, page 97) calls this 'the antique counterpart of St Francis kissing the leper's sores'. It may be so in part; and we may compare with this the words of Theseus to the blood-guilty Heracles in *Heracles* 1217 ff.; but to fifth-century Athenians this picture bore a more practical meaning. It expressed the desperate need, in the midst of a war which was destroying so many civilized standards, to cling to a minimal decency in treatment of the dead. This was perhaps the only decency which could always be afforded; and it was urgent, for the self-respect of Athens, that she should in this matter see herself as an example to other states.

We now come to one of the curiosities. The scene in which Adrastus, on Theseus' invitation, pronounces a funeral eulogy over the dead, is very puzzling. First, Theseus' remarks in 846–56 – apparently a criticism of a conventional type of Messenger's speech – seem out of place; and his politeness to Adrastus in 842–3, 'As a wise elder, you have knowledge . . .' makes a rather too obvious compensation for his earlier harshness, e.g., in 513. But chiefly the matter of Adrastus' eulogy is disconcerting. It is hard to believe that Euripides could not have composed something more significant, even about five men with whose personal characters the audience have no concern at all. The style of the whole speech is as dull as its content; and the fact that the author apparently could think of nothing whatever to say about the fifth man, Tydeus, and simply wrote down three versions of one trite remark, only deepens the mystery, since the MSS offer no formal grounds for questioning the authenticity of this passage.

However, in fairness to Euripides' reputation it should be noticed that a scene containing a speech in praise of the dead is of all kinds of scene the most likely to invite addition or substitution for the purpose of performance on some special occasion. There were still seventeen years of war to go, and a revival of this play either then or in the fourth century may well have been used for paying tribute to men known to the audience, with the result that what Euripides wrote here was replaced and eventually lost, perhaps up to line 931. The perfunctory nature of what Adrastus says about Tydeus (who had been a prime cause of his misfortunes), and of what Theseus says about Amphiaraus and Polyneices, makes it hard to concede that Euripides could ever have burdened this subtle play with so dull a passage. However, it must be recognized that the MSS give no hint of interference with an original text. If this eulogy is Euripides' work, since it is hardly credible that he thought it was good, he must have had some purpose in its dullness which we cannot hope to fathom.

The next scene presents the fourth contrast, and the second curiosity. The curiosity is the sudden appearance, in a self-contained scene, of two individuals as yet unmentioned, who then both disappear. Up to this point in the play we have been shown the communal suffering which a foolish and immoral war has inflicted on a state, in the persons of the crushed king and the mourning mothers; now comes Evadne, who has lost both husband and brother. Her response is not a formal dirge, but dramatic self-immolation. After her fiery passion comes the cold despair of her father Iphis – a result of war not less moving nor less usual. The indictment of war now seems to be complete; two powerful states have suffered miserably and gained nothing; two innocent lives have pictured for us the ruin which must be shared by thousands. The poet is addressing an audience in which the young men now entering the armed forces can only dimly remember a city at peace, ten years ago. What more remains to be said? One thing.

A second Chorus enters, the young sons of the dead heroes; they carry urns containing the ashes from the funeral pyres; and they join in the dirge. Presently they begin to speak of the revenge they hope to take as soon as they are old enough. They may or may not have been present when Adrastus with tears confessed his own folly (they were on stage at 106, but have not been mentioned since); or when the Theban Herald spoke of 'Hellas dying from war-mania', or when the Messenger told how Theseus had refused to lead his army into Thebes; or when Evadne threw herself into the flames. But they pray to the gods that their day of revenge may come. The Chorus in horror reply, 'This wrong sleeps not yet? . . . I have had enough. . .'; but the Sons continue, as if they had not heard, to picture themselves in bright armour advancing on Thebes. Thus Euripides foresaw the course which his own city would blindly pursue for the next seventeen years.

When the dirge is over, Theseus and Adrastus exchange expressions of trust and gratitude; but the representative of idealist Athens is interrupted in his farewells by the sudden appearance of contemporary Athens at war — in the familiar figure of Athena, with shield, helmet, and spear. Theseus, for the second time, has his error pointed out by a woman. Aethra told him to be less coldly rational and more compassionate. Now Athena tells him to be less trustful and more cautious, and to exact an oath from Adrastus with formal solemnity. More than this, Athena commands the young Argives, as soon as they become men, to lay Thebes in the dust.

Which is right, Theseus or Athena? Every citizen can answer for himself; the poet has left no doubt about his own belief. Yet he is sure that what he knows to be right will be defeated. The rising generation, learning, as always, more from instinct than from experience,

> . . . shall lay their city in the dust.
> This is the inescapable truth.

Pessimism has no illusions; despair is final.

Even after this the screw of irony can take one more turn. The honourable and humane Theseus, betrayed and debased by the unassailable power of Athena, surrenders unconditionally. The 'error' to which he confesses would seem, on the surface, to be his rashness in not demanding an oath from Adrastus; but this was a minor indiscretion. His central symbolic act, his humane declaration of faith, was to march home with the dead bodies leaving Thebes untouched. This decision Athena has specifically reversed; and Theseus responds with

Guide my decisions; while your favour rests on us,
Athens will live henceforward in security.

This is a fatuous faith which has been contradicted by all the
eloquence of the drama. A similar note is struck at the close of
Andromache, when Peleus, doubly bereaved in a desolate house,
takes pitiable comfort from the meaningless promise of his own
immortality. That folly involves only one person. Theseus'
renunciation of his ideal of humanity is the tragedy of a whole
people; and that people is the audience who sit to watch the
play, but only few of them know it.

THE PHOENICIAN WOMEN

Since the early plays of the war a decade and a half has passed;
and in wartime that represents, mentally and emotionally, at
least a whole generation. In *The Children of Heracles* the heroic
era as represented by the Elders and by the memory of Theseus
took our thoughts back sixty years to Marathon, while the
degenerate Demophon could stand for Athens demoralized by
the plague. In *Orestes* on the other hand we shall find a strong
hint that the poet looks back for the heroic age of Athens not
sixty years but twenty, and sees its embodiment in the splendid
figure of Pericles, using Orestes to typify the insane fever of
Athens in her death-struggle. The recognition that the war
against Sparta is already lost, which is a main theme of *Orestes*,
is already perceptible in *The Phoenician Women*. It is a strange
play, full of power but at first acquaintance bewildering in its
structure. Critics both ancient and modern have explained how
much better it could have been designed. As a pleasant change
from that discouraging tone Kitto's account in his *Greek
Tragedy* should be read; and if after reading it the student is
still unsatisfied, it is possible that he will find the key to a truer
account in a point which we have already noticed when

examining the first three plays in this volume. In eleven lively
pages Kitto mentions every scene, every character, every traditional criticism; and concludes that Euripides here achieves with
brilliant success a melodramatic entertainment – and we must
presume, though the point is not alluded to, that this was
directed towards an audience who were eagerly looking for
melodramatic entertainment. This is no doubt true in part; but
the part of the audience for which this is true was not the part
which included Euripides or any of the people with whom he
was most concerned to communicate. The various attitudes
and expectations of the Athenian audience have already been
described. What were their particular preoccupations in
409 B.C.?

Nearly four years had passed since the crushing blow of the
Sicilian disaster; twenty-one years since the plague; eighteen
years since wars and revolutions had begun to result in that
collapse of all moral restraints on behaviour, which Thucydides
noted when he described the temper of conflicting factions in
terms terrifyingly appropriate to our twentieth-century experience (III, 82–3); nine years since the Athenian Assembly
had voted for the annihilation of Melos without experiencing
the last-minute repentance which in the fourth year of the war
had saved Mytilene from a similar fate. In 409 the end of the
war, the total defeat and humiliation of Athens, was still five
years ahead, but it was clearly and inevitably coming. Athens
was a besieged city, and her strength was nearing exhaustion.
This is the background of the audience which gathers to see a
play called *The Phoenician Women* – a title which gives no hint of
its theme. Iocasta as Prologue soon assures the listeners that
the story will be a familiar one; and at the same time both the
style and the matter of her story – and not least the fact that she
is alive to tell it – create at once a new atmosphere. When she
has finished we know that the scene is Thebes, a besieged city,
and that the issue of the play is to be the quarrel between
Eteocles king of Thebes and his brother Polyneices who has

come with a foreign army to attack and destroy the place of his birth. This all too real situation is made more vivid by the short scene which follows, where Antigone sees from the wall the invading enemy – so close as to be individually recognizable; and we reflect that most members of the audience have for years past, every summer, watched from the walls of Athens the movements of Spartan troops. An ominous note is struck when her Tutor says to Antigone,

> Yet our enemies come with a just cause.
> My fear is that the gods may see this all too well.

It was of course known that in the legend Thebes had repelled the besiegers; yet the phrase is echoed by the Chorus in the closing words of the Parodos (259–60),

> He arms himself in a just cause
> Who fights to recover his home.

It will be natural for the besieged Athenian audience to identify themselves (as they did in Aeschylus' *Seven Against Thebes*, a play of fifty years before but very well known) with Eteocles and the Thebans rather than with Polyneices and the Argives. Are we then to be shown a difficult case of justice on both sides? This question will be answered when Eteocles appears. Meanwhile the Chorus enter; who are they?

They say they are 'choice spoils of war' who have been brought by Eteocles (292) and a Theban army to Thebes for presentation to Apollo, and that Eteocles was about to send them on to Delphi when the Argive army arrived. The nature and purpose of this military expedition is left entirely vague; so, more curiously, is the location of the 'Tyrian wave' or the 'Phoenician island' from which the girls were taken. It can hardly be Phoenicia proper, since they say in the same stanza that they sailed to Thebes past the Ionian Sea and Sicily, blown by the Zephyr, the south-west wind. The only reasonable conclusion is that they come from the Phoenician settlement of (in Greek Carchedon); and that the absence of any mention of the name suggests an intention to leave their identity vague, so that their function in the play is that of un-committed and impartial observers, though sympathetic be-cause of their connection with the family of Cadmus.* They regard themselves as already belonging to Delphi, whose status as a pan-Hellenic sanctuary sets her above the quarrels of other states.

There is a clear theme-pattern in the first three poems chanted by the Chorus. As Delphian votaries they are commit-ted also to Dionysus whose birth-place was Thebes. When they tell (638 ff.) the story of the founding of Thebes by Cadmus, they speak of 'this wheat-bearing plain watered by lovely rivers', and of Thebes as a place of fruitful and joyful life under the protection of Dionysus, a place of music and dancing. The opposite to this idyllic life is typified by 'the gory dragon of Ares' whom Cadmus had to kill before he could found his city. But the brood of Ares cannot be killed; the dragon's teeth produced, to found the new city, men whose 'hearts were as cruel as iron'. In time Ares uses them to win revenge for his dragon, and inflames Argos against Thebes, Thebes against Argos. In the magnificent first strophe of the second Stasimon (784 ff.) the destructive excitement of Ares is contrasted with the creative excitement of Dionysus; the two opposite worlds in which human communities may choose, or be fated, to live are presented in vivid pictures to the exhausted citizens of Athens, imprisoned now for more than a generation in the nightmare world of Ares, 'whose food is the fury of war'. Athenians, no less than Thebans, regarded themselves as a race sprung from the soil; and in the second Stasimon the story is told a second time (820–21) and is brought to a close in words which could hardly fail to make Athenians think how aptly,

---

* Why the further attempt is made to establish their connection with Io, whose familiar story makes her a princess of the enemy city of Argos, is a question to which I have so far seen no answer.

only ten years ago, such a description fitted their patriotic pride in Athens:

> And this city, enriched with numberless blessings,
> Grew from fortune to greater fortune,
> Till she stands crowned with the proudest garlands of war.

Finally the third Stasimon (the 'Sphinx Ode', 1018 ff.) applies the elements of this story, for the imaginative listener, still more closely to the experience of the Athenian *demos*. The ravages of the Sphinx may picture both the remembered terror of the plague in 430 B.C. and the repeated Spartan invasions of Attica which through the course of the war had steadily become more severe. Whether the second stanza of this Ode ('came Oedipus the accursed', etc.) bears any reference to political persons or events, is as uncertain now as Euripides surely intended it to be in his own day; but the analogy between the last five lines (1062–6) and the career of the Athenian people since the Battle of Salamis is pointed to by the invocation of Pallas Athene, under whose aegis they had first defeated the Persian invaders, then assumed the leadership of all Hellene states in the Delian League formed to resist Persian aggression, and later, by openly turning the League into an Athenian empire, had challenged other states to the trial of arms which was now slowly bringing Athens to her knees:

> . . . Pallas, dear goddess,
> Who cast the stone which laid the dragon in his blood,
> Who launched bold Cadmus on that enterprise
> From which there spread across the land,
> Devouring and destroying,
> A supernatural fury of blood and hate.

Now Polyneices enters, and immediately establishes a realistic wartime atmosphere of suspicion and defensiveness. Iocasta welcomes him with tender emotion. She has more intelligence and moral heroism than anyone else in the play (Menoeceus is a hero, but hardly a character); yet in her long first address to Polyneices she fatally exemplifies that want of tact and timeliness which is the simple cause of so much complex disaster both political and personal. When her one desire is to gain her son's compliance with her plea for a peaceful settlement, she must follow her warm greeting, before he has time to say a word, with bitter reproaches against his marriage with an Argive woman. In this she is comparable with Clytemnestra in *Iphigenia in Aulis*, who annuls any effect she might have had in pleading for Iphigenia's life by raising old quarrels with her husband. Here, the comment of the Chorus, 355–6, is innocuous, but leaves room for sardonic interpretation.

Polyneices in this play somewhat resembles Orestes in *Orestes*; he is desperately involved in a war to the death, but still retains the vestiges of a moral nature. (Eteocles, like Pylades, has successfully eliminated such encumbrance.) He is determined to secure 'justice' for himself, but is prepared in doing so to destroy his native city. Iocasta at first ignores this issue and asks him, 'What is an exile's life?' This apparently irrelevant passage has two points. First, one of the bitterest aspects of the war with Sparta was the very large number of Greek families broken by long and enforced exile. The second point is ironical. The most galling feature of exile, says Polyneices, is the fact that 'right of free speech does not exist'. This makes Polyneices an Athenian of 409 B.C., convinced, because he had never questioned it, that Athens, and no other Greek city, allowed free speech; but only the friends of Euripides would know what was in his mind when he wrote of exile. The poet was already contemplating final departure from Athens to the Macedonian court of King Archelaus, who had invited him more than once. And why did he think of leaving the city which prided itself on the right of free speech? Because his own practice of free speech had brought unpopularity and suspicion; it was only ten years later that Socrates was executed for encouraging the same kind of intellectual freedom which Euripides advocated by his plays. 'That's a slave's life –

to be forbidden to speak one's mind.' In this play, and the following year in *Orestes*, Euripides spoke his mind for the last time in Athens; and in 407 B.C. he went to Macedon.

Next comes the story, mentioned fifteen years before in *The Suppliant Women*, of the oracle given by Delphi to Adrastus: 'Marry your daughters to a lion and a boar.' In that play Theseus castigated Adrastus' folly in being enslaved to an obscure oracle of Apollo; here the point emphasized is rather the appropriateness of the analogy – the inhuman ferocity of Polyneices' resolve to sack his own city rather than submit to injustice. The comparison with two fighting beasts is used again several times in this play; its appearance here prepares us for the confrontation of two implacable enemies. Eteocles enters, and in six lines of brutal clarity indicates the spirit in which he has accepted his mother's offer of mediation.

Polyneices' statement of his case is what we expected – an appeal for just treatment, coupled with a threat of blood-thirsty violence if he does not get his way. The fact that the Chorus describe his words as 'reasonable' reminds us that in a group of states where war is endemic such threats, however outrageous, are taken for granted as a regular instrument of policy. Eteocles' reply is a focal point in the play. It states, with a lucidity close to that of Thucydides in the whole argument of the Athenian envoys against the Melians at the end of Book V, the fully developed conviction that the intelligent man regards might as the only right. If Thucydides, by half-way through the war, saw this conviction as the practical creed of the Athenian *demos*, there can be little doubt that Euripides in this play presents Eteocles, the resolute rationalist king of a besieged city, as a symbol of Athens. The 'absolute power' which he speaks of in 506 is *tyrannis*, the same word which both Pericles and Cleon had used to describe the Athenian empire; and for tyranny only one motto is feasible: What I have I hold, at whatever cost; and,

> since there must be wickedness,
> There is no nobler pretext for it than a throne.

Then, for those who recognize Athens in Eteocles, the eloquent reply of Iocasta, 528–67, is the appeal of the old poet to his fellow-citizens to be wise before it is too late, to recognize equity as a law not only of human society but of nature itself, and to see clearly and avoid the degradation and suffering which will accompany defeat. The *stichomythia* (line-by-line exchange) which follows this lofty speech offers a vivid picture of politicians dealing with a matter of life and death in a fashion which abandons dignity to score points in a battle of abuse.

The next scene is a short one consisting chiefly of Eteocles' haphazard and rash proposals for defensive strategy, followed by his ready acceptance of a sensible suggestion from Creon. It seems likely that such a dialogue contained for its first audience topical references which are lost to us. There is also, in 751 ('To name each one would be a foolish waste of time'), a reference to Aeschylus' *Seven Against Thebes*, where a third of the play is taken up with descriptions of the seven champions on either side. The significance of this is twofold. First, it is a reminder to the audience that, though this play treats the same story as that of Aeschylus, its character and purpose are different; it is concerned not with the nature of Fate and the tragic consciousness of the hero, but with a story picturing the present situation of Athens, a drama which extends forward from the stage to include as its tragic hero the whole audience of citizens, suicidally sticking to their stubborn creed of *tyrannis*. Secondly, this reference to the earlier play will be remembered by the audience presently, when the Messenger, by wasting time over his description of the attacking champions, ensures that Iocasta will come too late to save her sons' lives – an all too recognizable pattern of the chances and blunders which have decided major events in every war from Eteocles' day to our own. Two other points may be noticed in this scene. First, Eteocles voices in one line his resolve to kill his brother, and in the next a tender concern for his sister; secondly, having asserted in 502 that terms like 'equity' are meaningless words, he now goes off to battle proclaiming his confidence in 'Justice, my ally'.

The Athenian *demos*, the body politic, is by now identified with Eteocles; but the Phoenician Chorus are non-political women and in their second Stasimon they appeal to all those in the audience who are capable of human feelings deep enough to override politics. They invite them to join in heartfelt execration of the miserable destructiveness of war, which negates all the spontaneous joys of life. The last section of the Ode further strengthens that identification by summarizing the legend of Thebes and recounting, in terms which clearly recall the history of democratic Athens, a crescendo of glory which is now on the point of vanishing in the final collapse of the royal house. When the Ode is finished there appears – for once, un-announced – the unmistakable figure of Teiresias. It now begins to be clear what pattern Euripides is constructing for this long and variegated play. No story or set of characters was better known to the audience than this Theban saga. Its closing cata-strophe is the theme, and all its characters (except of course Laius) are to be included. Eteocles is given the central role in the play, and he is given the character of the Athenian *demos* in the last stage of its long struggle. All the familiar characters are grouped around Eteocles and the relation of each to him, and his to each, is displayed; and the pageant takes place in the last hour before death. The ironical last line of this Ode, 'crowned with the proudest garlands of war', is offered to an audience of citizens who still have it in their power to change their city's policy and save her from the humiliation of total defeat.

Teiresias' first speech contains warnings: 'the land has long been sick'; defeat is imminent; those who rule 'are possessed, and will destroy the state'. Any suggestion of irony in the treatment of Teiresias is avoided until after this message has been delivered. This done, the obvious pretence of reluctance to reveal a way of deliverance prepares us to receive the revelation with scepticism; so we are not surprised at the outworn, discredited, suspect remedy which is prescribed. It is as always – the innocent must suffer for the guilty, the honest for the false. This happens in all six plays in this volume, and in others too; the significance of such sacrifices is particularly set forth in *The Children of Heracles* and *Iphigenia in Aulis*, where Demophon and Menelaus respectively demonstrate how superstition enslaves the intelligence of brave men (as, for example, Nicias at Syracuse) or is used by the unscrupulous for their own ends. To sharpen the irony, Teiresias in his explanation talks seriously about Ares and his dragon, in an atmosphere which makes fairy-tales ridiculous; and adds some formal nonsense about the virginity of Menoeceus which is a palpable manoeuvre to accommodate the accepted legend about Haemon and Antigone. In fact Teiresias in this play is much the same kind of plausible fraud that he is in *The Bacchae*, though here he is more sinister. By his display of impressive and dangerous nonsense he dismisses himself as a serious character; his impact, unhappily, remains as a part of the traditional scene, and Menoeceus, who has no sophistic training, believes him. No one less young and innocent than Menoeceus could have believed this Teiresias; and Creon's unheroic reaction is hardly a 'bold stroke' on the dramatist's part, but rather a relief to the audience; and of course it is a finely dramatic preparation for Menoeceus' self-sacrifice. As he departs Menoeceus says, 'I will purge our country from her sickness.' But, as the audience know, he did not accomplish this; even if – as could never be proved – he saved his country from defeat, still in spite of his sacrifice the sickness raged as before, till it had obliterated the royal house and brought the history of early Thebes to an end in its destruction by the Epigoni (see the last scene of *The Suppliants*). We shall notice that when Creon reappears he cannot, even to comfort himself, consider any supposed connection between his son's sacrifice and the Theban victory as worth mentioning.

Now comes the First Messenger with his account of the battle; and we should ask; What is the significance of the particular way in which this account is given? It has been argued by some critics that, since the important thing in this play is exciting incident rather than universal truth, we should accept the vivid details of the battle, and equally the single combat of the brothers, merely as brilliant entertainment. It seems sounder criticism to try to relate such features first to the consciousness of the audience and next to other notable passages of the play. The narrative speech begins with a brief allusion to the ritual suicide of Menoeceus – an allusion so brief and banal as to suggest a sardonic dismissal of the whole episode as a piece of mumbo-jumbo. A subtle actor (and we must remember again that the dramatist directed the production) would have no difficulty in clothing such lines with an irony certain to elude those listeners who were not looking for irony. The enumeration of the leaders attacking the seven gates is relevant chiefly to the audience's despairing knowledge that they were menaced from every direction by the hatred of many different enemies. The provision of gory details, as in 1149–52, 1192–5, might indeed, in another context, or twenty years earlier, have aimed only at excited entertainment; but in the year 409, and after the irresistible eloquence of lines 784–800 ('O Ares, bringer of agonized exhaustion' etc.), the message must have worn an unpleasant realism for a fairly high proportion of those present.

The naming of Polyneices as merely fifth in the roll of seven attackers warns us that the final combat is not to come as a result of cosmic determinism. When the deliberate wickedness of both brothers is revealed, two points become clear. First, the slaughter hitherto inflicted has all been needless.* Secondly, whereas Thebes versus Argos and her allies is perhaps a cloudy

* One irony underlying the whole Trojan saga is that, had Athene suggested the wooden horse to Odysseus some years earlier, all the heroism of the *Iliad* could have been avoided.

symbol of Athens versus Sparta and her allies, Eteocles against Polyneices is a crystal-clear one. Euripides has invented the single combat not merely to vary his entertainment, but to isolate the fratricidal struggle and present it as a pattern of the desperate and exhausted war now going on a few miles outside the Athenian Long Walls. And when the fight is over and the brothers are dead, a third ironical comment is left staring bleakly at the spectator: after both sides had sworn to accept the result of single combat as decisive in the quarrel for 'sole possession', in the event they simply fell to fighting again. A final irony is heard in 1255 ff., where the description of the priests' solemnities, by recalling Aeschylus, *Prometheus* 493-8 (Prometheus' account of how he taught men the art of divination), reminds us that superstitions which may have been excusable thirteen generations before Heracles are in fact still being allowed to affect life-and-death decisions in the last decade of the fifth century.

By this time the analogy with the two combatants in the Peloponnesian War begins to be felt almost continuously:

> Two brothers are this moment reeling towards death,
> And we must stop each murdering the other's life.

The image of the fighting beasts recurs; and with 1285-7 ('Pity distracts my aching heart, Pity for a mother's misery') there first appears the possibility of a further symbol which still more powerfully underlies the situation in *Orestes*: the symbol of Hellas herself as the mother, ravaged and pitiable because of her sons' murderous hatred. Along with this, a dominating pattern of Greek religion begins to emerge in the rounded shape which Euripides gave to it. Man's duty is to *know himself* — as a mortal man, and neither a god nor a beast. Oedipus, both wittingly and unwittingly, had challenged Fate and the Sphinx and was seen as a god by his people; his two sons rejected the law by which alone man can survive as man (see Euripides, *Hecabe* 798-805), and became beasts. Iocasta knows herself, and the world, and the men of her family, and is, within limits, a wise mortal; but her wisdom cannot save, still less change, those who do not know themselves.

When Creon returns mourning for his dead son, he adds several touches to the developing complexity of his character. He knows (like the Messenger) that Menoeceus 'gave his life for Thebes and won for himself the name of hero', but never refers to any possible connection between the sacrifice and the victory. He emphasizes the importance of 'showing due piety to the gods of earth' by honouring one who is dead, thus preparing us for reflection later, when he forbids the burial of Polyneices. But his main function is to receive the Messenger's report of the battle between the brothers. The moral aspect of this battle is put in the most uncompromising terms: each prays to his chosen divinity, 'Grant that I may kill my brother'; but the political analogy is further confirmed when Eteocles offers this blasphemous petition 'gazing towards Athene's golden shield'. Again comes the image of fighting beasts; but the beasts are human, and their death causes the death of their mother.

Most editors agree that the end of the play is spurious. Some hold that 1581 is the last line of genuine Euripides; others place the change at 1643, 1703, or elsewhere. The textual and stylistic arguments are complex. Some of the objections to the general pattern of the text as we have it seem to me to lack force. That Oedipus, the central figure of the whole saga, the truly tragic and godlike hero, should appear, still full of nobility and courage, after his degenerate sons have fallen, at least softens the finality of despair. That Antigone should choose to accompany his exile may indeed sound like an idea derived from Sophocles' *Oedipus at Colonus*; but that may be because Sophocles' play is so much the better known to us. That she should set off with her father promising to slip back at night and bury her brother is reasonable enough in a passage where realism has ceased to be important and only poetry matters.

The style of the last 180 lines contains certain puzzles, but in general is not notably below standard (the spurious ending of *Iphigenia in Aulis*, for example, is a poor piece of composition). Even the last speech of Antigone is congruous with several earlier passages in this play, and similar in feeling to Agauë's words near the end of *The Bacchae*. What is certainly spurious is the final six-line speech of Oedipus, adapted from the end of Sophocles' *Oedipus Tyrannus*; it seems to replace an original ending now lost.

ORESTES

The strongest impression gained from studying the text of this play is that of a work written with passionate intensity. The author knew that it would be his last personal address to his fellow-citizens; for in the following year he left Athens for Macedon; and the closing lines of the first Stasimon sound like a farewell. From first to last the play is about Athens, her fall from greatness, her hopeless future. The final scene has often been called a 'happy ending', and scholars have tried to classify the play on this assumption; but this kind of classification is a sterile exercise. There may be several ways of interpreting the ironies of Apollo's appearance; but the ending is not happy. In the course of the action we find the tragedy of the Athenian *demos* set forth under various guises: Orestes and Electra, the house of Tantalus, the audience themselves, and in one aspect the Chorus, all offer their varied pictures of what is happening in Athens, and to Athens; but Orestes in his sickness and guilt is the clearest symbol of all – the symbol of a generation which has destroyed with the evils of war the land that gave it birth, and is now suffering the insanity consequent upon so unnatural an act.

Is this insanity curable? Can Orestes escape, either from himself or from the indignant citizens of Argos? At the beginning of the action he has three redeeming qualities. He is tenderly affectionate to his sister Electra; he still has some courage; and he retains enough moral sense to know that the killing of his mother was a hideous act which Agamemnon himself, were he alive, would have forbidden. On the other hand he has lost all stability and common sense. Though he knows his own guilt, he struggles to unload it on to some one else; first, on Helen (and it is his expression of contempt and anger against Helen which brings on him his raging fit); then on Clytemnestra; and lastly on Apollo. His panic in face of Tyndareos leads him into foolish and contradictory arguments. The theory that a mother is merely 'a field sown with another's seed' could hardly appear to any section of the audience as anything but a panic gesture of lost nerve, and the fact that it is an idea borrowed from the unsound pleading of Apollo in Aeschylus' *Eumenides* confirms the irony. In the opening scene, after recovering from his fit, Orestes said to Electra, 'I believe my father . . . would have . . . implored me not to lift a sword against my mother'; yet in defending himself to Tyndareos he says, 'Suppose I had approved my mother's act by silence, what would my dead father have done to me?' His approach to Menelaus is abject; his repulse of Menelaus' limited offer of help is abusive. When Orestes is thus at his extremity, Pylades arrives; and from that point on Orestes begins to lose the last vestiges of a moral nature. In addressing the Argive Assembly he employs the same paltry argument he had tried on Tyndareos: if women like Clytemnestra are not murdered, all wives will make slaves of their husbands. He readily embraces the murderous proposals of Pylades and Electra, and proceeds to carry them into effect with the ritualistic zest proper to mental derangement. After all this, any reader who can take the final theophany at its face-value as a happy ending must surely be impervious to theatrical experience. The insanity of Orestes is incurable except by death. The war-mania of Athens (diagnosed by Euripides in *The Suppliant Women*) from which she has been dying for twenty years, is incurable except by defeat; therefore the poet and prophet, like Apollo in *Alcestis*, will leave the doomed house, and is now speaking to the Athenians for the last time.

An important question must be settled before we go further in studying the play. What is the character of Helen? Helen speaks only thirty-six lines in one short scene; but throughout the action she is close at hand in the palace; her name is spoken on the stage again and again; she is the unseen centre of the climactic action described by the Phrygian slave in a long and unique narrative episode; and in the final tableau she is beside Apollo, an immortal goddess – which indeed legend had always accepted as her destiny. It is traditional to assert that in her short scene she shows herself as shallow, heartless, self-centred, self-excusing, spoilt. Is this in fact true? Is it even likely that a character of no worth or interest should hold such a consistently important place in the dramatic pattern? The style in which Helen speaks is reserved, formal, graceful. Any rendering which indicates by her language a stupid and shallow nature is unwarranted; judgement of her intended character should be based on the words the dramatist gave her to speak, considered in their context. In fact, however, it has almost always been assumed that Euripides intended us to accept the same estimate of her which he puts into the mouth of Electra.

This question properly involves a study not only of *Orestes*, but of the whole attitude of Euripides to the figure of Helen, which is too large a subject for this Introduction. Two considerations may be briefly alluded to here. First, the structure of the play seems clearly to invite a comparison between the two women: Electra, who has just murdered her mother, and Helen, who seventeen years ago deserted her husband. Both misdeeds are traditionally ascribed to divine influence. Helen is a mature woman of thirty-five; she has been brought to a city where most people have never seen her but nevertheless are ready to stone her in the streets; where she hoped to find one person who would welcome her – her sister Clytemnestra; and she arrives to find that Clytemnestra was a murderess, and has now herself been murdered. The young woman who murdered her curses Helen 'for the ruin you've brought on me, and on Orestes, and on all Hellas'. Before the end of the play Electra is evidently a homicidal maniac. There is little support here for the view that we should accept Electra's estimate of Helen. The second consideration is this: in two of his most celebrated plays, *Medea* and *Hippolytus*, Euripides took the stories of two women traditionally execrated for their crimes, and presented them without either extenuation or malice, but with sympathetic perception of their characters and situations. Would it not be natural that he should reassess this case as he did the other two? There are more arguments, some especially cogent; but the reader, once alerted, may more enjoyably pursue the inquiry for himself. The present translation assumes, in the absence of proper evidence to the contrary, that the author intended to present Helen as a dignified, gentle, and conciliatory person. This judgement affects our understanding of the whole play. If Helen is not the frivolous doll Orestes assumes her to be, but is rather what Aeschylus describes in *Agamemnon* 737 ff. as 'a still enchantment of sweet summer calm', with a mind to match her outward presence, then both the murder and the apotheosis have a doubled power and poignancy, which we shall consider in due course.

The Chorus now enter. They are women of Argos; their husbands are setting off for the Assembly where they will try Orestes and Electra for the murder of their mother; and the wives, though in no way condoning this act, come out of mere humanity to comfort Electra. She does not welcome them; and some have thought that her dialogue with the women as they enter was a hint by the poet that in the kind of play he is writing a Chorus is an irrelevance. This is surely mistaken. The Chorus of Argive women fill a vital role in the picture of Athens which is being presented. As Orestes and Electra stand for the active and powerful elements in Athenian life, so the women of the

Chorus are the ordinary people, good-hearted but uncritical, whose acceptance of the current leadership, good or bad, is an important factor in any nation's war-effort. When the first scene is over, they chant a moving prayer to the Furies, begging mercy for Orestes.

> Release him, let him forget
> The fury and frenzy of madness . . .
> The greatest happiness is not permanent
> In the world of men.

They are speaking of the house of Tantalus; but few could fail to think of the old prosperity of pre-war Athens, which they had known or been told of; and in the lines

> And this was the house of Tantalus . . .
> A house that claimed my reverence
> More than any house I have known

some would hear the voice of the poet himself, now at the age of seventy-two about to leave his home and city to die in exile.

In the second Stasimon, when they have witnessed the folly and the moral bankruptcy of Orestes, their condemnation is even stronger:

> 'Crime in a just cause' is an impious sophistry,
> An insanity breeding in evil hearts.

But a sinister change takes place in them after Orestes has returned from the Assembly condemned, and Pylades has taken the lead, appealing to Orestes' thirst for revenge on Menelaus (for an injury which is largely imaginary), and finally quenching in him the last traces of decent humanity. The Argive women have never seen Helen, only heard her reviled for as long as they can remember; but they are hypnotized at once into the fashionable attitude and offer excuses for the stupid and inhuman plan put forward by Pylades. When Electra proposes her equally revolting cruelty they make no protest; and after the mockery of the invocation (1225 ff.) they readily accept

Electra's commands and keep watch on the road to see that bloodshed is not prevented. A little later they are equally helpful in trapping Hermione; and just before the entry of the Phrygian they speak of their eagerness to see 'with our own eyes the dead body of Helen bleeding on the palace floor'. Euripides never used a Chorus, except perhaps in *The Bacchae*, with more powerful ironical effect. In his mirror he shows the ordinary decent people of Athens what happens to them under the stresses of war and unscrupulous leadership. The grotesqueness of that bloodthirsty wish achieves two effects. In the first place, coupled with the sudden comic spell-breaking line which follows ('Or heard a clear account from one of the servants'), it somewhat mitigates the painfulness of the dramatist's attack on the humbler members of his audience. Secondly, it relates itself to all the vicious, jealous gibes which Electra, Orestes, Tyndareos, and Pylades have lost no chance of flinging at Helen since the play began, and illuminates their true force and character: the hypocritical evasions of a guilt-ridden house.

Helen's husband Menelaus is an intriguing study. At his approach the Chorus, who have just been lamenting the imminent destruction of the disastrous house of Tantalus, suddenly turn – with a natural politeness – from sincerity to convention and say what is expected on such an occasion as this long-deferred homecoming; they greet Menelaus as 'a son of this glorious house'. They thus change the atmosphere back from one of stark truth to one of familiar, everyday pretence; which is surely a deliberate move, since there is a good deal of this pretence in Menelaus, though a good deal of sincerity as well. (The quality of pretence is underlined by his incongruous story of Glaucus' prophecy.) When in 372 Menelaus says that on landing at Nauplia he looked forward to embracing Orestes and Clytemnestra, he cannot be implying that he disbelieved Glaucus, since his words show that he knew Agamemnon was dead; the only conclusion is that he has made a slight slip in his conventional opening speech, forgetting for a moment that one does not embrace one's brother's murderess. A close study of the play makes it hard to believe that any of this is due to carelessness on the author's part. He knew exactly what he was doing; Menelaus is intended to be a puzzle, but one which will become clearer as the action proceeds. It is only fair to remember how long ago he left home; a noncommittal attitude is obviously the safest. And there is this further to be said for him: whereas Orestes, Electra, Tyndareos, and the Chorus, all deteriorate morally under the stress of fear, anger, and excitement, Menelaus does not.

As Orestes' story comes out, Menelaus commits himself to a clear judgement of Apollo's oracle as a denial of law and right; and this implies that Orestes ought to have been capable of the same judgement. Menelaus' position is certainly difficult. Argos is not his city; he is on his way to Sparta. Also he knows, and knows that others know, that he himself is next in succession, should Orestes not become king of Argos (see Note on line 1108). Whatever armed force he may have with him, to try to use it to influence the decision of the Argive Assembly in a matter like this would be extremely unwise; to let it be thought that he approved of Orestes' act would be equally foolish. His nettled reaction to his hectoring father-in-law shows that he is trying to be fair to Orestes and making full allowance for the weight of Apollo's command. He is a reasonably honest man trying to use his intelligence rather than his emotions in dealing with a complex situation.

Tyndareos, a generation older, also has some intelligence; but his emotions take a stronger part in governing his actions and reactions. He begins by talking some very sound sense; he brings the issue right into the fifth century – this indeed has already been hinted at by the democratic notion of having Orestes tried before the Assembly of citizens, who, if they can try Orestes, could equally have tried Clytemnestra. Our ancestors, Tyndareos says, established a sound principle: the crime of murder 'must be atoned by exile, not by blood for blood'.* He sees the folly of an endless chain of revenges; he exalts law above individual violence, and denounces anarchy no less in the cities of Hellas.

Orestes' reply to Tyndareos is, from first to last, the essence of folly. Tyndareos had advocated lawful proceedings against Clytemnestra, which 'would have preserved both law and piety'; Orestes can only say, 'I avenged my father; and for that act I am pure.' His arguments are all either irrelevant, or contradictory, or offensive; he finishes his speech with an implication that Menelaus' unstable marriage was the cause of his matricide. The Chorus make a sarcastic comment; and now Tyndareos in his indignant reply forgets all the rational restraint of his first speech, calls for death by public stoning for both Orestes and Electra, warns Menelaus against trying to save his nephew:

Reckon the cost of having me for an enemy –

and departs, while Orestes shouts after him, and then turns back to ask Menelaus why he is pensive and distracted. Menelaus is willing to listen to further pleas from Orestes, though he suggests that there are times when silence is better than speech. The truth of this could not be more clearly shown than by the hotch-potch of rigmarole and rhetoric in which Orestes then states his case.

Menelaus replies, in effect: 'I can't help you with armed force – it would be useless; but I will try to persuade Tyndareos and the Argive Assembly to moderate their fury.' This reasonable answer earns him the names of 'coward' and 'traitor', which would be enough to induce most men to change their minds and make no effort to influence the Assembly. Having discarded Menelaus as an ally Orestes now welcomes Pylades, who is a more kindred spirit; and within a few lines they are exchanging the stock gibes about Helen. What sort of person is

*See Note on lines 536–537.

Pylades, and what is his place in the pattern? His two noticeable qualities correspond to just those two features of the soldier's life which make war tolerable, exciting and acceptable to men in every century: comradeship in danger and daring, and a sense of freedom from every social or moral law. If, as seems probable, the symbolism of the whole play bears reference to Athens and the war, Pylades is surely the spirit of war itself, an embodiment of Ares. In the present scene he is all comradeship, and goes off with Orestes to support him in the trial. When they return and are joined by Electra, at the moment of their resigned despair Pylades seizes the initiative; and from then on the impetus of reckless violence carries all before it.

The speech of the Messenger seems to have had some fame in antiquity; Menander used it as a model for a long narrative in *The Sicyonian*. It beautifully illustrates Euripides' method. The speaker is a simple countryman, easily taken in, devoted to the royal family, and anxious to be as tactful as possible. His relaxed opening is a needed relief after the intensity which precedes it. He describes four speeches besides that of Orestes. The most sensible, that of Diomedes, he deals with in two and a half lines; evidently it gained little attention. The one he praises most is based on much the same kind of irrelevance as Orestes used at the beginning of his plea to Tyndareos – the 'deterrent' argument. It is implied that Tyndareos also spoke for the death-sentence; Menelaus is not mentioned. Orestes' own defence is as ill-judged, foolish, and falsely reasoned as it could well be. The listeners in the theatre are left to make their own judgement both on the Messenger and on the conduct of the trial as he reports it.

Electra's long monody of lament for the extinction of her family is difficult to accommodate in a modern production, which would probably be satisfied with the first two stanzas and cut the rest. But in the fifth and fourth centuries B.C. both the dramatist's music and the actor's performance would sustain the interest. The theme of the last two stanzas is the continuity of the present with the past through the inevitable sequence of cause and effect; this thought was very pertinent to the question so many Athenians must have asked as the final defeat approached: How did we reach this desperate strait? Where did we go wrong? The second stanza expresses most clearly the despair of Athenians at their city's hopeless outlook:

> Gone is the race of Pelops, root and branch,
> The prosperous home that was the world's envy;

and a few lines later, an echo from the first Stasimon:

> In the length of mortal life there is no permanence.

With the next scene sanity finally abdicates and Pylades takes over direction. The zest and grim wit that season his wickedness (e.g. 'Well, it's perhaps more suitable to leave her out') almost sound pleasant beside the sordid blood-lust which fills Orestes ('I want to hurt my enemies before I die') and the calculating cruelty of Electra. The proposal of cold-blooded murder causes not a second's hesitation. Once again there are gibes against Helen as an avaricious doll. Having made his plan with Orestes Pylades comes forward to sell it to the public. He is addressing Athenians whose families have during twenty-two years been again and again bereaved of sons, fathers, husbands. The killing of a bad woman, he tells them, as revenge for these losses, will bring joy and satisfaction to them all:

> There'll be cheering in the streets,
> Bonfires will blaze to all the gods . . .

To picture truly the effect of this in the theatre, we may remember that it was an Athenian audience three generations earlier, in a much less anguished situation than the present one, which fined Phrynicus a thousand drachmas for making them all burst into tears with his play about the capture of Miletus. Nevertheless it is this outrageous speech of Pylades which draws from the Chorus their comment in 1153–4 – a sentiment unhappily sincere, which both forgets and illustrates the more worthy irony of 605–6. Orestes' fulsome praise for Pylades leads naturally to his avowal that profitless revenge is his one desire. When he refers to Agamemnon he says of him exactly what was often said about Pericles, a man whom Hellas

> Chose for command by merit – no despot, but one
> Who had a god's strength in him;*

a man in whose day Athens had had a loftier concept of freedom than that which Orestes will claim by murdering Helen to punish Menelaus.

The crescendo of devilry reaches a suitable climax in the litany of invocation to Agamemnon's spirit (1125 ff.) – a travesty made more shocking by memories of the solemnity felt in the scene from Aeschylus' *Choephori* which is here parodied. But the power of ritual has its effect: the Chorus of Argive women are moved by it to whole-hearted cooperation in the murder; they turn not a hair when they hear Helen's dying cry; and Electra's insane ecstasy of hate which follows it troubles them no more than her treacherous plea to Hermione, 'My own mother brought you up'. When Electra has entered the palace, these good women, now thoroughly brain-washed, reach the nadir of their unreal, synthetic war-spirit, finding as object for their dutiful hatred the scapegoat who has so consistently been presented for their condemnation, Helen. 'How justly divine vengeance has fallen upon Helen!' The madman's murder has become the act of a god; and these women have never seen Helen. How can they be made to see her, to see what has been done in the name of that hatred which they so glibly endorse?

The Phrygian is one of Euripides' most brilliant dramatic strokes. Of course he is funny, outlandish, irrelevant, extravagant – a natural rhapsodist; his language glitters with oddities

---

* Since Agamemnon was obviously a *tyrannos*, it is hard to see the point of this phrase unless such a reference was intended.

and ineptitudes; we laugh – but if, by half-way through his scene, we are not crying too, he is an incompetent actor. Though he is Helen's servant, he is not specially beholden to her; she was a cause of his country's downfall – 'Hell-Helen'; but he saw her killed – in line 1456 he says, 'I saw, I saw'; implying, possibly, that he was not one of those locked up in the outhouses. What does it matter whether he saw? He is there to make the audience see, and this he does. They heard Helen scream; they have the Phrygian's story; and to clinch belief, out comes Orestes with a bloody sword in his hand, playing a lunatic game with the trembling Phrygian.

Menelaus returns. The Chorus, still seeing only with Orestes' eyes, call him 'a man proud in success'. Since his last appearance, he has allowed Orestes' trial to go through without saying a word. What else could he do, even if Orestes' defence had shown some shred of dignity? Some commentators on the play assume that Euripides presents Menelaus' character exactly as Orestes sees it. The truth is that, here as elsewhere, the dramatist leaves his audience to think out for themselves a question which is not central to the main message of the play. In any case, the phase of realism is past, and nightmare succeeds; even before Menelaus arrived, flames and smoke were seen in the palace; the death of Helen is veiled in supernatural mystery; Orestes' claim to govern Argos is plain lunacy; from the nightmare Menelaus appeals to the remaining source of sanity, the citizens in the audience; and Apollo appears above the palace wall, and with him immortal Helen. The world has become too sordid and brutal a place for the most perfect beauty ever created; insanity now rages everywhere, and its crowning triumph is the wanton destruction of beauty. Irony follows irony; the Trojan War may have been due to the gods' beneficent design, but Athens and Sparta are diligently purging the bloated earth of its mortal burden without Helen to inspire them; if one irritant has been removed, the arrangements made for Hermione and Electra seem calculated to supply another;

and Apollo unconvincingly contradicts what the whole drama
has asserted, that Orestes' obedience was Orestes' own responsibility. This is neatly confirmed by the final cynicism of the
whole performance, Orestes' words:

> Yet, I confess, I felt uneasy, lest the voice
> I heard, and took for your voice, was in truth the voice
> Of some accursed fiend.

And sincerity speaks in a simple, unemphatic statement of the
story's moral: 'Go, then, honouring the most noble of goddesses, Peace.'

The play is a magnificent climax to the series of protests
which for a generation Euripides had continued to launch
against the war; first, against the dereliction of honourable and
humane standards of behaviour which resulted from the first
years of conflict; later, against the suicidal folly and blood-lust
which, long after the real causes of the war had ceased to be
relevant, made Athens again and again reject opportunities for
peace, and continue to inflict upon her civilian population
hardships, bereavements, and anxieties which grew worse
every year. For the victims of such unmerited miseries these
plays plead successively in the persons of Macaria, the Chorus
of Suppliants, Evadne, Iphis, Andromache, Iocasta, Hermione,
and Iphigenia. There was one last denunciation yet to come – in
some ways the most direct and complete denunciation of all,
though an unfinished play: *Iphigenia in Aulis*.

IPHIGENIA IN AULIS

This play was written at the very end of Euripides' life, after
he had left Athens and was living at the court of King Archelaus
of Macedon. He died probably before it was completed, certainly before he had time to revise it. The incompleteness of
the manuscripts is frustrating, but does not, to my mind, ob-

scure the impression which Euripides intended the play to make upon its audience. His creative art was at its zenith; he had just finished writing *The Bacchae*. That play clearly shows what stimulus he had received from the change of scene, of company, of environment, when the anxiety and privation of a city exhausted by war was replaced by the privileged ease of a palace surrounded by mountains and solitude; and there is no reason to suppose that his genius was any less active in the months that followed, though *Iphigenia in Aulis* is as different as possible from *The Bacchae* in its whole character, theme, and treatment. The manuscript was found after the author's death by his son, who brought it to Athens and produced it on the stage, and was probably responsible for at least some of the alterations and additions which can be recognized in our present text.

The play is a tragedy, but an unorthodox one – as indeed most tragedies are. The present ending (which some commentators curiously insist on calling a 'happy' one) was written by someone else at some time within the next two centuries. There are several comedic passages, such as the arrival of Clytemnestra and her first encounter with Achilles. These are almost certainly not by Euripides, though Euripides, if he left these passages incomplete, may well have intended to use comedy at those points. There were also two different versions of the opening, and these are put together in our MSS in an unsatisfactory patchwork. A close and fascinating study of the text (for which some knowledge of Greek is necessary) is to be found in *Actors' Interpolations in Greek Tragedy*, by Professor Denys L. Page; and it is evident from the conclusions there reached that enough of the author's genuine work remains to form the basis of a clear interpretation.

Such comments, however, as are available for the non-Greek reader prove disappointing. For example, Kitto says (*Greek Tragedy*, page 362) that by the standards of Greek tragedy *Iphigenia in Aulis* 'is a thoroughly second-rate play'. He suggests

(pages 315, 365) that 'the happy ending replaces tragic cathar-
sis', and compares the play with *Alcestis*, *Ion*, and *The Merchant
of Venice*. This is misleading. Those three plays all contain
passages in a serious or painful mood, but they are classifiable as
comedies; in *Iphigenia* the mood of harsh and sombre bitterness
intensifies throughout the action, in spite of occasional relief;
and the final act of Artemis in substituting a deer for the
human victim, if it spares Agamemnon the ritual pollution,
spares him none of his shame, nor Iphigenia her ordeal, nor
Clytemnestra her loss. True, there is no tragic hero or heroine,
no pattern of crime and retribution; and we are not invited to
take divinity seriously. The play is about human suffering, its
modes and its causes; and the fact that none of the three suffer-
ers is of heroic stature – Agamemnon a moral coward, Clytemnestra a selfish and foolish woman, Iphigenia a brave child – this
fact cannot possibly make the play a comedy, whatever ending
the author intended for it.

What did Euripides mean to say in composing this piece? Did
he wish simply to entertain an audience with a good plot? or is
some 'tragic illumination' to be found here? In considering this
question we must bear in mind which passages are certainly
Euripidean and which are later additions (see below, pages 84,
89, 92 et al.); and we should be ready to recognize that some
of the additions (perhaps those made by the poet's son) not
only contain first-rate dramatic writing (e.g., the opening dialogue 1–48) but also echo and develop both the irony for which
the author was well known and the particular direction of it
which seems to have been his purpose in this play – as in the
first long speech of Achilles, 919–74. What, then, was this
purpose? For a comparison we may look back to *The Women of
Troy*. There the 'tragic hero' is the Greek nation, shown in the
Prologue as doomed already for acts of *hybris*, and through the
action earning their fate by successive crimes, till in the closing
lines they set sail for destruction; but the 'hero' never appears,
except impersonally in the figure of Talthybius (Menelaus is

there on private business). He is an unseen background of which we are constantly aware; but the play itself is concerned with his victims. In *Iphigenia in Aulis* the 'tragic hero' is once again the Greek nation (cf. Menelaus' remark in 370), whose folly has involved it in war; but here it appears in the persons of three of its leaders, while its total strength is near at hand and both seen and heard by persons on the stage – in the shape of a superstitious, brutal, and mutinous rabble of men whom the leaders call their army, but whose slaves they know themselves to be (450, 517, 1020, 1269–71, 1346 ff.). As in *The Women of Troy*, the centre of interest is the victims, though pity must expand also to the wretched ring of anti-heroes who surround them. This is the pattern of war as Euripides saw it after a generation of experience. The former play was composed between a crime and a disaster, and still its message proved ineffectual; the latter was composed when the poet had been driven by despair over the follies and prejudices of his fellow-Athenians to leave his home at the age of seventy-three and accept a new one in an unfamiliar country, while they continued to drag out a generation of war to its agonizing close. Before beginning to study the play scene by scene, let us look at a single passage which illustrates the mood in which the poet was writing. The Chorus paint a vivid picture (773–92) of what the Greek heroes are going to Troy to do.

> There will be heads forced back, throats cut,
> Streets stripped, every building gutted and crashed;
> Screams and sobs from young women . . .
> God grant that neither I nor my children's children
> Ever face such a prospect . . .

These lines the poet wrote in 407, knowing well that, as he wrote, Athenian wives were sitting 'before their looms, and asking each other, Who will be the man who twists his hard hand in my silken hair, and like a plucked flower drags me away, while my tears flow hot and my home burns?' If this play was indeed performed in Athens a year or so before the final disasters, what can have been the effect of this voice from the unheeded poet now dead?

Two recurring themes are noticeable. The first is insanity, used as a symbol both for war itself and for the kind of action to which war commits those who become involved in it. This symbolism appears as early as *The Suppliant Women*, where the Theban Herald speaks of Hellas as 'dying from war-mania'; and in *Orestes* it is central. In *Iphigenia in Aulis* Agamemnon's behaviour is repeatedly called insane (as it is by the Chorus in Aeschylus' *Agamemnon*); so is the whole impulse which has launched the expedition against Troy. The other recurring theme is the question, Who is a free man, and who is a slave? In *Hecabe*, the enslaved queen confronting the victorious king says, 'A free man? – There is no such thing. All men are slaves . . .'; and in *Iphigenia* this truth is variously illustrated, chiefly by Agamemnon, who tells his daughter that he is the slave of Hellas, and three lines later, that the sacrifice is necessary because 'Hellas must be free'; while behind the scenes, destroying everyone's freedom, is the mutinous army, itself slave to superstition and the lust for loot.

The Prologue as it stands is a patchwork. Euripides wrote a Prologue in his traditional style, lines 49–105. This has been clumsily fitted into the other passage – in itself an excellent scene – with which the play now begins; but this arrangement does not work on the stage – I have seen it well tried, and the long speech completely ruins the atmospheric opening. Agamemnon's account of the situation does not give any reason, except the word of Calchas, why Artemis was believed to require the sacrifice of Iphigenia. (One reason is given in the Prologue of *Iphigenia in Tauris*, and legend offered others.) He simply says, 'The weather was unsuitable for sailing' (88). As the play proceeds it becomes clear that what makes the murder inevitable is the superstition of the common soldiers, whom their leaders are quite unable to control; and Euripides takes care in various ways to leave the state of the weather, and the conditions of the oracle's command, as vague as possible. The later additions follow the same line. There is no mention of the storm which figures in Aeschylus' *Agamemnon*, nor even of adverse winds (1323-4 is a very dubious exception). There is a calm (10-11, 813). This difference is nowhere emphasized, but nowhere contradicted. Warships would be equipped with both oars and sails. Normal practice was to use oars for entering or leaving harbour, and sails in the open sea; but in emergency oars were available; and a position grave enough to demand human sacrifice was surely an emergency. The text of this play mentions oars repeatedly (e.g. 174, 765, 1388), and never sails (again a dubious exception in 1326). When Achilles comes to protest to Agamemnon about the delay in sailing, he implies that the Myrmidons, at least, attributed it to the indecision of the leaders, not to the weather. All this does not prove anything, except that our interest is being quietly kept away from the cosmic or the divine, from the question of the weather or the will of Artemis, and directed always to the demands of the mutinous mob and the scheming of those who use them as the tools of power-politics – Calchas, Odysseus, and Menelaus. In other words, the author presents to us as the primary source of evil and suffering in this play neither natural nor supernatural causes (though the leaders use traditional phraseology, 809, 126 4), but first the war, secondly the combined errors and follies of a group of people involved in it; and shows all these causes converging to destroy the one life in the story that is entirely innocent.

The character of the Old Man is, of course, partly at least the creation of the interpolator; but, whether this was the poet's son or some later writer, the role is in the style of Euripides. (The slave who owes loyalty rather to the misused wife than to the deceitful husband has an important part in *Ion*.) He is not merely a tool for the development of the plot; he is there as the one single-hearted adult in the play, to show clearly at the outset the duplicity and cowardice of the 'king of men'. How are we to interpret Agamemnon's true thoughts in this scene? His feeble habit of wishing that he were not a king is properly rebuked by the slave (28); but there is worse failure than this. Passages later in the play (e.g. 538–41, 749–50, 1273–5, and his line of argument in the quarrel with Menelaus) make us look very closely at the Prologue. 'I made a wrong decision then; now I'm reversing it,' he says. This at once engages sympathy. Agamemnon, however, knew pretty well how long it would take his first messenger to reach Argos, and how long it would take his daughter and her attendants to reach Aulis. He has delayed reversing his decision until a day when he must have known that the royal party could arrive at any minute; so he has been forced to the point of sending the second letter only by the immediate prospect of having to kill his daughter. This may seem harsh reasoning; but since later in the play Euripides shows us Menelaus relenting as soon as it is quite safe to do so, and Achilles airily promising with bombastic oaths what he knows he cannot fulfil, we can hardly acquit Agamemnon of dealing falsely with his own conscience in sending this letter at a time when there is little chance of its getting far. There is nothing in his later behaviour to suggest that a more charitable view should be taken of his actions in the Prologue.

However, at this early stage there is much that we do not know, and to think charitably of Agamemnon is natural; so that when the Chorus introduce themselves and say, 'We have come to see the Achaeans, heroes descended from gods', we do not yet feel the prick of irony; and when they mention that they 'ran quickly up past the altar in the grove of Artemis' with the eagerness of young girls (line 188 indicates that they are very young, though some (176) are married) to see heroes in armour, it takes a quick mind in the audience to feel the prick of apprehension anticipating the final scene at that same altar. The glory of warlike patriotism is a thing visible here to the romantic eyes of young girls, and later visible, apparently, to the doomed and resolute Iphigenia before she vanishes; but not in evidence when adults are conducting their serious business. Besides the general splendour of the camp and the harbour, the Chorus mention two other things. First, the legend of the Judgement of Paris, and the purpose of the expedition – 'to bring back Helen'. As a feature in the emotional design of the play we may notice that in the second Stasimon (773–800) the description of this purpose has become realistic: it is to sack a town and slaughter a population; while myths have come under question as a 'false and foolish fancy in the pages of poets'. Secondly, the girls from Chalcis give a full-length picture of the godlike Achilles in his physical perfection, which will sharpen the unpleasantness of surprise when he arrives and expresses himself in speech. The later part of this *Parodos* (entrance-song of the Chorus) is certainly an addition, written in imitation of the 'catalogue of ships' in the second book of the *Iliad*.

Menelaus now enters in a scuffle with a slave, and half a minute later the heroic joint-commanders are engaged in a fraternal dispute in which no holds are barred and both rake the disreputable past to find matter for abuse. When the speeches are over, eight lines of *stichomythia* follow, in which Menelaus' whining tone rings entirely false – as we realize at line 413.* The sudden return to threats as he hears the Messenger approaching should make an alert audience aware that before Menelaus entered, when he was watching the road from Argos (348), he had already assured himself that the royal chariot was near; so that the surprising repentance of 471 ff., though it seems to convince the distracted Agamemnon, and possibly the Chorus too, is not out of character after all, but of one piece with 337–75, compact of calculating pretence. Whatever Menelaus says, he knows that there will be no saving Iphigenia once she has arrived. If the Myrmidons will draw sword against Achilles (1353), what can discipline be like in the rest of the

---

* Menelaus behaves in a curiously similar way in a somewhat parallel situation in *Andromache*, 729–38.

camp, with the unsavoury Odysseus (526, 1364), the scheming
Calchas (518–20), and the ruffianly soldiers (914), all clam-
ouring for excitement and blood? Menelaus can well afford any
degree of repentance. The proposal to murder Calchas is an
artistic touch in the picture of Menelaus' villainy; all through
513–27 Menelaus knows what conclusion Agamemnon will
reach in 536–37: 'Such is my pit of misery, the blind despair
in which the gods now have me trapped.' Agamemnon is a
pretty despicable figure; it needed this refinement of brutality
on the part of Menelaus to ensure that for the present we still
feel some vestige of pity for the elder brother. It has also been
pointed out that after reminding himself (492) of his relationship to Iphigenia, Menelaus carefully guards himself (498–9)
against any imputation of guilt for kindred blood: 'My share I
give to you.' One cannot help wondering (though I doubt if
the question can be answered) whether the comment of the
Chorus in 524–5 is ironic; among the crimes which legend
recorded as having earned Tantalus his famous punishment
were infanticide and perjury.

   The charming, innocent Ode which follows provides a welcome rest between the harshness just ended and the painful
pathos to come. The first stanza describes two kinds, and two
effects, of love, 'One to bestow lifelong content, the other,
ruin and confusion'; and the reference implied is of course to
the unlawful love of Paris and Helen. Perhaps in speaking of
calm and moderate love these girls are thinking of their own
marriages; but an ironic reference to the conjugal relationship
of Agamemnon and Clytemnestra can hardly be escaped. After
the two husbands whose encounter we have just witnessed, the
loveliness of love as described in 581 shines out as well worth
any cost – the one piece of truth in the whole tangle. The antistrophe too contains a number of innocent references to jolt
the alert listener. Where on this stage is 'real goodness clearly
seen'? or the scrupulousness which is wisdom? In the coming
scenes we shall observe two instances of 'a childhood nurtured

by sound training', and be able to compare Achilles, who tells us about his moral education, with Iphigenia, whose actions speak for her when eventually she fulfils 'the vision of duty revealed by reflection'. In 571 the word translated 'discipline' is *kosmos*, 'order'; and we cannot miss the gentle allusion to the picture provided in this play, of an army whose four chief leaders are hating, opposing, and threatening each other, and all either terrorized by, or busy exploiting, the insubordination of the rabble.

Considering what the Chorus already know about Agamemnon's intention, we can hardly take as Euripides' work the lines in which the Chorus greet Clytemnestra on her arrival; most commentators assume that this was a passage the author left incomplete. The first speech of Clytemnestra too is probably a late addition; but it is partly modelled on Clytemnestra's arrival in *Electra*, and is an entertaining piece of comedy in the manner of Menander; it is not incongruous with the subsequent development of the character. In twenty-four lines she includes twelve imperatives, ten stage-directions, and other fussy chat showing her excitement at the occasion. She is so busy with all this that Agamemnon's entry must take place unobtrusively, somewhere in the second half of her speech; and she only remembers to greet him politely some lines later.

This pattern is skilfully used – whether by Euripides or by the interpolator – for a double purpose: it illustrates Agamemnon's embarrassment, and it makes clear Iphigenia's extreme youth – she is probably not more than fourteen. This immaturity is the key to her role, and in particular to the brilliant combination of tenderness and irony which the poet shows in her last scene. For the moment, a point of structure in the present scene is worth noting. In 693 Clytemnestra nearly precipitates the crisis by implying that *she* will lead Iphigenia to her bridegroom in the wedding ceremony, thus carefully correcting Agamemnon's statement in 690 that *he* will give away the bride. The postponement of the crisis suits Agamemnon's

abjectness, but also gives opportunity for the fifteen lines de-
tailing the divine and miraculous origins of Achilles, which
comprise the whole gamut of mythical fancy from Zeus to the
nymphs and centaurs. This fantastical world is alien to the
pragmatic atmosphere of the play, and alien to Agamemnon,
who supplies the answers to his wife's questions like a Classical
Dictionary, evidently speaking *ad feminam*; for Clytemnestra,
like Creusa in *Ion*, finds belief in religious myth no problem,
and *credit quia incredibile*. At the end of all this comes the last
gleam of comedy: 'Such is the man who will marry your child.'
– 'Not bad.' The close of the scene, with Clytemnestra defiant
and Agamemnon beaten, could appear funny, if we did not
know that the end of all this was the altar and the knife.

In the second Stasimon the Chorus, immature girls as they
are, try to face reality, compelled to it by the harshness of the
scene they have just witnessed. The heroes they so admired are
going to Troy with the deliberate purpose of committing murder and rape, on a huge scale, against people like themselves
and their own families in Chalcis. If Euripides had intended this
play as a comedy, its purpose would have been to provide for
the besieged Athenians a brief escape from the prospect which
every month grew closer and grimmer: defeat and capture.
Instead we have (762–92) the very pictures of horror which,
while Euripides was writing, kept Athenian women awake at
night. And the Ode is rounded off with realism of another kind,
as these innocent but intelligent girls, of a different generation
from the credulous Clytemnestra, open the door of scepticism
a narrow crack, to let in the flood of reason which in half a line
(800) reduces Achilles' lineage, Paris' judgement, Artemis'
oracle, and all such lies, to 'a false and foolish fancy'.

Now, after his imposing build-up by Agamemnon and by the
Chorus, enters the young man whom Clytemnestra, when she
meets him, will insist on addressing repeatedly as 'son of the
goddess'. He orders an attendant at the tent-door to summon
the Commander-in-Chief to speak to him; and then tells the

audience how impatient his Myrmidons are with 'the delays of the sons of Atreus'. He mentions the 'light winds over Euripus', which his men seem to regard as no impediment ('What are we waiting for?') to getting out the oars and starting for Troy. He refers to the fever of eagerness which has driven Greek men to join the expedition in such numbers – 'not without the gods' (Agamemnon echoes this 1264–5); and implies that he is not the only leader in the army who has complaints to make to the general. Altogether his opening speech contains more self-importance than dignity, and as the scene develops he does not correct this impression.

The character of Achilles as established in the *Iliad* was well known to Athenian audiences. He was the perfection of manly virtues, combining eloquence – which implied both mental and moral qualities – with courage and skill in arms. What Euripides is showing in this play is the pretence and falsity inseparable from war: the commanders who cannot command, the alleged reasons which are not real reasons, the loyalty which is expedient, the resolves which are provisional; and his Achilles fits the pattern. His tone in speaking to Clytemnestra is usually taken for a comedic exhibition of shyness, and the cross-purpose conversation would be funny in most circumstances; but here the imminence of cold murder is so close that Achilles' ineptitudes and Clytemnestra's adulation offer only the kind of relief which makes pain more painful.

His reply to her greeting as she enters is curiously phrased. The word *aidōs* means 'a sense of being overawed'; it is used for what we feel when confronted with some person whom we revere, or with some proposed act which we know would be dishonourable. Here Achilles addresses 'the goddess *Aidōs*', and proceeds to compliment Clytemnestra as 'a woman possessing a comely form'. We cannot be sure whether this cumbersome phrase is merely 'poetic diction' (which certainly can go to remarkable lengths) or if it represents the coarse embarrassment of a soldier at meeting a well-dressed woman in the camp.

Perhaps the ambiguity is deliberate. Achilles' behaviour must surely appear gauche to the audience; but Clytemnestra, unaware of this, sees only what she was expecting to see, the 'son of the goddess'. When she tells him who she is, his rudeness becomes more pronounced; he will not attempt chivalry towards a woman with whose husband he is barely on speaking terms (cf. 869). Clytemnestra still interprets his boorish manner as due to shyness. Only when it becomes evident that both he and she have been treated outrageously by Agamemnon does Achilles drop his hostility; but he still shows the self-centred insensitiveness which characterizes him – 'Don't worry; give it not another thought.' Then come the Old Man's revelations and Clytemnestra's appeal; followed by Achilles' long speech.

Unfortunately it seems probable that neither this speech nor the remainder of the scene was written by Euripides. The style falls below his usual standard; it is crude and exaggerated; there are many usages which are obscure or exceptional. A few lines of genuine quality, however, together with the ironical treatment of the situation, suggest that this passage may have been modelled fairly closely on a draft left incomplete by the author. The best we can do is to study it on this assumption; especially since the general tenor of our text leads naturally to the conclusion drawn by the Chorus at the end of the next Stasimon – a passage whose genuineness is not questioned.

Achilles' first seven lines are pretentious and irrelevant; to whom do his platitudes about misfortune and success and 'a well-governed life' refer? When he goes on to 'recklessness' and 'sound judgement' we can see that he is wondering whether the situation just revealed to him can be used to reinforce his already defiant attitude to his Commander-in-Chief. In 928–31 we hear him gaining courage and edification from his own picture of himself as a champion of freedom. In 932 he commits himself to this attractive role, and warms to his theme as he develops it, finally giving his oath, backed by pompous comparisons, that he will accomplish what Agamemnon, with far more reason for desiring it, knew he could not accomplish. Two lines are allowed to Clytemnestra's suffering, two to Iphigenia's; the rest of the speech, up to 958, is devoted to Achilles' own principles, his training, his intentions, his honour, his name, his courage, his family, his city, his jealousy of Agamemnon, and his contempt for Menelaus and Calchas. Three times he swears that no one shall lay a finger on Iphigenia. Taking breath after 958 he proceeds to more momentous ineptitudes; even Clytemnestra must feel the blow of 959–61, and in 965–7 he declares that he has no objection in principle to the slaughtering of Iphigenia, or to the use of a lie to lure her to Aulis, so long as his permission was asked. He ends with two pictures of himself which give him obvious satisfaction: in one he is terrorizing Agamemnon with a reeking sword (970), in the other he is being honoured as not merely the son of a goddess but a god (974).

When he has finished, the admiring comment of the Chorus may perhaps be innocent enough; though if we recall the closing lines of the last Ode we may notice that what they do not say is, 'Son of Peleus, your words are worthy of your father' (cf. 504); and if we look at the next Ode, lines 1081 ff. indicate clearly enough what they think of his promises. As for Clytemnestra, the bewildering crassness of the speech she has just listened to makes it hard for her to find any reply which can hope to achieve her one purpose; yet she cannot, must not, do or say anything to weaken the frail hope that this blusterer will help her and save her daughter. The repetition of her appeal when Achilles has already promised help is a fault which we need not ascribe to Euripides. Clytemnestra feels her way, plays to his vanity. The ambiguity of 990 should be noted. It could mean, 'Your speech was admirable from beginning to end'; but it could also mean more nearly what it says, which is, 'The moral sentiments you began with were admirable; so was the promise of help with which you ended' – omitting mention of all that went between. Clytemnestra's closing lines are a

piece of technical competence: it is sufficient here to mention
the *idea* of Iphigenia kneeling to beg for her life; she will
actually do this in the scene with Agamemnon. Before he departs, Achilles repeats his promise (1007) with an over-confi-
dence which does not convince Clytemnestra; and a few lines
later makes it clear that the necessity of keeping in with the
general and with the army is still an important consideration.
When Clytemnestra asks, 'Where shall I find you if I'm desperate?' he will say no more than, 'I'll be on the look-out for
you'. The mother trying to save her daughter from the knife
must be a slave (1033) ruled by the spoilt and empty youth
obsessed with self-importance. When he has gone, she speaks
her bitter despondency: 'If there are gods . . .' She who has
revelled in the thought of Achilles' divine parentage is forced
to acknowledge the possibility that neither Thetis nor any
other divinity exists. If that is so, then death and weeping must
be endured.

The third Stasimon (1036-97) is a lovely poem; it is also a
significant step in the development of the drama. It firmly removes the action further away from comedy. The first two
stanzas describe the wedding of Peleus and Thetis, when Cheiron foretold the greatness of Achilles and the exploits he and
his Myrmidons would accomplish against Troy. But the third
stanza reminds us to doubt the innocence of the Chorus's comment on Achilles' long speech (975-6); apparently they saw in
it what Clytemnestra saw and what some at least of the audience surely could not miss – though many modern commentators could. This Ode does not entertain a shred of hope that
Achilles can or will carry out his boastful promises. Nor does it
suggest that there is anything either sacred, or beautiful, or
true, in the notion that Artemis requires the blood of a girl, or
that the whole cruel crime is anything other than a pandering
to brutal superstition for the purpose of keeping mutinous
soldiers in order.* The girls from Chalcis waste no time pro-

---

* In Aeschylus, *Agamemnon* 803-4, the Elders interpret it similarly.

pounding the theology which in *Iphigenia in Tauris* (380–91) criticizes Artemis for her human sacrifices. They condemn outright the murder demanded in the goddess's name, and proceed, without bothering to explain that of course the goddess does not really want a girl's throat cut, to denounce the ruthlessness of powerful men who forget that they are mortal and tread down goodness and overrule law because they no longer tremble at the terror of God. The last eight lines of this Ode are as passionate a cry against the triumph of wickedness as any in Euripides – and Achilles has not yet been put to test. Could there be a clearer guide to the interpretation of Achilles' speech (whether as it stands, or as the poet designed it), and of his part in the drama?

Now Clytemnestra confronts her husband. The advice Achilles gave her – to use all her power of persuasion to make him save his child's life – was well enough. She is a woman of some sense, and the moment is desperate. She, if anyone, ought to know how to handle Agamemnon. She challenges him with what she knows, calls out Iphigenia, and shatters his prevarications to dumbness. Then begins her speech of sixty-two lines; and we must ask, With what effect in mind did Euripides compose this speech? Is it, as commentaries tend to assume, just another 'law-court harangue' like so many that this author wrote? Did he, in fact, write law-court harangues only because people liked them? or did he sometimes use them to say what he meant to say? Admittedly, our notion of what is appropriate at such a moment will not necessarily coincide with the notion held by our counterparts in the original audience. With this caution in mind, let us attempt an objective account of the speech.

'First – that this may be the first reproach I cast at you . . . I never wanted to marry you at all; you forced me to.' Is this the most persuasive opening Euripides could give her? Has her own quarrel with her husband pushed their daughter's peril to one side? 'I was a model wife to you, little as you deserved it; and such wives are rare. In return you rob me of one of my daughters.' The crime, apparently, is a crime against Clytemnestra rather than against Iphigenia. The next point made (1166-70) arises from jealousy of her sister; and the next (1171-84) is entirely concerned with the suffering Clytemnestra will undergo when deprived of her child. The disillusionment we felt when looking at Achilles as a possible rescuer for Iphigenia is repeated, and with more bitterness, as we observe how Clytemnestra uses the last possible chance of averting murder. Nearly forty lines have been spoken, and still no appeal to Agamemnon's manhood, no reference to the sacredness of a young life, or the bond of the marriage-bed. Lines 1185-95 at least appeal to a sense of right and wrong, and to the relationship of a family with a father; but 1201-5 plunge us back into despair over this unworthy mother: 'Let Menelaus, the cause of the whole war, kill his daughter Hermione. I've always behaved properly, yet I'm to lose my child; Helen's an adulteress, yet she can keep hers.' Let a girl's throat be cut, so long as it's my niece and not my daughter; and if there's anything wrong with my argument, tell me (1206). In the ascending scale of irony, here is the keenest yet – though the ultimate is still to come. Agamemnon may be despicable, but we have seen enough of him to know that what he feels for Iphigenia is a more worthy and humane emotion than anything Clytemnestra has expressed to him. Her inner feelings may be creditable; but what she has put into words is not; and more than that, it must fail totally to move Agamemnon – no line of this speech ever had a hope of success. Thus we see completed the pattern of the play, which shows four people in high position, all behaving in a way that makes us, the audience, blush for them. This is in the Euripidean tradition. Admetus in *Alcestis*, Xuthus in *Ion*, Agamemnon in *Hecabe*, Hecabe in *The Women of Troy*, Cadmus in *The Bacchae* – the unconscious shame of the great is one of Euripides' preoccupations.

The speech of Iphigenia comes at a point where any reader or member of an audience who has entered deeply into the play must feel as we feel when in *Romeo and Juliet* the Nurse says, 'I think it best you married with the County' – when the last hoped-for adult support has betrayed youth and truth. This is (except for Clytemnestra's first appeal, 900 ff.) the only simple and sincere speech in the play. It is fully in character; yet all its childish qualities have perfect dignity and conviction. Love of both father and mother, and the love of life, comprise the whole theme.

The first line of Agamemnon's reply seems to hint at his sense of the difference between Clytemnestra's speech and Iphigenia's: 'I am well aware what's pitiable and what is not.' He points to the unruly army; he is the slave of Hellas – which means, of a bloodthirsty rabble exploited by Odysseus and Calchas. He repeats what Achilles said about the mad impatience of the army to get to Troy, again hinting at divine influence. The hypocritical nonsense of his last three lines – an all too natural result of the irritation Clytemnestra has caused him – is his final moral abdication:

> So far as lies in you, child, and in me, to ensure,
> Hellas must be free, and her citizens must not
> Have their wives stolen forcibly by Phrygians.

He has ceased to think and speak as a person; he is indeed a slave, with whom no free man or woman can hold converse. We shall remember this parting falsity with a further shock when we come to Iphigenia's last scene, 1378–84.

About the lyric passage which follows here (1283–1335) it is probably impossible to reach a definite judgement. Perhaps the last twenty-five lines were intended as a substitute for the first part; some editors assign them to the Chorus. The passage in its full length does not seem essential to the pattern of the play: and a lyric performance of this kind is likely to have been added or extended to give scope to some particular actor. The lengthy description of the Judgement of Paris (already referred to at 580), and the tedious sentence about Zeus' disposal of the winds, seem equally inappropriate to Iphigenia.

Presently back comes Achilles, having discovered that his rescue of the maiden, though an attractive idea, is impracticable, since even his own Myrmidons have drawn sword against him, along with the whole army. In spite of this experience Achilles continues to repeat his promises (1358–65). There might, presumably, have been a chance, if after his earlier appearance he had immediately galloped off with the girl in his chariot; now there is plainly no chance at all. The words and behaviour which before convinced the Chorus that his promises were worthless, have now led Iphigenia to the same conclusion about Achilles. She has seen Agamemnon's cowardice matched by Clytemnestra's selfishness. The rest of the adult world is represented by Menelaus, Odysseus, and Calchas. Iphigenia knows for certain that she will die today at the altar. She will not be dragged off with ignominy (1459, 790). The family tradition of royalty has come to her aid and stiffened her; she rejects the indignity of having this glib young man lend her a mock protection. She is capable of facing death bravely – if she can but grasp at some plausible *rationale* for it;* and here Euripides produces his final exquisite irony. The hollow, fatuous words with which Agamemnon departed (1270–75) now in this critical moment give Iphigenia what she needs. The false and crude material of wartime propaganda, which in every millennium leaders elaborate and soldiers mock at, can help a helpless child caught in this unsoldierly trap. With courtesy and with restraint she utters words which every scene in the play has revealed – to the adults who do not have to die just yet – as nonsense. In the mouth of the child who has to die now, this very nonsense becomes the vehicle of a dignity and courage which puts the adults to shame. When she has finished her speech, the other children present, the girls from Chalcis,

* Compare Antigone's words uttered in a similar extremity: Sophocles, *Antigone* 904–20.

suddenly see the whole truth; and the couplet in which they comment on Iphigenia's speech, while phrased in the familiar convention, clinches in its final word the reality of the whole situation. 'Your spirit and behaviour, Iphigenia, is noble; but that of chance and of Artemis is diseased.' 'The [spirit and behaviour] of chance' means simply 'the events that have led to this crisis'; and that means the behaviour of every person named in the play. 'The [behaviour] of Artemis' means oracles and the machinery of religion as adapted to military necessity. Modern usage offers a suitable rendering for the last word. 'The child alone can still show dignity and courage; the action of responsible adults, and their use of religion, stinks.' More briefly, 'Events fester, and divinity is sick.' If that was Euripides' conclusion after twenty-four years of wartime Athens, we understand why at seventy-three he set out for Macedon.

What of the two short speeches given to Achilles before he goes? Achilles may be vain, coarse, unreliable; but he has courage, and now he suddenly recognizes courage where he did not expect it. He is moved, shaken into a genuineness of feeling which is rare to him. When he tells Iphigenia to 'call upon his promise even at the altar', does he at last mean what he is saying? Euripides did not intend us to know, since Achilles himself does not know, being in the grip of a quite unfamiliar, because unselfish, emotion. There are a number of speeches in Euripides which are dramatic for this reason, that we cannot tell how far they are meant by the speaker. Achilles goes; and whatever the true ending of the play may be, we know that he was not called upon.

Iphigenia's farewell is quiet and dignified like her speech of decision; but her theme has changed from one discredited myth to another, from the liberation of Hellas to the traditional reverence for Artemis. When she has gone, the girls from Chalcis sing in her praise. Their abhorrence of the sacrifice is muted, but still expressed (1514–15, 1524–5); they extol Artemis in deference to Iphigenia's attitude, which they must honour but cannot share.* Of Agamemnon they speak with respect and goodwill, since nothing is to be gained by anything else.

There remains only the fragmentary last scene. A writer of the second century A.D., Aelianus, quotes two and a half lines as from this play: 'I will put into the hands of the Achaeans a horned deer, and sacrificing this they shall say confidently that they are sacrificing your daughter.' It is evident that this quotation came from a version of the final scene in which Artemis appeared immediately after the exit of Iphigenia, and foretold the traditional miracle. Such a version is incompatible with a Messenger recounting the sacrifice. But Aelian's quotation is as certainly not from Euripides' pen as the ending given by our manuscripts; so that if Euripides ever wrote a final scene it may have been different from both. He may have intended to offer a 'happy' ending, or at least a bearable one, to those who could so far suspend their disbelief; while those who could not must accept the play as reflecting a world which at times is not bearable. If he used Artemis *ex machina*, though we cannot guess what she said, we may be fairly sure, from the analogy of other plays, that her words were ironical. In any case the general meaning of the play is already complete by the time Iphigenia departs for the grove of Artemis.

* The Greek particle *hōs*, 1523, has a meaning which can be either 'assuming' or 'knowing'; English cannot preserve the ambiguity.

THE CHILDREN OF HERACLES

CHARACTERS

IOLAUS, *formerly a friend of Heracles*
COPREUS, *herald of Eurystheus*
CHORUS *of old men of Marathon*
DEMOPHON, *king of Athens*
ACAMAS, *brother of Demophon*
MACARIA, *daughter of Heracles*
SERVANT *of Hyllus, Heracles' eldest son*
ALCMENE, *mother of Heracles*
EURYSTHEUS, *king of Argos*
Several young sons of Heracles

*

Scene: Marathon, before the temple of Zeus.

IOLAUS *sits on the steps of an altar, with a group of boys*

IOLAUS: I have long held the opinion that an honest man
  Lives for his neighbours; while the man whose purpose
     drives
  Loose-reined for his own profit, is unprofitable
  To his city, harsh in dealings, and a valued friend
  Chiefly to himself. This is not theory; I know it.
  I could have lived quietly in Argos; yet from a sense
  Of honour, and family loyalty, while Heracles
  Still lived among us, I took a greater share in all
  His labours than any other man. And now, when he
  Lives in the sky, I take his children under my wing,
  To seek for them the safety I need no less myself.

    When Heracles passed from the earth, Eurystheus planned
  To kill us; so we fled. Our city is lost to us;
  But we still live – exiles continually moving on,
  Wandering from this city to that. For in addition
  To all our other troubles Eurystheus has seen fit
  To do an outrageous thing: no sooner does he learn
  That we've found refuge in some city, than he sends
  Heralds to demand our extradition, have us denied
  Asylum; pointing out that friendship or enmity
  With Argos is no trifling matter, and he himself
  Is a powerful king. So, when they see that I am powerless
  And the children young, lacking a father's help, they bow
  To the stronger party, and debar us from their land.
  So these children and I are fellow-refugees,
  And every blow that falls on them falls on me too.
  If I abandoned them, you know what would be said:
  'When Heracles died, what help did Iolaus give
  To his uncle's fatherless children?' I will not have that.

    Now, barred from every place in Hellas, we have come
     here

To Marathon and its neighbour towns; and here we sit
As suppliants at the altars of the gods, praying
For help. We have been told that in this neighbourhood
Live Theseus' two sons, who received it from Pandion
As an inheritance; they are related to these children —
And that is why we have come here to the boundaries
Of famous Athens. This convoy of refugees
Is under aged leadership: I'm taking charge
Of these boys, with a heavy heart; and Alcmene
Is in the temple, her protecting arm thrown round
Her great son's daughters, since we could not let young girls
Sit suppliant at an altar in full public view.
Hyllus and his elder brothers have set off to seek
Some place where we can build a stronghold and a home,
Should we be forcibly expelled from Marathon.
     O children, children, come here, cling to my cloak! I see
Eurystheus' herald coming to capture us, the man
Who drives us homeless and helpless through the length and
     breadth
Of Hellas!
     [*Enter* COPREUS.]
                              You abominable wretch, a curse on
     you
And the man who sent you! Too often you have carried vile
Messages to the noble father of these boys!
COPREUS: No doubt you think you have chosen a fine place
     to sit,
And come to a country that will help you. You are a fool.
No man alive is going to choose your feeble strength
Against Eurystheus. March! Why all this fuss? Get up,
And back to Argos, where you shall be stoned to death.
IOLAUS: No, never! The god's altar will avail for me;
So will the soil on which we stand: this land is free.
COPREUS: Do you wish to give me trouble? Must I use my
     hands?

IOLAUS: I swear you'll not take me or these children off by
force.

COPREUS: You will find out. You're no true prophet on this
point. [*He seizes two of the children.*]

IOLAUS: Leave them alone! You'll not do this while I'm alive.

COPREUS: Keep off! Whether you like it or not, I'm taking
them
As being Eurystheus' property; and so they are.

IOLAUS: Help! You who have lived in Athens since the ancient
days,
Help! We are suppliants to Zeus of the Market-place.
We are molested; violence tears our holy wreaths,
Bringing disgrace on Athens, slander to the gods!
[COPREUS *throws* IOLAUS *to the ground. Enter the*
CHORUS.]

CHORUS: This way, come quickly. Who was that shouting for
help
Near Zeus's altar? What trouble shall we hear of now?
   – Look there, stretched on the ground,
       An old, helpless man – a pitiful sight!
   – Are you hurt by your fall?
       Who was it attacked you?

IOLAUS: Friends, it was this man here; with no respect for
your gods
He was dragging me by force away from the altar of Zeus.

CHORUS: But from what region, friend,
             Have you come to the people of the Four
                 Towns?
             Have you come here by boat
             Across from the cliffs of Euboea?

IOLAUS: Why, no, friends; I've not spent my life as an
islander.
We came to Attica from Mycenae; that is my home.

CHORUS: And by what name, old friend,
             Did the Mycenaeans call you?

IOLAUS: You may have heard of Iolaus, who was the friend
 And helper of Heracles. My name is not unknown.
CHORUS: We know your name since long ago. But whose are
        these
                Young boys holding your hand? Tell us.
IOLAUS: These, my friends, are the sons of Heracles. They
        have come
 As suppliants to beg help from Athens and from you.
CHORUS: Tell me, do you wish to plead your cause
                Before our people? What is your request?
IOLAUS: Not to be handed over. Not to be dragged off
 By force to Argos, to the disgrace of Attic gods.
COPREUS: So; but your master will not be content with this.
 His right over you is valid; and he finds you here.
CHORUS: Stranger, respect is due to suppliants of the gods.
                No violent hand must drag them
                Away from altar or statue.
                Justice is holy, and will not allow this.
COPREUS: Then send them away. They are Eurystheus'
        property.
 Do as I tell you, and I will use no violence.
CHORUS: They are suppliants and strangers
                Who look to our city for help.
                To reject them is to defy the gods.
COPREUS: It's also a good thing to keep your feet well clear
 Of trouble, and when good counsel's given, to follow it.
CHORUS: This land is free. You should have shown enough
        respect
 To address her king, before you so presumptuously
 Defied the gods, and laid hands on these strangers here.
COPREUS: Who is the king, then, of this region and this city?
CHORUS: The son of the famed hero Theseus: Demophon.
COPREUS: With him alone, then, I'll pursue this argument.
 All other talk is idle.
CHORUS: Look, he is coming now

In haste, with his brother Acamas, to hear your claim.

[*Enter* DEMOPHON *and* ACAMAS, *with attendants.*]

DEMOPHON [*to the* CHORUS]: Since you, for all your years,
    outran us younger men

To answer the cry that called you to this shrine of Zeus,

Tell me now, what occurrence has gathered all this crowd?

CHORUS: These suppliants, who, as you see, my lord, have hung

    The altar round with wreaths, are sons of Heracles;

    And this is Iolaus, their father's trusted friend.

DEMOPHON: And why should that demand this outcry of
    despair?

CHORUS: This man, trying to pull them from the altar,
    caused

    The outcry; then he flung Iolaus to the ground –

    A pitiful sight that moved my tears.

DEMOPHON: The man's attire

    And style are Greek; his violence, barbarian.

    – Tell me what place you come from, then; and waste no
    time.

COPREUS: I am – since you ask this – an Argive. Why I come,

By whom sent, I will tell. Eurystheus sent me here,

King of Mycenae, to arrest these fugitives.

And, Sir, I come well furnished with just arguments

For deed and word. I, as an Argive, come to fetch

These, also Argives, on the run from my own city,

Condemned to death by Argive law. We are a state,

And have the right to implement a sentence passed

On our own citizens. These persons have approached

Altars in many other towns; and in each case

We have, from the same reasons, urged the same demand;

And none has dared to call down trouble on his own head.

They came here, either counting on some folly in you,

Or staking all their desperate fortune on one throw,

To win or lose. They'd hardly hope, when they have
    travelled

Hellas from end to end, that you alone, being
No fool, would pity their ill-advised predicament.

 Weigh the advantages you gain by either course –
Letting them stay, or letting us convey them home.
Here is your gain from us: you range on Athens' side
The mighty Argive power and all Eurystheus' strength.
But if, through listening to these piteous arguments,
Your heart turns soft, the matter becomes one that swords
Will settle. Don't imagine that we shall forgo
This issue without trial of steel. Then what excuse,
What rape of lands or property could you allege,
For war with Argos? What ally do you defend?
The dead men you must bury – in whose cause will they fall?
Do you think your citizens will applaud you, if for the sake
Of this old shadow, this walking coffin – why, what else? –
And these few boys, you get bogged down in war with us?

 The gain you'll no doubt speak of is, at best, mere hope;
And what is hope, compared with actuality?
When these are grown men – if that's what you're counting
  on –
They'll show but puny fight against Argives in arms;
Meanwhile there's ample time for you to get wiped out.

 Listen to me: give nothing; let me take what's mine –
And gain Mycenae for your ally. Don't commit
Once more your favourite folly, which is this – to choose
Feebleness for your ally, when you could choose strength.
CHORUS: Who can give judgement, who discern an argument,
 Before he hears from both sides an exact account?
IOLAUS: King, in your country I enjoy this privilege:
 I may hear and be heard in turn; and until then
 I shall not be rejected, as from other states.

 We have nothing in common with this man. Since, then,
The bond we *had* with Argos is now null and void,
And we, by their vote, exiled from our native earth,
What right has he to take us prisoner, calling us

Mycenaeans, whom they themselves drove from their land?
To him we are aliens; — or do you claim that banishment
From Argos bars against us every Greek frontier?
Athens is not barred; nor will Athenians, through fear
Of Argos, drive Heracles' children from their soil.
This is not Trachis, nor some Achaean hill-fortress —
From such refuges you've been hounding us, with threats
Of Argive force as your sole right, the same you used
Just now, though we were suppliants claiming sanctuary.
No, this is Athens; if you win your way, and she
Allows your claim, then the free Athens I knew once
Is dead. But I know the inborn temper of these men.
They will die sooner than betray us. Where men's hearts
Are noble, they prize honour above life itself.

Of Athens I have said enough; to praise too much
Ends in offence. Often, I know, I too have been
Irked by excessive praise. I wish next to explain
How you yourself are under bond to save these boys,
Being prince of Attica. Pittheus was King Pelops' son;
Aethra was Pittheus' daughter; and the son she bore
Was Theseus, your own father. Let me trace again
These children's family: Heracles their father was
Son of Zeus and Alcmene; she was Pelops' daughter;
Sons of first cousins, then, were these boys' father and yours.

So near to them in kinship are you, Demophon;
But now I tell you, ties of blood apart, how great
Your debt is to them. For their father claims to have sailed
With Theseus when he went to get that blood-bought belt,
And borne his shield; he brought your father up to the light
From the dread keep of Hades. This all Hellas knows;
And for such benefits the thanks that these boys ask
Is, that they be not given up, nor torn away,
Nor denied refuge here in defiance of your gods.
Yours is the shame, your city bears the dire effects,
If homeless suppliants, and, alas, your kinsmen too —

Look at them now, but look! – are violently dragged off.
I beg – like suppliant garlands, see, my hands wreathe yours –
These sons of Heracles are in your power: do not
Turn them away, but be their kinsman, be their friend,
Their father, brother – even their master; better that
Or anything, than to fall into Argive hands!

CHORUS: My lord, their hard lot wins my pity. Never yet
Have I seen nobleness so vanquished by mischance.
A great man's sons do not deserve this misery.

DEMOPHON: Three paths of reason meet to induce me, Iolaus,
Not to reject your suppliant strangers. First of these
Is Zeus, by whose altar you and this youthful group
Are sitting. Then, our kinship, and these children's right
To kindly treatment from me for their father's sake.
The third, which weighs most heavily, is my fear of shame.
If I allow this altar to be violated
By a foreign hand, to Hellas it will seem that my
Country is no free country, and that I betray
Suppliants through fear of Argos. I'd sooner hang myself
Than hear that said. I wish you had come with happier
Auspices; but, even so, have confidence. No man
Shall ever drag you and the children from this altar.
– Go back to Argos, herald, and tell Eurystheus this;
And further, if he wishes to charge them in our courts,
Justice is free; but you shall never touch them here.

COPREUS: Not if both right and reason are stronger on my
          side?

DEMOPHON: How can it be right or just to arrest a suppliant?

COPREUS: The crime is mine, then; and from it you receive
          no harm.

DEMOPHON: No, it is mine, if I let you drag them away.

COPREUS: Banish them past your border – we'll arrest them
          there.

DEMOPHON: You are a fool to think you can quibble with a
          god.

COPREUS: It seems, then, Athens welcomes criminals on the run.

DEMOPHON: A temple offers sanctuary to every man.

COPREUS: That argument may not convince the Mycenaeans.

DEMOPHON: But this is Athens; here I hold authority.

COPREUS: If you are wise, you will not use it to their hurt.

DEMOPHON: Be hurt, then, Argos! I will not outrage the gods.

COPREUS: I do not wish to see war between you and us —

DEMOPHON: I am of your mind; but I'll not give these children up.

COPREUS: However, since they're mine, I'll take them with me now.

DEMOPHON: Then you'll not find it easy to get home again.

COPREUS: I'll learn if that is so by making the attempt.

[COPREUS *moves to take hold of the children.* DEMO-
PHON *confronts him with a raised weapon.*]

DEMOPHON: Lay hand on them, and you'll regret it this very moment.

CHORUS: Be prudent, king! Don't strike a herald, for God's sake!

DEMOPHON: I will, if the herald cannot learn how to behave.

CHORUS: Go back to Argos. — Demophon, don't touch the man.

COPREUS: I'm going; one man does not make an attacking force.
But I'll be back, bringing War with me — the great army
Of Argive spearmen mailed in bronze. Ten thousand men
Wait for me, shield on arm, and at their head the king
Himself, Eurystheus. On the Megarian frontier
He waits, expecting my report from Attica.
Told of your arrogance, he will blaze forth against
You and your citizens, against your land, your crops.
The warlike youth of Argos flocks to arms — and all
Their might a mockery, if we fail to punish you.

DEMOPHON: Go hang yourself! Your Argos holds no terror
for me.

[*Exit the* HERALD.]

Your hope was to bring shame on me by dragging off
These suppliants; that was not for you. This city of mine
Owes no subservience to Argos; she is free.

CHORUS: It is time to prepare, before Argive arms
                 Press on our frontiers.
                 The warlike rage of Mycenae is hot,
                 And more hot than before, for events of today.
                 All heralds alike build up a tall tale,
                 Bend double each fact.
                 Can you hear him unfold to his Argive king
                 What outrage he suffered, and by a bare inch
                 Escaped being torn into pieces?

IOLAUS: Sons have no richer endowment than the quality
A noble and brave father gives in their begetting.
High birth has greater strength to fight calamity
Than common blood. When we were fallen into the depth
Of danger and misery, we found for friends and kindred
These men here; they alone, in all the peopled breadth
Of Hellas, have stood up for us. Children, give them
Your right hands; and you, Elders, come near, join your
hands.

Children, we have received the proof of friendship here.
One day you'll see the sun rise on your native earth,
Live honoured in your father's home and heritage;
Remember then, these were your friends who saved your
lives.

This I command; never lift spear against this land,
But cherish Athens as the dearest of all cities.
These men deserve our reverence; they took on them
Our danger – the enmity of the great Argive state,
The Pelasgian race. They saw us outcast, helpless; yet
They would not give us up, or drive us from their land.

Whether I live, or die — whenever that may be —
With endless praise, dear boy, I will exalt your name,
Setting you next to Theseus, to rejoice his heart;
Telling what generous welcome, what protection you
Offered to Heracles' children; how your nobleness
Upholds your father's fame in Hellas — you're no less
A man than Theseus! — It's a rare thing nowadays
When quality begets its like; you'd hardly find
One in a score who's not a worse man than his father.

CHORUS: To help the helpless in the cause of right has been
Our long tradition, and is always our desire.
Often before, this land has for the sake of friends
Faced peril; now I see this new struggle looming near.

DEMOPHON: Your words I welcome; and these boys, I am
confident,
Will keep your bidding, and remember what we have
done.
I'll go and muster all our citizens in arms,
And take the field, to meet the army of Mycenae
In full force. And I'll send out scouts to guard against
Sudden attack — Argos is quick to mobilize.
I'll send for prophets and make sacrifice. Meanwhile,
Quit sanctuary, and take the boys inside my palace.
You'll find there those who will attend your needs, even if
I must be elsewhere. Come, Iolaus, go indoors.

IOLAUS: I will not leave this altar; here we must remain
Sitting, in supplication for your victory.
Once you emerge triumphant from this trial, then
We will go indoors. The gods on whose help we rely
Are no less strong than those who back the Argive cause.
I know that Hera, wife of Zeus, helps them; but we
Have great Athena. Mark my words: in such issues
To be allied with stronger gods weighs heavily.
Pallas Athena never will accept defeat!

[*Exit* DEMOPHON.]

CHORUS: Not all your boastful threats,
Stranger coming from Argos,
Gain one more ear to heed you;
No proud words of yours
Can strike terror to my heart.
May Athens great and lovely, city of dances,
Yet be far from such a destiny!
You are a fool, and the man who sent you,
Despot of Argos.

You come to a city no less great than yours,
Where homeless suppliants call on the gods
And pray to my land for help;
And you, a foreigner, try to take them by
    force,
You ignore our king's rebuke,
You offer no justification.
Could this win the approval
Of any right-minded man?

Our first desire is for peace;
But I tell you, evil-minded king,
If you march to our city
You will be surprised by your reception.
You are not the only man who can handle a
    sword
Or a bronze-bound shield.
You men who are in love with wars,
Never let your weapons threaten our city,
This masterpiece of the Graces.
Pause, and refrain.

[DEMOPHON *returns*.]

IOLAUS: Why have you come, my son? Your eyes are eloquent.
  You bring news of the enemy? Do they take their time,

Or are they on us? What have you heard? That herald, I
    think,
Will not disappoint us. In the past the Argive king
Has met good fortune; and in his pride of heart, I know,
He'll march on Athens. When presumptuous arrogance
Swells above mortal measure, Zeus will punish it.
DEMOPHON: The Argive army is here, and King Eurystheus
        too.
I've seen them for myself; a man who claims to know
A general's business can't rely on mere reports. —
Well, he's not sent his troops down yet into the plain,
But holds a position on a rocky brow, meaning —
This is my guess — to spy out the best route to bring
His army safely down and camp right in our midst.
As for defence — my preparations are all made,
Athens is armed, victims ready for slaughter stand
Beside the altars of the appropriate gods; prophets
Have filled the city with sacrifices. I have assembled
All the chanters of oracles, and questioned them
About ancient predictions, whether publicly
Delivered, or in secret, which might indicate
A course of safety for this country; and the experts
Differing in many other points, are all agreed
On this one clear pronouncement: they insist that I
Must sacrifice to Persephone, Demeter's Maid,
The virgin daughter of a royal family.

    Now, for myself, I am most anxious, as you see,
To help you; but I will not kill my own daughter,
Nor will I compel any of my citizens
To such an act — and, if not forced, what father would
Be so insane as to give up his own dear child?
At this moment there are angry gatherings to be seen,
Where some say I was right to promise sanctuary
To foreign suppliants, others hold this was an act
Of folly. I have only to carry out this promise —

And civil war is on us. So, consider this,
And help me find some way to save at once your lives,
This country, and my good name among my citizens.
I hold my throne not as a Persian king holds his;
I win fair dealing as I give it, deed for deed.

CHORUS: Can this be true? When strangers are in need, and
    Athens
  Is willing, do the gods forbid us to give help?

IOLAUS: Oh, children! We are like seafarers who have escaped
The violent cruelty of the storm, whose clutching hands
Reach for the shore – and then the strong wind drives them
    back
To the open sea. Now we are pushed out of Attica
Just when we thought at last we had come safe to land.
O bitter Hope! Why did you come to cheer me, when
You had no mind to carry your fair promise through?
Demophon will not slaughter his own subject's child:
Well, who can blame him? The Athenians' attitude
Is also reasonable. If heaven decrees that I
Must suffer, this does not revoke my thanks to you.

    But you, dear sons – what is there I can do for you?
Where shall we turn? What god have we not garlanded?
What place is there whose shelter we have not implored?
We shall die, children; yes, we shall be handed over.
My own death, if it must come, moves me not at all –
Save for the pleasure it will give my enemies;
It is your fate, children, that melts my heart to tears –
Yours, and Alcmene's, aged mother of Heracles.
O sad Alcmene, to whom long life came as a curse!
And wretched Iolaus, for all my fruitless toils!
This was ordained and sealed, that we should fall into
An enemy's hands, and die in shame and misery.

    Wait – not all hope of their deliverance is lost yet;
I have a thought, and you can help to make it work.
Give *me* up to the Argives, king, instead of them;

That puts you out of peril, and I shall know them safe.
My life is not a thing to care for; let it go.
Nothing would please Eurystheus more than to lay hands
On me, Heracles' ally, and satisfy his rage –
Yes, he's a savage. A civilized man should pray to make
Civilized enemies, not brutish ones; at worst,
Then, one would meet some sense of decency and right.

CHORUS: Iolaus, do not lay the blame upon this city.
To say we gave up strangers to their enemies
Might be false rumour, yet would bring us deep disgrace.

DEMOPHON: What you have said is noble, but unpractical.
The king has not marched here in force to capture *you*.
What would Eurystheus profit from an old man's death?
He wants to kill these children. Young lives that grow up
Conscious of their high lineage and their father's wrongs
Strike terror to their enemies' hearts. All this the king
Has to provide against. But, if you can unfold
Some timelier counsel, let us hear it. These oracles
Terrify me; I cannot think what's best to do.

[*Enter, from the temple,* MACARIA.]

MACARIA: Friends, do not think it forwardness in me to come
Here to you – this I must beg first. The part that best
Befits a woman is silence and modesty,
And to stay quietly indoors. But, Iolaus,
It was your anguished voice that brought me out, and not
Any sense of my importance in this family.
Yet, since I have some measure of concern, and love
My brothers dearly, I want to know their fate and mine.
My dread is that some new disaster has appeared
Beyond our former sufferings, to wring your heart.

IOLAUS: Dear daughter, of all Heracles' children you are the
    one
Whom I have always praised the most, and with good cause.
Just now it seemed to me our way was prospering;
Now all is changed, and once again we are in despair.

Chanters of oracles, the king says, all command
The sacrifice to Demeter's Maid – not of a bull
Or calf, but the virgin daughter of a royal house,
If we, and Athens, are to live. Here, then, we stand
Helpless; for Demophon insists he will not kill
Either his own child or any other citizen's.
He does not say in plain words, but says none the less,
If we can't find some way to untie this knot ourselves,
Then we must seek some other land to shelter in,
Since his own first concern is to keep Athens safe.

MACARIA: The fact is, then, our lives depend on this condi-
          tion?

IOLAUS: Yes, that is so – provided all the rest goes well.

MACARIA: Then you need no more dread the attack of
          Argive spears.

Before you bid me, Iolaus, I am myself
Ready to die, and give my blood for sacrifice.
What could we say, when Athens is prepared to face
Great peril for our sake, if we ourselves, who laid
This burden on their shoulders, having it in our power
To bring them victory, draw back and shrink from death?
Never! We should command not sympathy but scorn
If we, who sat here weeping as suppliants to the gods,
Demonstrate that a father such as Heracles
Can beget cowards! We think better of ourselves.
I would choose rather that this city – which God forbid! –
Were captured, I a prisoner in my enemies' hands,
Suffering outrage – I, the daughter of a king –
And after all this shame were doomed still to face death.
Or suppose that I wandered banished from this land:
Would I not blush when those I asked for help replied,
'Why come to us with suppliant boughs, you who so loved
Your own lives? We will not help cowards; away with you!'
Again, suppose my brothers lost their lives, and I
Was spared – many in such ways have betrayed their friends –

Even so, I have no hope of a good life; for who
Will choose for wife a girl so destitute, or wish
To beget children from me? Better then to die
Than meet a fate I have not deserved, a fate which might
Better become a girl less notable than I.
   Here I am: lead me to the place where I must die;
Garland me, if you will; perform your ritual.
Defeat your enemies. Readily, not reluctantly,
This life is offered; here I pledge myself to death.
Because I did not count my life dear, I have won
This dearest prize of all – to meet death gloriously.

CHORUS: I hear this maid's sublime words, as she gives her
    life
To save her brothers, and I am held speechless. Who
Could show greater nobility in word or act?

IOLAUS: Dear child, your spirit flowered from no other root
But from the godlike heart of Heracles: you are
His very seed. My grief at what you must endure
Is matched by the great pride with which I hear your words.
Yet listen – there is a juster way to have this done:
    [*He turns to the* CHORUS.]
We should call here Macaria's sisters and draw lots,
And let the one chosen die for her family.
It isn't fair that you should die without this chance.

MACARIA: I will not die by choice of hazard. If I should,
The willing gift has vanished; speak of it no more.
If you accept me, if you will whole-heartedly
Use what I offer – my life for my brothers' lives,
This I give with free will, and under no constraint.

IOLAUS: Ah, noble child!
Your former words were wonderful; but you speak now
Even more royally than before. Courage outshines
Courage, and word surpasses glorious word. My daughter,
Indeed I neither bid you nor forbid you die;
But yet in dying you will help your brothers live.

MACARIA: That is wise bidding. Have no fear that any guilt
  Will fall on you for my death; freely let me die.
  Come with me; I would wish to fall with your arm near.
  Be there, Iolaus, to wrap my body in my dress,
  Since I am going to meet the terror of the knife —
  Being his daughter whom I proudly call my father.

IOLAUS: I could not stand beside you there and see you
  killed.

MACARIA: Then ask the king to see to it that I breathe my last,
  Not in men's hands, but women's.

DEMOPHON: O brave, helpless girl!
  I promise this. I should myself be shamed, if you
  Lacked any mark of deep respect, both for your own
  High courage, and for justice' sake; since of all women
  I have ever met, you are the first in steadfastness.
  So, if there is any last word you would speak to these
  Elders, or Iolaus, before you go, speak now.

MACARIA: Good-bye, old friend, good-bye! And listen:
      teach these boys
  To be like you, with right judgement in everything —
  No more than that; it is enough. And do your best —
  I know you will — to save their lives. We were brought up
  By you — we are your children. Now you see me go
  To death, giving up my flower of marriage for their sake.
  And you, my brothers gathered here, I wish for you
  A good life, full of all those gifts which my heart's blood
  Will flow to win for you. Honour old Iolaus;
  Honour Alcmene our father's mother, and these Elders.
  If in the gods' good time you win clear of these troubles
  And live secure in your own home, remember then
  Your burial-debt to one who saved you. I have not
  Failed in my duty; for you all I gave my life.
  Therefore a glorious tomb is my just due; and this
  Shall be, for babes unborn, maidenhood unfulfilled,
  My great reward and treasure — if there is a world

Below the earth; I hope there is none. For if we
Whose short life ends in death must there too suffer pain,
I do not know where one can turn; since death has been
Thought of as our great remedy for all life's ills.

IOLAUS: Peerless in courage, noblest of all women born,
Be sure that we shall honour you, in life or death,
Above all others. Now farewell. Reverence forbids
That I should speak ill of divine Persephone,
Demeter's daughter, to whom your blood is dedicated.

    [Exit MACARIA.]

Dear sons, I am fainting; sorrow has unnerved my limbs.
Lift me and set me on a chair, and wrap my gown
Over my head. This cruel day will break my heart;
Yet, if we ignore the oracle, we cannot live.
That means the greater ruin; yet this is terrible.

CHORUS: I believe that no man becomes prosperous,
        No man falls into disaster,
        Except by the will of heaven;
        Nor does good fortune always attend
        The same house, but differing fortunes
        Follow close upon one another.
        Fate brings low those that were high;
        The unhonoured Fate makes prosperous.
        To evade destiny is forbidden;
        Not by wisdom shall a man resist it;
        He who attempts this will spend
        His length of life in fruitless struggle.

        Then, Iolaus, do not fall prostrate
        Or rack your heart with grievous thoughts,
        But endure the will of heaven.
        The part of pitiful death which she has chosen
        Will bring her glory as the saviour
        Of her brothers and of Athens.
        Praise on the lips of the world awaits her;

> For the course of a noble life must pass through
> pain.
> Her act honours her father,
> Honours the royalty of her line.
> All the reverence you feel
> For the passing of noble lives, I share with you.

*

[Enter a SERVANT *of Hyllus.]*

SERVANT: Good day to you, children. Where is old Iolaus?
And has
Your father's mother Alcmene left her suppliant seat?

IOLAUS: I am here – what still remains of me.

SERVANT: Why lying there?
And why so downcast?

IOLAUS: Wrapped in new grief for this house.

SERVANT: Lift yourself up; look up.

IOLAUS: I am old. I have no
strength.

SERVANT: I've brought you great news.

IOLAUS: Who are you? I've
seen you before –
I forget.

SERVANT: Hyllus's man. Look – don't you know me now?

IOLAUS: Dear friend! You have come to save us from our
misery?

SERVANT: Yes; and good fortune brings you our return as
well.

IOLAUS [*calling at the door of the temple*]: Alcmene, mother of
an heroic son, come out!
Here's welcome news. Stop worrying over their return,
Eating your heart out with anxiety: they've come back!
[Enter ALCMENE.]

ALCMENE: What is this shouting, Iolaus? The whole temple
Echoes with it. Is this another herald from Argos

Come to arrest you? [*She turns to the* SERVANT] I've no
   strength at all; but this
You should know, stranger: you'll not take these boys away
While I am living, or may I never again be called
Heracles' mother! Touch them, and — old as we are —
You'll have to fight *us*. It won't bring you much credit.

IOLAUS: All's well, Alcmene; fear nothing. This man is not
   An Argive herald; he bears no hostile messages.

ALCMENE: Then why raise such a clamour, and terrify us all?

IOLAUS: You were in the temple. I just called you to come
   out.

ALCMENE: Well, I know nothing about that. Who is this
   man?

IOLAUS: He comes to tell us that your grandson has arrived.

ALCMENE [*to* SERVANT]: Then you are welcome too for your
   good news. But why,
   If he has set foot in this land, is he not here?
   What hindered him from coming with you to cheer my
      heart?

SERVANT: He's pitching camp, and marshalling the troops
   he's brought.

ALCMENE: That sort of thing does not concern me.

IOLAUS: Indeed it
      does;
   But questions on such matters are for me to ask.

SERVANT: Then what do you wish to know? Much has been
   happening.

IOLAUS: What size of army has he brought to fight for us?

SERVANT: I can't give the exact number; but it's a strong
   force.

IOLAUS: I presume that the Athenian leaders know he's here?

SERVANT: They do. He is already placed on their left wing.

IOLAUS: What, is the army drawn up ready to engage?

SERVANT: Yes; and the victims have been brought for sacrifice.

IOLAUS: What distance lies between them and the Argive
          line?

SERVANT: Near enough for their chief to be clearly recog-
          nized.

IOLAUS: Engaged, no doubt, in placing out the enemy's ranks.

SERVANT: We reckoned so; what they were saying could not
          be heard.

    But I must go; I should be sorry if my chief,

    When marching into battle, saw my place unfilled.

IOLAUS: I am coming with you. We both share the same de-
          sire,

    To stand beside our friends and help them as we should.

SERVANT: It does not suit your dignity to make foolish jokes.

IOLAUS: With my friends fighting, shall I fail to play my part?

SERVANT: Fierce looks hurt no one; the hand must hold a
          sword and strike.

IOLAUS: Well? Do you think I have not the strength to pierce
          a shield?

SERVANT: Perhaps: but you'd fall down yourself before you
          struck.

IOLAUS: There's not a man of them will look me in the eye.

SERVANT: But, honoured sir, your strength is not what it
          once was.

IOLAUS: Yet I'll fight with as long odds as when I was young.

SERVANT: Your weight in your friends' ranks will hardly turn
          the scale.

IOLAUS: See – I'm all set for action; don't you hold me back.

SERVANT: Action's beyond you, however willing you may be.

IOLAUS: Talk on, then, if you wish to. I'll not stay behind.

SERVANT: You'll stand there without armour in the hoplite
          ranks?

IOLAUS: Inside this temple there is armour, taken in war;

    I'll use that. If I live, I'll give it back; the god

    Won't ask it of me if I'm killed. Go in at once,

    Take down a suit of hoplite armour off the nails

And bring it quickly. I'm no coward stay-at-home;
This hanging back while others fight – it's a disgrace!
[*The* SERVANT *goes into the temple.*]

CHORUS: Your spirit is not yet laid low by time,
              It is youthful; but your body's strength is gone.
              Why undertake all this, to your own hurt,
              And little profit to the Athenian cause?
              Be wise, admit that you are old. Do not
              Attempt the impossible. Youth is a thing,
              Once lost, a man can never find again.

ALCMENE: What's this? You're not in your right mind! Do
    you propose
To leave me unprotected with these children here?

IOLAUS: Fighting is men's work; looking after them – is
    yours.

ALCMENE: Well, and suppose you're killed? Who will look
    after *me*?

IOLAUS: Your son's remaining children will take care of you.

ALCMENE: And if – which God forbid! – they were unfortu-
    nate?

IOLAUS: Our hosts here – have no fear! – they'll not abandon
    you.

ALCMENE: They are my sole hope; besides them – I've noth-
    ing else.

IOLAUS: Yes, there is Zeus. I know he cares for your distress.

ALCMENE: Zeus shall get no hard words from me; but he best
    knows
Whether his conduct towards me is above reproach.
    [*The* SERVANT *comes out of the temple.*]

SERVANT: Look, here you are now: armour! – a complete
    outfit.
Get inside that, and lose no time. The battle's just
Beginning; and there's nothing Ares hates so much
As dawdlers. However, if you dread the weight of it,
Go unarmed for the present, and when you reach the ranks

Put all this gear on there. Meanwhile I'll carry it.

IOLAUS: A good suggestion. Bring the armour, then, and have
it

Ready for me. Give me a spear to hold; and now,
Grip my left elbow firmly, so that I walk straight.

SERVANT: Must I lead an armed soldier like a little child?

IOLAUS: To stumble would be unlucky. I must tread carefully.

SERVANT: I only wish you had strength to match your eagerness.

IOLAUS: Press on – if I miss the battle I'll not forgive myself.

SERVANT: It's you who are slow, not me. You're full of
make-believe.

IOLAUS: What? See my stride now: don't I show more speed
than you?

SERVANT: I see you showing imagination more than speed.

IOLAUS: You won't say that when you see me on the battlefield.

SERVANT: What will you do? I hope to see some doughty
deeds.

IOLAUS: You'll see me drive this spear clean through an
Argive shield.

SERVANT: If we ever get there – that's the thing I'm doubtful
of.

[IOLAUS *has progressed slowly across the stage, down to the
orchestra, and over to the exit. Before disappearing, he
turns back for his final speech.*]

IOLAUS: O my right arm, how I remember your young
strength,

When you, with Heracles, sacked Sparta! Ah, could you
But offer now the same true service, what a rout
I'd give the coward Eurystheus – he's no man to stand
And face a spear. Wealth and position bring this false gain,
Repute for courage; for we attribute every kind
Of valuable knowledge to the successful man.

[*Exit* IOLAUS *followed by the* SERVANT. ALCMENE *remains.*]

CHORUS: O Earth, and night-long Moon,
   And dazzling beams divine
   That light our mortal race,
    Bring me your message!
   Send forth the victory-shout
   To fill the sky, and reach
   The august throne where reigns
    Grey-eyed Athene.
   Now, for our native soil,
   For our homes, and for the suppliants
   We sheltered, we are ready
   To take grey steel in hand
    And cut through danger.
   That a state so strong, so admired
   In warfare as Mycenae
   Should nurse anger against Athens —
    This is distressing;
   But my city would be disgraced
   If we handed over refugees
    At the bidding of Argos.
   Zeus stands at our side;
   We are not afraid; for Zeus
   Justly grants us his favour;
   And never, I trust, can the power of a god
    Yield before mortals.

   Since yours is this land, Athene,
   Yours our city, and you
   Its mother, mistress, guardian —
   Send about his business
   This lawbreaker from Argos
   With his hurricane of spears!
   This is not what our deeds have deserved —

      To be driven from our homes.
      For sacrifice without ceasing
      Is offered in your honour;
          Nor is forgotten
      The day of the moon's waning,
      With music of youthful voices
          And songs of dancers;
      While on the windy hill
      Rapturous cries ring forth
      And the beat of the feet of girls is heard
          In night-long rhythm.

   [*Enter the* SERVANT.]

SERVANT: Madam, the news I bring won't take you long to
     hear,
  And gives me joy to tell: we have the victory
    Over our enemies; trophies are now being raised
  Displaying armour and weapons of the Argive dead.
ALCMENE: O best of friends! For such news this day sends
     you forth
  A free man. But first, set me too free from one dread:
  Are those whose safety I most long for still alive?
SERVANT: Alive, and honoured by the whole army for their
     deeds.
ALCMENE: But is not this man here the aged Iolaus?
SERVANT: It is he. The gods have given him a rare privilege.
ALCMENE: What is it? Did he execute some glorious deed?
SERVANT: He has left old age behind, become a youth once
     more.
ALCMENE: You speak of a miracle! But the thing I would
     hear first
  Is, how the battle turned to victory for our friends.
SERVANT: One speech of mine shall give you the whole story
     plain.
  When we were drawn up, and the two fronts of armed men,
  Fully extended, faced each other eye to eye,

Hyllus leapt from his four-horse chariot and went out
Mid-way between the lines of spears, and spoke these words:
'You who have led this army here from Argos, why
Should we not leave this land unharmed, [and spare the
    blood
Of many brave men? This dispute can be resolved
By two alone. I willingly will risk my life
As thanks to Athens for her hospitality;]
And if *you* fall, and rob Mycenae of one life,
You do her no great injury. So, man to man,
Fight with me. If you kill me, the sons of Heracles
Are yours to take; if I kill you, then yield to me
My father's throne, his palace, and his royal rights.
    The ranks cried out, 'Well said!' – they hoped a bloody
        battle
Might be avoided, and they liked his courage. But
Neither the thousands who had heard the challenge, nor
His own cowardice made evident before his troops,
Could shame Eurystheus into venturing within reach
Of a hero's spear. This is the nature of the man,
The complete coward, who came here hoping to enslave
Heracles' children! Hyllus moved back to the line;
And the priests, learning that no settlement would be
    reached
By single combat, with no more delay drew knife
And loosed from victims' throats the blood that bodes suc-
    cess.
    Then some were mounting chariots, some fencing their
        ribs
Behind ribbed shields. The king of Athens raised his voice
To address his army with a king's encouragement:
'This land, my fellow-citizens, has nurtured you,
This land has given you birth; now pay your debt to her.'
On the other side their leader implored his fighting-men
Not to bring Argos and Mycenae to disgrace.

Then, when the shrill voice of the Tyrrhenian trumpet
    spoke,
And the armies locked in battle, can your imagination
Tell you how deafening was the roar as shield met shield,
The swell of mingled screams and groans? At first the hail
Of Argive spears shattered our ranks; then the enemy
Gave back, and so, foot braced against unyielding foot,
Man fronting man, the fight raged fierce; and many fell.
Two shouts went up: 'You men of Athens' – 'You who
    plough
The soil of Argos – save your city from disgrace!'
With supreme effort and long agony, at last
Our men prevailed; the Argive line broke, turned, and fled.
    Old Iolaus caught sight of Hyllus charging on,
And waved his arm, and begged that he would take him up
Into the chariot. Then he took the reins himself
And drove hard after Eurystheus. And that's as far
As I saw for myself; the rest I heard described
By others. When he passed the Pallenian Hill, sacred
To Athene, there he saw Eurystheus' chariot;
And he prayed to Hebe and to Zeus, that for one day
He might be young again, and take just vengeance on
His enemies. Now you will hear a miracle.
Over the horses' yoke two stars appeared, and hid
The chariot in a sombre cloud. Those who should know
Say they were Hebe and your son Heracles; but he,
Iolaus, from that sinister gloom emerged showing
A man new-moulded, strong-armed with the vigour of
    youth!
    And glorious Iolaus pursued and overtook
Eurystheus' chariot near the Scironian Rocks.
He has bound his arms with cords, and has returned bringing
That once successful general here a prisoner.
So now Eurystheus' fate gives warning to all men
That we should envy none his seeming happiness

Till his last hour. Fortune may vanish in one day.

CHORUS: O Zeus, giver of victory! Now fear and dread
Depart, now dawns the bright day of deliverance.

ALCMENE: So, Zeus, at last you take heed of my sufferings;
It is late; yet I am thankful for this victory.
Until now I did not believe my son had joined
The company of gods; now I know this is true.
    Dear children, now you are freed from all your troubles,
        now
Freed from Eurystheus, who shall die a shameful death.
Now you shall see your father's city; you shall stand
On soil of your inheritance, and after long years
Of wretched exile, now return unhindered home
To pay glad sacrifices to your father's gods.
        [*She turns to the* SERVANT.]
But tell me, what concealed purpose had Iolaus
In sparing Eurystheus' life instead of killing him?
I see no sense in this myself – when you have taken
Your enemies prisoner, not to make them pay their debt.

SERVANT: He did this for your pleasure, so that your own
        eyes
Might see him captive, subject to your hand and will.
We brought him here by force – he did not want to come;
He had to, on compulsion. It was not his choice
To live to meet your eye and suffer your revenge.
    So now, good-bye, Alcmene; and remember, please,
The thing you promised me when I first brought my news:
To set me free. In matters of this kind, a tongue
That keeps its word brings credit to a royal name.
        [*Exit the* SERVANT.]

CHORUS: Dancing is my delight, and the clear note
               Of flutes finely played at a festival;
               And love, and loveliness, should be there too.
               And pleasant it is to see,
               When, beyond expectation,

Friends at last have found good fortune.
Many events are brought to birth
By Fate, who gives fulfilment,
And Time, child of creation.

A certain path belongs to you, my city:
The path of fairness; never lose hold of this.
The gods require their honour;
The man who bids you otherwise
Drives within danger of insanity.
Today's events provide a lesson;
Plain is the warning given by God, as once and
     again
He trims the pride of the wicked.

Aged mother, your son
Has taken his place in heaven;
Legend says that consumed by ruthless fire
His flesh went down to the house of death.
He has escaped this tale;
Now in the courts of gold
He enjoys the touch of love in Hebe's bed,
Where you, Hymenaeus, have honoured
The marriage of Zeus' son with Zeus'
     daughter.

How often events are interwoven!
Athena once, they say,
Came to the help of these boys' father;
Now today they are saved
By the same Athena's city and people.
The violence which set Justice aside
Falls by the sword of Athens.
A relentless nature, obsessive hatred —
God keep me guiltless of these!

[*Enter the* SERVANT *followed by* EURYSTHEUS *led in chines.*]

SERVANT: My mistress, let me announce what you yourself
  can see:
 He is here. Eurystheus stands before you prisoner.
 You looked for no such joy, nor he for such defeat.
 When from Mycenae, with ten thousand toilsome shields,
 He marched, proudly defying justice, to destroy
 Athens, he little thought to fall into your hands.
 But God decreed the contrary to his thought, reversed
 The event he hoped for. Hyllus and noble Iolaus
 I left raising a statue of Zeus Conqueror
 In thanks for victory; and to delight your heart they send
 This man here in my charge; for nothing gives such pleasure
 As this – to see a prosperous enemy cast down.

ALCMENE: Loathed creature, have you come? After so long,
  has Justice
 Caught you? Come, turn your head this way and dare to look
 Your enemy in the face. Once you were powerful; now
 You are overpowered. Are you the man – I wish to know –
 The man without shame who saw fit to load outrage
 On my son – be he now where he may be? Was there
 A wickedness you did not perpetrate on him?
 You sent him living down to Hades, ordered him
 To destroy hydras, lions – it would take long to count
 What other cruelties you contrived. But all of these
 Were not enough, or cruel enough, for you; you must
 Drive out of every state in Hellas me and mine,
 Who sat – some aged, some still children – suppliant
 At holy altars. Here at last you met free men
 And a free city, that did not fear you. Now your death
 Comes with dishonour, yet, on all counts, is your gain;
 You owe not one death, but a score, for all your crimes.

CHORUS: This is unlawful; you cannot put this man to death.

SERVANT: What, did we take him prisoner for nothing, then?

ALCMENE: Indeed? What law forbids him to be put to death?

CHORUS: This country's rulers hold it undesirable.

ALCMENE: What's this? They call it wrong to kill your
enemies?

CHORUS: Those taken alive in battle we do not put to death.

ALCMENE: Then what of Hyllus? Did he accept this principle?

CHORUS: Had he the right to challenge Athens on this point?

ALCMENE: I'm sure Eurystheus has no right to stay alive.

CHORUS: To spare his life *then* was not just; but it was done.

ALCMENE: Then is it not right that he should be punished
now?

CHORUS: You'll find no hand here willing to take this man's
life.

ALCMENE: You're wrong: here's mine. I have a hand as well
as you.

CHORUS: If you do this, a storm of censure falls on you.

ALCMENE: I love this city; no one shall deny me that.
But now my enemy has fallen into my hands;
And there is no man living who shall rescue him.
So let whoever will, hear this and point at me,
Call me harsh, arrogant beyond a woman's right;
What needs to be done shall be done, and I will do it.

CHORUS: The hatred that possesses you is fearful; yet
It has strong reason – this I fully recognize.

EURYSTHEUS: Do not expect me to plead humbly for my life,
Or to speak any word that might be thought to show
Fear. Yet, to take up this feud was not my choice.
I knew that I was born your cousin; therefore I was
Kinsman to your son Heracles. But whether I wished
To be his enemy or not, our enmity
Was a plague sent by Hera – yes, a god's to blame;
This was a sickness. And, the feud once taken on,
Knowing that I must fight this fight out to the end,
I made myself the inventor of successive toils,

And Night and I put heads together to hatch schemes
For scattering and destroying all my enemies;
Else I must live with fear behind my every step.
    I knew, of course, that your son was a man above
The common run; a hero. Though my enemy,
I'll yield him all praise as a great and noble man.
Once he was gone, what choice had I? These children here
Hated me; I recalled their father's enmity.
I had to leave no stone unturned — use murders, plots,
Banishments — to ensure my own security.
If you had been in my position — you, perhaps,
Would not have persecuted the angry lion-cubs,
Your hereditary enemies, but used self-restraint
And let them live in Argos? Few would believe that.
    So, since they did not kill me in the field, when I
Was ready, now by all the Hellene laws the man
Who kills me is a polluted murderer. Athens
Counted divine law weightier than my enmity,
And wisely spared me. You have spoken, I have replied.
If you kill me, my spirit will haunt you with revenge,
And I shall be called noble. My attitude is this:
I do not crave death, nor would I be loath to die.

*

SERVANT: Alcmene, I would offer one word of advice:
    Let the man go unharmed; this is the city's wish.
ALCMENE: What if I obey the city's wish, and still he dies?
SERVANT: That would be excellent. How can it be arranged?
ALCMENE: A simple matter; listen. I will kill the man,
    Then give his corpse back to his friends who come for him.
    Thus I fulfil the letter of the Athenians' wish,
    And at the same time I am revenged by killing him.
EURYSTHEUS: Kill me; I ask no mercy. But since Athens
        spared
    My life, and was ashamed to kill a prisoner,

I will bestow on her an ancient oracle
Of Loxias, which in time shall benefit her more
Than you might think. Inter my body in the place
Chosen by Fate, near the Pallenian Virgin's shrine;
And there for ever I shall lie, a guest, your friend,
Athens' protector, under Attic soil. And when
These children's children, forgetful of your kindness, march
Against you in arms, I shall be their implacable
Enemy; for these are faithless guests whose cause you saved.
Since, then, I knew this, why (you ask) did I neglect
The oracle's word, and march to Athens? I supposed
Hera was stronger than an oracle, and would not
Betray me. Therefore allow no one to pour out wine
Or blood to sanctify my tomb; such offerings
I will repay with sorrow at their homecoming.
Thus from my death you will receive a double gain:
For yourselves, blessing; and injury for your enemies.

ALCMENE: Then why delay, now you have heard his proph-
ecy?
Ensure success for Athens and our posterity
And kill him now, since his own words point out the path
Of fullest safety. He is an enemy, and his death
Will profit us. Men, lead him off; kill him, and throw
His body out to feed the dogs. You shall not live
To drive me out of my father's country ever again!

*

CHORUS: I hold the same opinion. Men, march on.
              At least no act of ours
              Shall fasten guilt upon our king.

Fragments from missing parts of the play:
  (1) The man who lives devoted to his parents gains,
      Whether in life or death, the favour of the gods;
      But let the man who would dishonour his own father

Keep far from me! I would not pray at the same shrine,
Nor cross the sea in the same ship with such a man.

(2) My son, there are three virtues you should practise. First,
Honour the gods; second, honour your parents; third,
Honour the common laws of Hellas. Practise these,
And you'll possess the noblest crown of lasting fame.

(3) True – to be killed is terrible, but glorious;
While not to die is cowardly – but we long for it.

ANDROMACHE

CHARACTERS

ANDROMACHE, *widow of Hector, now slave of Neoptolemus*
Old female SLAVE
CHORUS *of women of Phthia*
HERMIONE, *wife of Neoptolemus, daughter of Menelaus*
MENELAUS, *king of Sparta*
MOLOSSUS, *son of Andromache and Neoptolemus*
PELEUS, *father of Achilles, grandfather of Neoptolemus*
NURSE *of Hermione*
ORESTES, *nephew of Menelaus*
MESSENGER, *servant of Neoptolemus*
THETIS, *an immortal sea-nymph, once the wife of Peleus*
mother of Achilles

The scene is before the palace of Neoptolemus, king of Phthia. On one side is a shrine with a statue of Thetis. ANDROMACHE *is seated as a suppliant before the shrine.*

ANDROMACHE: My home! Thebe, the loveliest city in all
        Asia!
  I left my home; and with me came a golden hoard
  Of treasures for my dowry. Then we reached the royal
  Palace of Priam; there I became Hector's wife,
  To bear him true sons. My name is Andromache.
  It was an envied name in those days; now there is
  No woman living whose life holds such bitterness.
  I saw my husband Hector killed by Achilles' sword;
  And on the day the Greeks took Troy I saw my son
  Astyanax thrown to death from the high battlements.
  And I, the famous daughter of a noble house,
  Was brought to Hellas as a slave, a chosen prize
  From the spoils of Troy, awarded to the island prince
  Neoptolemus, for valour. Now my home is here
  In the level pastures lying between Pharsalia
  And Phthia. Here Thetis used to live as Peleus' wife,
  Aloof from mortals, shunning the public eye; and now
  The people of Thessaly call this region Thetideion
  After the immortal who was married to their king.
  Achilles' son Neoptolemus came to live here, leaving
  Peleus to rule Pharsalia, since he had no wish
  To claim the throne while his grandfather was alive.
      And here in Neoptolemus' house I have borne a son,
  My master's son. At first, in spite of the misery
  In which I lived, I hoped always against hope that if
  He grew to manhood he would find some way to mend
  My shattered fortunes; but my master took a wife,
  Hermionè, from Sparta; he had no further need

For his concubine, who now became the target for
Hermione's malice. She says that by secret spells
I make her barren, make her husband tired of her;
That I mean to oust her from her lawful marriage, and take
Her place in his house. When I had that place, it was
No choice of mine; now I have quitted it. Great Zeus
Be witness, I had no wish to be his concubine.
Hermione won't believe this; she desires my death.
In this her accomplice is her father Menelaus,
Who has come from Sparta for this very purpose, and
Is now in the house. He frightens me; so I've come here
For sanctuary to the shrine of Thetis, which is close
To the palace, hoping this may save my life. Peleus
And all his family hold this place in reverence, as
A symbol of his marriage with the immortal nymph.

    My only son I am sending secretly away
To another house, since I am fearful for his life.
His father is not here either to rescue me
Or help the boy; he is in Delphi, where he has gone
To make amends to Apollo for his reckless act
Of long ago, when he went to the Pythian oracle
Demanding reparation for his father's death.
His hope is, by entreating pardon for past sin,
To ensure Apollo's friendship for the years to come.
    [Enter an old female SLAVE.*]*

SLAVE: My mistress! — that's what I still call you, as I used
  To call you — and proud to do so — when we lived in Troy
  In your old home. I'm loyal to you now, as I was
  To your good husband while he lived. I've got some news.
  I was terrified someone from the palace might see me come;
  But I was sorry for you. Menelaus and his daughter
  Are working out some vicious plot. You must take care.
ANDROMACHE: My dear friend! True, I was your queen in
    the old days
  Of happiness; now you and I are fellow-slaves.

Tell me, what are they doing? What cruel treachery
Are those two scheming now against my wretched life?
SLAVE: Your little son, whom you sent secretly away —
Oh, my poor lady! — they are resolved to murder him.
ANDROMACHE: Oh, no! Then they discovered he'd been
    sent away.
Who can have told them? Oh, poor child! What shall I do?
SLAVE: I don't know who; but I heard this from their own
    lips.
Menelaus has gone off himself to fetch him back.
ANDROMACHE: Then there's no hope. My little boy, this
    pair of hawks
Will catch and kill you; Neoptolemus, who is called
Your father, stays in Delphi when we need him most.
SLAVE: You'd not be treated in this way if he were here,
I'm sure of that; but now you're left without a friend.
ANDROMACHE: Was there no word from Peleus saying he
    would come?
SLAVE: Why, he's too old, even if he came, to give much help.
ANDROMACHE: I've sent to ask him, more than once, to
    come to me.
SLAVE: And do you think your messengers pay heed to you?
ANDROMACHE: Why should they? — Well, then — will *you* be
    my messenger?
SLAVE: What excuse shall I make for being away so long?
ANDROMACHE: Aren't you a woman? You'll find twenty
    things to say.
SLAVE: It's quite a risk; Hermione keeps her eyes open.
ANDROMACHE: There, now: your friend's in need of help,
    and you say no.
SLAVE: I do not; never cast that at me. I will go;
And if I suffer for it — a slave-woman's life
Is no great matter.
ANDROMACHE: Go, then.
    [*Exit* SLAVE.]

                    Meantime I'll renew
The groans and tears to which I dedicate my life,
And cry my griefs to heaven. All women do the same —
Tell over and over each day's fresh calamity;
It is their nature, and their pleasure. But *my* griefs
Clamour unending for lament: my city gone,
Hector my husband killed, this harsh and joyless life
To which I've been bound fast since first I left my palace
To become a slave. How wrong it is ever to call
Any mortal happy until he's dead, and you have seen
In what condition he passed through his final day
Of life, before departing to the world below.

    When Paris brought back Helen
        To share his home and bed,
    No bride, but a blasting Fury
        Through Troy's high gates he led.

    For Helen Greece vowed vengeance:
        A thousand swift ships came,
    And Argos' angry armies
        Took Troy with sword and flame.

    Struck by the cruel Achilles
        I saw my husband fall,
    And in the dust his body
        Dragged bleeding round the wall.

    The hateful hood of slavery
        About my head I wore,
    And from my palace bound I went
        Down to the crowded shore.

    My cheeks were wet with weeping
        The day I left them there —
    My city, home, and husband,
        One dusty tomb to share.

Why must I drag out further
  My wretched life, a slave?
O Goddess, see my torment;
  O Thetis, hear and save!

My hands plead on unceasing,
  My tears flow still undried,
As mountain streams for ever
  Flow down the steep rock's side.

[*Enter the* CHORUS.]

CHORUS: Are you still here, Andromache?
    You have sat so long by the altar
    On the holy floor of Thetis.
    Although I am Greek, and live here in Phthia,
    While you are an Asiatic, I have come
    Hoping we may concoct some remedy
    To help you out of your dilemma.
    We are grieved that you and Hermione
    Should be matched in this deadlock of hate –
    Two women claiming one man's bed,
    A rival to the wife of Achilles' son.

    Face the facts; take a reasoned view
    Of your present plight, and realize where you
      stand.
    You belong to Hermione; she
    Is a Spartan princess, you a woman of Troy;
    Can you fight against her?

    Leave the temple; this is the altar
    Where they sacrifice sheep to the sea-goddess.
    What help can it be
    To let distress waste and disfigure you
    Because those who command are cruel?
    Power will overtake you; you are nothing;
    Then why bring trouble on yourself?

Come, then — this beautiful place
Belongs to the immortal sea-nymph;
Come away! Accept your position;
You are a slave, on foreign soil,
In a city that is not yours,
With not a friend of your own in sight.
Your situation is most unfortunate;
You are a woman greatly to be pitied.

I at least have felt sorry for you
Since first you came to this house from Troy;
But for fear of my lady I have kept quiet,
Though you have my truest sympathy;
But I would not wish Hermione
To know that I am your friend.

[HERMIONE *has already entered.*]

HERMIONE: This rare and fine gold coronet which adorns my
      head,
This handsome gown that glows with rich embroidery,
Are not this house's treasured heirlooms handed down
From Peleus and Achilles. No; they come from Sparta —
Just two of many gifts my father Menelaus
Gave me when I was married. For this reason I
Say what I please; and that [*she turns to the* CHORUS] is
      answer enough for you.
[*To* ANDROMACHE] But as for you — a slave-woman, a prize
      of war —
You want to own this palace; to get rid of me;
Your witchcraft makes my husband hate me; for your
      gain
My womb is barren, dead. You oriental women
Are expert in such devilry — but I'll stop you.
You'll find no help in Thetis, neither temple nor
Altar will save you; you shall die. Or if someone,
Divine or mortal, wants to save you, your best way

Is to leave off your queenly airs of long ago,
Learn to bow low, kneel humbly to me, sweep the floors,
Sprinkle my house with water from the golden jars;
And learn where you live now – there is no Hector here,
No Priam decked in gold; this is a Greek city.
And you have the effrontery, you immoral wretch,
To sleep with the man whose father killed your husband, bear
Children with the blood of his murderer in their veins!
You orientals are all alike – incest between
Father and daughter, brother and sister, mother and son;
And murder too – the closest family ties outraged,
And no law to forbid any such crime! You can't
Import your foreign morals here. It's a disgrace
In Hellas for one man to be master of two women;
Unless a man wants trouble at home, he must enjoy
The pleasures of marriage with one wife, and be content.

CHORUS: Women have a genius for malice; and against
A rival wife their enmity is worst of all.

ANDROMACHE: How vividly youth shows humanity's worst side –
The immature mind, tempted to unscrupulousness!
I am your slave: I fear this leaves me little hope
Of a fair hearing, however clear my case may be;
And if I win it, I merely sign my own sentence.
Nothing makes arrogant people angrier than being
Worsted in argument by the weaker party. Still,
No one shall say that I don't stand up for my rights.
    Can you, young woman, name one valid reason which
Might stir me to desire your place as lawful wife?
Is Sparta a less powerful or less fortunate
City than Troy? Are you addressing a free woman?
Am I so elated with my own young, supple flesh,
So confident in my country and my friends, that I
Threaten your tenure as the mistress of this house?

Am I to take your place in bearing sons – who will
Be slaves, a mere encumbrance to my wretched life?
You say I make you barren – will your barrenness
Make anyone accept my son as king of Phthia?
No doubt the Hellenes love me – I was Hector's wife,
My name was royal, and not unknown in Phrygia.
Your husband hates you, not because I practise magic,
But because you are not congenial company.
There's magic even in mere pleasantness; it's not
Beauty, but character, that wins a husband's heart.
You, if something annoys you, begin praising Sparta,
Belittling Scyros. In a modest house you flaunt
Your wealth; you set your Menelaus above Achilles.
Naturally Neoptolemus dislikes you. A wife,
Even if she has married beneath her, ought to make
The best of it, and not pit her pride against her husband's.
If you were married to some king in snowy Thrace,
Where one man shares his bed in turn with several women,
Would you kill all your rivals? You'd be named the one
Who branded our whole sex with jealous lustfulness –
A shameful malady to which women are more prone
Perhaps than men; but we disguise it decently.

 Beloved Hector! When Aphrodite snared your heart,
I have even loved your other lover for your sake,
Even nursed your love-child at my breast, sooner than speak
One word to grieve you! – So, by being a good wife,
I drew my husband to me; but you, for sheer panic,
Won't let the dew of heaven fall on your precious man!
Your mother Helen, my girl, was much too fond of men;
Don't you try to outdo her. Look at your mother's bad
Example, and avoid it, if you have any sense.

CHORUS: Dear mistress, will you not – it is quite possible –
Be ready to make terms with her as best you can?

HERMIONE: What do you mean by lecturing me and arguing?
Do you tell me you are self-controlled and I am not?

ANDROMACHE: You – after all you've just said to me – self-controlled?

HERMIONE: You talk of 'sense' – I want none of your 'sense' in my house.

ANDROMACHE: You're just an adolescent with a vicious tongue.

HERMIONE: It's vicious practice I complain of, not your tongue.

ANDROMACHE: Still your sex-troubles! Why won't you stop airing them?

HERMIONE: Why? Doesn't sex come first in every woman's life?

ANDROMACHE: Rightly, if she's chaste-minded; if not, nothing's right.

HERMIONE: In Greece we have different standards from you foreigners.

ANDROMACHE: Shameful is recognized as shameful, east or west.

HERMIONE: You're very good at arguing; it won't save your life.

ANDROMACHE: Thetis is looking at you – do you see?

HERMIONE: I do;
It is your Troy she hates. You Trojans killed her son.

ANDROMACHE: Your mother killed him, not I. Helen killed Achilles.

HERMIONE: Do you think I have not suffered? Must you probe the wound?

ANDROMACHE: No, I have done. I'll hold my tongue and say no more.

HERMIONE: Say one thing – answer the question I came here to ask.

ANDROMACHE: I will tell you this: you lack common intelligence.

HERMIONE: Will you get out of here? This is a sanctuary.

ANDROMACHE: Yes, if my life is promised me; if not, never.

HERMIONE: You die, that's settled; I won't wait till he comes back.

ANDROMACHE: Till he comes back, neither will I give myself up.

HERMIONE: I'll burn this place down. I don't care what happens to you.

ANDROMACHE: Go on – burn the place down. The gods will witness it.

HERMIONE: I'll scar your flesh, I'll mangle you and torture you.

ANDROMACHE: Cut me to pieces, drench this altar with my blood;

Thetis will punish you.

HERMIONE: You brazen foreign beast,
Do you defy death? I shall shift you soon enough;
You'll leave that altar of your own accord. I have
A bait to fetch you. What it is I'll not say yet;
You'll soon discover what I mean. So now sit on;
If you were fixed there like a statue set in lead,
I'd make you move. You rely on Neoptolemus;
But I shall get my own way before he comes back.
     [*Exit* HERMIONE.]

ANDROMACHE: Yes, I rely on Neoptolemus. How strange
That nature provides remedies against deadly snakes,
But against a bad woman – deadlier far than snakes,
Crueller than fire – no one has found a remedy.
To that extent we are a plague to the human race.

CHORUS: That day was the beginning of great sorrows,
         When Hermes, son of Zeus and Maia,
         Came to the shady slope of Mount Ida,
         And like a charioteer leading his team
         Led the three lovely goddesses,
         Armed for the battle of beauty,
         Plumed with jealousy,
         To a cowherd's shed, to a solitary shepherd-lad
         Who made his home in a lonely cottage.

So when they reached the leafy glen
They bathed their glistening bodies white
In the cold gush of mountain springs,
And came to the son of Priam;
And each against other staked vast promises
Loaded with foreboding;
And Aphrodite won, with words
To dazzle thought, enchant the ear —
And plunge high-towering Troy and her
    doomed people
Deep in confusion and ruin.

Oh! If only his mother had destroyed him!
Not let him live to haunt the high rocks of Ida,
But at once, while Cassandra cried, 'Kill
    him!' —
Stood by the prophetic bay-tree, crying
'Kill the destroyer of Priam's city!'
Kneeling to one after another,
Entreating every elder and councillor,
'Kill that child!'

If Troy had listened! Her women would have
    been
Spared the chain of slavery; you, Andromache,
Would have inherited a throne and palace;
Hellas too would have been spared the agony
Of those ten years when her young men
Fought to and fro before the walls of Troy;
Spared the widow's lonely bed,
And old men's tears for their dead sons.

[*Enter* MENELAUS *with two soldiers leading* MOLOSSUS.]

MENELAUS: You sent your son away to another house without
  My daughter's knowledge. I found him, and I've brought him
  back.

To save your life, you trusted to this statue here;
For his, to your accomplices; but the result
Shows you to be less clever, my lady, than Menelaus.
And now, if you refuse to abandon sanctuary,
This child's throat shall be cut instead of yours. So choose:
Either your life, or your son's life, shall pay what's due
For your practices against my daughter and myself.
ANDROMACHE: Oh, fame! How many thousand nobodies
          there are
Whom fame blows up to importance and authority!
Heaven bless the man whose splendid reputation's based
On truth; but when it lives by lies, I'm not deceived;
Fame hides an empty fabric of pretence and luck.

   You! Did a coward like you lead the picked fighting-men
Of Hellas against Priam to conquer Troy? And has
Your childish daughter talked such spirit into you
That you dare challenge a defenceless slave-woman?
You – took Troy? Troy deserved a different conqueror.
Menelaus, come now – let us reason the matter out.
Suppose your daughter has her way, and I am killed:
She's branded forthwith as a murderess; you too
In most men's eyes would be held guilty of my death
As her accomplice. Or if I escape with my life,
Do you propose to kill my son? And will his father
Accept his son's death lightly? That is not how Troy
Remembers Neoptolemus; he'll know where to look
For his revenge. He has Achilles' blood in him,
And Peleus' – and he'll show it. He will turn your daughter
Out of his house. Then, when you try to marry her
To someone else, what will you say? That her pure soul
Could never stomach a bad husband? Truth will out.
Then who will take her? Will you keep her in your house,
A sexless, grey-haired widow? Pitiful, reckless man!
Do you see the deluge of disaster threatening you?
Sooner than put up with such injury, you would see

Your daughter supplanted in her marriage ten times over.
Why, then, invite calamity for so slight a cause?
Or, if we women are a plague and curse, why must
Men mould their natures to our pattern? Now, if I
Am, as your daughter says, bewitching her with spells
To make her barren, I will go willingly – not fly
For refuge to an altar, but without demur
Will stand my trial before Neoptolemus; my crime,
If I rob him of children, is chiefly against him.
That's all I have to say to you. I fear one thing,
Menelaus, in your nature; when you levelled Troy
With the dust, that quarrel too was for a woman's sake.

CHORUS: You have said more than a woman ought to say to a
    man;
    Your self-control has reached the end of its resource.

MENELAUS: Andromache, these are trivial matters, as you say,
Unworthy of the attention of a king like me
Or of any Greek. But let me tell you this: the thing
That a man happens to want always means more to him
Than taking Troy. Now, for a woman to be deprived
Of her rights in marriage, I don't regard as trivial;
So I'm here to take my daughter's part. Some other things
A woman has to put up with rank as secondary;
To lose her husband is to forfeit her whole life.
My son-in-law has a right to assume authority
Over my slaves; and I claim equal authority
For myself, and for my daughter, over his. With friends –
I mean true friends by nature – private property
Does not exist; the wealth of each belongs to all.
To wait, then, for the absent to return, instead
Of settling matters to my satisfaction now,
Would be feeble and foolish. So, get up and leave
This temple. If you die, your son's life shall be spared;
If you prefer not to be killed, I shall kill him.
One of you, or the other, must depart this life.

ANDROMACHE: This is a cruel choice and lottery for lives
    You set before me. If I win the draw, my prize
    Is misery; if I lose, there is despair and death.
        Menelaus, why move mountains for a trivial cause?
    Listen: why are you killing me? What have I done?
    Have I betrayed your city? Killed a child of yours?
    Or burnt your home? I was my master's concubine
    Because he forced me. Why kill *me*, then, and not him?
    The fault was his; yet you pass by the source of wrong
    And turn against its victim with your cruel rage.
    Oh, oh! My dear, dead country! Oh, what misery!
    Why did I have to bear a child, grief heaped on grief?
        What joy can living bring me? Which way must I look
    For comfort — to the present or the past? I saw
    Hector dragged dead behind his victor's chariot.
    I saw Troy crumble in the pitiless flames. Men held
    Me by the hair, and hauled me to the Argive ships.
    When I came here, it was to live as concubine
    To the man whose father killed my husband. But why waste
    Tears on the past? Here is today's agony, weighed
    And counted to its full bitterness. This boy was all
    I had left, the one light of my life. Now those who make
    Decisions will kill him. No! Not if my wretched life
    Can save him. There is still hope here, if he can live.
    My life is mere shame if I will not die for him.
    Menelaus, I leave the altar; I am in your hands;
    Now bind me, hang me, cut my throat, do what you will.
    — My son, my own child, see — I am going to my death
    To save you. If you escape alive, remember me,
    How cruelly I was killed. Go to your father, and
    Kiss him, and weep, and put your arms around his neck,
    And tell him what I have done. Children are more than life;
    I always knew. A burden, childless women call them;
    They suffer less; but their good fortune is all loss!
CHORUS: Your words move my compassion. It is sad to see

Anyone in such grief, even a foreigner.
Menelaus, you should persuade Hermione to reach
Some agreement with her, to relieve her misery.

MENELAUS: You men, get hold of her and tie her arms. She
won't
Like what I have to tell her. I threatened to kill
Your son, to induce you to abandon sanctuary
And freely give yourself into my hands to kill.
That explains *your* position. As regards your son,
My daughter shall decide either to kill him or
Not kill him, as she pleases. Now, into the house;
And learn that free men take no insolence from slaves.

ANDROMACHE: Oh! Then you lied, your promise was all
treachery!

MENELAUS: Proclaim it from the housetops: I deny nothing.

ANDROMACHE: And this, with Spartans, passes for intelligence?

MENELAUS: Troy too respects the principle, 'An eye for an
eye'.

ANDROMACHE: Are there no gods? Do you not fear divine
justice?

MENELAUS: We will endure that when it comes. I'll kill you
first.

ANDROMACHE: But will you take my little boy and kill him
too?

MENELAUS: Oh, no; my daughter, if she wishes, will do that—
He's hers.

ANDROMACHE: Child, it's already time to mourn for you.

MENELAUS: The outlook for him is perhaps discouraging.

ANDROMACHE: Spartans! The whole world hates you above
all other men!
Lies are your policy, treachery your accomplishment,
Your craft is crime and cruelty; your hearts warped and sly,
Your minds diseased, you lord it over the Hellene world;
Justice lies dead! What wickedness is not in you?

You add murder to murder, you make gold your god;
The whole world knows your speech is one thing, your
    intent
Another. My curse on you! Death is less terrible
To me than you imagined. I died long ago
When my dear city died, when my great Hector died,
Who many times drove you at sword's point to your ship
In panic! Now, the figure of grim-visaged war,
You come to kill a woman! Not one cringing word
Shall you get from my lips, nor your Hermione.
If you are royal in Sparta, so was I in Troy;
If I'm defeated, make no boast; your turn will come.
        [ANDROMACHE *and* MOLOSSUS *are led into the house;*
        MENELAUS *follows.*]

CHORUS: I think it wrong that a man should love two
                women,
           That his two sons should have different
                mothers.
           The result is that his house
           Is split with quarrelling and sore with sorrow.
           I hold that a man should be content with one
                wife;
           Marriage cannot be shared.

           The same holds good in cities:
           Two kings are a worse imposition than one;
           For burdens are doubled and loyalty is divided.

           If two poets work together in composing one
                song,
           The Muses will certainly make the result a dis-
                cord.
           When a ship flies before a fresh breeze,
           The work of steering is not helped by two
                opinions.

Again, in government, a large assembly of wise
    men
Is less effective than a single autocrat,
Even if he is of mediocre ability.
In the home and in politics it is equally true:
Authority must be single
If the right thing is to be done at the right time.

An example of this is the Spartan general's
    daughter.
She was flaming with rage against her rival,
Filled with resentment and jealousy, resolved
To kill the unhappy Andromache and her
    son.

This killing is a godless, barbarous business;
It is revolting.
My lady Hermione, what you are doing
Will recoil in time on your own head.

Look now! I see them coming from the house,
Their two fates joined in one sentence of
    death.
Andromache, we weep for you,
Child, we pity you –
Dying because your father loved your mother!
You have no part in this quarrel;
You have not injured the royal house.

[*Enter* ANDROMACHE *and* MOLOSSUS, *guarded.*]

ANDROMACHE: You see me sent to my grave
                Bound, with wrists bleeding under the
                    cords.

MOLOSSUS: Mother, let me come close at your side.

ANDROMACHE: You rulers of Thessaly,
                You have left me a prey to my enemies.

MOLOSSUS:	O father, come and save us!
ANDROMACHE:	Dear child, you shall lie on my breast;
	In death we shall be together.
MOLOSSUS:	Death? Oh, mother what will they do?
	What will happen to us both?

[MENELAUS *has entered.*]

MENELAUS:	Away with you to the depth of the earth!
	You both belong to an enemy town;
	But you have had separate judgement: I
	Passed sentence on you, Andromache, and
	My daughter Hermione on your son –
	And rightly; to leave
	Your enemies' children to take their place
	When you could kill them off, and relieve your house
	Of a burden of fear,
	Is mere inexcusable folly.
ANDROMACHE:	O Hector, son of Priam, if I could only call
	Your strong arm and your spear to fight for me!
MOLOSSUS:	Mother, what can I say to save us from death?
ANDROMACHE:	Go to him, kneel to your master and implore him.
MOLOSSUS:	Dear, dear master, save me from death.
ANDROMACHE:	My eyes stream tears, like drops that roll
	Down some smooth, sunless face of rock.
MOLOSSUS:	Dear mother, what way can I find
	To bring us out of all our troubles?

MENELAUS: It is no use kneeling there, for you may
                 As well say prayers to the rocks or
                     waves.
                 I am here in my own child's interests,
                 And I've nothing for you.
                 I've spent a great part of my life and soul
                 In capturing Troy, and your mother
                     here;
                 And you may thank her
                 That you're bound for the darkness of
                     Hades.

CHORUS: Why, look, look! I see Peleus coming! Yes, it is —
The aged Peleus hurrying this way; he's come!
    [*Enter* PELEUS, *attended*.]

PELEUS: Now, tell me, all of you — and you there with the
    sword —
What is all this? Has the whole house gone mad? Well,
    what's
At the bottom of it? Is this execution without trial?
Just hold your hand, Menelaus; you go beyond your rights.
[*To Attendants*] Come on, this is no time for dawdling. Now,
    if ever,
I had best summon my strength of younger days. And first
I must come up like a fair wind and fill the sails
Of this poor vessel. — Andromache, by whose sentence
Have these men bound you and brought you here, and the
    boy too?
What does it mean — like a ewe and her lamb led to slaughter
When I'm not here, and in your master's absence too?

ANDROMACHE: Sir, as you see, these men have brought me
    and my child here
To die. What can I say? I sent you messages
Not once, but many times, urgently begging you
To come. I think you know the quarrel here between
Me and Hermione, and the reasons why they want

To kill me – she no doubt has told you. I came here
To the altar of Thetis, mother of your noble son,
Whom you devoutly worship; but they dragged me away
And sentenced me, without any trial, without waiting
For Neoptolemus to come home. They knew that I
Was unprotected, and my son too; and they are going
To kill him with me, though he is wholly innocent.
Sir, I implore you – see, I fall at your knees; my hands
Are bound, or they would reach your beard to plead with
     you:
Save me, in the gods' name! Otherwise my death will bring
Shame on you all, and to my sad life a sadder end.

PELEUS: Untie these cords, I tell you – obey me instantly,
     Before someone feels sorry; set this woman free!

MENELAUS: I forbid it. I'm not under your authority;
     And over *her* I've easily the prior right.

PELEUS: What? You come here and organize my house for me?
     You're king of Sparta; can't you be content with that?

MENELAUS: This is my prisoner; I brought her back from
     Troy.

PELEUS: You mean, my grandson won her as his lawful prize.

MENELAUS: My property is his, and likewise his is mine.

PELEUS: Yours to treat rightly, not to abuse, to seize and kill.

MENELAUS: Let this be clear: you'll not take her out of my
     hands.

PELEUS: Won't I? You see this stick? You'll get a bloody
     head.

MENELAUS: Touch me, and you'll soon see. Come nearer,
     take one step.

PELEUS: You blackguard, son of a blackguard! Are you called
     a man?
What claim have you to count as a man? A man from Troy
Made you a cuckold when you left your house unlocked,
Unguarded, as though your wife were chaste; though the
     truth is

A wickeder woman never lived. No Spartan girl
Could grow up modest, even if she wanted to.
You never find them staying at home; no, they go out
With bare thighs and loose clothes, to wrestle and run races
Along with the young men. I call it intolerable.
Then can you wonder that your women don't grow up
Modest? You should ask Helen about that – Helen,
Who left your home, all sacred ties, and cheerfully
Went gadding off with her young man to foreign parts.
Then what do you do? For her sake you collect that vast
Army of Greeks and march them off to Troy. You ought
To have spat her out, not stirred a single spear for her,
Once you had learnt what kind of woman she was; you
        ought
To have let her stay in Troy, you ought to have paid her
        money
Never to ask to be taken back. But oh, no! You
Never thought of that; the wind was blowing the other way.
No; you must send brave men by thousands to their deaths;
Old women, waiting for their sons' return, you made
Childless. Grey-headed fathers – I am one of them –
Were robbed by you of noble sons. Yes, Menelaus,
I see Achilles' blood spread like a guilty stain
On your hands! – Yet, of all the Hellenes, you alone
Came back from Troy not even wounded! You brought
        home
Your splendid armour in its fancy case unmarked,
As fresh as when you took it there! Oh, yes, I warned
My grandson, when he had a mind to marry, not
To make alliance with you, not to bring home a girl
Whose bad ways would reflect her mother's infamy.
– Take my advice, you who would marry: choose the
        daughter
Of a good mother. – Then again, how monstrously
You behaved towards your brother, when you insisted on

The sacrifice of his most innocent child! – and all
Because you could not bear to lose your worthless wife!
When you took Troy – no, even there you shall not escape –
And laid hands on her, then you did not kill the woman.
She only had to bare her breast, and you threw down
Your sword, you let her kiss you, gave the treacherous bitch
Loving caresses – you contemptible, amorous
Weakling! To crown all, you come here and create havoc
In my grandson's house when he's away, with a dastardly
Attempt to kill an unfortunate woman and her son.
If that boy were three times a bastard, yet he'll live
To make you sorry, and that daughter you have indoors.
There's many a stony field gives fatter crops than loam,
And a bastard may be a better man than the true-born.
So take your daughter back to Sparta! I'd rather have
As a son-in-law, or friend, an honest man who's poor,
Than any wealthy blackguard. You're beneath contempt.

CHORUS: Some trifling cause can lead men to a violent quar-
    rel
    Simply through talking. Any sensible person takes
    Great care not to start disagreement between friends.

MENELAUS: How can they say that there is wisdom in old
    men?
    Or in some individuals once thought to have
    Intelligence? You are Peleus, and your father was
    Well known. You have made alliance with my family;
    Yet now you disgrace yourself, and insult me, and all
    For the sake of a foreign woman! You should have turned
        her out,
    Sent her to the other side of the Nile or Phasis, where
    She belongs; and I would have helped you. She comes from a
        land
    Where untold thousands of Hellenes lie fallen in war.
    She had her share too in your son Achilles' death:
    Paris, who killed your son, was Hector's brother, and she

Was Hector's wife. Yet you don't hesitate to come
Under the same roof with her, eat at the same table;
You let her bear sons in your house – your enemies!
And when I try, both in your interest and in mine,
To prevent such risk by killing her, I find the woman
Snatched out of my hands! Here's a further point well worth
Considering. Suppose Hermione remains
Childless, while *she* produces sons; do you propose
To recognize them as royal, and let barbarians
Rule over Greeks? Am I a fool if I refuse
To tolerate such wrong? and are you sensible?
You're an old man, you know; yes, old! And, by the way,
When you speak of my generalship, you support my case
Better than if you said nothing. Then, Helen's trouble
Came by divine volition, not from her own choice;
And through it she conferred great benefits on Hellas.
Weapons and fighting formerly were unknown to them;
The war brought out their manly qualities, and, further,
Brought different kinds of Greeks together – contact is
A great teacher. As for the fact that I refrained
From killing Helen the moment I set eyes on her,
That was just self-control. I wish that you, Peleus,
In the case of Phocus, for example, had shown the same.
I came here not to quarrel with you, but in a spirit
Of friendliness; and if you lose your temper and shout,
You'll only make yourself hoarse, without robbing me
Of the advantage of my prudent policy.

CHORUS: Now both of you give up this useless argument
Before you both regret it. This would be far better.

PELEUS: I'll tell you a bad custom which obtains in Hellas:
When an army wins a victory over the enemy,
No one gives credit to the men who sweat and fight;
The general reaps the glory. Yet he, after all,
Can only wield one sword, being one man among
Ten thousand; but he gets more fame for the same work.

And then, in public life your generals take their seats
In office – self-important nobodies who despise
The common people; yet ten thousand heads contain,
Surely, ten thousand times more common sense – given
The necessary daring and initiative.
So, you and your brother – I can see you sitting there
In your headquarters before Troy, swollen with pride,
Exalted by the sweat and pain of other men.
You'll soon find Peleus a more dangerous enemy
Than ever Paris of Ida was, if you won't take
Yourself and your barren daughter out of my son's house
Immediately; otherwise, as sure as he's my son,
He'll take Hermione by the hair and throw her out.
Being barren, she can't bear to see another woman
Happy with children, when she has no child herself.
Well then, because of your daughter's incapacity
For children, must my house be left without an heir?
[To MENELAUS' *guards*] Hands off her, curse you! I'll soon
    see if anyone
Will stop me setting her free. [To ANDROMACHE] Stand
    up, now; I'll untie
These knots, although my hands are shaking. Look at this!
Did you think you were tying up a bull or lion,
To maul her so? Or were you afraid she'd get a sword
And defend herself? – Come close beside me, child, and help
To free your mother. I'll take care of you in Phthia;
I know you'll grow up a great enemy to *them*.
– Apart from fame in fighting and success in war,
The Spartans are no better men than other Greeks.
CHORUS: Old men are liable to be so uncontrolled
That once they are in a rage there's no resisting them.
MENELAUS: You fly too easily into mere abusiveness.
For my own part, as a stranger here I don't intend
Either to commit violence or submit to it.
For the present, since I've not unlimited time to spare,

I am going home. Not far from Sparta a certain city
Which once was friendly has turned hostile; I must now
Lead out a force to attack them and regain control.
When I have arranged that matter to my satisfaction
I shall return; and I hope to meet my son-in-law
In person, both to state my views and to hear his.
If he will punish Andromache and act reasonably
For the future, he will find me reasonable in turn.
If he gets angry, he will find me angry too;
In other words, he will be paid in his own coin.
As for your blatherings, they leave me undisturbed.
What are you? A walking ghost endowed with a loud voice,
Incapable of everything but endless talk.

    [*Exit* MENELAUS.]

PELEUS: My boy, come and stand by me here, and we'll go in.
  You too, poor soul; you have endured the raging storm;
  But now at last you're safe in harbour, and all's calm.

ANDROMACHE: Peleus, may the gods bless you and all your
    family
  For rescuing my child and me in our distress.
  But do take care; they see that you are old, and I
  Am weak, and he is a child – they may be lying in wait
  To attack us on some lonely path and carry me off.
  We're safe for the moment; later we might still be caught.

PELEUS: Now do stop talking like a terrified woman. Come on,
  Who's going to touch you? The first to lift a hand will be
  Sorry for it. My power is backed both by the gods
  And by a numerous body of troops, both horse and foot.
  Besides, I'm not the old man you think me. I stand straight;
  I only need to look a man like that in the eye
  To make him run, for all my white hair. One old man,
  If only he shows a stout heart, is a match for twenty
  Young men. Why, what's the use of muscle to a coward?

    [PELEUS, ANDROMACHE, *and* MOLOSSUS *go out in
    the direction from which* PELEUS *arrived.*]

CHORUS: The kind of life that I would choose,
            The only kind worth living,
            Is to inherit some great and honoured name
            And be brought up in a wealthy house.

            When trouble comes, and there appears no
                escape,
            Help can always be found if you are of noble
                blood.
            If your family is of high repute,
            If your name is heard in ceremonial announce-
                ments,
            You will enjoy consideration and respect.
            Time takes no toll of the remembrance of
                great men,
            And their virtue is a beacon over their grave.

            I would rather forgo the success which involves
                dishonour
            Than earn men's hate by perverting right with
                force.
            For though tyranny tastes sweet for the
                moment,
            Yet of its freshness time takes toll,
            Till it lies yet one more burden on a disgraced
                house.
            The life I admire, the way that I would choose,
            Either in marriage or in ruling a city,
            Is to wield no power beyond what is just and
                fair.
            Peleus, old hero, I can well believe
            That when you were young and a famous
                fighter
            You went into battle with the Lapithae against
                the Centaurs;

That you sailed with the Argonauts on that
    world-famed voyage
Out through the Clashing Rocks into the
    Inhospitable Sea;
And that long ago, when the glorious Heracles,
    son of Zeus,
Stretched a girdle of blood about the walls of
    Troy,
You shared his exploits and brought home to
    Europe
A fame as notable as his.

[*Enter Hermione's* NURSE.]

NURSE: Oh, friends, dear friends! The troubles that pour
    down on us
Today, one after another! There's my mistress now,
Hermione, indoors – her father's just gone off
And left her! What with that, and feeling full of guilt
For her wickedness in trying to kill Andromache
And the boy – she wants to kill herself! She's terrified
That her husband will disgrace her and turn her out of the
    house
For what she did, or even kill her for attempting
Such a dreadful murder. She was trying to hang herself;
The servants told to watch her barely prevented it.
She found a sword; they snatched it from her and took it
    away.
Remorse torments her; she knows now that what she did
Was criminal. She'll hang herself – I'm just worn out
With trying to stop her. *You* go in, and see if you
Can save her life. She knows me too well and won't listen;
Someone she isn't used to might have more success.

CHORUS: Yes, I can hear the servants' voices; and they're
    saying
Just what you told us. Now we shall see her for ourselves,
Distracted with remorse and terror. Here she comes,

Escaping from her servants' hands, resolved to die!

[*Enter* HERMIONE *followed by Servants.*]

HERMIONE: Get away, let me alone!

    I'll tear my hair, I'll tear my face with my nails!

NURSE: Dear child, what are you going to do? Don't hurt yourself.

HERMIONE: Take it away –

    Why should I tie my hair in a fine-spun veil?

    Throw it to the winds!

NURSE: Dear child, cover your breast, pull your gown together.

HERMIONE: Why cover my guilty breast?

    I have wronged my husband, there's no hiding it;

    Everyone knows, everyone saw!

NURSE: If it's because you plotted against your rival's life –

HERMIONE: It was cruel, it was criminal; that's why I'm crying.

    I am accursed, before all the world accursed!

NURSE: Don't grieve; this is a fault your husband will forgive.

HERMIONE: Why did you wrench the sword out of my hand?

    Give it me, dear Nurse, give it back to me;

    Let me strike one straight blow.

    Or the rope – let me go; I will have it.

NURSE: You are out of your mind; it would be murder to let you go.

HERMIONE: Oh, how can I bear it?

    Where is a fire? The flame will be welcome.

    Where is a cliff I can climb to,

    By the sea or on the wooded mountain?

    There I would die and have nothing to fear from the living.

NURSE: Why give yourself all this distress? The gods send trouble

At one time or another to every human being.

HERMIONE: Father, why did you leave me, abandon me,

Like a derelict stranded ship, not an oar left?

My husband will kill me, I know he'll kill me.

I won't stay in his house another hour.

Could I not kneel before some statue for sanctuary?

Or shall I go and fall

Like a slave at my own slave's feet?

Oh, if I were a bird,

To soar on dark wings away from Thessaly!

Or Jason's pine-wood ship, the first that ever sailed

Out through the purple cliffs, and away, away!

NURSE: Hermione, listen: to go to extremes is always wrong.

You went too far in plotting against Andromache;

And now in this foolish terror you make the same mistake.

Your husband is not going to disown you as his wife

Because some wretched foreign woman complains of you!

You're not a prisoner of war brought back from Troy; you are

His wife. He received you with a large dowry from Menelaus,

Who belongs to a royal house and a rich powerful state.

And will your father simply abandon you and let you

Be driven out of your home? You need fear no such thing.

Now come indoors; you must not show yourself out here

In front of the house. People will slander you, my girl,

If you're seen standing in this state outside your door.

CHORUS: Why, look! Here comes a stranger, from a distant part

Of Hellas, by his appearance. He has been travelling fast.
  [*Enter* ORESTES.]
ORESTES: Ladies, is this the royal palace, and the home
  Of Neoptolemus?
CHORUS: Yes, it is. But who are you?
ORESTES: I am the son of Agamemnon and Clytemnestra;
  My name is Orestes. I am travelling to Dodona,
  To Zeus's oracle; and since Phthia lies on my way
  I would like to inquire about my cousin, Hermione
  Of Sparta, if she is well and all goes happily
  With her. She lives at a great distance from us now,
  But we at home still think of her affectionately.
HERMIONE: Orestes! Oh, to see you come here is like find-
      ing
  A harbour in a storm! I kneel entreating you
  To pity me, when you learn of my predicament.
  I am in despair. My arms clasping your knees must serve
  As suppliant wreaths, to sanctify my appeal for help.
ORESTES: I am astonished. Do my eyes deceive me, or
  Is this in truth the daughter of Menelaus, the queen?
HERMIONE: Yes, yes, indeed it is true. I am Hermione,
  The only child that Helen gave to Menelaus.
ORESTES: Apollo defend us, and deliver us from evil!
  What's happening? Who is injuring you, god or man?
HERMIONE: In part it's my own doing, in part my husband's
      fault,
  And the gods' too – I'm persecuted on all sides.
ORESTES: What has gone wrong? You have no children yet;
      the source
  Of trouble, then, can only be one thing: your marriage.
HERMIONE: You have said the words for me. It is that very
      thing.
ORESTES: There is some other woman he prefers to you?
HERMIONE: Yes, Hector's wife. My husband brought her
      home from Troy.

ORESTES: That's a bad thing — for a man to live with two
women.

HERMIONE: That's how it is. I took steps to defend myself.

ORESTES: One woman against another — you contrived some
plot?

HERMIONE: I did; I meant to kill her and her bastard son.

ORESTES: Did you kill her? Or were you stopped by some
mischance?

HERMIONE: Yes, Peleus stopped me. He supported the guilty
cause.

ORESTES: Was anyone helping you in this plot to murder
them?

HERMIONE: My father came from Sparta for this very purpose.

ORESTES: Then did the old man get the better of him by
force?

HERMIONE: My father showed respect for his old age. But
now
He has gone away and left me alone.

ORESTES: I understand.
You are terrified of your husband, after what you have done.

HERMIONE: You are right; he will be justified in killing me.
What can I say? In the name of Zeus and family love,
I beg you to take me away as far as possible
From here, or to my father's palace. The very walls
Of this house seem to shout at me to drive me away,
The earth itself detests me. If my husband comes
Back here from Delphi before I can escape, he will
Lay dreadful charges against me, and either kill me, or
Make me a concubine in the house where I was queen.
You may well ask what made me plan this murderous act.
Foul-minded women were my undoing; they would come
To visit me, with their endless chatter: 'Are you going
To allow that wicked slave-woman to share your house
And share your husband? By Queen Hera,' they would say,

'If she were in *my* house stealing my rightful place
She would not live long – she would not!' I listened to
Their siren-songs, their clever, twisted, wicked gossip;
It puffed me up with folly. Why, what need had I
To be jealous of my husband? I had everything
I wanted – comfort, wealth, a home where I was queen.
My children would have been my husband's lawful heirs,
My rival's bastards would have been almost their slaves.
A married man should never – I repeat, never
Let women come to the house to gossip with his wife.
If he allows it he is a fool. Such visits are
A school of malice. One of them will have taken a bribe
To upset her marriage; another, being guilty, wants
Someone to share her guilt; while many take delight
In scandal for its own sake. As a consequence,
Their husbands' homes are wrecked and ravaged. No good
      comes
Of women visiting your house, but untold harm.
CHORUS: You go too far in speaking ill of your own sex.
I understand your feelings; still, we women ought
To put a decent front on woman's difficulties.
ORESTES: He was a prudent man who said one ought to hear
Both sides of a dispute. I knew affairs had reached
A crisis here, and about the quarrel between you
And Hector's widow. So I watched the situation,
To see if you would stay here, or if, terrified
By the attempted murder of Andromache,
You'd want to quit this palace once for all. Then I
Came, disregarding your instructions, and resolved –
If you would allow me to speak with you, as you have –
To take you away with me from Phthia. You were mine first;
It's through your father's broken promise that you live here
With this man. Menelaus, before he went to Troy,
Promised that you should be my wife; but later on
He promised you to your present husband, in return

For his help in taking Troy. So when Neoptolemus
Came home, I could not blame your father; but I begged
Neoptolemus to renounce his claim to marry you.
I pointed out how fate and circumstances then
Were adverse to me; how it was possible that I
Could find a wife among my circle of relatives,
But hardly elsewhere, on account of my exile and
The special reasons for it. He was insolent;
He abused me as a matricide and victim of
The gory-eyed goddesses. My family circumstances
Forced me to take a humble tone. It galled me – yes,
Deeply; but there it was, and I put up with it;
Robbed of my marriage, I reluctantly withdrew.
Now, since your fortunes are turned upside-down, and you
Find yourself in this desperate predicament,
I'll take you away and bring you safe to your father's house.
Well, blood is thicker than water, and in difficulty
There's nothing better than a friend of your own blood.

HERMIONE: I can't decide about my marriage; my father will
Assume responsibility for that; but please
Take me out of this palace as quickly as you can,
For fear my husband comes and finds me still at home,
Or someone tells old Peleus that I've disappeared
And he sends horsemen after me to bring me back.

ORESTES: Ha! Peleus – he won't touch you! As for Achilles'
    son –
After his insults to me, have no fear of him.
My plans for Neoptolemus are laid; my net
Is round him, firmly fastened: he dies by this hand.
I will not speak before it is time; but when the deed
Is being performed, the Delphian Rock shall know of it.
If my comrades-in-arms at Delphi keep their oaths,
I'll teach Neoptolemus – yes, I, the matricide –
To beware of marrying a woman who belongs to me.
He shall regret that he demanded satisfaction

For his father's death from Lord Apollo; if he now
Has changed his mind, and *offers* satisfaction for
His insolence, that shall not help him. By the hand
Of Apollo, and by my slanders, he shall die like a dog,
And learn what it is to have me for an enemy.
For the powers immortal turn the way of their enemies –
Or of mine – upside-down, and subjugate their pride.

[*Exeunt* ORESTES *and* HERMIONE.]

CHORUS: Apollo, whose immortal hand
                 Reared the strong towers and walls of Troy!
                 Poseidon, driving your chariot-horses
                 Grey-blue over the salt ocean!
                 Why did you dishonour what you had made,
                 Surrender the work of your own hands,
                 Unhappy Troy, unhappy Troy,
                 To the murderous misery of war?
                 By the river-bank on the Trojan plain
                 Many a horse was harnessed well,
                 Many a man you summoned
                 To the trial of strength and valour;
                 But the prize was death and the garland blood.
                 And the princes of Troy have gone to the home
                      of the dead,
                 And the altars of Troy are cold,
                 The smoke of incense vanished,
                 And the holy flame quenched.

                 Gone too is the victor, the son of Atreus,
                 Felled by the strength of his treacherous wife;
                 She in turn, receiving death for death,
                 Earned her reward at her son's hands.
                 And this was a god's command; an oracle
                 Given by a god rounded upon her,
                 When Orestes came to Argos
                 Straight from the holy temple

To be his mother's murderer.
O Fate, O Phoebus, how can I believe?

And in the streets of Hellas many mothers
Raised the sad music of mourning for their
    sons;
Many widows left their homes behind
And went to another husband.
Not alone on you and yours, Andromache,
The bitterness of sorrow has fallen;
This plague — Hellas too has endured the
    plague.
The thunder that shattered Troy
Has passed to our pleasant fields,
And death is with us in a rain of blood.

[*Enter* PELEUS.]

PELEUS: Ladies, please tell me just what has been happening.
  I've heard a confused rumour that Hermione
  Has left the palace, that she's gone! I want to know
  At once if this is true. My grandson is away,
  And we at home must strictly guard his interests.

CHORUS: The rumour was true, Peleus. It would not be right
  To conceal a trouble which concerns me equally.
  The queen has left the palace, she has fled and gone.

PELEUS: Fled? What was she afraid of? Give me more details.

CHORUS: Afraid Neoptolemus would turn her out of doors.

PELEUS: No! Why? Because of their design to kill the boy?

CHORUS: Why, yes; she was afraid too of Andromache.

PELEUS: Well, did her father take her with him? Or who did?

CHORUS: No; Orestes, Agamemnon's son, took her away.

PELEUS: What is he after? Does he hope to marry her?

CHORUS: Yes, that — and more; he's plotting against your
    grandson's life.

PELEUS: But how? By secret treachery, or in open fight?

CHORUS: He swore to kill him in the holy oracle

Of Loxias, with the assistance of the Delphians.

PELEUS: Then there's real danger. [*To an* Attendant]
     Here, you! Go immediately
To the Pythian temple, and warn my grandson of all this
Quickly, before he's murdered by his enemy's sword!
     [*Enter a* MESSENGER.]

MESSENGER: Oh, Sir! I am the unhappy bearer of bad news,
     To fill with grief both you and all who loved my master.

PELEUS: I know already what you have to say, I know it.

MESSENGER: Then, Peleus, here it is: you have no grandson
     now.
His body is pierced and hacked to pieces by the swords
Of Orestes of Mycenae and his Delphian friends.
     [PELEUS *falls to the ground.*]

CHORUS: Peleus, what will you do? Have courage, don't give
     way!
Lift yourself up.

PELEUS: My life is over. I am dead.
I cannot speak or stand; my legs sink under me.

MESSENGER: Come, Sir, do you not want to avenge him?
     Then stand up
And listen while I tell you everything that happened.

PELEUS: Could Fate even now not spare me, when I stand so
     close
To the utmost limit of old age? Must I still be
Besieged by sorrow on all sides? My only son's
Only son! Tell me how he met his end. Your story
Will be unfit for hearing; yet I wish to hear.

MESSENGER: When we first reached Apollo's famous
     sanctuary,
We spent three whole days, dawn to sunset, gazing at
The sights of Delphi. This, it seems, aroused suspicion.
The citizens of the holy city began to gather
In knots and groups. Orestes went the round of them,
Whispering to this one and to that, setting them all

Against us. 'Do you see this man Neoptolemus,'
He'd say, 'everywhere visiting the temple vaults,
All packed with gold, the treasuries of the whole race?
He has come again for the same purpose as before:
He means to rob Apollo's temple.' Words like these
Stirred up an ugly excitement. Magistrates began
Flocking to council-chambers; those responsible
For the sacred treasures posted guards in the colonnades
Around the buildings. We as yet were unaware
Of all this. We took with us sheep for sacrifice
From the pastures of Parnassus, and stood with our hosts
And the Pythian diviners near the altar-steps.

   One of them asked, 'Sir, what prayer shall we make for
     you
To the god? What have you come to seek?' Neoptolemus
Replied: 'I wish to make amends for my past fault
To Apollo. I once demanded of him reparation
For my father's death.' It now became clear how effective
Had been Orestes' slander – that Neoptolemus
Was lying, that he had come to Delphi bent on crime.
My master stepped inside the threshold of the temple
To pray to Apollo before the oracle. The omens
From the burnt sacrifice were good; but close at hand,
Screened by the foliage of the laurel-trees, a group
Of men with drawn swords waited. Clytemnestra's son,
Who plotted this whole treachery, was one of them.
Neoptolemus stood, his face to the altar, praying; they,
Holding their sharp swords ready, from their hiding-place
Stabbed at his unarmed body. He sprang round; his wound
Was only a flesh-wound. There was armour hung from pegs
In the temple-porch; he dodged aside and snatched it down,
Then leapt on to the altar; and a grim fighter
He looked. He shouted to the Delphians, 'I am here
On a pious pilgrimage; why should you kill me? What
Have I done to merit death?' Of all the thousands there

Not one uttered a word. They picked up stones, and began
To throw them. A thick hail of missiles pelted him
From all directions. He had a shield on his left arm,
And held it before him, now on this side, now on that,
To protect himself. It was no use. Weapons came at him
Flying in a mass — arrows, spits, sacrificial knives—
And fell at his feet. As he avoided each attack
He looked like one performing a ghastly Pyrrhic dance.

   By this time they had hemmed him round in a close ring,
Giving him not a moment's respite. Seeing this,
He abandoned the altar — where victims are sacrificed —
And with the famous Trojan leap he went for them;
And they, like doves at sight of a falcon, turned their backs
And fled. Men fell in struggling heaps, wounded by him,
Or in the narrow doorways trampled underfoot;
And from that holy temple issued an unholy
Shrieking, which the cliffs echoed back. My master stood
There, his bright armour gleaming; an unearthly calm
Fell for a moment; till from the temple's inmost shrine
A voice, dreadful and terrifying, sounded forth,
Rallied the Delphian ranks and turned them again to fight.
Then the son of Achilles fell, his body pierced
With a sharp sword-blade wielded by a Delphian, who
Was yet but one among his many murderers.
When he had fallen, then not a man of them but came
With his weapon, or with a stone, to strike and hack at him;
His splendid body was all destroyed with savage wounds.
They took him from beside the altar where he lay
And threw him outside the court of sacrifice. Then we
Lifted him up as quickly as possible, and have brought
Him here, so that you, Sir, may lament and weep for him
And give him burial with due honour.
                              This is what
Apollo, the divine dispenser of oracles,
Whom the whole world reveres as judge of right and wrong,

Did to the prince who came to make his peace with him.
This god, like any evil-hearted man, remembered
An ancient grievance: how can he be wise and good?

[*Exit* MESSENGER. *A group of men approaches bearing the
body of Neoptolemus.*]

CHORUS: Now he is near. Look, our king is coming,
            Carried from Delphi to his home.
            His death was cruel;
            This day, Peleus, is cruel to you.
            This was not the welcome home
            You had hoped to give to Achilles' son.
            You and he, victims of one fate,
            Are one in suffering.

PELEUS: And I have lived to see this sight!
            For this my arms were open,
            And my house waiting.
            O pity, O grief, O misery! O city of Thessaly!
            Life is gone and hope dead.
            Not one of my family is left,
            Not one to bear my name.
            What a wretched, ravaged creature I am!
            Where is a friend whose eyes hold comfort for
                me?
            Dear face, dear hair and hands!
            Had you but died by the fortune of war
            Under the Trojan walls, by the banks of
                Simois!

CHORUS: True, Peleus; to have died at Troy would have
                assured
            Honour to him, and made your grief more
                tolerable.

PELEUS: O marriage, marriage, that destroyed
            My house and my city!
            Dear boy, son of my son!
            It was an evil day for me

When you made Hermione your wife.
Her fatal heritage ensnared
My house and children in a net of death.
Better to have died at once
By a bolt from heaven, before you went
To lay your father's death at Apollo's door,
To voice a mortal's indignation
At the god who guided the deadly arrow,
Phoebus the son of Zeus!

CHORUS: Weep, weep for the king;
            Join with me, raise the dirge of the dead.

PELEUS: I weep, weep in turn,
            Tears that sear aged eyes,
            For grief weighing the grey head.

CHORUS: God alone ordains,
            God alone fulfils.

PELEUS: You have left your home, dear son, orphaned
                and empty;
            You have left an old man helpless, childless,
                and desolate.

CHORUS: It is hard that the old should live
            To see the death of the young.

PELEUS: May I not cry my grief,
            Stretch out indignant hands,
            Kneel in the dust and groan?
            Listen, my own people!
            I had two sons, and Apollo
            Has taken them both from me!

CHORUS: Old and skilled in Fortune's ways,
            Sorrow seen and sorrow felt,
            What shall be your portion
            In the years remaining?

PELEUS: Friends departed, children lost,
            Death my only end and hope,
            I shall drink my cup

To the last bitter dregs.

CHORUS: Little good the gods bestowed
When they blessed your marriage-feast.

PELEUS: All my life's achievement gone like wind,
All my proud ambition laid in dust!

CHORUS: You will live a lonely ghost
Creeping through deserted rooms.

PELEUS: My native land has no more place for me,
My kingly power is no more use to me.
Thetis! Look from your dark ocean-caves,
See my bowed head and my broken heart!

[Enter THETIS.]

CHORUS: Look there, look! What is moving?
Is this a supernatural vision?
Look, friends, see what is happening –
The goddess hovers on the shining air!
Here on these plains of pastures
She stands to speak to us.

THETIS: Peleus! In remembrance of our marriage in days past
I have left my father's house to visit you – I am
Thetis. My first advice to you is: Do not let
Today's calamities cause you undue distress.
I too had hoped to be happy in my children; yet
I lost the son I bore you, Achilles fleet of foot,
The hero of Hellas. Now, listen to what I came
To tell you. Carry the body of Achilles' son
To Apollo's temple at Delphi, and there bury him
For a reproach to the Delphians, that his tomb may bear
Witness to his violent murder at Orestes' hands.
Fate orders that the captive woman Andromache
Shall find a home in Molossia as the lawful wife
Of Helenus, and shall take with her her son, who is
The sole survivor of the line of Aeacus.
He shall beget a prosperous dynasty of kings
To rule in long succession over Molossia.

This sad day does not mark the final overthrow
Of your family and mine, nor yet the end of Troy;
For though, because Pallas demanded it, Troy fell,
Yet even to Troy the gods extend their kindly care.
  Next, learn what blessings wait upon the marriage you
Enjoyed with me, a goddess: I will set you free
From all the ills which trouble mortals, and confer
On you divine, unfading immortality.
Thenceforward, god and goddess, you and I shall live
Together in the palace of Nereus till time ends.
Dry-footed you shall rise from the ocean, and behold
Achilles, your dear son and mine, where he now has
His island home by the White Sands of the Friendly Sea.
  So, first go to the city of Delphi, built by gods,
Bearing this body with you, and there bury him.
And afterwards go to the ancient Sepian Rock
And sit down in its vaulted cave, and wait until
I come out of the sea with fifty dancing nymphs
To escort you home. What is ordained you must perform
In full; this is the will of Zeus. Now end your grief
Over the dead; for this decree the gods have fixed
For ever: death is a debt which every man must pay.
PELEUS: Divine daughter of Nereus, noble wife, farewell!
Your acts are worthy of yourself, and of your son
And grandson. At your bidding, goddess, I will end
My grief; and when I have laid this body in the earth
I will go, as you command, to the Bay of Pelion,
Where first I took your lovely body in my arms.
    [Exit THETIS.]
There, now! Have I not always said how right it is,
How wise, to look for a wife, or choose a son-in-law,
From a family of noble blood, what a mistake
It is to marry beneath you, even if your bride
Brings with her wealth unlimited? Trust in the gods;
That is the surest way to safety and success!

CHORUS: Gods manifest themselves in many forms,
Bring many matters to surprising ends:
The things we thought would happen do not
       happen,
The unexpected God makes possible;
And that is what has happened here today.

THE SUPPLIANT WOMEN

CHARACTERS

AETHRA, *mother of Theseus*
CHORUS *of Argive mothers and their Attendants*
THESEUS, *king of Athens*
ADRASTUS, *king of Argos*
THEBAN HERALD
MESSENGER

EVADNE, *widow of Capaneus*
IPHIS, *father of Evadne*
SONS *of the seven dead chiefs*
ATHENA, *tutelary goddess of Athens*
Athenian soldiers and herald

The scene is before the temple of Demeter at Eleusis. On the altar steps
AETHRA *is seated. Suppliant branches lie on the altar, and from*
them garlands of flowers are stretched, symbolically binding AETHRA
in her place. Around the altar are ADRASTUS, *with a group of boys,*
and the CHORUS, *seven women in mourning attire, with a similar*
number of female attendants.

AETHRA: Divine Demeter, you who guard this holy ground
   Eleusis, and you servants of her sanctuary,
   Grant years of blessing to myself, Theseus my son,
   The city of Athens, and to Pittheus' town, Troezen,
   Where he, my father, brought up in a prosperous home
   His daughter Aethra, till, obeying Loxias' word,
   He gave me to Aegeus, Pandion's son, to wife.
   I pray thus, troubled by the sight of these grey heads.
   These women here, leaving their homes in Argos, come
   To kneel with suppliant branches, and entreat my help
   In their calamity. They are childless. Round the gates
   Of Cadmus' walls their seven noble sons lie dead.
   Adrastus led them against Thebes, resolved to gain
   For his exiled son-in-law Polyneices the due share
   Of Oedipus' inheritance. And when these mothers
   Desired to bury those who had fallen by the sword,
   The victors, dishonouring the gods' law, turned them back
   And would not let them take up the dead bodies. Here,
   Sharing the stress of their appeal to me, his eyes
   Flooded with tears, Adrastus lies, and mourns aloud
   His conquered sword, the ill-fated force he led to Thebes.
   He urges me to entreat my son to undertake –
   Whether by negotiation or by force of arms –
   The rescue of those bodies, and to bear his part
   In burying them. Upon my son alone he lays
   This task, and on the city of Athens. When they arrived,
   It happened that I had come here to make sacrifice,

For a good harvest, at this holy shrine, where first
Bristled above the soil the fruitful ears of corn.
Here these weak leafy chains I dare not break bind me
Fast to the sacred altar of the two goddesses,
The Maiden and Demeter, both for pity of these
Grey mothers who have lost their sons, and for respect
To these religious wreaths of laurel. I have sent
A herald up to the city to summon Theseus here,
Either to banish this distressful company
Out of the land, or loose their suppliant constraint
By rendering some holy service to the gods.
For women, the part of wisdom is to act through men.

CHORUS: Aged queen, we implore you!   [Strophe
             We too are old, our voices tremble.
             Look, we kneel at your feet.
             Ransom our sons' lifeless limbs
             From the lawless enemy who leaves
             Dead bodies to feed the mountain beasts.

             Have pity! Look first at our eyes   [Antistrophe
             Bleared and sodden with weeping;
             See then how these ashen fingers
             Have torn the flesh of our wrinkled cheeks.
             What should we do?
             Our sons are dead; but they have not come
                  home.
             We have not composed their limbs;
             We see no mound heaped for burial.

             You too, Queen, have borne a son,   [Strophe
             Making your husband glad that he married you;
             Now share your heart with us.
             Let the help you give be as great
             As our grief for the sons we bore, now dead.
             Persuade your son, we entreat you,

To march to Ismenus, and bring
Those lost, unburied bodies
Home to our arms, the dead to the living.

[*Antistrophe*

Though grief has no place before the flame
That burns on a god's altar, yet necessity
Makes us come kneeling and beseeching.
Our plea is just: you are strong, for your son
    lives;
You can relieve our sorrows.
Out of the depth of pain I cry to your son
To give my dead into my arms,
That I may embrace and mourn the body that I
    bore.

An echo rises, groan for groan;   [*Strophe*
Our maids' lament is matched with ours.
Come, our partners in mourning,
Come, you who share our anguish,
Tread out the ritual which Death regards;
Let blood flow from our cheeks
To redden the white finger, stain the skin;
Let us but see those dues our dead require –
For us, that will be beauty enough.

I cannot slake this thirst for tears; [*Antistrophe*
Grief overflows to ecstasy,
Ceaseless in weeping as the flow that falls
Over a dank cliff-face.
The bitter toll of tears for children dead
Is a burden women are born to.
Could I but die, and my heart be numb to pain!
    [*Enter* THESEUS.]
THESEUS: I heard the sound of dirges for the dead, the beat

Of hand on breast. What were those cries of grief, coming
From near the temple? I greatly fear some accident
May have befallen my mother, whose long absence from
    home
Has brought me here to fetch her. – Why, what do I see?
There's some strange story lies behind this sight – my mother
Sitting at the altar, and with her, women of other cities
Picturing grief in varied forms; tears fall to earth
From aged sorrowing eyes; their shorn hair and black gowns
Ill suit this temple. Mother, what does this mean? It is
For you to speak, for me to hear, some strange account.

AETHRA: My son, these women here are mothers of the seven
    Chieftains who fell in battle at the Cadmean gates.
    Now they have circled me with boughs of supplication
    And, as you see, my son, they hold me prisoner here.

THESEUS: And who is this, whose groaning fills the sacred
    porch?

AETHRA: Adrastus, so these women say, the Argive king.

THESEUS: The group of boys there at his side – are they his
    sons?

AETHRA: No; these boys are the children of the seven who
    died.

THESEUS: Why have they come as formal suppliants to us?

AETHRA: I know; but further questions are for them to
    answer.

THESEUS: You, muffled in your cloak – then I must question
    you.
    Leave your laments, unveil your head, and answer me.
    No bridge is crossed unless your tongue be road to it.

ADRASTUS: Theseus, victorious king of the Athenian race,
    I kneel to you and to your city, entreating help.

THESEUS: What goal do you pursue? What is your need of me?

ADRASTUS: You know that I led an army to defeat and death.

THESEUS: Indeed, your way through Hellas was no silent
    march.

ADRASTUS: Argos' best soldiers perished under my command.

THESEUS: This is war's daily work; war deals in agony.

ADRASTUS: I went to Thebes to beg for their dead bodies back.

THESEUS: Did Hermes' heralds urge your claim to bury them?

ADRASTUS: Indeed yes; but the men who killed them still refuse.

THESEUS: What do they say in answer to your pious demand?

ADRASTUS: What should they? Victors do not know what suffering is.

THESEUS: Have you then come for my advice? What do you wish?

ADRASTUS: To ask you, Theseus, to bring home these Argive sons.

THESEUS: Where is your Argos? Is she nothing but empty boasts?

ADRASTUS: We failed; we are defeated. Now we come to you.

THESEUS: Did you alone decide to come, or your whole state?

ADRASTUS: All Argos begs you to give burial to her sons.

THESEUS: What made you lead those seven armies against Thebes?

ADRASTUS: It was a wish I granted my two sons-in-law.

THESEUS: You gave your daughters – to what Argive citizens?

ADRASTUS: I linked my royal house with men not native-born.

THESEUS: Ah! You bestowed your Argive girls on foreigners?

ADRASTUS: On Tydeus, and on Polyneices, prince of Thebes.

THESEUS: What made you eager to join kinship with these men?

ADRASTUS: An obscure oracle of Phoebus influenced me.

THESEUS: What did Apollo say, then, to direct their marriage?

ADRASTUS: This: Give your daughters to a lion and a boar.

THESEUS: What sense did you unravel from this divine command?

ADRASTUS: One night, outside my palace gates, two exiles came —

THESEUS: Tell me their names; who were these two?

ADRASTUS: Tydeus was one,
  And Polyneices; and they fought each other there.

THESEUS: You took them for those two beasts, and so chose them?

ADRASTUS: Yes;
  The way they fought seemed like two savage animals.

THESEUS: And how did these two come to leave their native land?

ADRASTUS: Tydeus was banished; he had shed a kinsman's blood.

THESEUS: Why did the son of Oedipus quit Thebes?

ADRASTUS: He feared
  His father's curse, which said that he should kill his brother.

THESEUS: Then he was wise in this self-chosen banishment.

ADRASTUS: Yes; but his brother robbed him of his rights in Thebes.

THESEUS: Secured control of his possessions?

ADRASTUS: Yes. So I,
  To claim them, marched on Thebes; and there I met defeat.

THESEUS: Did you consult prophets, and observe altar-flames?

ADRASTUS: Alas, no; that was my error. You have found me out.

THESEUS: You went, it seems, lacking the favour of the gods.

ADRASTUS: Still worse: Amphiaraus warned me, yet I went.

THESEUS: Was it so light a matter to ignore the gods?

ADRASTUS: The young men clamoured at me, and I lost my head.

THESEUS: You sacrificed sound judgement to bold enterprise.
ADRASTUS: A choice which has brought many a leader to his
    knees.
  Great king of Athens, chief in power through all Hellas,
  I am ashamed to fall thus on the ground, and clasp
  Your knees in supplication. I am old, and once
  I was a prosperous king; now I must yield to hard
  Necessity. Have pity on my misfortunes,
  And on these mothers mourning their lost sons. Bring home
  Our dead to us. See, how old age condemns their life
  To childlessness. They have endured long, weary days
  Of travel, weak and slow with years, to this strange soil;
  Not to observe Demeter's joyful mysteries,
  But to seek burial for those sons, by whose strong hands,
  Instead, their own frail bodies should have been interred.
  Wisdom will prompt the rich man to regard the poor,
  And the poor man to look with emulation towards
  The rich, to keep alive love of prosperity;
  So, those whom pain has spared should look on misery.
    (For gods are cruel, and men pitiable; but we
  Most pitiable of all men. This is why my voice
  Breaks, and my words falter, as I plead with you,
  And so betray my cause. A strong pleader should show
  Confidence in himself, and wisdom) – as a poet
  Should take joy in creating the songs that he creates.
  If he feels no such joy, how can he, from his own
  Distress, give joy to others? It is impossible.
    Perhaps you ask me, why I pass by Peloponnese
  And come to lay this enterprise at Athens' door.
  The question's just, and I will answer it. Sparta
  Is harsh; her policies are always changeable;
  The other cities there are small and weak. Athens
  Alone can undertake this task; for she regards
  Compassion; and in you she has a leader both
  Young and courageous. Many a city before now

Has perished because her leader lacked these qualities.

CHORUS: Theseus, we in our turn echo the same appeal:
    Take up our cause, have pity on our sufferings.

THESEUS: Often with others I have striven in argument
    Upon this question: men say that in human life
    The worse outweighs the better; but I hold the view
    Which contradicts them, that the blessings man enjoys
    Outnumber his disasters. If this were not so,
    Our life would not continue. So I praise whatever
    Immortal power took man's life from its primal chaos
    And brutishness, disposed it in an ordered state,
    Endowed it first with understanding, then bestowed
    The tongue to convey meaning through articulate speech;
    Gave us earth's fruit for food, and, lest supply should fail,
    Sends rain to nourish growing plants, and fertilize
    The womb of earth; provides shelter in storm, and shade
    To shield us from the sun-god's heat; taught men the arts
    Of navigation, so that, by trade, what one land lacks
    Others may furnish. Even such things as are obscure
    And hard to judge, prophets have skill to expound, whether
    By scanning fires, or entrails' folds, or flight of birds.

    Then, since God makes such rich provision for our life,
    Are we not wanton, showing discontent? Men's pride
    Seeks to outmatch the strength of gods, their truculent
       hearts
    Claiming a wisdom higher than divinity's.

    And of this company your unwisdom makes you one.
    Enslaved to Apollo's riddle – as if belief in gods
    Urged it – you gave your daughters to these foreigners;
    Fouling a pure stream with impure, you dealt your house
    A dangerous wound. No wise man should betray his blood,
    Mingling corrupt with virtuous, but rather seek
    Those whose sound fortunes will befriend his family.
    For gods regard our human state as shared by all:
    They involve in one destruction both the evil man's

Doomed life, and his who shared the taint, though innocent.
You led the entire army of Argos out to war;
You ignored a prophet's warning, sought no favour of
The gods, and brought defeat and ruin on your state;
Misled by young men, who love popularity
Above all else, multiply wars unscrupulously,
And corrupt our citizens – one, to obtain a generalship,
Another, to gain office and use it for his pleasure,
A third, for money, heedless of what injury
His act may cause to the whole people. Citizens
Are of three orders. First, the rich; they are useless, and
Insatiable for more wealth. Next, the very poor,
The starving; these are dangerous; their chief motive is
Envy – they shoot their malice at those better off,
Swallowing the vicious lies of so-called champions.
The middle order is the city's life and health;
They guard the frame and system which the state ordains.
    Shall I then form alliance with you? What sensible
Reason for this could I offer to my citizens?
Go then; farewell; and since you chose an imprudent
    course,
Fight with your fate yourself, and do not trouble us.
CHORUS: He was at fault. The young men acted as young men
    Will always act; but this man – you should pardon him.
ADRASTUS: I did not ask you to pass judgement on my faults,
    Theseus, nor did I come to you for chastisement,
    Nor for rebuke, of such mistakes as I have made.
    I came for help. So, if you will not give me this,
    I must accept your answer. What else can I do?
        Come, mothers; let us go. Leave your green branches
            here,
    And by their leafy presence on this altar call
    As witnesses the gods, and Earth, and Demeter,
    Divine torch-bearer, and the sun's pure light, that prayers
    Uttered in the gods' names did not avail for us.

CHORUS: Consider, great king: Pittheus is your grandfather,
　　The son of Pelops; and we come from Pelops' land,
　　And share with you one race, one blood. What will you do?
　　Will you deny this kinship? Will you send away
　　Out of your land old, helpless women, and refuse
　　All we so justly ask? No, no! A beast can flee
　　For refuge to the rock, a slave find sanctuary
　　At an altar, a city in trouble shelters safe beside
　　A neighbour city. For in human life nothing
　　Enjoys for ever quietness and prosperity.

　　　　[THESEUS makes no response.]
　　－ Rise from the holy floor of Persephone,
　　　　Go, bend to him, cling around his knees;
　　　　Our sons are dead! Have pity on us;
　　　　Under the Cadmean wall we lost our sons.
　　－ By your beard, Theseus, dear friend,
　　　　Greatest of the Greeks, I implore you!
　　　　An unhappy woman clasps your knee and your hand.
　　－ I cry for my son; I beseech you,
　　　　Hear my lament and pity my wailing.
　　－ Theseus, our sons were young like you:
　　　　Would you see them lie there unburied
　　　　On Cadmean soil, for beasts to enjoy their flesh?
　　　　No, no, I implore you!
　　－ Turn your eyes to the tears that fill my eyes;
　　　　See, I fall at your feet.
　　　　Fulfil our hopes, win for our sons a grave!

THESEUS: Why, mother, do you weep, with your fine mantle
　　　　drawn
　　Over your eyes? Have their sad voices caused your tears?
　　I too was somewhat moved. Lift up your head; you sit
　　At the holy altar of Demeter; do not weep.

AETHRA: Alas!

THESEUS:　　It is not for you to mourn these womens'
　　　　griefs.

AETHRA: Unhappy women!

THESEUS: But — you are not of their race.

AETHRA: May I speak what concerns your honour and the city's?

THESEUS: You may; wisdom is often heard on women's lips.

AETHRA: Yet the word hidden in my mind still gives me pause.

THESEUS: It is not well to hide good words from those you love.

AETHRA: Then I will speak, lest I should later blame myself
For keeping cowardly silence now. Even good advice
From women, they say, is worthless: I'll defy this gibe,
And forbid fear to make my wisdom impotent.

First, then, my son, I bid you look well lest you act
In error, thus rejecting their appeals to the gods.
Wise in all other matters, here alone you erred.
More than this — were it not man's duty to be bold
In helping the oppressed, I would have said nothing.
But this, my son, is for your honour; nor do I
Shrink from exhorting you, when pride of power denies
Dead men due burial and the rites of decency,
To force them to their duty by the might of arms,
And stop them undermining the established laws
Of all Hellas. This one bond makes all cities one:
Free, honourable respect for universal rights.

Why, some will say faint heart made feeble hand* — that you,
Faced with the chance to win a crown of fame for Athens,
Declined — through fear; that you accepted readily
The easy challenge of the wild boar, but when asked
To meet helmets and javelin-points in sweat of battle
You failed your duty, and performed a coward's part.
Theseus, you are my own son: do not act like this.
You have seen how, when sneered at for rash policies,

* This phrase is borrowed from Way's translation; I cannot better it.

Your country, greatest when in greatest danger, turns
Upon the sneerers her grim glare of hardihood;
While laggard states pursue their dark manoeuvres, cold
With caution, and blink weakly at their enemies.

    Will you not go, son, and bring help, first to the dead,
And then to these sad women in their desperate need?
You'll march with Justice at your side; I have no fear
For you. And though I see Thebes now proud in success,
My trust is, at the next throw she will find the dice
Fall otherwise. The gods stretch greatness in the dust.

CHORUS: O dearest queen, here is a double joy; your words
    Win honour for your son, and from us, gratitude.

THESEUS: Mother, the words I spoke to Adrastus here were
        words
Of truth; I pronounced frankly upon those policies
Which caused his downfall. Yet I clearly see the force
Of your reminder, that to avoid a dangerous task
Is not my nature. I have, by honourable deeds,
Chosen and claimed this character among the Greeks,
To be always the punisher of injustice. So,
I cannot now refuse this task. Why, if I should,
What will my enemies say of me, when even my mother,
Who has most cause to fear on my behalf, is first
In urging me to undertake this enterprise?

    Then I will do it. I will go and redeem their dead,
If I can, by persuasion; if words fail, the sword
Shall gain the same end, and no jealousy of gods
Will haunt us. I desire that all my citizens
Shall give their free assent; they will uphold my wish,
But their hearts will be stronger in this cause, if I
Have given them reason. When first I assumed leadership,
I gave my people freedom and the equal vote,
And on this basis instituted monarchy.
I will take Adrastus with me, and, to illustrate
My words, appear before the assembled citizens.

When their assent is given, I will return bringing
A picked force of Athenians; and we'll wait here armed
While I send word to Creon to yield those bodies up.
    Women, set free my mother from these holy wreaths,
That I may take her hand and lead her home. A son
Is a wretched creature, if he will not lovingly
Repay his parents' care with service; all he gives
He receives again in just measure from his own sons.

    [*Exeunt* THESEUS *and* AETHRA, *with* ADRASTUS.]

CHORUS: Argos, pastureland of horses,   [*Strophe*
            Argos, home of my fathers,
            You heard these words spoken,
            Words of a king who reveres the gods,
            A promise of hope for Pelasgia,
            Acclaimed in Argos.

            May he relieve our sorrows,   [*Antistrophe*
            Achieve his goal, and more;
            Rescue for each mother her dear treasure
            Slaughtered and stained;
            And receive as his worthy reward
            The love of the land of Inachus.

            A pious and perilous undertaking   [*Strophe*
            Is an honourable treasure in a city's memory
            And earns eternal gratitude.
            What decision shall we hear from Athens?
            Will they give their oath to befriend us?
            Shall we win burial for our sons?

                                              [*Antistrophe*
            Come, city of Pallas, come to a mother's aid;
            Save from dishonour the laws of mankind.
            You reverence Justice;
            Injustice you despise;
            To those in distress you bring deliverance.

[*Enter* THESEUS *with an Athenian Herald;* ADRASTUS
follows.]

THESEUS: Your sacred office, Herald, obeys the state and me
In constant duty, bearing at large our public words.
Go now to where Asopus and Ismenus flow
And give this message to the haughty king of Thebes:
'Theseus requests you graciously to give up the dead
For burial. His land neighbours yours; and in this right
He asks. Consent, and make Erechtheus' race your friends.'
If they grant this, thank them and speed you home at
    once.
If they will not, give them my second message, thus:
'Expect a Bacchic whirlwind of Athenian shields;
My army is close at hand, encamped and disciplined,
Ready for action, by the banks of Callichoros.'
        [*He turns to the* CHORUS.]
With warm goodwill the Athenian people, when they saw
That I desired it, undertook this enterprise.
– Why, who is this that comes to interrupt my words?
I cannot yet be certain, but he appears to be
A Theban herald. [*To the Athenian Herald*] Wait; maybe he
    comes to save
Your journey, and to anticipate my purposes.
        [*Enter a* THEBAN HERALD.]
HERALD: Who is king absolute here? To whom must I convey
The words of Creon, who rules the land of Cadmus since
Eteocles died defending Thebes, killed by the hand
Of his brother Polyneices at the seventh gate?
THESEUS: First, stranger, you began your speech on a false
    note,
Enquiring for a king absolute. This state is not
Subject to one man's will, but is a free city.
The king here is the people, who by yearly office
Govern in turn. We give no special power to wealth;
The poor man's voice commands equal authority.

HERALD: There you concede a point which gives me half the
    game.
  The city that I come from lives under command
  Of one man, not a rabble. None there has the power
  By loud-mouthed talk to twist the city this way and that
  For private profit – today popular, loved by all,
  Tomorrow, blaming the innocent for the harm he's done,
  Getting away with every crime, till finally
  The law-courts let him off scot-free! The common man!
  Incapable of plain reasoning, how can he guide
  A city in sound policy? Experience gives
  More useful knowledge than impatience. Your poor rustic,
  Even though he be no fool – how can he turn his mind
  From ploughs to politics? The worst pestilence of our time,
  As every sane man knows, is the unscrupulous
  Upstart whose glib tongue brings him fame and popular
    power.
THESEUS: An accomplished herald, this – dabbling in
    rhetoric!
  – Since it was you who challenged me to this debate
  And chose the subject for an argument – listen.
    A state has no worse enemy than an absolute king.
  First, under such a ruler there is no common law.
  One man holds the whole law in his own grasp; that means
  An end to equality. When laws are written down,
  Both poor and rich possess their equal right; the weak,
  Threatened or insulted by a prosperous neighbour, can
  Retort in the same terms; the humble man's just cause
  Defeats the great. Freedom lives in this formula:
  'Who has good counsel which he would offer to the city?'
  He who desires to speak wins fame; he who does not
  Is silent. Where could greater equality be found?
    Further: the people, vested with authority,
  Values its young men as the city's great resource.
  An absolute king regards them as his enemies;

The best of them, and those he thinks intelligent,
He kills off, being afraid of rivals to his throne.
How can a city grow in strength, when all its young
And bold spirits are mown down like fresh stalks in spring?
Why should a man win wealth and substance for his sons,
When all his labour only swells a tyrant's hoard?
Why should he bring up daughters virtuously at home,
To serve as dainties for a king's caprice, with tears
For those whose care ended in this? I'd rather die
Than see my children forced so to a lustful bed.

    Thus much in answer to the points you aimed at me.
Now tell me what you have come to seek; indeed, if you
Were not your city's envoy, your uncalled-for speech
Would cost you dear. A herald's business is to say
What he's been told to say, and go straight home again.
Let Creon, then, in future dealings with my city,
Employ a messenger less garrulous than you.

CHORUS: When success favours evil men, their insolence
    Assumes the same good fortune will be theirs for ever.

HERALD: I'll give my message. As for the points we've argued
    on,
You hold to your opinion, and I'll hold to mine.

    But now, in the name of all Cadmean citizens,
I warn you not to receive Adrastus in your land;
And further, if he is here, to remove those suppliant wreaths
From the goddess' altar, and before today's sun sets
To expel him from your limits; and further, not to use
Force to retrieve those corpses, since you have no concern
With the Argive state. If you obey me, your city will
Sail in calm seas. If not, both we and you and all
Our allies will be involved in one vast surge of war.

    Consider, then; do not let indignation at
My words, because you claim to have a free city,
Lead you, the weaker, to answer in inflated terms.
Hope's a deceptive thing, and often locks two states

In combat, fanning their fury to excessive heat.
For when an issue of war hangs on the people's vote,
Then no one reckons that his own death may be involved;
This mournful prospect he assigns to someone else.
If Death stood there in person while men cast their votes,
Hellas would not be dying from war-mania.
Yet we know — all men know, which of two arguments
Is more valid; we know what good, what evil is;
How far peace outweighs war in benefits to man;
Peace, the chief friend and cherisher of the Muses; peace,
The enemy of revenge, lover of families
And children, patroness of wealth. Yet these blessings
We viciously neglect, embrace wars; man with man,
City with city fights, the strong enslaves the weak.

And do you now help our dead enemies, bring home
For burial men who died through their own insolence?
Was it, then, unjust punishment — the thunderbolt
That scorched the scorner Capaneus as he set his ladder
Against our gates, and swore he'd sack Thebes whether the gods
Liked it or not? Was it unjust — the chasm that seized
And swallowed the seer Amphiaraus, engulfing man
And chariot together? or the downfall of other chiefs
Whose disjointed, rock-mangled frames lie round our walls?

Either, then, claim a wisdom higher than Zeus, or else
Acknowledge that gods justly overthrow the wicked.
A wise man's love is owed first to his children, then
To his parents; and to his native land, which he should strive
To build, not to dismember. Whether on land or sea,
A rash leader is a risk; timely inaction, wise.
Discretion too, I think, may be a brave man's part.

CHORUS: The punishment Zeus has inflicted was enough;
    Must you Cadmeans add to that this insolence?

ADRASTUS: You vicious villain —

THESEUS: Silence, Adrastus; hold your
    words,

And don't thrust in your answer before mine. This man
Is messenger to me, not you. I'll answer him.

   To take first, then, your first demand: I am not aware
That Creon possesses either authority over me
Or power to compel Athens to obey him. Streams
Will run uphill, when we accept Creon's commands.
This war is none of my making; I did not march
With the Argive army against Thebes. I bring no harm
To your town, nor challenge you to a slaughterous trial of
       strength.
I claim the right to fulfil the law of all Hellas
In burying those dead bodies. Wherein lies the offence?
If you were injured by those Argives – they are dead.
You fought your foes with glory to yourselves, and shame
To them. That done, the score is paid. Permit their bodies
To hide below ground, and each part to return there
Whence first it came into this light; breath to the sky,
Flesh to the soil. For we have in our own bodies
But a life-tenancy, not lasting ownership;
At death, the earth that bred us must receive us back.
Do you think that you hurt Argos by not burying them?
Far from it; this is a hurt done to the whole Hellene race,
When dead men are denied their proper rites, and left
Unburied. Should such practice become general,
Brave men would shrink from battle. And do you, who hurl
At me these threatening speeches, tremble at dead men
Unless they lie unburied? What fear troubles you?
Do you think that from their graves they'll undermine your
       town,
Or in their earthy chambers beget sons, from whom
Vengeance will haunt you? But this is idle waste of speech,
To tell you such fears are unworthy and untrue.

   Come, quit this folly. Think how men's existence is
Beset with hardship – our whole life a wrestling-match.
Some win success soon, others later, some at once;

While Fortune grows capricious. From the unsuccessful,
Who hope to prosper, she receives worship as a god;
The prosperous man exalts Fortune because he fears
The approach of death. Then we should recognize these truths,
Meet wrongs with calmness, not with furious rage, and see
That wrongs we offer cause no injury to the state.

    How shall it be, then? Yield us the bodies to inter;
We wish to give them pious rites. If you will not –
In plain terms, I will come with arms and bury them.
It never shall be published through the Hellene lands
That I and this city of Pandion, called upon
To uphold this ancient, divine ordinance, let it die.

CHORUS: Take heart; while you guard justice like a gleaming torch,
A thousand slanderous rumours cannot touch your fame.

HERALD: Shall I reply in brief?

THESEUS: Speak, if you wish; you don't
Lack words.

HERALD: You will never take those Argives from our soil.

THESEUS: Then hear my answer too.

HERALD: It is your turn to speak.

THESEUS: I will bring home those dead from Thebes and bury them.

HERALD: First you must face death shield to shield.

THESEUS: I have faced already
Many such battles.

HERALD: Were you born invincible?

THESEUS: By arrogance, yes. Against just men I lift no sword.

HERALD: You and your people are busy with other men's concerns.

THESEUS: Our business spreads wide; so does our prosperity.

HERALD: Come, then; be caught by an army bred from dragon's teeth.

THESEUS: A dragon! What hardy soldiership can that pro-
        duce?
HERALD: You'll learn its force by feeling it. You are still
        young.
THESEUS: You will not move my anger with your boastfulness.
    Now leave this land. The idle words you brought with you —
    Take them back home; we're getting nowhere.

    [*Exit the* THEBAN HERALD. *Some Athenian soldiers
    appear.*]

                                              Every man,
    Hoplite or chariot-fighter, at top speed to Thebes!
    Horsemen, let your wild bridles streak your mounts with
        foam!
    Soon at the seven gates of Cadmus, wielding this
    Sharp steel in my right hand, I'll be my own herald.
    Adrastus, you must stay here; your fortunes must not
    Be mixed with mine. This enterprise I undertake
    In my own fortune, which is fresh and innocent
    As my sword is. One thing I need: that all those gods
    Who respect justice shall be with me. Their alliance
    Brings victory. In this world valour itself is dumb,
    Ineffectual, unless it have the gods' good will.

    [*Exit* THESEUS *with soldiers.*]

CHORUS: Listen, mothers of our lost leaders,
               Pitiful mourners for the pitiful dead,
               Pale fear lodges deep in my heart —
               — You have some further thought; what is it?
               — For the army of Pallas. What will be the out-
                   come?
               — Do you mean, of a battle? Or of negotiation?
               — That would be welcome; but if we are to see
               Bloodshed and death in battle,
               And in Athens, grief beating the breast,
               Since our misfortune caused their loss,
               What will they call us, what will they say of us?

— Though a man be radiant with success,
Yet in turn his destiny may destroy him.
This thought gives me good heart and comfort.
— You speak of gods who are just.
— Who else but they govern the events of our
     lives?
— I observe that the ways of gods to men are
     various.
— You are discouraged by fears already felt.
Yet justice calls to justice, blood to blood,
And the gods grant to mortals respite from
     suffering;
For they hold all issues in their own hands.

I long to leave Demeter's river, Callichoros,
And fly to the plain where noble towers rise —
— If some god would but grant us wings! —
— To Thebes, the city between two rivers;
To see, only to see, how Fortune deals with
     our friends!
— What fate, what chance is in store
For the courageous king of Athens?

Yet again we cry to the gods we called before;
They are our first trust in the hour of terror.
— Hear us, Zeus, whose son was born
Of the daughter of Inachus, the cow-maiden,
Mother of our ancient race!
— Come as a friend, fight on the side of Argos,
The city you loved, the city you founded;
The dead who lie dishonoured —
Bring them home to their funeral-pyre!

[Enter a MESSENGER.]

MESSENGER: Women, I have much to tell you, and good
news. The first

Is my own safety; I was made prisoner in the battle
The seven squadrons of our dead captains fought beside
The river of Dirce. Next, I tell of victory
For Theseus. — To forestall your questioning, I served
Capaneus, whom Zeus blasted with a lightning-flash.

CHORUS: Friend, we rejoice at your return, and at your news
    Of Theseus. Add that the Athenian army too
    Is safe home, and your words are unmixed happiness.

MESSENGER: The army is safe; its fortune — such as we all
        prayed
    For Adrastus and the Argives, when he marshalled them
    On Inachus' banks, and set off to make war on Thebes.

CHORUS: How went the battle? Tell us! How did the son of
        Zeus
    And Aegeus conquer, and those who shared the fight with
        him?
    We who were not there long to hear from one who was.

MESSENGER: The morning sun shot down straight shafts of
        light to earth,
    When near Electra's Gate, on a high pinnacle,
    I took my stand to watch the battle. And I saw
    Three companies of armed men, each a separate tribe;
    The first stretched up the hill they call Ismenian;
    The second, on the right wing, was the royal guard,
    Men of the race of Cecrops, under the king himself,
    The famous son of Aegeus; these in number matched
    The first. Then came the spearmen of the Coastal Force,
    And all the chariots, next to Ares' Fountain, with
    The mass of cavalry placed on the fringes of the camp.
    The Cadmean army was drawn up before the walls;
    Behind them lay the bodies, causes of the dispute,
    Under Amphion's holy tomb. So horseman challenged
    Armed horseman, four-horsed chariot faced chariot.
        Then Theseus' herald called on all the marshalled ranks
    For silence, and said, 'Listen. We have come to bring

Those bodies home for burial, in accordance with
The law of all Hellenic states. We have no wish
For further bloodshed.' To this Creon made no reply,
But waited silent, sword in hand. The chariot-chiefs
At once began the battle. Down the opposing files
They hurled their chariots; spearmen leapt to earth, en-
     gaged
The enemy hand to hand, while chariots, wheeling round,
Came back to help the fighters. Phorbas, who commanded
The Athenian horse, seeing the confusion of the chariots,
Charged in to help; the Cadmean cavalry did the same,
And success swayed now this, now that way. I was there,
Near where the chariots and the spearmen fought it out;
I saw it all with my own eyes, and hardly know
Where to begin in telling the horrors that I saw –
The dust that towered to heaven, so thick it rose; men's
     bodies
Slung up and down, tangled in reins, the streams of blood
From corpses, or from those who, tossed like acrobats
Out of their shattered chariots headlong to the ground,
Were killed by spokes and splinters. Soon, when Creon saw
That Theseus' horse were winning on one flank, he advanced,
Grasping his shield, to check despondency among
His allies. In the centre, all along the line,
They clashed, killing and being killed; a mighty roar
Swelled as they cheered each other on: 'Hard at them!
     Drive
The Athenians home!' Theseus held high his glittering
     shield,
And charged ahead; with him there was no weakening,
Though the array of men who sprang from dragon's teeth
Were a grim adversary, and pushed our left wing back;
While on the right their men were worsted and driven off.
The fight hung in the balance. Then our leader showed
His generalship; scorning a partial victory,

He flew to help his hard-pressed men on the other wing,
And the whole earth re-echoed with his bursting roar:
'Come, lads, if you can't hold the advance of the earth-born,
Athens is beaten!' Then through the army of the Rock
Courage flared up in every heart. Theseus himself,
Grasping that fearful weapon, his Epidaurian mace,
Brandished it round him like a sling; necks, helmets, heads,
The weighty wood mowed down or lopped. Then, at long
     last,
The enemy line broke, and they fled. I danced, I clapped,
I yelled for joy. Now they were making for the town gates.
All over Thebes there was shouting, wailing of young and
     old;
Terrified thousands filled the temples. But Theseus,
With the way clear before him, would not enter the gates.
'I have not marched from Athens to destroy this town,'
He said, 'but to demand the dead for burial.'

    There is a general! He is the kind of man to choose –
Hardy in danger; an enemy to arrogant states
Who exploit success, burning to reach the topmost heights,
And throw away the good life that was theirs to enjoy.

CHORUS: O friends, this is a day I never hoped to see!
  Now I believe that gods exist. I feel my grief
  Lighter, since arrogance has paid its penalty.

ADRASTUS: O Zeus, why do they say our wretched human
     race
  Has wisdom? We are fast bound to you, and all our acts
  Are such as your will chooses. Once Argos to us
  Seemed irresistible, we ourselves superior
  In numbers and in youth; so when Eteocles
  Offered us peace on fair conditions, we refused,
  And then we were defeated. Next, the tables turned,
  Victorious Thebes acts like a poor man newly rich,
  Grows insolent; and in turn insolence leads the whole
  City of Cadmus through stupidity to ruin.

O fools, who strive for untimely and mistaken ends,
Suffer hard blows at the hands of Justice, learn nothing
From friendly counsel, much from the cruelty of events!
O foolish states, who have the power by conference
To avert disaster, yet choose the ordeal of blood!
– Why speak of these things? What I wish to learn is, first,
How you escaped; then I will ask for other details.

MESSENGER: In the confusion caused by the defeat, I slipped
    Out through a gate where Theban soldiers were coming in.

ADRASTUS: And are you bringing home the bodies for which
        they fought?

MESSENGER: Yes, all who led those seven famous companies.

ADRASTUS: Where then are all the others laid who lost their
        lives?

MESSENGER: They have been given burial on Cithaeron's
        slopes.

ADRASTUS: Who buried them? and on which side of the
        boundary?

MESSENGER: Theseus, beneath the high cliff of Eleutherae.

ADRASTUS: Where did you leave those bodies Theseus did not
        bury?

MESSENGER: Near by; we have here all that's needed for their
        pyres.

ADRASTUS: But were not slaves reluctant to lift them from
        the ground
    Where they were slaughtered?

MESSENGER: No slave undertook that task.

[ADRASTUS: Surely not Theseus? Was his piety so rare?]

MESSENGER: You would have said so, had you seen his work
        of love.

ADRASTUS: Did he then wash the blood-stains from their
        pitiful wounds?

MESSENGER: Yes, and prepared their biers; then covered
        them with veils.

ADRASTUS: A fearful load to lift, leaving a mark of shame.

MESSENGER: What shame from one man's fate can mark
    another man?

ADRASTUS: I should have died beside them. How I wish I had!

MESSENGER: Your grief is idle; you distress these mothers
    here.

ADRASTUS: So it may seem; yet it was they taught me to
    weep.

    Enough. I raise my hand in welcome to the dead,
    And pour sad dirges in a flow of tears, to greet
    My friends, whose loss I mourn, alone and desolate.
    Wealth lost may be retrieved; but this most dear treasure,
    Once spent, is never found again: the life of man.

    [*Exit* ADRASTUS.]

CHORUS: Joy shares this day with grief.
           Athens is crowned with glory,
           And her leader in the battle
           Has doubled his former fame.
           But to us comes the sorrow
           Of beholding our sons' lifeless limbs;
           Yet, if we but see them, the sight is welcome;
           Since this is a day unlooked for,
           Bringing the sharpest pain of all.

           I wish that Time, the ancient father of days,
           Had kept me all my life unmarried.
           Why did I need children?
           Had I never been joined to a husband,
           I would have supposed that I suffered
           The worst of all disasters;
           But now that my dear son is taken from me
           My suffering is not imaginary; it is real.

           See! They are bringing the bodies of our sons.
           How gladly I would leave this grievous life
           To share our children's home in the dark
             world!

[*The procession bearing the dead bodies enters, led by* ADRASTUS, *with* THESEUS *following.*]

ADRASTUS: Mothers, cry out your lamentation
             For the dead who live below the earth;
             Let your mournful voices echo mine.

CHORUS: Dear son, it is sad that a mother
             Must use such words to the child she loves:
             I call your name, and you are dead.

ADRASTUS: The pain we have suffered —

CHORUS: — Is the worst of
             all pain.

ADRASTUS: City of Argos, do you not see my fate?

CHORUS: Argos beholds our childless sorrow too.

ADRASTUS: Bring to their grave these bodies marked
                 with blood.
             They did not deserve this death,
             Nor did those who slaughtered them deserve
             The victory Fate bestowed.

CHORUS: Give me my son;
             Let my arms hold him fast;
             Let my embrace rest and enfold him.

ADRASTUS: There, you have him.

CHORUS: My loss is burden enough.

ADRASTUS: I weep for them.

CHORUS: Have you no word for us who bore them?

ADRASTUS: Listen to me.

CHORUS: Your tears are for them, and for us.

ADRASTUS: I wish that the Cadmean ranks
             Had destroyed me in the dust.

CHORUS: I wish that my flesh had never
             Been mated in a husband's bed.

ADRASTUS: Behold an ocean of suffering —
             Mothers desolate, children lost!

CHORUS: Our cheeks are furrowed with rending nails,
             Dust and ashes cover our heads.

ADRASTUS: Let the earth engulf me,
                 Let the storm ravage me,
                 Let the scorch of Zeus's fire fall on my head!

CHORUS: To your own hurt you gave your daughters in
                    marriage;
                 To your own hurt you listened to Apollo's
                    voice.
                 The mournful curse of Oedipus
                 Which made his house desolate
                 Has lighted upon you.

THESEUS: Since you have voiced in full the tears due for these
    dead,
  I spare the questions I would else have asked, and look
  Instead to Adrastus. Of what lineage were these men,
  So graced with courage? Speak to my young citizens
  As a wise elder; you have knowledge, for you saw
  Those exploits, outbidding description, by which they
  Had hoped to capture Thebes. Lest I be thought a fool,
  I will avoid one question – what antagonist
  Each of these warriors met in battle, or whose spear
  Wounded him. Such tales can as well be told by those
  Who ask, as those who offer them. When a man stands
  In battle, with spears flying thick before his eyes,
  How can he clearly say who's brave and who is not?
  I would not ask such questions, nor could I believe
  One who presumed to tell me. Fighting face to face,
  A man can see enough to keep alive – no more.

ADRASTUS: Listen, then; since you ask me, I most willingly
  Will speak in praise of these my friends. I wish to tell
  Only the truth, and do full justice to their merits.
    See this wound, where the violent thunderbolt shot
    through:
  This man was Capaneus. He was rich, but in no way
  Made arrogant by wealth; of pride he had no more
  Than the poor man; avoided those who spread their feasts

With ostentation, and despise frugality.
'The good life is not gluttony,' he would say; 'enough
Is all that's needed.' To his friends — and they were many —
He was a true friend, absent or present. He was frank
In nature, friendly in speech; whether to servants or
To citizens, he left no duty unfulfilled.

  Next, Eteoclus; in whom a different excellence
Was perfected. A young man with no wealth, but held
In highest honour throughout Argos. When his friends
Offered him gold, he would refuse it, lest the weight
Of debt should hamper and enslave his free spirit.
He hated wrongdoers, not their city; since no state
Corrupted by a bad ruler should be held to blame.

  Of a like nature was the third, Hippomedon.
From boyhood, his bold spirit never turned aside
To seek those soft allurements which the Muses offer.
Wild places were his home; his joy was to pursue
Courage through hard endurance, and his one purpose,
By skill in hunting, archery, and horsemanship,
To train himself for useful service to his city.

  Next, Parthenopaeus, son of the huntress Atalanta,
A man unmatched in beauty. Arcadian by birth,
He came to Argos, and grew up beside the stream
Of Inachus, avoiding, as a newcomer,
All causes of offence or jealousy in the place
Of his adoption; in contentious argument —
By which both citizens and aliens earn reproach —
He took no part. As though a native born, he stood
In our armed ranks, and fought for Argos. When our cause
Flourished, he was glad, and sick at heart for each reverse.
Many, both men and women, held him in affection;
But he stood guard over himself, and did no wrong.

  The praise of Tydeus in few words I will make great.
He did not shine in speech; but in debate of shields
Was formidable, unwearied in resource and skill.

Then do not wonder, Theseus, hearing what I have said,
That these men dared to die before the walls of Thebes.
A noble upbringing bears honour for its fruit;
And every man trained in brave deeds will feel ashamed
To prove a coward. Courage is teachable, just as
A child is taught to speak and hear matters as yet
Not understood. Things learnt in youth are often stored
Till old age; therefore give sound training to the young.

CHORUS: My child, it was for sorrow
            I bore you in my body
            And laboured at your birth.
            The son my pain delivered
            The god of death has taken.
            I shall grow old as a forsaken mother
            Without a son to tend me.

THESEUS: The noble Amphiaraus received his eulogy
Openly from the gods themselves, who seized him and
Entombed him with his chariot in the depths of earth.
The son of Oedipus, Polyneices, I will praise
With true words. When, in voluntary exile from Thebes,
He crossed to Argos, on his journey he was my guest.
Do you know, now, what I wish to do for these dead men?

ADRASTUS: I know this only: that your word shall be my
            guide.

THESEUS: First, then, for Capaneus, whom the fire of Zeus
            struck down –

ADRASTUS: To a sacred corpse you would give separate
            burial?

THESEUS: Yes; and consign the others to a single pyre.

ADRASTUS: Where will you set the separate tomb for
            Capaneus?

THESEUS: Here near this temple I will build his monument.

ADRASTUS: This task my men will undertake immediately.

THESEUS: The rest I'll see to. Lift the biers and carry them.

ADRASTUS: Come now, sad mothers, stand beside your sons.

THESEUS: Not so,
   Adrastus. Your suggestion is unsuitable.
ADRASTUS: Why? Is it wrong for a mother's hand to touch
   her son?
THESEUS: They are disfigured; the sight would be too great a
   shock.
ADRASTUS: True; blood and wounds of dead men are a dread-
   ful sight.
THESEUS: Then why inflict distress on these women?
ADRASTUS: I agree.
   [*To the* CHORUS] Wait patiently. Theseus is right. When we
   have given
   Their flesh to burning, you shall gather up their bones.
     O wretched race of mortals! Why must men get spears
   And spill each other's blood? Stop! Lay this rage to rest;
   Live quiet with quiet neighbours, and preserve your towns.
   Life is a brief affair; such as it is, we should
   Seek to pass through it gently, not in stress and strain.
   [*The funeral procession moves towards the pyres.*]
CHORUS: No longer a happy mother blest in my son;
            No longer sharing with women of Argos
            Joy and pride in the young men we bore.
            Artemis, helper of childbirth, will not speak
            Her word of cheer to our barren lives.
            Through weary days and years I wander
            Like a lost cloud driven by wintry blasts.

            Seven mothers, we bore seven sons to our
               sorrow;
            They were foremost of the men of Argos.
            Now in childless misery
            I tread the lonely road to old age;
            Numbered neither with the dead nor with the
               living
            I inhabit the world of the outcast.

All that is left to me is tears.
At home there are pitiful reminders of my son,
Locks cut for mourning, garlands for the head,
Offerings of wine for lifeless souls,
Songs that golden Apollo will not accept.
When I rise each morning I shall weep,
And the folds of the dress on my bosom
Will be wet with tears.

Look now, look there – outside the temple
I see the consecrated pyre, the resting-place
Of Capaneus, killed by the thunderbolt;
And the offerings brought by Theseus to the
      dead.
And I see the hero's wife, Evadne,
Daughter of Iphis. Where is she going?
Why is she standing on that lofty rock
That towers over the temple?

[EVADNE *appears on a cliff above the pyre of Capaneus.*]

EVADNE: What brightness was it that flashed that day
From the sun's chariot, or what gleam
Flowed from the moon in the deep sky
Where stars ride fast through the dark –
The day when the city of Argos
Raised a high tower of song and of blessing
Upon my ill-fated marriage
And my bronze-mailed bridegroom Capaneus?
To be with you, husband, I have come
Running in wild frenzy from my home
To share with you your flame, your monument,
To dispel in death my afflictions
And the labours of living.
To die one death with our beloved
Is the dearest death of all;
And this may heaven grant me!

CHORUS: That is indeed the pyre you see close at your
                  feet;
              A treasury of Zeus, on which your husband lies,
              His victim, overpowered by the fierce light-
                  ning-flame.

EVADNE: In this I see my end, here at my feet.
              May Fortune guide my fall!
              For the sake of an honoured name
              I shall plunge from this rock into the heart of
                  the fire;
              And as in the bright heat my flesh shall join my
                  husband's,
              Limb with limb in close embrace,
              So I shall come to my marriage-bed
              In the house of Persephone;
              And in your lifeless grave
              My spirit shall never desert you.
              Farewell light, farewell love!
              It may be my sons will find in Argos
              Joyful brides and worthy marriage;
              But I shall not see them. . . .

CHORUS: Look now, Evadne! The aged Iphis is approach-
                  ing,
              Your father himself, in time to hear your
                  frenzied words.
              He does not know yet — but to hear will break
                  his heart.

[*Enter* IPHIS.]

IPHIS: Women, as full of sorrow as my aged self,
  I come weighed down with double grief for my own kin;
  First, to sail home with my dear son Eteoclus,
  Killed by a Theban spear; and next, to find my daughter,
  The wife of Capaneus. She suddenly left home —
  Rushed from the house, resolved to die beside her husband.
  I had for some time guarded her indoors; but then

These troubles came, and I relaxed my care, and she
Has gone. This seems the place where she most probably
Would come; so please tell me if you have seen her here.

EVADNE: No need to ask them; I am here, perched like a gull
On this high cliff, swayed by the wind, and hovering
In dark despair over the pyre of Capaneus.

IPHIS: Dear child, what impulse guided you? Why did you slip
Out of your home, to make so long a journey here?

EVADNE: To learn what I intend, father, would anger you;
Therefore I do not wish that you should know my mind.

IPHIS: I am your father; is it not right for me to know?

EVADNE: Father, you would be no wise judge of my intent.

IPHIS: Why do you array yourself in this triumphal garb?

EVADNE: There is a glorious meaning, father, in my dress.

IPHIS: You do not seem like a widow mourning for her husband.

EVADNE: I am robed in readiness for a strange, unheard-of deed.

IPHIS: And should you stand, so dressed, beside a funeral pyre?

EVADNE: Indeed, I am come here for a noble victory.

IPHIS: What victory are you speaking of? Explain to me.

EVADNE: A victory over every wife under the sun.

IPHIS: In skills and crafts of Pallas, or in wise judgement?

EVADNE: In courage. I will die, and share my husband's grave.

IPHIS: This is a ghastly riddle. Tell me what you mean.

EVADNE: I'll leap down on the pyre of my dead Capaneus.

IPHIS: Daughter, don't speak like this – in front of all these people!

EVADNE: That is my dearest wish, that all Argos should hear.

IPHIS: Shall I stand by and see you do this? I will not!

EVADNE: It is all one; you cannot reach me here. I fall,
I let go. See my end – to you, a grief; to me
And to my husband with me in the fire, a joy.

[EVADNE *throws herself on to the pyre.*]

CHORUS: Evadne! Oh! Oh, what a terrible thing!

IPHIS: O misery! Women of Argos, I am lost!
CHORUS: How fearfully you have suffered!
            And now an appalling sight awaits you.
IPHIS: Where is there suffering more bitter than
                mine?
CHORUS: We weep for you. Your old age has inherited
            The curse of Oedipus; and in that curse
            Argos, my city, has an equal share.
IPHIS: For pity's sake – why are not wretched mortals given
    A second chance, to be young twice, then old again?
    In affairs at home, if errors have been made, we can
    With later judgement set them right; not so with life.
    Were it but possible to be twice young, twice old,
    Mistakes could be amended in life's second round.
    If I had learnt the anguish a bereaved father feels,
    I never would have reached this day of misery.
    But I begot a son, a splendid youth, handsome
    And brave; now I am left alone to mourn for him.
        So, what am I to do now with my wretched life?
    Must I go home – to contemplate room upon room,
    One desert? or the uselessness of my own life?
    Or shall I go to Capaneus' house? It's true, I once
    Loved it, when my dear daughter was alive. She used
    Often to pull my face to hers and kiss me; then
    She'd fold my old head in her arms. And now she's gone.
    When a man's old, there's no one dearer than his daughter.
    Sons have more strength of character, but no gentle touch,
    No sweet endearments. Take me home – quickly, at once!
    Stow me away in darkness; there alone I'll waste
    And starve this aged body to its proper end.
    What use in waiting to compose my daughter's bones?
        Old age, grim wrestler, how I hate your strength! Those
            too
    I hate, who try to drag out life with foods and drinks
    And magic charms to turn Time's stream out of its course,

And put off death. Since they're no use to the earth, they
    ought
To die, take themselves off, and make way for the young.
    [*The young* SONS *of the dead heroes appear in procession.
    They carry the urns containing their fathers' ashes.*]

CHORUS: Here in these urns are borne
            The bones of our dead sons.
            I am a feeble old woman;
            Tears for my son have drained my strength;
            Take my arm and help me.
            I have lived a long time; grief upon grief
            Melts my soul away in tears.
            Can you find in human life any greater suffering
            Than to see your children dead?

SONS: I bring you, mourning mother,
            I bring you from the fire my father's bones,
            A burden of heaviness, weighted with sorrow;
            My world contained within a little urn.

CHORUS: Why do you bring, sad son,
            Gifts of tears for the dead
            To the mother who loved him,
            A little handful of ash for the living man
            Once famous in Mycenae?

SONS: You are childless, childless;
            And I shall inherit a deserted house,
            A lonely orphan mourning my father's fate,
            Missing the protection of his hand.

CHORUS: Where now are the years
            Of toil spent for my children!
            What reward for the pains of birth?
            Food and care, the routine of sleepless eyes,
            The tender pressure of face to face?

SONS: All this is lost with my dear father's life;
            Lost, and will not return.
            Fire has wasted them to dust.

CHORUS: Their home is the wide sky;
            They have flown on wings to the world of
                death.

SONS: Father, your son mourns for you:
            Do you hear? Shall I one day,
            Shield in hand, avenge your death? God grant
                it!
            Justice for my father's blood —
            It will yet come, with the favour of God.

CHORUS: This wrong sleeps not yet.
            Why must we always weep?
            I have had enough of disasters and of misery.

SONS: The day will come when Asopus gleams in
                welcome
            As I march bronze-clad at the head of a Danaid
                army
            To avenge my father's death.
            It seems to me that I still see you, father —

CHORUS: — Placing a loving kiss upon your cheek —

SONS: But the encouragement of your words I cannot
                hear;
            Your voice is blown to the winds.

CHORUS: Sorrow for us both:
            Sorrow is his bequest to his mother;
            Sorrow for your father will never leave you.

SONS: The burden that I bear has crushed me.

CHORUS: Give me the urn;
            Dear ashes — let me clasp them to my breast.

SONS: Your pitiful words bring tears to my eyes,
            Pain to my heart.

CHORUS: My son, light of your mother's life,
            You are gone. I shall never see you again.

THESEUS: Adrastus, and you women of Argive race, you see
    These boys bearing the remnants, rescued by my hand,
    Of honoured fathers. To their sons I and my city

Present their ashes. It is for you to bear this gift
Always in thankful memory; let your eyes witness
Your debt to me; repeat this story to your sons,
And they to theirs in turn. Teach them the honour due
To Athens; let them recall in perpetuity
Kindness received. May Zeus and all the heavenly gods
Witness that not in vain you came as suppliants.

ADRASTUS: Theseus, our hearts know the great kindness you
          have shown
To Argos, and the help you gave her in her need.
Our gratitude will not grow old; your acts to us
Were noble; therefore in turn we owe you nobleness.

THESEUS: Is there some further service I can render you?

ADRASTUS: Farewell; you and your city deserve happiness.

THESEUS: So be it; and may the same good fortune follow you.

[ATHENA *appears above the temple.*]

ATHENA: Theseus, I am Athena; listen to my words
And hear what you must do — and do for Athens' good.
You must not lightly yield these bones up, to be taken
Without condition back to Argos by these boys.
First, in repayment of the exertions you and Athens
Undertook for them, make them swear an oath. Adrastus,
As king, is competent to pledge his whole country;
So he must swear. And this shall be the form of the oath:
'Never shall Argives march against Attica in arms;
If others march, Argos shall interpose her sword.
And if they break their oath and march, then let them bring
Down upon Argos shame, destruction, and defeat.'
    Now hear where you must kill the sacrifices which
Shall guard this oath. You have at home a bronze tripod
Which Heracles once, after the sack of Ilion,
Hastening upon another task, bade you set up
At the Pythian altar. Sacrifice three sheep, and catch
Their warm blood in this tripod; afterwards inscribe
The words of the oath there in the hollow of the bowl.

Then give the tripod to the Delphian god to keep,
To record the oath, and call as witness all Hellas.
And when you slaughter victims for the sacrifice
Take the sharp knife with which you lay the entrails bare
And bury it deep in earth close to the seven pyres.
If Argives ever march to Athens, they shall be shown
This monument, and march home again in shame and fear.
When you have done this, only then let the dead go
From Attic soil. The precincts where, at the meeting-place
Of these three roads, their flesh was purified with fire,
Leave untouched, consecrated to the Isthmian god.

　　Thus much to you. I speak now to the Argives' sons.
When you reach manhood you shall sack the city of Thebes
In vengeance for your fathers' blood. You, Aigialeus,
As a young commander-in-chief, shall take you father's place;
And with you Diomedes, from Aetolia,
The son of Tydeus. Once your beards darken your cheeks,
Lose no time – launch a bronze-armed force of Danaids
Against the towers and seven gates of Cadmus' town.
Bitter to them shall be your coming; the lions' whelps,
Grown to full strength, shall lay their city in the dust.
This is the inescapable truth. And you shall be
Called throughout Hellas 'The After-Comers', and your
　　deeds,
Your mighty army, led by the gods to victory,
Posterity shall remember in heroic songs.

THESEUS: I will obey you, Queen Athena; by your voice
Alone I am saved from error, led in the right path.
I will bind down Adrastus with an oath. Only
Guide my decisions; while your favour rests on us,
Athens will live henceforward in security.

CHORUS:　　It is time to go, Adrastus. Let us give
　　　　　　To Theseus and to Athens the oath they ask for.
　　　　　　The battle which they fought on our behalf
　　　　　　Has earned our gratitude and devotion.

THE PHOENICIAN WOMEN

CHARACTERS

IOCASTA, *wife and mother of Oedipus*
TUTOR *in charge of Antigone*
ANTIGONE, *daughter of Oedipus and Iocasta*
CHORUS *of Phoenician women*
POLYNEICES, *second son of Oedipus and Iocasta*
ETEOCLES, *elder son of Oedipus and Iocasta*
CREON, *brother of Iocasta*
TEIRESIAS, *a blind prophet of Thebes*
MENOECEUS, *son of Creon*
FIRST MESSENGER
SECOND MESSENGER
OEDIPUS, *formerly king of Thebes*

*

Scene: before the royal palace of Thebes.

Enter IOCASTA.

IOCASTA: You who among the stars carve your celestial way,
Riding your gold-compacted chariot, whose swift
Horses bestride earth with their arc of fire: O Sun!
How full of doom for Thebes your brightness shone that day
When from the Phoenician coast to this spot Cadmus came
And took to wife Aphrodite's daughter Harmonia;
She bore Polydorus; he in turn, they say, was father
Of Labdacus; his son was Laius. I and Creon
My brother are both children of Menoeceus, by
One mother; and the name my father gave me was
Iocasta. Laius married me. After some time,
Seeing that I had given his house no child, he went
To enquire of Phoebus, and entreated for us both
Male children to succeed to our inheritance.

  Phoebus replied: 'King of the glorious chariots
Of Thebes, do not defy the gods; beget no son.
If ever your seed sees the light, your son shall take
Your life, and your whole house shall drown in kindred
      blood.'
Laius, yielding to pleasure and to drunkenness,
Begot our son; then, having begotten him, aware
Of disobedience to the god's command, he pierced
His ankles with an iron skewer (hence his name
Oedipus, 'Swollen-foot') and gave the child to shepherds
To expose on Mount Cithaeron, on the rocky slope
Called Hera's Meadow. There, servants of Polybus,
Stablemen, found him; took him home, and presented him
To the queen, their mistress; she suckled the infant born
Of my pain, making the king believe it was her own.

  Now when in time my son was grown, and his man's
      beard
Gilded his cheek, then – whether through intuition or

Through some word spoken – he set off for the oracle
Of Phoebus, eager to learn his parentage; and Laius
My husband also was on that same road, resolved
To find out if the son he exposed were still alive.
Where the road forks for Phocis, there the two men met.
Laius's driver shouted, 'Make way for the king!'
My son was proud; he made no answer, and strode on.
The shod hooves gored his feet. Then he – but why prolong
The fatal story? Son killed father. Carriage and team
He captured, and gave to Polybus who had fostered him.

 Then, with my husband dead, with Thebes ravaged and
  cowed
By the mysterious Sphinx, my brother Creon proclaimed
My hand in marriage as the prize for whatever man
Should solve the Sphinx's riddle. And it so happened
That Oedipus my son interpreted her song,
And for reward received the throne of Thebes, and so
Became his mother's husband, and she her son's wife,
Each miserably unwitting in whose bed we lay.

 I bore my son four children; two boys, Eteocles
And stalwart Polyneices; then two girls; the younger
Her father named Ismene, and the elder I
Named Antigone. But when he learnt the truth, that he
Was married to his mother, Oedipus, distraught
With extreme anguish, took a brooch of beaten gold
And stabbed, destroyed, and drenched in blood his own two
  eyes.

 Now when my sons grew men, they kept their father
  hidden
Behind locked doors, hoping his dreadful story, which
Taxed all invention to conceal, might be forgotten
With time. He still lives, here in the palace; and this fate
So maddened him that he invoked upon his sons
The wickedest of curses, that they should divide
The inheritance of their father's house with sharpened steel.

So they, afraid lest, if they lived under one roof,
The gods might bring this curse to fruition, made a pact:
That the younger, Polyneices, should of his own will
Go into exile for one year, while Eteocles
Remained in Thebes as ruler; and at each year's end
They should change places. But, once firmly on the throne,
Eteocles would not budge. When Polyneices came,
He repelled and banished him. He went to Argos then,
Married Adrastus' daughter, gathered a large force
Of Argive soldiers, and has led them here against
These very walls of seven-gated Thebes, demanding
His father's throne, and due share in his native land.
Trying to solve this quarrel, I have induced my sons
To agree to meet here under truce before they fight.
My messenger reports that Polyneices will come.

   Then save us, great Zeus, you who dwell in the bright folds
Of heaven, and grant that my two sons be reconciled.
If gods are wise, wisdom should not let misery
Settle unchangeably upon one mortal's life.

   [*Exit* IOCASTA. *Enter* TUTOR *and* ANTIGONE.]

TUTOR: Antigone, loveliest flower of your father's house,
Since you desired it, your mother has permitted you
To leave your room and stand here on the edge of the roof
To see the army of Argos. Wait while I go first
To scan the road, in case some citizen appear,
And I be blamed — which doesn't matter for a slave;
But you, the princess, may be blamed as well. And then
I'll give you a full account of what I saw and heard
When I went, under truce, from Thebes to meet your
    brother
In the enemy camp, and came back through their lines to
    Thebes.

   [*He goes up the stair to the roof.*]

I see no Theban walking anywhere near; so come,
Climb up. See how the huge hordes of the enemy

Swarm by the river Dirce and on Ismenus' banks.

ANTIGONE: Come, give me your hand,
             Reach your arm down from the stairway;
             Help me, I'm coming up.

TUTOR: Here, take my hand, child; that's the way. You're
     just in time;
  The army's moving, forming in separate companies.

ANTIGONE: Divine Hecate, Lato's daughter!
             Look there, what a sight!
             The whole plain flashes with polished
             bronze.

TUTOR: True, it's no puny force that Polyneices brings;
  Horses in thousands, shields and swords in myriads.

ANTIGONE: What of the stone walls Amphion built?
             Are the gates closed fast,
             And the bronze bolts all secure?

TUTOR: Rest easy; everything inside these walls is safe.
  Look at that man in front there; do you know his name?

ANTIGONE: – With a white crest to his helmet, who is
               he? –
             Marching at the head of his men
             Lightly holding on his arm
             A shield of solid bronze.

TUTOR: He is a captain, princess.

ANTIGONE: Who? From what city?
  Tell me, what is his name?

TUTOR: He is a Mycenaean,
  And lives by the Lernaean river – King Hippomedon.

ANTIGONE: Oh! How haughty he is! His look speaks
               terror.
             He is like an earth-born giant,
             Not like any mortal creature.

TUTOR: Do you see a man fording the stream of Dirce?

ANTIGONE: Yes; his armour is different,
             Quite different. Who is he?

TUTOR: He is Tydeus, son of Oeneus; and his heart is full
  Of the warlike spirit of fierce Aetolia.

ANTIGONE: He must be the man who married
          The sister of Polyneices' bride,
          When they shared their wooing.
          How strange his armour appears, half bar-
            baric!

TUTOR: All the Aetolians, child, have shields like that,
  And hurl their lances with unerring aim.

ANTIGONE: And who is the man now passing Zethus'
            tomb,
          A young man with long hair
          And eyes to make hearts tremble?
          He must be a captain; hundreds of men
          Are ranked behind him in full armour.

TUTOR: That is Parthenopaeus, Atalanta's son.

ANTIGONE: Then may Artemis and her mother Lato
          Come with her bow swiftly over the moun-
            tains
          To humble and destroy him;
          For he comes to plunder my city.

TUTOR: Amen, child; yet our enemies come with a just
  cause.
  My fear is that the gods may see this all too well.

ANTIGONE: Where is my own mother's son,
          My ill-fated brother? Tell me, old friend,
          Where is Polyneices?

TUTOR: See there! He is standing next to Adrastus, near the
  tomb
  Of Niobe's seven daughters. Do you see him?

ANTIGONE: Not clearly;
  And yet I think I see the outline of his body;
  That looks like him.
          Oh, how I wish I could fly like a cloud on
            the wind,

Run through the air to my own dearest
    brother, and fling
My arms round his neck!
So long he's been absent, an unhappy exile!
Look, how splendid he is in his armour of
    gold,
Like flames of the rising sun!

TUTOR: He's coming here to the palace – this will delight
    your heart –
Under safe-conduct.

ANTIGONE: Tell me now, who is that man
  Standing in a white chariot, handling the reins himself?

TUTOR: That, princess, is the prophet-priest Amphiaraus;
  Near him stand beasts for slaughter, blood-offerings to the
    earth.

ANTIGONE: Selene, circle of gleaming gold,
              Daughter of the radiant-belted Sun!
              How calmly, how steadily he drives,
              Goading each horse in turn!
              But where is Capaneus, the man
              Who would terrify Thebes with his insults?

TUTOR: There, measuring with his eye, from ground to para-
    pet,
Our city's walls, to get his ladder the right length.

ANTIGONE: Come, Nemesis,
              Come, violent thunders of Zeus,
              Come, white-hot lightnings!
              When man's proud speech swells beyond
                  measure
              You lay his boasting to rest.
              Is this the man who shall capture Theban
                  women,
              Make them slaves to matrons of Mycenae,
              Or dedicate them to the Lernaean trident
              By Amymone's fountain?

Never, O divine Artemis, golden-haired
    child of Zeus,
Never may I endure such slavery!

TUTOR: Dear child, come into the house now, go back to
    your room
And stay there; you have seen everything you wished to
    see.
Here comes a crowd of women, driven towards the palace
By the sudden alarm that fills the city. Women love
To criticize – it's their nature. Give them half an excuse
To talk about you, they'll improve it twenty-fold.
In slandering other women they find a strange delight.

    [*The* TUTOR *and* ANTIGONE *go indoors. Enter the*
    CHORUS.]

CHORUS: From the Tyrian sea-coast,
    From an island of Phoenicia,
    I have come as a picked offering to Loxias,
    To be slave in Apollo's temple,
    Where the god has made his home
    Under the snow-bound peaks of Parnassus;
    Brought by ship across the Ionian Sea,
    While over the fruitless plains
    Which circle the isle of Sicily
    Zephyrus rode his wind-white horses
    And the sky was loud with his song.

    Chosen from our town as the flower of beauty,
    Fit for the service of Loxias,
    We have come to the Cadmean country,
    Sent here to Laius's fortress,
    Being kindred to the house of Agenor.
    Now we are servants of Apollo,
    To stand before him like golden statues;
    It yet remains for me to dip my hair
    In the Castalian fountain,

And thus dedicate my maiden glory
To the service of Phoebus.

We greet you, rocky ridge of Parnassus,
Where twin peaks kindle and blaze
With the dancing torches of Dionysus!
We greet you, vine of Delphi,
Yielding each day a fresh-bloomed cluster
Rich with the ritual wine!
Sacred cavern of the earth-serpent,
Lofty pinnacles god-haunted,
Snow-blown slopes and summits!
May we come to the folds of Apollo's moun-
    tain,
And there as servants of immortal Artemis
Dance at the earth's centre,
Safe from the terror of Thebes!

But now raging war
Stands at this city's ramparts
With a blaze of blood
Threatening death to Thebes, which God
    forbid!
Friend suffers with friend;
If these seven towers should fall,
Our country too is struck to the heart.
We and they are one family,
Descended alike from Io;
Their fate, then, is ours too.

All around this city
Gleaming shields mass like a dense cloud,
A signal of bloody battle;
This Ares shall soon learn
When he brings fulfilment of the Furies' curse

On the two sons of Oedipus.
O Pelasgian Argos,
I tremble before your fierce strength
And before the hand of heaven;
For he arms himself in a just cause
Who fights to recover his home.

[*Enter* POLYNEICES.]

POLYNEICES: The guards on duty readily unlocked the gates
And let me in at once; which makes me wonder if
I've stepped into a trap, and won't get out again
With a whole skin. It's up to me to keep my eyes
Alert this way and that, for fear of treachery.
I am armed, and with this sword I'll offer a good account,
If need be, of my readiness to fight. – Who's there?
Do I jump at noises? Well, there's danger everywhere
On such a desperate venture, and on enemy ground.
And yet I trust my mother – and mistrust her too;
She induced me to come here under flag of truce.
Well, help's not far off; there are altars here to give
Sanctuary; and the house won't be deserted. Now
I'll sheathe my sword – it's better out of sight; and ask
These women gathering round the palace who they are.
– You ladies, tell me, please – I see you're foreigners –
From what land have you come to make your home in
Hellas?

CHORUS: The home where I grew up is a Phoenician land;
But we were brought here as the choicest prize of war
By a Theban army, for an offering to Apollo;
And King Eteocles, son of Oedipus, was about
To send us on to the temple and holy oracle
Of Loxias, when the Argive army came and laid
Siege to this city. You, in turn, tell me your name
And what you seek here in the fortress of seven gates.

POLYNEICES: My father is Oedipus, son of Laius, and my
mother

Iocasta. I am known in Thebes as Polyneices.

CHORUS: Oh, Polyneices! Son of Agenor's race, and brother
Of my own king, who brought me here!

        Prince, I kneel at your feet –
        This is the custom of my home;
        Welcome, after so long, to your native land!
        – Iocasta, Queen! Where are you?
        Come out here, fling the doors wide!
        Do you hear us? Mother, your son has come!
        Run through the rooms, come out,
        Clasp him in your arms!

[Enter IOCASTA.]

IOCASTA: I heard you call, I knew your voice.
        I am old, I can't move quickly;
        I am shaky on my feet. – Oh, my son!
        After all this time, thousands of days,
        I see your face!
        Put your arms round me, hold your mother
            close;
        Your cheek on mine, your hair,
        Your dark curls, clustering my neck!
        I did not dare to think
        Or hope that you would come;
        Now I see and hold you.
        What shall I say to you?
        How shall I grasp the joy of seeing you?
        By touch, by speaking,
        By dancing in wild delight?
        All the happiness of the old days!

        Oh, son, your father's house
        Was lonely when you went away
        Exiled by your brother's wickedness;
        We who loved you longed for you,
        Thebes longed for you.

So I cut my white hair short
And let it fall loose, shedding tears for you.
I never wear a white robe now;
Instead I put on this old and shapeless thing,
Murky as midnight.

Your old blind father is indoors.
He says you and your brother were the twin
        horses
That drew the chariot of our house,
And now you have both broken from the yoke;
And he weeps in longing despair.
Once he rushed about trying to find a sword
To stab himself, or to fix a rope from the roof-
        beam,
Groaning for the curse he laid on his sons.
Since then he hides himself day after day,
And all we hear is wailing and cries of pain.

Now you, my son — they tell me
You have yoked yourself with a wife
To pleasure your bed and bear you children
In an alien home;
You are involved with a foreign alliance!
How can this win your mother's blessing?
Will it not bring on you
The anger of Laius from his grave?
Your marriage brings with it an alien curse.
I did not light the marriage-torch for you —
A mother's privilege and joy;
Ismenus gave no cleansing water
For the ritual bath when your marriage-song
        was sung;
When your bride stepped over your threshold
The music of Thebes was dumb.

I curse whatever cause brought this about,
Whether iron, or anger, or your father,
Or whether the genius of the house of Oedipus
Mocked us in mad sport;
I am the one who endures
The pain of all these troubles.

CHORUS: Motherhood sets strange forces in motion, and some kind
Of love for children characterizes our whole sex.

POLYNEICES: Mother, it is partly wisdom, partly folly, that brings
Me here among my enemies. There's no help for it —
Every man longs for his own country, and to say
Otherwise is a form of words with no meaning.
I was so full of dread as I entered Thebes, fearing
My brother would try to have me killed by treachery,
That I walked with sword drawn through the streets, turning
my eyes
In all directions. One thing gave me confidence:
The sworn truce, and your promise, which had summoned
me
Inside my father's walls. As I came in, and saw,
After so long, my home, and the gods' altars, and
The wrestling-ground where I grew up, the river Dirce —
Tears filled my eyes at the injustice which deprives
Me of so much, condemns me to an exile's life
With all its miseries. And now, wretched as I am,
To see you no less wretched doubles my own pain.
What a foul, fearful thing, mother, is enmity
Within a family! My poor father, old and blind —
What part does he take? And my sisters — do they weep
Because I am exiled?

IOCASTA: Some immortal power is bent
To destroy the house of Oedipus. At the beginning
I bore the son I was forbidden to bear; this son,

Your father, sinned in marrying; you, in being born.

What help in saying this? The gods' will must be endured.

There is a question I have a great desire to ask;

But — how to ask? I am anxious not to cause you pain.

POLYNEICES: Mother, your wish is my wish; so ask everything,

Leave nothing out.

IOCASTA: This above all I long to know:

What is an exile's life? Is it great misery?

POLYNEICES: The greatest; worse in reality than in report.

IOCASTA: Worse in what way? What chiefly galls an exile's heart?

POLYNEICES: The worst is this: right of free speech does not exist.

IOCASTA: That's a slave's life — to be forbidden to speak one's mind.

POLYNEICES: One has to endure the idiocy of those who rule.

IOCASTA: To join fools in their foolishness — that makes one sick.

POLYNEICES: One finds it pays to deny nature and be a slave.

IOCASTA: What keeps exiles alive is hope — or so they say.

POLYNEICES: Hope wears a kind face, always full of promises.

IOCASTA: Yet surely time teaches the emptiness of hope?

POLYNEICES: Hope beguiles misery with a strange seductive charm.

IOCASTA: What did you have to eat before you married wealth?

POLYNEICES: Some days I ate, and other days I ate nothing.

IOCASTA: But did your father's friends and guests give you no help?

POLYNEICES: There is one rule — succeed. Friends vanish if you fail.

IOCASTA: But royalty gave you some position?

POLYNEICES: It's a mistake

Not to be rich. My royal blood bought me no bread.

IOCASTA: It seems, there's nothing dearer than one's own
city.

POLYNEICES: You could not find words to express how dear
it is.

IOCASTA: But what took you to Argos? What plan had you in
mind?

POLYNEICES: I don't know; some power beckoned me to my
destiny.

IOCASTA: The gods are wise. In what way did you win your
bride?

POLYNEICES: Adrastus had from Apollo a certain oracle.

IOCASTA: What was it? Tell me.

POLYNEICES: Loxias gave him this advice:
Marry your daughters to a lion and a boar.

IOCASTA: And what could you, son, have to do with those two
beasts?

POLYNEICES: It was night when I reached Adrastus' palace-
gate.

IOCASTA: In search of a bed – like any exiled vagabond?

POLYNEICES: Just so; but then another exile turned up too.

IOCASTA: Another no less wretched than yourself – who was
it?

POLYNEICES: Tydeus the son of Oeneus.

IOCASTA: What resemblance
then
Did Adrastus see between you men and those two beasts?

POLYNEICES: The way we fought over this matter of a bed.

IOCASTA: Adrastus so interpreted the oracle?

POLYNEICES: Yes, he gave his two daughters to the two of
us.

IOCASTA: And is your marriage fortunate or unfortunate?

POLYNEICES: I have no complaint at present.

IOCASTA: How did you
induce

The Argive army to march with you against Thebes?
POLYNEICES: Adrastus swore an oath to us his sons-in-law
  To bring back each from exile to his native land,
  And me first. Many leading men, both Danaans
  And Mycenaeans, are here, and for my sake they give
  Their service – I've no choice but to accept, though this
  Distresses me, for I march against my own city.
  And I call heaven to witness that I come in arms
  Against my kin and country most unwillingly.
  So, mother, the solution of this rests with you,
  If you can bring two brothers to agree on terms,
  And end my sufferings, and yours, and our city's too.
  Let me repeat you an old platitude: the thing
  That gets most honour in this world, and wields more
      power
  Than anything else, is money. That's what I've come here
  To get, with twenty thousand spears to press my point.
  A royal prince without money counts for nothing at all.
CHORUS: Look, here comes Eteocles to join the conference.
  Now, Queen Iocasta, play a mother's part, and speak
  Words that may lead your two sons to a compromise.
      [Enter ETEOCLES.]
ETEOCLES: Mother, I have come; this was your wish, and I am
      pleased
  To obey. What must I do? Let someone begin talking.
  I have to plan defences, and coordinate
  Our fighting units; I broke off this work to come
  And hear your mediation, for which, at your request,
  This man is allowed to enter Thebes on safe-conduct.
IOCASTA: Less haste, my son. Justice does not consort with
      haste.
  Slow speech most often achieves wisdom. So relax
  Your fierce frown, this belligerent air. What you see here
  Is not the Gorgon's severed head; it is your brother
  Who has come. And you too, Polyneices, turn your face,

Look at your brother. If you see each other's eyes
You will speak better, and better understand his words.
I want to give this sober counsel to you both:
When a man has an angry quarrel with his friend,
And comes at last to meet him face to face, it is well
To stick to the one issue for which they have met,
And nurse no bitter memory of feuds long past.

It is for you, then, Polyneices, to speak first,
Since you have led the Argive army here, and claim
To have been unjustly treated. And may some divine
Power judge between you, and resolve your enmity.

POLYNEICES: Truth by its nature tells a plain tale; and a just
Cause needs no subtle presentation. Both these bear
A fitness in themselves; but the unjust cause is sick
In its own essence, and needs devious remedies.

I valued my own well-being, and my brother's, higher
Than the possession of my father's house, and wished
To avoid the curse which he called down upon us both.
I therefore of my own free will left Thebes, giving
My brother one full year to hold the royal power,
It being agreed I thereupon should take my turn
And rule one year – not fall to hate and jealous rage
Leading to mutual injury and grievance, which
Today we do. He gave consent, and took his oath;
And now performs none of his promises, but keeps
The throne of Thebes, and my share of our patrimony.

Now I am ready, when I receive what's mine by right,
To take my army out of Theban territory,
To receive my house and live in it one year by turn,
And duly render it for another year to him,
And not plunder my native country, nor assault
The walls of Thebes with scaling-ladders; all which, if
My full rights are not granted, I shall attempt to do.
To seal my words, I call the gods as witnesses
That all my acts are just, and that I have been deprived

Of my own country unjustly and outrageously.

So, mother, I have composed my fair claim, point by
point,
Not wrapped in subtle words, but, as I think, a case
To approve itself as just with wise and simple alike.

CHORUS: It is true, we are not native born to Hellas; yet
To us it seems that what you say is reasonable.

ETEOCLES: If men all shared one judgement of what's noble
and wise,
All wordy quarrelling would vanish from the earth.
But as it is, there's no such thing as 'equal right'
Or 'justice'. These are words; in fact – they don't exist.

Mother, I'll be quite open with you. I would go,
If it were possible, to the regions of the stars,
Explore the sunrise, probe the depths of the earth, to win
That greatest of all goddesses, absolute power.
This valuable possession, mother, I will not
Let go to another, when I can keep it for myself.
For a man to yield the greater and accept the less
Is cowardice. Besides, it is a disgrace to me
If he gains everything he wants by coming here
With an army and plundering the land. What reputation
Would Thebes have, if through fear of Argive spearmen I
Gave up my throne to him? It was a mistake, mother,
For him to seek a settlement by force of arms;
Everything that a military attack could gain
May well be achieved by conference. Therefore, if he wishes
To live in Thebes on other terms, he may do so;
But what he asks I will not yield him till I must,
Nor be his slave while to be king is in my power.

So now, let fire and sword be let loose; yoke your teams,
Fill the whole plain with chariots. I will not give up
My throne to Polyneices. In all other matters
Piety is well; but, since there must be wickedness,
There is no nobler pretext for it than a throne.

CHORUS: Only a noble action shall deserve my praise;
  This action is not noble; it affronts justice.
IOCASTA: My dear son Eteocles, not all the qualities
  Of age merit contempt; experience has words
  Wiser sometimes than youth. Oh, son, why set your heart
  Towards the most evil of divinities, ambition?
  She is a corrupt power; shun her. Many prosperous
  Cities and homes have entertained her, and thereafter
  In degradation and despair watched her depart.
  She has possessed you. There is a nobler course: to honour
  Equity, which binds for ever friend to friend, city
  To city, ally to ally. Nature gave to men
  The law of equal rights. Want is the inevitable
  Enemy of wealth, and works towards war. Equality
  Settled for men fair measure and just weight, and fixed
  The laws of number. Night's dark face shares equally
  With the bright sun the travelling of each yearly round;
  Each yields in turn, and neither burns with jealousy.
  Shall day and night give equal service to mankind,
  And shall you scorn your lawful share of your own home,
  Deny your brother equal right? And is this just?

    Why set so high, so extravagant a value on
  Sovreignty – this injustice crowned by good fortune?
  Is admiration precious? It is an empty gain.
  This wealth you long for – what advantage comes with it?
  For a mere name, it brings you endless trouble. Enough
  To supply need contents the man who knows himself.
  A man's possessions are not his in private right;
  We hold in trust, as stewards, what belongs to the gods,
  Who, when they will, in turn take from us what is theirs.

    Come, let me put before you this alternative:
  Which do you choose, to rule, or to save Thebes? Will you
  Answer, To rule? What if your brother wins the battle?
  Then you will see this city under an enemy's heel;
  You will see Theban girls, in hundreds, captured, raped

By enemy troops. The wealth you crave will agonize
Thebes, when she pays the price of your ambitious pride.
　So much to you. And, Polyneices, this to you:
The favour Adrastus showed you was sheer folly; and you,
In marching to destroy Thebes, showed yourself insane.
Think now: suppose — which God forbid — you capture Thebes,
In God's name how will you, destroyer of your own city,
Set up trophies to Zeus, and offer sacrifice?
Over your spoils heaped by the banks of Inachus
What will you write? 'Polyneices burnt the city of Thebes
And dedicates this armour to the immortal gods'?
Dear son, let Hellas never make such report of you!
Say you're defeated, driven from the field by Theban arms,
And, leaving thousands dead, return to Argos: what
Will be your welcome? You will hear them say, 'A curse
On Adrastus for the son-in-law he chose! Our lives
Pay for his daughter's wedding.' Oh, my son, you steer
Straight for two evils: Argos will reject you, Thebes
Will see you fall a corpse. — Both of you, cast away
This violent passion, let it go! When headstrong fools
Meet two together, the outcome is most horrible.

CHORUS: Avert, O gods, the miseries which we foresee;
　Grant that the sons of Oedipus be reconciled!

ETEOCLES: Time for argument is ended, mother; any further words
　Will be wasted. All your goodwill can have no effect, since I
　Will accept no terms but those I stated: that I hold the throne
　And continue king of Thebes. So spare me any further long
　Speeches of advice. And you — get out of Thebes at once, or die.

POLYNEICES: Die, indeed! Why, who will kill me? Are your men invulnerable?
　Who takes arms against me without dying for it? Where's the man?

ETEOCLES: Close beside you; look no further. Here's my
        sword-arm, do you see?

POLYNEICES: Yes, I see a rich man and a coward quick to
        save his skin.

ETEOCLES: So, against a coward you come leading this vast
        armament?

POLYNEICES: Care and caution are more use than boldness in
        a general.

ETEOCLES: Mighty words, you braggart – trusting in the
        truce to save your life.

POLYNEICES: It saves yours too. Once more, I demand my
        throne and heritage.

ETEOCLES: I hear no demands. I tell you, I remain in my own
        house.

POLYNEICES: Keeping what you've stolen?

ETEOCLES: Yes, I say so.
        Now get out of Thebes.

POLYNEICES: Altars where my fathers worshipped . . .

ETEOCLES: You
        came here to throw them down!

POLYNEICES: Hear me!

ETEOCLES: You take arms against your country –
        who will hear your prayers?

POLYNEICES: Temples of the white-horsed riders!

ETEOCLES: You are
        their hated enemy.

POLYNEICES: See me – hounded from my country!

ETEOCLES: – which
        you came to loot and burn!

POLYNEICES: I claim justice!

ETEOCLES: Call on gods of your Mycenae,
        not of Thebes.

POLYNEICES: Blasphemer!

ETEOCLES: Maybe; but not, like you, my
        country's enemy.

POLYNEICES: You take my inheritance –

ETEOCLES: I'll take your life
too, willingly.

POLYNEICES: Father, hear what's done to me!

ETEOCLES: He also hears
what you are doing.

POLYNEICES: You too, mother!

ETEOCLES: Silence! To name *her* is to
flout decency.

POLYNEICES: Hear me, O my city!

ETEOCLES: Go to Argos – that's
your city now.

POLYNEICES: I'm going, don't fret. – I thank you, mother.

ETEOCLES: Out of my territory!

POLYNEICES: I will go – but let me see my father.

ETEOCLES: You shall
not see him.

POLYNEICES: My young sisters, then?

ETEOCLES: Your sisters you shall
never see again.

POLYNEICES: Oh, my sisters!

ETEOCLES: Why do you call on them? You
are their enemy.

POLYNEICES: Then, farewell to you, dear mother.

IOCASTA: I've no
hope of faring well.

POLYNEICES: You have lost a son.

IOCASTA: I have lost everything.
This is my fate.

POLYNEICES: He is the cause; he has destroyed our lives.

ETEOCLES: I
repay like with like.

POLYNEICES: In the battle, where will you be stationed?

ETEOCLES: Why do you ask that?

POLYNEICES: I'll be there to kill you.

ETEOCLES: Be there; that will
     please me equally.

IOCASTA: Oh, for pity! Sons, what are you doing?

POLYNEICES: The event
     will show.

IOCASTA: Surely you will shun your father's curse?

ETEOCLES: No! Perish
     our whole house!

POLYNEICES: Soon my sword no longer shall rest idle, but
     shall reek with blood.

   First I call as witness Thebes, my childhood's home, and all
     the gods,

   How with cruelty and dishonour I am driven from this land —

   I, the son of Oedipus, as he is — treated like a slave.

   Therefore, for the fate you suffer, Thebes, the blame is his,
     not mine.

   It was not my will to march against you, nor to be driven out.

   You too, Phoebus, god of journeys, farewell; ancient home,
     farewell;

   Boyhood's friends, farewell; you marble gods to whom we
     sacrificed,

   Farewell. Who knows whether Fate will let me speak to you
     again?

   But my hope is lively, and with heaven's help I am confident

   I shall kill my enemy and be ruler of this land of Thebes.
     [Exit POLYNEICES.]

ETEOCLES: Out, beyond my borders, traitor! Oedipus was
     god-inspired

   When he named you Polyneices, full of hate and jealousy!
     [Exit ETEOCLES.]

CHORUS: When Cadmus came from Phoenicia to this
                    country
                 An untamed heifer bounded before him
                 Till, flinging herself to the ground on this very
                    spot,

She gave the sign the oracle promised,
Showing where it was fated he should make
      his home
In this wheat-bearing plain
Watered by lovely rivers,
Where the stream of Dirce feeds the green
      pasture
And quickens the deep-sown furrow;
Here Semele, fostering the seed of Zeus,
Gave birth to Dionysus; and immediately
A garland of ivy blessed the new-born babe,
Twining a shady bower with its green tendrils;
And all the maidens of Thebes,
And women shouting with the joy of Bacchus,
Celebrate this birth with a holy dance.

There by the Spring was the gory dragon of
      Ares,
His keen eyes rolling this way and that,
Fierce and cruel, guarding the bright water
And the green-reflecting fountain.
Cadmus came to the spring to purify his hands;
He lifted a crystal rock in his hunter's arm,
Hurled it at the dragon's ravening head
And killed him; then, instructed
By Pallas the motherless goddess,
He sowed the dragon's teeth in a deep furrow
And up through the surface of the soil
The earth shot forth men in full armour;
And their hearts were as cruel as iron,
And slaughter joined them again with their
      mother earth,
And soaked with blood the soil that had sent
      them forth
To the warm sun and the winds of heaven.

You too, Epaphos son of Zeus,
Born long ago to Io our ancestress,
I invoke with a song of the east,
With prayers in the Phoenician tongue:
Come, come to this city!
For you Thebes was founded by your descend-
     ants
And by the two goddesses, Persephone
And Demeter who rules all living things
And is Earth, the nurse of all living things;
Escort them here with ritual torches
To defend and save this city;
For to the gods all things are possible.

[*Enter* ETEOCLES *with a Soldier.*]

ETEOCLES: Go and fetch here Menoeceus' son, my uncle
     Creon.
Say I wish to consult him on both personal
And public matters, before the battle and all the cares
Of strategy are upon us. – Why, look! You may save
Your legs a journey. I see him coming towards the palace.

[*Enter* CREON.]

CREON: King Eteocles, I have hunted for you all through
     Thebes;
I went to each gate in turn, each fortified position,
Hoping to see you.

ETEOCLES: I too wish to speak with you.
I had an interview under truce with Polyneices,
And found he had nothing satisfactory to offer.

CREON: They say his army, and his alliance with Adrastus,
Swell his ambition against Thebes; he'll offer nothing.
That we must leave to the disposal of the gods.
I came to tell you of the chief problem we must face.

ETEOCLES: Which problem? I don't know what you're refer-
     ring to.

CREON: A prisoner has arrived here from the Argive camp.

ETEOCLES: And what fresh information has he about their plans?

CREON: He says they plan an immediate assault on Thebes
Launched from all sides at once against our towers and gates.

ETEOCLES: Then Thebes must sally forth and fight in the open field.

CREON: Sally forth where? Is this the short-sightedness of youth?

ETEOCLES: Outside our trench-works, to give battle without delay.

CREON: Our army is small; their numbers are unlimited.

ETEOCLES: I know they are full of boasts.

CREON: Argos is reckoned formidable
In Hellas.

ETEOCLES: Is it? I'll fill these plains with Argive dead.

CREON: I hope so; but I see that as a gruelling task.

ETEOCLES: I tell you I won't keep my men inside these walls.

CREON: Good counsel and foresight are the springs of victory.

ETEOCLES: You think I should explore other proposals, then?

CREON: Examine all, sooner than risk all on one throw.

ETEOCLES: A surprise attack at night, from ambush: would that work?

CREON: Given a secure retreat in case of failure – yes.

ETEOCLES: Night levels chances, and favours the attacking side.

CREON: If things go wrong, darkness can be disastrous too.

ETEOCLES: Shall I attack while their whole army's having supper?

CREON: There'd be some panic; but what we need is victory.

ETEOCLES: They'd have to cross the Dirce to retreat. It's deep.

CREON: Guard against every chance; all plans that don't – are bad.

ETEOCLES: How if we mount a full-scale cavalry attack?

CREON: Their army too has chariot-squads on either flank.

ETEOCLES: What's left, then? Hand Thebes over to the enemy?

CREON: By no means. Work a scheme out – you're a prudent man.

ETEOCLES: Where is a scheme more prudent than what I proposed?

CREON: They have seven men appointed, as I understand –

ETEOCLES: Seven men – a meagre force! Appointed to do what?

CREON: To lead seven companies to attack our seven gates.

ETEOCLES: What plan, then? When they attack us it will be too late.

CREON: You too must pick seven men to oppose them at the gates.

ETEOCLES: In single combat? Or with regiments at their back?

CREON: With regiments. Choose out the hardiest men you have.

ETEOCLES: I agree; they'll deal with any attempt to scale the walls.

CREON: Choose deputies for them; one man can't see everything.

ETEOCLES: Shall I choose them for their courage or their intelligence?

CREON: For both, since neither quality is any use alone.

ETEOCLES: I'll do that. I'll go now to the city and appoint
Captains for all the seven gates, as you suggest –
For each attacker his appropriate opposite.
To name each one would be a foolish waste of time
With the enemy encamped here at our very walls.
My hands must not be idle; I will go at once –
And may Fate send me my brother as my opposite,
Matched shield with shield, till with this spear I strike him dead!
    Now, for my sister Antigone, if Fortune today

Deserts me, you must take thought for her marriage with
Haemon your son. As I go out to fight, I now
Ratify the betrothal already made. You are
Her mother's brother; so what need for many words?
Give her such care as honours both yourself and me.
I've little sympathy with my father; when he destroyed
His sight he was guilty of wicked folly against himself;
And his curse, if Fate wills it, may yet kill us all.

    One thing I've not yet done is to discover from
The prophet Teiresias if he has any word
Of divine guidance for us. I will send your son
Menoeceus, named after your father, to conduct
Teiresias here. The old man will talk happily
To you; but I have criticized his prophetic art
Before now to his face, and he's displeased with me.

    And, Creon, I now give you, and Thebes, this strict
        command:
If I am victorious, Polyneices' body must
Never be given burial here in Theban soil.
Any who inters him, even of our family, shall die.
Bring me my weapons, case me head to foot in bronze!
The trial of blood awaits me now; as I set forth,
Justice, my ally, promises me victory;
And to Precaution, that most helpful deity,
I pray, to grant success and safety to our land.
    [*Exeunt* ETEOCLES *and* CREON.]

CHORUS: O Ares, bringer of agonized exhaustion,
            Why are you dedicated to blood and death?
            Why does your trumpets' blare
            Untune the songs of Bacchic festivals?
            When the ripeness of youth is crowned with
                flowers,
            And girls dance together,
            You are not with them, tossing your hair to the
                wind;

When breath fills the flute
You sing no song to make the Graces dance;
You assemble warriors and weapons,
You inflame the fighters of Argos with thirst
    for Theban blood;
No music of pipes sweetens your merrymaking;
Your running is not graced
With the wild whirl of thyrsus and fawnskin;
You rush with a rattle of chariots, ringing of
    bridles,
Thunder of hooves beside the quiet Ismenus;
You inflame the earth-sown race of Thebes
With hatred for the men of Argos;
You marshall your joyful dancers,
Whose food is the fury of war,
To match their massed bronze against walls of
    stone.
Hatred, that god of terrible power,
Has devised this misery for the royal house,
To exhaust with anguish the descendants of
    Labdacus.

God-haunted glen of wild Cithaeron
Where countless creatures move through the
    leafy stillness,
Snow-covered heights that Artemis loves;
When Iocasta's babe was cast out of his home,
When they left him to die – Oedipus,
His flesh incised with the sign of a golden
    brooch:
If only you had not preserved his life!
If only the Sphinx, that winged monster from
    the mountains,
Had never cursed this country with her baleful
    song,

When she lighted on these walls with her
    beast's claws,
Sent from hell to plague this city,
And carried off Cadmus' sons to the trackless
    depths of light!
And now springs into life a new hatred
To curse the city and home of the sons of
    Oedipus.
For never can bad be good, dishonour honour;
Nor can sons whom, to their father's shame,
Their mother bore in unlawful wedlock
Ever prove true sons.

I heard the legend told in my Phoenician home
Of the purple-crested, beast-devouring dragon
Whose teeth were sown in this soil;
And how from the dragon's teeth
The land gave birth to a race of men,
A glory and a reproach to Thebes;
And then to Harmonia's wedding came the
    heavenly gods,
And the walls of Thebes rose high to the harp's
    music;
And at the bidding of Amphion's lyre,
On ground between two rivers her towers
    stood straight,
Where Dirce and Ismenus side by side
Moisten the lush green plain.
Thereafter Io, mother of our race,
Bore kings for the line of Cadmus;
And this city, enriched with numberless
    blessings,
Grew from fortune to greater fortune,
Till she stands crowned with the proudest
    garlands of war.

[*Enter* TEIRESIAS, *led by his young daughter, and*
MENOECEUS.]

TEIRESIAS: Lead on, my daughter; you're the eye for my
   blind feet,
As the north star to sailors. Guide me on smooth ground.
There, go in front; don't let me slip; I've little strength.
Hold carefully these written tablets which I took
As I interpreted the omens given by birds
In the holy chamber where I practise divination.
   Tell me, Menoeceus, how far have we still to go
To Thebes, to find your father? My old legs are tired;
We've come a long way. Walking is too much for me.
   [*Enter* CREON.]

CREON: Courage, Teiresias; you are close now to your
   friends;
You can drop anchor here. Menoeceus, take his arm;
Old bones look for the strong help of a younger hand.

TEIRESIAS: We're here, then. Why did you send for me in
   haste, Creon?

CREON: My mind is full of it. But you, first collect your
   strength,
Get your breath, and recover after your long walk.

TEIRESIAS: I am indeed exhausted; only yesterday
I travelled here from Athens. There was war there too,
Against Eumolpus; and I made the Athenians
Victorious. This golden garland which I wear
They gave me, chosen from their spoils taken in war.

CREON: I take your garland as an omen of victory.
We, as you know, are in great peril. Argos has sent
An army against us; Thebes has a hard fight ahead.
Already King Eteocles, fully armed, has gone
To meet the Mycenaean attack. He instructed me
To ask you by what act we can best help our city.

TEIRESIAS: From Eteocles I would have withheld the oracles
And spoken no word. Since *you* ask me, I will speak

To you. Creon, the land of Thebes has long been sick,
Since Laius, disobeying the gods, begot a son,
The wretched Oedipus, to become his mother's mate;
That gory havoc he performed upon his eyes
Was heaven's design, that Hellas might see it and take heed.
Oedipus' sons, who thought they could elude the gods,
Hiding him away, to blunt men's memory with time,
Committed a disastrous folly. Giving him
Neither respect nor freedom to depart, they stung
His wretchedness to fury. Sick, degraded, he
Poured out on them his vicious curse. I warned them both
Time and again, by act and word; and for my pains
They hate me. Creon, death for each by the other's hand
Is very near. Bodies on bodies heaped, laid low
By Argive or by Theban spears in confused ruin,
Shall rouse wild wailing and despair through all this land.
And you, doomed city, shall be levelled with the ground
Unless my words be heeded. It were best for Thebes
That none of Oedipus' race remain here, whether as ruled
Or ruler; they are possessed, and will destroy the state.
But, since evil now holds advantage over good,
One other way to win deliverance yet remains.
To tell this is unsafe for me, and terrible
For those to whom Fate gives the power to offer Thebes
The price of safety. Therefore I will go. Farewell;
And if what shall be, must be, I will suffer it,
One Theban among many. What else can I do?

CREON: Wait, stay here, Teiresias.

TEIRESIAS: Do not lay hands on me.

CREON: Why must you leave us?

TEIRESIAS: Fortune leaves you, Creon,
     not I.

CREON: Tell Thebes and all our people which way safety lies.

TEIRESIAS: You long for knowledge; you will soon long for
     ignorance.

CREON: How so? Do I not wish to save my native land?

TEIRESIAS: You wish to hear, then? This is truly your desire?

CREON: It is indeed. What should I wish for, more than that?

TEIRESIAS: Then listen while I speak the word revealed by
  heaven.
 But tell me this first: where is Menoeceus, who just now
 Guided me to this place?

CREON: He is here, close at your side.

TEIRESIAS: Then let him stand removed from what I have to
  tell.

CREON: He is my son, and will keep secret what he should.

TEIRESIAS: I am to speak, then, in his presence? You wish
  this?

CREON: If you speak of deliverance, this will give him joy.

TEIRESIAS: Listen then to my oracle, which way it tends,
 Since you yourself demand it. You must sacrifice
 Your son Menoeceus, if you would save your country's life.

CREON: What are you saying? Teiresias, what do your words
  mean?

TEIRESIAS: This is decreed by Fate, and this you must perform.

CREON: Immeasurable evil, spoken in two words!

TEIRESIAS: Evil to you; to Thebes, words of deliverance.

CREON: I was not listening, did not hear. Let Thebes perish!

TEIRESIAS: This is a changed man now; he looks the other
  way.

CREON: You may go home. I have no need of your oracles.

TEIRESIAS: Does truth lose force because *you* are unfortunate?

CREON: I implore you – by your white hair – see, I kneel to
  you!

TEIRESIAS: Why kneel? You pray for suffering which will
  surely come.

CREON: You are to make no such statement to the citizens.

TEIRESIAS: You bid me betray the city. I will not be silent.

CREON: What are you doing to me? Will you kill my son?

TEIRESIAS: That is for others. My part is to speak the
    words.

CREON: Whence comes this horror which destroys my son
   and me?

TEIRESIAS: You are right to question, and insist on fair reply.
 In that den where the earth-born dragon lay on guard
 Watching the spring of Dirce, there your son must give
 His blood as a libation to the earth, and die
 To appease the anger which, in ancient times, Ares
 Nursed against Cadmus, which now drives him to avenge
 The dragon, offspring of the earth, which Cadmus killed.
 If you do this you will gain Ares for your ally.
 And if the earth receive now fruit for fruit bestowed
 And blood of man for blood once spilt, earth too will be
 Your friend, the same that once sent up for us a crop
 Of sown warriors, gold-helmeted. He who dies now
 Must be of that same stock, sprung from the dragon's jaw.
 You, Creon, are sole survivor of that race, unmixed
 On both father's and mother's side – you and your sons.
 Haemon is barred from sacrifice as one destined
 For marriage. Though not married yet, he is betrothed
 And thus not counted virgin. But your second son,
 An unbroken colt, can save his country by his death.
 He can ensure for Adrastus and the Argive arms
 A bitter homecoming, benight their eyes with doom,
 And clothe great Thebes in glory. Of two prospects choose
 One: you may save either your city or your son.
  So, you have heard my message. Daughter, lead me home.
 To practise divination by burnt sacrifice
 Is folly. Offer unwelcome words, and those for whom
 You practise hate you. If you speak falsely, in compassion
 For your inquirers, you offend the gods. Phoebus
 Fears no one: he should speak his oracles himself.

   [*Exit* TEIRESIAS.]

CHORUS: Why silent, Creon? Speech starts, but no word
     comes. I too
  Am struck to dumbness.

CREON: What is there a man can say?
  Well, this at least is clear: I've not yet reached such depths
  As to allow my son's throat to be cut for Thebes.
  A man's sons are a part of his own life; no man
  Who loves his son would hand him over to be killed.
  No man shall kill my sons and praise my patriotism!
  I'll die myself, and willingly, to save the city;
  I've had my full time. – Son, come here. You must escape
  Before the whole city hears this irresponsible
  Oracle. Ignore it, and get out of Thebes and away
  Immediately. Teiresias will go the round
  Of the city gates, and tell our officers and generals.
  If we act quickly, there's a chance yet for your life;
  If you delay a moment, it's the end, you die.

MENOECEUS: Where should I go? What city?

CREON: Anywhere, as far
  From Thebes as possible.

MENOECEUS: You suggest some place, I'll try
  To get there.

CREON: First, to Delphi.

MENOECEUS: Yes; where after that?

CREON: Aetolia.

MENOECEUS: Yes; and then?

CREON: Up to Thesprotia.

MENOECEUS: To the temple at Dodona?

CREON: Yes.

MENOECEUS: And how will that
  Protect me?

CREON: Heaven will guide you.

MENOECEUS: How shall I get money?

CREON: I'll send you gold.

MENOECEUS: All's well, then. Go now; I must first

Speak to Iocasta, who nursed me when my mother died
And brought me up. Go, father; there's no time to waste.
    [CREON *embraces him and exits.*]
See, women, how well I've allayed my father's fears,
Using deceit to bring about what I intend.
He means to get me away, commit me to an act
Of cowardice which would rob Thebes of her victory.
In him, at his age, this is forgivable; but not
In me. How can I betray the city of my birth?
Be sure of this, then: I will go and save the city,
Giving my life for Thebes. I should be ashamed, if men
Not named in oracles, not compelled by divine powers,
Take sword in hand and face death in the battle-line
Fighting before the walls of Thebes, while I betray
My father, brother, and my city, and slink off
A coward; no matter where I lived, the world would know
Me as a traitor. Zeus, who lives among the stars,
And fierce Ares, who raised the Sown Men from this soil
And made them kings over our land, be witnesses:
I am no traitor! I go now to our battlements,
To stand and look down to the murky den where once
The dragon lay; and there, as Teiresias commanded,
I'll kill myself and save my country. All is said.
I will present to Thebes a death – no paltry gift;
And purge our country from her sickness. If each man
Would take the noblest gift of which he's capable,
Reckon it fully, and offer it for his country's need,
Our Hellene cities would be less experienced
In misery, and the future would be bright with hope.
    [*Exit* MENOECEUS.]
CHORUS: You came, Sphinx, winging the air you came,
           Born from Earth's womb,
           Begotten by a snake of hell,
           To ravage the town of Cadmus,
           Death before, tears following;

Half-beast, half-maiden,
A monster of terror, of ranging wings
And claws red with raw flesh.
By the river of Dirce in those days
You snatched up young men from the farms,
And carried them aloft, carried them away,
Chanting your sinister music,
A song of doom and despair
Filling the land with deadly pain;
Deadly was the divinity that brought this on us.
In every house was wailing,
Mothers and maidens wailing,
A mournful refrain, a pain-racked roar,
As through the city house answered house,
Street echoed street,
In succession of endless sorrow.
Like a thunderstorm that groaning rose and
      fell,
As another vanished and yet another,
While dread wings hovered above.

In course of time came Oedipus the accursed,
Sent by the Pythian god,
And brought to the land of Thebes
First rejoicing, but afterwards grief.
In the glory of success when he solved the
      riddle
A miserable fate married him to his mother
And polluted the city.
In his misery he cursed his sons,
Set their feet on a path of blood,
Their hands to an unholy conflict.
Noble and glorious is he
Who has gone to his death for the sake of his
      native land,

And has left to Creon crying and tears,
But will bring the joy of victory
To the city's seven gates.
May my son be like him!
May we be mothers of noble sons,
We pray, Pallas, dear goddess,
Who cast the stone which laid the dragon in
      his blood,
Who launched bold Cadmus on that enterprise
From which there spread across the land,
Devouring and destroying,
A supernatural fury of blood and hate.

[*Enter a* MESSENGER.]

MESSENGER: Hullo, there! Who's on duty at the palace gate?
Open! Tell Queen Iocasta to come out. Hullo!
Better late than never – come out here and listen to me;
No more lamenting, Queen Iocasta; dry your tears.

[*Enter* IOCASTA.]

IOCASTA: Good friend, what news? My son Eteocles is not
dead?
You are the man who stands beside him, to keep off
The enemy spears – come, tell me, is he alive or dead?

MESSENGER: Alive – there's comfort for you; set your heart
at rest.

IOCASTA: And what of our defences? Do the walls and gates
Stand strong?

MESSENGER: They are unbreached and firm; the city is safe.

IOCASTA: Were our men ever in danger of defeat?

MESSENGER: They were,
Within a hair's breadth; yet they proved the better men.

IOCASTA: Next tell me, for the gods' sake, if you have any news
Of Polyneices. I must know if he too lives.

MESSENGER: Yes; so far, both your sons are living.

IOCASTA: God bless
      you!

Now tell me of your victory, how the defenders
Beat off the Argives from our gates. I want to bring
This glorious news to gladden old blind Oedipus.
MESSENGER: When Creon's son, who died to save his native
          land,
     Had stood on a high tower and through his throat had
          plunged
The deadly sword which brought deliverance to Thebes,
Your son Eteocles was selecting seven chiefs,
Each with his share of troops, to man the seven gates
Against the assault. Behind the cavalry he set
Supporting ranks of horsemen, while the hoplites had
Hoplite reserves, so that help could be quickly brought
Wherever our defence was weak. From the towers' height
We saw the white shields of the Argive army advance
From Teumessus; close by our trench they quickened pace
And charged towards our bastions. The mingled roar
Of paean and trumpets from their side and ours rose high.

     And first, against the Neistean Gate Atalanta's son
Parthenopaeus led his bristling ranks of shields.
On his own shield he showed the emblem of his house,
Atalanta with her bow shooting the Aetolian boar.
Against the Proetian Gate the prophet Amphiaraus
Advanced, with altar-victims on his chariot;
His modest armour flaunted no proud emblem. Next,
Against the Ogygian Gate came Prince Hippomedon.
The device he bore was Argus the all-seeing, his shield
Stippled with eyes; some, with the rising of the stars,
Open, and others closed as the stars set – the truth
Of this sign appeared later, when the man was dead.

     Then Tydeus took his place at the Homolean Gate.
Over his shield a lion's hairy hide was draped,
And, for device, Titan Prometheus held aloft
A torch to burn this city. At the Fountain Gate
Your son Polyneices led his soldiers to the attack.

His painted shield showed horses in a wild stampede,
Mounted on pins near the shield-handle, and rotated
From inside the shield, so that in front they seemed to leap
In frenzied panic. Then Capaneus, with spirit to match
Fierce Ares, led his men towards the Electran Gate.
On the iron ridges of his shield there was engraved
A giant supporting on his shoulders a whole city
Which he had heaved with iron bars from its foundation —
Meant as a picture of the fate he promised Thebes.

At the seventh gate Adrastus stood. His coloured shield
Displayed the boastful Argive emblem, a hundred snakes
Which in their jaws were snatching from the Theban walls
The sons of Cadmus. Each man's symbol I could observe
When I took round the password to our fighting chiefs.

Well, then the battle began; first at long range, with bows,
Thong-javelins, slings and crashing stones. We pushed them
    back.
A rallying shout went up from Tydeus and your son:
'Danaans, why wait until you're torn to shreds? Come on,
All of you, light-armed, cavalry, charioteers, charge now
And force the gates!' They heard, and every man obeyed.
There in front of the walls bodies were falling, heads
Laid open, corpses somersaulting everywhere
As the thick dust grew sodden with the streams of blood.

Atalanta's son — no Argive, an Arcadian —
Fell like a hurricane on the gates, shouting for fire
And crowbars to annihilate the town. But he
In his mad rage was stopped short by Poseidon's son
Periclymenus, who hurled down from the battlements
A coping-stone, itself a waggon-load in weight,
And shattered Parthenopaeus' head, and broke apart
The sutures of the skull, and soaked in blood his bright
Hair and his newly-growing beard. The Arcadian
Huntress will never welcome back her son alive.

Seeing the fight successful at this gate, your son

Went on to others, and I followed. Then I saw
Tydeus and his close-ranked Aetolians hurl their spears
So thick against our towers that the defenders fled
And left the crests unguarded. Your son rallied them
As a hunter does his hounds, and once again they took
Their perilous place. The danger thus averted, we
Pressed on to the other gates. But how can I describe
The raging fury of Capaneus? He advanced holding
A scaling-ladder of prodigious length; and this
Was his boast, that not the immortal lightning-flame of Zeus
Should stop him laying our highest towers low in the dust.
These words he shouted as he climbed up, with his body
Crouched close under his shield to avoid the rain of stones.
Still, foot by foot, from rung to smooth rung, up he came;
And at the moment when he topped the rampart's crest,
Zeus struck him with a thunderbolt. The trembling earth
Roared, terrifying everyone; and from the ladder
Flung far, his whirling corpse, fire-blackened, crashed to the
    ground.
    Now when Adrastus saw Zeus hostile to his cause
He withdrew the Argive army back beyond the trench;
While our men, seeing this sign of favour sent by Zeus,
Charged in a mass, with chariots, hoplites, cavalry,
And struck the Argive centre. Death and horror then
Were let loose; men were falling from their chariot-rims,
Crashing to earth; axle was fouling axle, wheels
Leaping in the air, corpses on corpses heaped together.
    So for today at least we have held at bay the ruin
That threatened Thebes. Whether her fortune is to hold
For time to come, rests with the gods. Her present safety
She owes, for certain, to divine deliverance.

CHORUS: Victory is good; if in their purpose the gods hide
Yet greater good – I pray for blessing on us all.

IOCASTA: The gods and fortune have alike proved favourable;
My sons live, and the city stands. On Creon, I fear,

Is laid the bitter load of grief which Oedipus
And I engendered by our marriage. He has lost
His son; the city is saved, the father's heart broken.
– Resume your story. What do my sons now mean to do?

MESSENGER: Question no further. So far all the news is good.

IOCASTA: Your words make me uneasy. How can I not ask?

MESSENGER: What more is needed than to know your sons
    are safe?

IOCASTA: Am I to hope good fortune can continue still?

MESSENGER: Let me go. Your son is left without his shield-
    bearer.

IOCASTA: You are hiding something dreadful, keeping me in
    the dark.

MESSENGER: It's true – I don't want to undo good news with
    bad.

IOCASTA: You will tell me now, unless you can find wings to
    escape.

MESSENGER: For pity's sake, could you not let me go after
  My good news? Must you force my tongue to cruelty?
  Your sons intend – foolhardy wickedness – to meet
  In single combat, separated from their troops;
  And in the hearing of all, both Argives and Cadmeans,
  They have spoken such words as should never have been
    uttered.
    A herald was bidden call for silence; then, standing
  On a high battlement, Eteocles spoke first:
  'You Danaan chieftains who have travelled here, and you
  Soldiers of Cadmus, do not, either for Polyneices
  Or for myself, bargain away your lives; for I
  Will free you of this danger, and alone make trial
  Of battle with my brother. If I take his life,
  I will be sole possessor of my house; but if
  I am defeated, I yield him the sole possession.
  Then, Argives, drop your weapons, go back to your land,
  Leave no more lives behind you in the Theban dust;

Already of our earth-born race enough lie dead.'

    When he had finished, Polyneices leapt from the ranks
To approve his words; and from both armies rose a loud
Roar of assent. Half-way between the lines they made
Agreement on these terms, which both chiefs swore to keep.

    Now the two sons of Oedipus were covering
Their bodies, head to foot, in armour all of bronze,
With friends to dress them – nobles of Thebes armed Eteocles,
And Argive princes Polyneices. There they stood
Shining; not pale, each madly eager to let fly
His spear at the other. And their friends came out to them
From either side to encourage them: 'It lies with you,
Polyneices, to set up a statue of Zeus in thanks
For victory, and bring glory to the state of Argos!'
To Eteocles they said, 'It is for Thebes you fight;
Now conquer, and be sole possessor of your throne.'
With such encouragements they cheered them on to battle.
Priests offered sheep at the altar, duly interpreting
The flame single or forked, the ominous flickering,
The fiery tip whose character distinguishes
Promise of victory from presage of defeat.

    So come, Iocasta, use whatever wisdom, art,
Or power you have; go quickly, speak, and draw your sons
Back from this dread encounter; for the danger is great,
And for yourself the prize in tears intolerable
Should this disastrous day rob you of both your sons.

IOCASTA: Daughter, Antigone! Come out here! The ordi-
    nance
Of heaven forbids you celebrate this day with dancing
Or such-like innocence; two heroic warriors, your
Two brothers, are this moment reeling towards death;
And we must stop each murdering the other's life.
    [Enter ANTIGONE.]
ANTIGONE: Dear mother, why are you calling here before the
    palace?

Have you some unexpected shock to tell me of?

IOCASTA: Yes, child; it is the destruction of your brothers'
lives.

ANTIGONE: What can you mean?

IOCASTA: The two are meeting in
single fight.

ANTIGONE: Mother! What are you saying?

IOCASTA: Nothing pleasant.
Come.

ANTIGONE: Come? Where? I have just left my room.

IOCASTA: To the
battlefield.

ANTIGONE: How can I, before everyone?

IOCASTA: This is no time
For modesty.

ANTIGONE: What can I do?

IOCASTA: Persuade your brothers
To stop this fight.

ANTIGONE: But how can I?

IOCASTA: Fall on your knees;
I'll do the same.

ANTIGONE: Lead on, then, to the battlefield;
Let's lose no time.

IOCASTA: Come, hurry, child. If I get there
Before they fight, my life still holds a ray of hope.
If they are killed, I too will lie beside them, dead.

          [*Exeunt* IOCASTA *and* ANTIGONE.]

CHORUS: My heart shudders and trembles,
               My thought chills with horror;
               Pity distracts my aching heart,
               Pity for a mother's misery.
               O Zeus, what pain! O earth, what anguish!
               Which of her sons shall lay the other
               Bleeding on the ground,
               Pierce a brother's throat,

Ravage a brother's life,
Strike at a brother's shield,
Shed his blood?
Which of the two is dead?
Over whose pitiable body
Shall I raise the outcry of mourning?
Zeus, Zeus, have mercy!
There stands a pair of wild beasts,
Minds full of murder,
Hearts poised for the killing blow;
In one moment of violence
Flesh will fall and blood will pour.
Wretched, reckless men, what led your
          thoughts
To single combat?
With oriental wailing, with wild cries of pain,
With tears I will lament the dead.
Chance stands on the brink of slaughter;
What shall decide the outcome?
Save us, O Fate,
Save us from the blood of vengeance!

Hush! Break off this lamentation; wait in silence – here I see
Creon coming towards the palace, clouds of sorrow on his
          face.

[*Enter* CREON.]

CREON: What shall I do? Shed tears for my own misery,
Or for my city, wrapped now in so dark a cloud
As should convey her past the very river of death?
My son is dead; he gave his life for Thebes, and won
For himself the name of hero, but for me despair.
I found him where he lay below the Dragon's Cliff,
Slaughtered by his own hand. I carried him in my arms
Home, where each room resounds with crying; and I have
          come,
Old Creon, to find my sister, old Iocasta. She

Will wash and lay out the body that was once my son.
When a man is dead, one who is not yet dead should show,
By honouring him, due piety to the gods of earth.

CHORUS: She has gone out, Creon; your sister and Antigone
Went both together.

CREON: 　　　　　　　Where? Has something happened? Tell
me.

CHORUS: Yes, news was brought her, that her two sons were
resolved
To meet in single combat for the throne of Thebes.

CREON: Is it true? Being so preoccupied in caring for
My son's body, I did not hear this further news.

CHORUS: It is some time now since Iocasta left the house.
I think, Creon, that deadly battle must already
Have reached its issue for the sons of Oedipus.

CREON: You speak the truth; for here comes evidence – I see
A messenger with haggard face and anguished eyes
Coming towards us. He will tell the whole story.
[*Enter a* SECOND MESSENGER.]

MESSENGER: Oh! What words, what tears can tell the story
of this dreadful day?

CREON: There is death in your beginning; nothing good can
follow now.

MESSENGER: Nothing good; but tears, and dread, and death.
My news is terrible.

CREON: Tears and terror fill this day already. What have you
to add?

MESSENGER: Creon, they are both dead; your sister's sons
have left the light of day.

CREON: 　　　　This is a word of sorrow,
　　　　　　Bitter for me, bitter for Thebes.
O royal house! Has this word reached you? Oedipus'
Two sons are gone; one mutual death destroyed them both.

CHORUS: The house itself, if it had heart to feel, would weep.

CREON: 　　　　O grievous destiny, O dreadful deed!

MESSENGER: Too true, did you but know what more there is
    to tell.

CREON: What can there be more grievous to endure than
    this?

MESSENGER: She is dead too; your sister lies beside her sons.

CHORUS: Wail aloud, howl and cry,
             Let white arms batter the head for grief!

CREON: O miserable Iocasta! To this piteous end
  The Sphinx's riddle brought your marriage and your life!
  – Tell me, how came fulfilment of this double death,
  The duel foretold by the curse of Oedipus?

MESSENGER: The victory won by Thebes before her battle-
    ments
  You know already, since the walls are not far off.
    When the two sons of aged Oedipus were cased
  And weaponed all with bronze, they came and stood between
  The two armies, prepared to match their strength, and fight
  Sword against single sword. Then Polyneices prayed,
  'Hera, great goddess – for I am yours, since I have wed
  Adrastus' daughter, and live in Argos on your soil –
  Grant me to kill my brother; let my fighting arm
  Be reddened with the blood of victory.' At this,
  Many shed tears of shame, to think that such a thing
  Could happen, and looked this way and that uneasily.
  Eteocles, gazing towards Athene's golden shield,
  Which shone before her temple, prayed: 'Daughter of Zeus,
  Grant me to hurl from this right hand my conquering spear
  Into my brother's heart, and kill the man who came
  To lay my city in the dust.' Then, when the blare
  Of the Tyrrhenian trumpet, like a beacon-flame,
  Leapt forth to sound the signal for the trial of blood,
  The two charged at each other with tremendous force.
  Like boars whetting their savage tusks they clashed together;
  Foam flecked their beards; their spears lunged out; behind
    round shields

They crouched, so that the blade should glance off harm-
    lessly.
If one saw the other's eye peer over the shield's rim,
He thrust, intent to drive his spear-point home in time;
While each still kept an eye close to the eyelet-holes
In the rim, so that the other's spear dealt idle blows.
Those watching them, in terror for their champion's life,
Were dripping sweat more freely than the combatants.
    Then Eteocles misjudged his footing on a stone
Which rolled under his tread, and placed his leg outside
His shield's protection. Seeing the offered chance, where
    steel
Could strike, Polyneices thrust, and drove his Argive spear
Right through the shin, while the whole Argive army roared
In triumph. But in that effort Polyneices left
His shoulder bare; his wounded enemy saw, and struck
His lance with fierce force through Polyneices' chest, and
    gave
Joy to the Thebans; yet he broke his lance off short.
So, with his lance useless, retreating step by step,
He picked up a crystal rock, flung it, and broke the shaft
Of the other's spear in the middle; and now both had lost
Their spear-shafts, and the struggle was on even terms.
They gripped their sword-hilts then, and closed, clashing
    their shields
And circling, while the clangorous din of battle swelled.
Then Eteocles used the Thessalian feint, which he
Had learnt when visiting that country. He sprang clear
Of the close grapple, drew his left foot back, and crouched,
His eye fixed on the other's belly; then he lunged
With right foot forward, and through the navel drove his
    sword,
Wedging it in the spine. Polyneices doubled up,
Clutching his middle in agony and spouting blood;
Then fell. Eteocles, jubilant at his victory,

Threw down his sword, and began to strip the armour off
His enemy – all intent on that, giving no heed
To his own safety. This was his undoing. The sword
Was still in Polyneices' hand, where he had fallen.
With his last painful gasp, with all his ebbing strength,
He stretched, and thrust the blade into Eteocles' heart.
There, side by side, biting the dusty earth, they lie;
And which has gained the victory is still unknown.

CHORUS: My heart grieves for your sorrows, Oedipus; and
yet
This surely was your curse, which heaven has now fulfilled.

MESSENGER: Now listen further; there is more grief yet to
tell.
While her two sons lay dying, their unhappy mother
In desperate haste came with Antigone, and fell
To her knees beside them. When she saw that both their
wounds
Were mortal, she sobbed out, 'Dear sons, I came to save
Your lives, but came too late.' Bent over each in turn,
She wept and mourned, with tears recalling all her care
When they were infants. By her side Antigone
Was mourning too: 'O dearest brothers, to your love
Our mother looked for comfort in old age, and I
For hopes of marriage. You have left us solitary!'
King Eteocles heaved from his breast one dying gasp;
He heard his mother, laid his chill damp hand on hers.
His lips uttered no sound, but from his eyes the tears
Sent her a loving message. Polyneices, still
Breathing, looked at his sister and his mother, and said:
'Mother, my life is finished. I am sorry for you,
And for my sister, and my dead brother. For he was
My brother, and became my enemy, yet was still
My dear brother. I beg you both – you, mother, and
You, sister: bury me in my native land; and soothe
The resentment of the citizens, that I may gain

Thus much at least of my own heritage, though I
Have lost my home. Now close my eyelids with your hand,
Mother' — with this he placed her hand upon his eyes —
'And so, good-bye. Darkness begins to wrap me round.'
Then both together they gasped out their piteous lives.

But when their mother saw their end come, in excess
Of anguish, she snatched up a sword that lay by them,
And did a fearful thing: right through her throat she drove
The iron blade; and there between her two dear sons
She lies now, with a lifeless arm thrown around each.

At once both armies started to their feet. Our men
Shouted that Eteocles was victor; their men said
Polyneices; and the officers too were arguing,
Some pointing out that Polyneices had drawn first blood,
While others claimed neither had won, since both were
    dead.
Antigone slipped away unnoticed. Both sides then
Took to their weapons; with a fortunate foresight
The Theban army had halted in their fighting-lines,
And so we took the Argive enemy by surprise
And charged before they could present an armoured front.
No stand was made; they ran — the plain was thick with
    them;
Blood flowed in streams from thousands massacred by our
    spears.
So, when we had beaten them in battle, some set up
A statue of Zeus as trophy, while some took the shields
From the Argive dead, and brought the spoils inside our
    walls.
Others now, with Antigone, are coming here
Bringing the dead, for those who loved them to lament.

So, today's agony has brought to Thebes one way
A joyful issue, another way profoundest grief.
CHORUS: The disasters of the house of Oedipus
            Are no longer a tale that we have heard;

Now we may see, nearing the palace,
Three bodies fallen together in death,
Three lives that have entered the world of
　　darkness.

[*Enter* ANTIGONE *with a procession bearing the three
bodies.*]

ANTIGONE:　No seemly veil covers
The curling hair and soft cheek;
No maidenly reserve hides
The flush under the eyes, the hot forehead,
As I come, a Bacchant of the dead,
Tearing loose the band that held my hair,
Flinging free my saffron robe of silk,
To lead the march of mourning for these
　　dead.
Wail aloud, weep and cry!
Polyneices, Man of Strife, so truly named
(Alas unhappy Thebes!),
Yours was the quarrel - and yet
No quarrel, but murder matched with
　　murder -
Which, accomplished in a horror of blood,
In an anguish of blood,
Has overwhelmed the house of Oedipus.
What music, what chorus of tears,
What song of weeping shall I summon
To mourn for you, my home, my home?
Here I bring three killed with the sword,
Of one family, a mother and her sons,
A welcome sight to the spirit of vengeance
Which doomed our house to utter ruin
On that day when the wisdom of Oedipus
Found easy the hard riddle of the cruel
　　Sphinx
And destroyed her life.

Father, dear father, I cry aloud your
    sufferings!
What other man of our mortal race,
Hellene or barbarian, or hero of ancient
    royalty,
Endured before all men's gaze
The torment of such disasters?
What bird, hidden aloft
In the leafy boughs of oak or pine,
Mourning for a mother dead,
Will sing in tune with my sorrow,
With my dirge of despair
For the long life of solitary days that awaits
    me,
And the tears that will not cease?
On which body shall I cast first
The offering of hair torn from my head?
On the two breasts of my mother
Where once I was fed?
Or on the piteous wounds of my dead
    brothers?

Father, father! Leave your room,
Blind as you are, and old,
Come, Oedipus, show your unhappy self,
Drawing the slow breath of a long life,
You who once in this palace
Plunged your eyes in misty darkness,
And now grope your feeble way along the
    walls,
Or rest on a bed of pain;
Do you hear me? Come!

[Enter OEDIPUS.]

OEDIPUS: My daughter, why have you brought me
    With your pitiful wailing out into the light,

> Your hand in mine like the blind man's
>   stick,
> From the darkened room where I lay on my
>   bed,
> A dim grey ghost made of air,
> A dead soul from the depths, or a hovering
>   dream?

ANTIGONE: There is cruel news, father, for you to hear.
            Your two sons no longer see the light;
            Gone too is your wife, who laboured always
            To guide your blind steps and care for you.
            Weep with me, father.

OEDIPUS: Weep for the blows that bow me down!
            Here indeed is matter for groans and tears;
            Three lives have left the sun's light.
            Tell me, child, what fate overtook them.

ANTIGONE: I speak, not to reproach you or rejoice over
                you,
            But in bitter pain. It was your curse,
            Heavy with swords and fire and insatiable
                enmity,
            That came upon your sons, unhappy father.

OEDIPUS: My calamitous curse!

ANTIGONE: For whom are you groaning?

OEDIPUS: For my sons.

ANTIGONE: You suffer indeed;
            But what if you still could raise your sight
            To the striding sun, and see with a clear gaze
            The bodies of these dead?

OEDIPUS: How my sons died I understand;
            But tell me, Antigone,
            What stroke of death ended Iocasta's suffer-
                ings?

ANTIGONE: Heart-rending tears flowed down her face
            As, heedless who saw her,

She ran, she ran to her sons,
To kneel and show her breast in supplica-
    tion.
She found them by the Electran Gate
In a meadow bright with lotus-flowers,
Locked in mortal combat spear to spear,
Fighting like lions loose from their dens;
And from their wounds already flowed
The chill, gory libation offered by Ares,
Received as his due by the god of the dead.
From beside the bodies she snatched a sword
    of hammered bronze,
Buried it deep in her flesh, and fell,
Her heart broken for her sons,
Her lifeless arms enfolding her sons.
These many sorrows, father, in a single day
Are heaped upon this house
By the god who fulfils our destiny.

CHORUS: Today sees the enactment of great misery
  For the royal house. May happier times await us now.
CREON: No more lamenting; it is time to turn our thoughts
  To burial rites. And this word, Oedipus, you must hear:
  Your son Eteocles left to me the rule of Thebes,
  To pass to Haemon as a dowry with your daughter
  Antigone, whom he gives to my son as his wife.
    Henceforth, then, I forbid you to remain in Thebes;
  For Teiresias said plainly that, while you live here,
  This city has no hope of peace and happiness.
  So you must go. I say this with no harsh intent,
  No hostile feeling, but because I fear those spirits
  Of vengeance which attend you may destroy our land.
OEDIPUS: O Destiny! You created me, beyond all men,
  For life-long wretchedness and pain. Before I came
  Forth from my mother's womb Apollo prophesied
  To Laius that his unborn son should murder him.

Cruelty followed cruelty: after begetting me
My father saw in his new-born son an enemy,
Since prophecy made me his killer; and cast me out –
An infant torn from the breast – to make a meal for beasts.
Cithaeron spared me – should not a just punishment
Have sunk Cithaeron to the pit of Tartarus? –
Cithaeron did not kill me . . . And my guiding fate
Gave me a slave's home in the palace of Polybus.
When my accursed hand had shed my father's blood
I took my miserable mother to my bed as wife,
Bred sons who were my brothers, whom I have destroyed,
Tainting them with the curse which Laius left to me.
I am not such a lost fool as to perpetrate
That outrage on my eyes and on my own sons' lives
Without being forced to it by divine malevolence.
   So be it; what should such a wretch as I do now?
Who will come with me and guide my groping feet? Here
    lies
One who would help me were she living; she is dead.
I had a brace of fine sons once; where are they now?
What of that robust strength I once had? Will it get
My daily food? – Creon, why must you kill me outright?
Yes, you will kill me, if you banish me from the land.
I am no cringing suppliant, to wind my hands
About your knees. I was a king; and I will not,
Because fortune is false to me, betray myself.
CREON: You say well, that you will not clasp my knees; and I,
For my part, will not let you stay on Theban soil.
[*To Attendants*] Take up Eteocles' body and carry it indoors.
Throw out the other body beyond our boundaries
To lie unburied – a fit end for one who came
With allies to destroy the city of his birth.
And let this be proclaimed to all our citizens:
'Whoever is found covering this corpse with earth
Or laying ritual wreaths, shall answer with his life.'

Now cease your tears over these bodies, Antigone,
And take yourself indoors. Live a maid one day more;
Tomorrow Fate gives you as bride to Haemon's bed.

ANTIGONE: Dear father, pain and misery enclose us round.
My heart is torn for you even more than for the dead;
Your sorrows are not light and shade, but, from your birth,
The pattern moves through one unvaried sombreness.
— You, Creon, the new king of Thebes, I ask you why
You inflict the cruelty of exile on my father?
Why must you, for a helpless corpse, rewrite old laws?

CREON: These are Eteocles' decisions, not my own.

ANTIGONE: A madman made them, and a fool now honours
them.

CREON: How so? Am I not right to carry out commands?

ANTIGONE: Wicked commands spoken in malice — no, you
are not!

CREON: Is it not justice that he should be thrown to dogs?

ANTIGONE: All law forbids the kind of justice you demand.

CREON: He was no foreigner, yet became Thebes' enemy.

ANTIGONE: And for that, he has forfeited his life to Fate.

CREON: Then let him forfeit burial too.

ANTIGONE: He came to Thebes
To claim his just inheritance: was that a crime?

CREON: I tell you, he shall not be given burial.

ANTIGONE: Then let the state forbid it! I will bury him.

CREON: Then you will bury your own body at his side.

ANTIGONE: A title of honour — one grave for two faithful
friends.

CREON [*to Attendants*]: You there! Arrest this woman, take
her into the house.

ANTIGONE: My arms are round my brother, I will not let go.

CREON: The decree of fate, my girl, runs counter to your
choice.

ANTIGONE: Learn this decree too: You shall not outrage the
dead.

CREON: No living hand shall spread the damp dust on this
　　　corpse.

ANTIGONE: Relent, I beg you, Creon, for his mother's sake.

CREON: Begging is useless; you will gain nothing.

ANTIGONE:　　　　　　　　　　　　　　At least
　　Let me bring water and wash his body.

CREON:　　　　　　　　　　　　　No; this too
　　The state forbids.

ANTIGONE:　　　　Then let me bind his gaping wounds.

CREON: Impossible. All pious duties are forbidden.

ANTIGONE: Dear brother! Then I give your lips a farewell
　　　kiss.

CREON: Silence! These tears are unpropitious for your
　　　marriage.

ANTIGONE: You think I'll marry Haemon? No, not while I
　　　live!

CREON: Oh, yes, you'll have to. Where and how can you
　　　escape?

ANTIGONE: That night shall number me among the Danaids.

CREON: Brazen defiance! Do you hear that, Oedipus?

ANTIGONE: See here – I swear it with my hand on this sword-
　　　blade.

CREON: And why are you so desperate to avoid this marriage?

ANTIGONE: I will share my unhappy father's banishment.

CREON: That is a noble thought, but somewhat foolish too.

ANTIGONE: And this you may know further – I will die with
　　　him.

CREON: Away now, leave this country! You'll not kill my
　　　son.

　　[Exit CREON.]

OEDIPUS: Dear daughter, your love warms my heart. And
　　　yet –

ANTIGONE: Father,
　　How could I marry, while you wander forth alone?

OEDIPUS: Stay here, be happy. I'll endure my own troubles.

ANTIGONE: And who will give you all the care a blind man needs?

OEDIPUS: My fate will lead me. Where I fall, there I will lie.

ANTIGONE: Where is the famous solver of riddles, Oedipus?

OEDIPUS: Dead. One day raised my fortune, one day cancelled it.

ANTIGONE: Then I must share your fortune.

OEDIPUS: For a child to share
In her blind father's exile is a shameful fate.

ANTIGONE: Not shameful; noble rather, if her ways are wise.

OEDIPUS: Then – guide me, so that I may touch your mother's face.

ANTIGONE: Reach out your hand and touch her – old, and dearly loved.

OEDIPUS: Dear mother, dear wife, what long suffering you bore!

ANTIGONE: A world of grief is gathered in this piteous frame.

OEDIPUS: Where is Eteocles' body? Where is Polyneices?

ANTIGONE: They lie close by you, stretched out at each other's side.

OEDIPUS: Now lay my sightless hands upon the face of each.

ANTIGONE: These were your sons; there, touch them with your hand.

OEDIPUS: Dear sons,
I mourn your grievous death, as grievous as my loss.

ANTIGONE: O Polyneices! Your name is always dear to me.

OEDIPUS: Now, daughter, comes the truth of Loxias' oracle.

ANTIGONE: What oracle? Have you more misery to tell?

OEDIPUS: I shall reach Athens as a wanderer, and there die.

ANTIGONE: Which of the Attic fortresses shall welcome you?

OEDIPUS: Colonus, where Poseidon's sacred horses graze.
But come, we must be going. Since you are resolved
To share my exile, take my arm and lead the way.

ANTIGONE: To exile, then, with all its weariness.
               Take my hand, father; I'll be your fair wind
               And give you a safe voyage.

OEDIPUS: There, daughter, I am coming.
               You must now be my sorrowful guide.

ANTIGONE: Sorrowful indeed I am,
               More than any other girl in Thebes.

OEDIPUS: Where shall I find safe footing?
               Child, give me my stick.

ANTIGONE: This way, this way, where I am guiding you.
               Place your foot this way, this way.
               Your strength is faint as a dream.

OEDIPUS: Do you hear me, Creon, do you see me –
               You who drive an old man from his native
                   soil?
               Let the world hear and see what I suffer!

ANTIGONE: Why harp on suffering, suffering?
               Justice does not see suffering,
               Still less does she punish
               The insensate folly which inflicts it.

OEDIPUS: I am the man whose name was exalted to
                   heaven
               In grateful songs of triumph
               When I solved the baffling riddle of the dog-
                   maiden.

ANTIGONE: Why hark back to the dark days of the
                   Sphinx?
               That victory was long ago – enough of it!
               This dark day's misery, this anguish of
                   exile,
               This wandering search for a place to die,
               Was waiting for you, father.
               I leave behind girls who are my friends,
               Who weep to see me go far from my home,
               Far from protection or comfort.

Alas! I shall reap fame
For my example of duty
Towards my father in his misfortunes.
On me the burden falls
Of cruelty meted out to you, and to my
    brother
Carried forth a helpless corpse, unburied.
Father, I will go at night and bury him,
If I have to die for it!

OEDIPUS: Say good-bye to the girls you knew here.

ANTIGONE: No; my own tears are enough.

OEDIPUS: Then cry for help at altars of the gods.

ANTIGONE: The gods are weary of my troubles.

OEDIPUS: Appeal to Dionysus at Semele's tomb
             Where Bacchants dance in the hills.

ANTIGONE: Appeal to Dionysus?
             To the god for whose honour, in days past,
             I dressed in a Theban fawnskin
             And danced the holy mountain-dance of
                 Semele –
             An act of worship that won me no reward?

ORESTES

CHARACTERS

ELECTRA, *daughter of Agamemnon*

HELEN, *wife of Menelaus and sister of Clytemnestra*

CHORUS *of women of Argos*

ORESTES, *son of Agamemnon*

MENELAUS, *brother of Agamemnon*

PYLADES, *friend of Orestes*

TYNDAREOS, *father of Clytemnestra and Helen*

HERMIONE, *daughter of Helen*

MESSENGER, *an old servant of Agamemnon*

A PHRYGIAN, *a slave of Helen*

APOLLO

*

The Scene is in the royal palace at Argos.

ORESTES *lies asleep on a bed*; ELECTRA *is beside him*

ELECTRA: There is no fate so terrifying to describe,
   No bodily pain or heaven-sent cruelty so sharp,
   Which human flesh may not be destined to endure.
   Tantalus, 'the fortunate' – I do not mock his fall –
   The son of Zeus (so legend has it), floats in mid air
   Dreading the rock that leans and lours above his head,
   And, as they say, suffers this punishment because,
   When the gods welcomed him, a man, to equal place
   At their own table, he did not discipline his tongue –
   Unmanly weakness! Tantalus begot Pelops;
   His son was Atreus – and for him the spinning Fates
   Drew out a thread of anger, doomed him to make war
   On his own brother Thyestes. Why should I spell out
   The horrible story? Atreus killed Thyestes' sons,
   And set their flesh before him at a feast. I pass
   In silence the aftermath of that; and then Atreus
   Had two sons by his Cretan wife Aërope:
   The famous Agamemnon – if 'fame' is the word –
   And Menelaus. He became husband of the woman
   The gods hate, Helen; Agamemnon's infamous bride
   Was Clytemnestra, whose name every Hellene knows.
   By her he had three daughters, Chrysothemis, Iphigenia,
   And me, Electra; and one son, Orestes – all
   Calling that execrable fiend mother. And she
   Devised and cast a woven snare without escape
   And killed her husband – with what purpose, is no matter
   For an unmarried girl to tell; this mystery
   I leave to the world's judgement. Then Apollo spoke
   He induced Orestes – was the god wrong? Why should I
   Accuse him? – to perform an action which has not
   Gained universal applause: to kill his own mother.
   And yet he killed her in obedience to Apollo;
   And in the killing I took what part a woman could.

Since then Orestes, wasted with a fierce disease,
Lies where he fell, here on this pitiful fevered bed,
His mother's blood like a charioteer wielding the whip
Of insanity – for I will not name those Powers whose terror
Ravages him, the 'Kindly Goddesses'. Today
Is the sixth day since fire consumed and purified
Our mother's murdered body; all this time no food
Has passed his lips; he has not washed; he lies huddled
Under his cloak, and in short periods of relief
He knows himself, and weeps; then suddenly, like a colt
Throwing off the yoke, he leaps from bed and rages round.

The assembly of Argive citizens has decreed that we,
As matricides, shall be debarred from shelter, fire,
Or speech, by everyone; and today they meet to cast
Their votes, whether or not we must be stoned to death.

We have indeed one hope, such as it is, of living:
Menelaus has come back from Troy. After long years
Of storm-tossed wandering, he has reached Nauplia, where
   his ships,
Riding at anchor, crowd the harbour. And his wife
Helen, source of all sorrow, he has sent on ahead
To our house – last night; he knew that, if she came by day,
She would be stoned by those whose sons were killed at Troy.
She is indoors, weeping for her sister Clytemnestra
And all the misery of our house. Yet in her grief
She has some comfort; when she sailed to Troy, she left
At home her daughter Hermione; Menelaus then
Brought the girl here from Sparta, and entrusted her
To my mother to bring up; and now Hermione
Is a joy to Helen and helps her to forget her troubles.

I gaze down the whole length of the road, hoping to see
Menelaus come. Unless he finds some way to save
Our lives, all other hopes are built on shifting sand.
A house gripped by misfortune is in desperate straits.

   [*Enter* HELEN.]

HELEN: Daughter of Clytemnestra and of Agamemnon,
    Electra, so many years deprived of womanhood –
    Oh, how could you? and how could your unhappy
        brother,
    Orestes, be the man to take his mother's life? –
    Speaking with you, I catch no taint from what you did;
    The blame for that I lay on Phoebus. But I weep
    For Clytemnestra. She was my sister. Since that day
    When, in a god-sent ecstasy – that was the truth –
    I sailed to Troy, I had not seen her. Now I feel
    Lonely and lost, and weep for what has happened to us.

ELECTRA: Why need I tell you, Helen, what you can see
        yourself –
    That Agamemnon's son lies crushed by circumstance?
    I sit here sleepless by this pitiable corpse –
    A corpse he is, save for a tenuous catch of breath.
    For what he suffers, why should I blame *him*? But you –
    You and your husband, crowned with happiness and success,
    Come home to find *us* overwhelmed with misery.

HELEN: How many days has he been lying on this bed?

ELECTRA: Ever since the day he shed the blood that gave him
        life.

HELEN: Pitiful son! Pitiful mother, to die so!

ELECTRA: The agonies he suffers have exhausted him.

HELEN: Electra, will you – please – do something that I ask?

ELECTRA: I would – but I am not free; I must stay with my
        brother.

HELEN: Will you go for me, Electra, to my sister's grave?

ELECTRA: You mean – my mother's grave? What for?

HELEN: To pour out wine,
    And to lay on the mound an offering of my hair.

ELECTRA: What law prevents *you* visiting your sister's grave?

HELEN: I shrink from being seen in Argos.

ELECTRA: Good: it's time
    You felt some shame for leaving home the way you did.

HELEN: What you have said is just, Electra, but not kind.

ELECTRA: What is this shame you feel before the citizens?

HELEN: I am afraid of the men whose sons were killed at Troy.

ELECTRA: You may well be; your name is execrated here.

HELEN: So, save me from this fear; do for me what I ask.

ELECTRA: To stand and see my mother's grave – I could not do it.

HELEN: To send these gifts by servants would show disrespect.

ELECTRA: Then why do you not send your daughter Hermione?

HELEN: A young girl should not walk alone through crowded streets.

ELECTRA: But she could pay the gifts due for her bringing-up.

HELEN: You are quite right, Electra. I'll do as you say. –
Hermione! Come out here, my dear.

[*Enter* HERMIONE.]

Now take this jar
For a libation, and these locks cut from my hair,
And go and stand by Clytemnestra's tomb, and pour
Round it this honey mixed with milk and bubbling wine;
Then climb the mound and say these words: Your sister Helen
Sends this libation as a gift, being herself
Afraid to approach your monument, through terror of
The Argive citizens. Beg her to have kindly thoughts
For me, and you, and for my husband, and for these
Two unhappy children, whom Apollo has destroyed.
And speak my promise that I will discharge in full
All gifts and ceremonies due to a sister dead.
Go quickly, dear child, and when you have paid these rites
Over the grave, remember, come straight home again.

[*Exit* HERMIONE. HELEN *goes indoors.*]

ELECTRA: What potent evil lives in native quality –
While sound and noble natures possess enduring strength.

You saw how she had cut her hair off near the ends
So as not to spoil her beauty? She's the same woman
She always was. – May the gods hate you, for the ruin
You've brought on me, and Orestes, and on all Hellas!
Oh, miserable life!

    [*The* CHORUS *begin to enter.*]

              Now here come my friends, to join
Their sad voices in sympathy with mine. I fear
They'll wake him from his rest, and make me drown my
    eyes
In tears, to watch my brother in his raving fit.
– Dear friends, tread softly! Hush! No noise! It's kind of you
To come, friends; but if you wake him you'll break my
    heart.

CHORUS: Hush! Tread lightly in soft sandals;
            Make no noise, no sound.

ELECTRA: Keep over that side;
            Further, please – well away from his bed.

CHORUS: Of course, we'll go over there.

ELECTRA: Quieter, softer, friends! Make your voice
            As thin as the breath of a reed pipe.

CHORUS: All right, I will whisper like a muted flute.

ELECTRA: Like that – quieter still!
            This way; come with hushed steps.
            Explain to me, what has brought you?
            All this time he has lain there, where he fell.

CHORUS: How is he? Tell us about him, dear Electra.

ELECTRA: What can I say, but that he is deadly sick?
            He still breathes; sometimes he cries out in
                pain.

CHORUS: How terrible! Poor boy!

ELECTRA: You will kill him, if you make him open his
                eyes
            Now, when at last
            The gentle blessing of sleep has come to him.

CHORUS: For his horrible deed, done at a god's com-
        mand,
        And for his suffering, I pity him.

ELECTRA: Apollo had no right to speak such words;
        The thing he commanded was a crime,
        When from the tripod of Themis
        He prescribed the unnatural murder of my
        mother.

CHORUS: Do you see? He stirs under the cloak.

ELECTRA: It was you who broke his sleep,
        With your thoughtless shouting.

CHORUS: I think he moved without waking.

ELECTRA: Can't you leave us alone?
        Get away from the house quickly,
        And stop making a noise.

CHORUS: He's fast asleep.

ELECTRA: I think he is.

CHORUS: Divine night, holy night,
        Giver of sleep to mortals in their pain,
        Rise from the deep dark
        On hurrying wings to Agamemnon's palace.
        Trouble has crushed us, pain overwhelms us,
        Life has gone from us, died in us.

ELECTRA: You are disturbing him. Hush! Take care.
        If you speak loudly, keep away from his bed.
        Dear friend, allow him the gentle gift of sleep.

CHORUS: How will his suffering end? Tell us.

ELECTRA: In death. What other end?
        He has no desire for food.

CHORUS: It is clear, then, what must follow.

ELECTRA: Phoebus made our lives a sacrifice
        When he laid upon us
        This unnatural, this heart-rending deed,
        To kill our mother, who killed our father.

CHORUS: Just it may have been.

ELECTRA: Right it was not.
              My mother, you who brought me into the
                  world,
              You killed, and you were killed:
              You destroyed our father, and
              Destroyed us too, the children of your blood.
              We share the death we dealt you; we are
                  dead.
              You dwell in the lifeless world;
              My greater part of life is spent already
              In cries of sorrow, night-long tears.
              Husbandless, childless, I drag out my life
              In misery from year to endless year.

CHORUS: Come here, Electra – close; look at your brother
    now.
  Could he perhaps have died, and we not notice it?
  I am uneasy; he lies too inert, too still.

      [ORESTES speaks without stirring.]

ORESTES: O magic charm of sleep! With what comfort you
      came
  To help me in my sickness! How I needed you!
  O sovereign Lethe, death of sorrow! With what skill
  You tend the sufferer who invokes your heavenly help!
  – Why am I here? How did I get here? When did I –?
  I can't remember anything. The past is blank.

ELECTRA: Dear brother, I am happy that you have had some
      sleep.
  Would you like me to hold your hand, and lift you up?

ORESTES: Yes, hold me, hold me. Wipe my lips clean; they
      are sore
  And foul with sticky froth. So are my eyes. Wipe them.

ELECTRA: There; is that better? I will nurse you like a slave –
  Why not? I am your sister; I do it willingly.

ORESTES: Let my back rest against you, so. My hair is damp;
  Push it back off my face. My eyes don't see clearly.

ELECTRA: Poor head – your soft, curled hair all dirty and
    uncombed,
  Like a wild man! It's so long since you washed yourself.

ORESTES: Lay me down flat again. After the raging fit
  Has passed, my nerves die, my limbs have no strength in
    them.

ELECTRA: There now. When one is ill, one's thankful for a
    bed;
  To lie in bed is wearisome, but necessary.

ORESTES: Help me sit up again and face the other way.
  I'm hard to please; being ill makes me feel desperate.

ELECTRA: Perhaps you'd like to stand; it's a long time since
    you
  Set foot to earth. You need a change from lying there.

ORESTES: I will. To stand up feels like being well. It's good
  To *feel* well, even when the feeling's far from true.

ELECTRA: Now, brother dear, I want to tell you something,
    while
  The Furies still let you remain in your right mind.

ORESTES: You have some news? If it's good news I'm glad of
    it;
  If it's more trouble, what I have now is enough.

ELECTRA: Your father's brother Menelaus has come home;
  His ships lie anchored in the harbour of Nauplia.

ORESTES: Menelaus home? He has the power to save us both!
  He is our uncle, and deeply in our father's debt.

ELECTRA: Yes, he has come; and listen – here is proof of that:
  He has brought his wife Helen back from the walls of Troy.

ORESTES: If he had come alone he'd be a happier man;
  If he's brought her, he has brought a load of trouble home.

ELECTRA: Oh, what a vicious pair of daughters Tyndareos
  Fathered, two names of infamy throughout Hellas!

ORESTES: Then you be different from that wicked pair. You
    can.
  And don't just *say* you will be; let your heart be good.

ELECTRA: Oh, brother, brother, your eyes are wild. How rapidly
　You change – one moment, health; the next, insanity!
ORESTES: Mother! No, no! Don't set them at me, I implore you –
　Those female fiends with bloody faces wreathed in snakes!
　They're here! They're coming closer! Now they leap at me!
ELECTRA: Brother, don't break my heart; stay quietly on your bed.
　These sights you see are not real; you imagine them.
ORESTES: Phoebus Apollo! They have dog's jaws and gorgon's eyes;
　They'll kill me – priestesses of hell, dread goddesses!
ELECTRA: I will not let you go! I'll wind my arms round you –
　Stop struggling like a miserable madman, stop!
ORESTES: Let go! You're one of these same Furies killing me.
　You've gripped me fast, to fling me into Tartarus!
ELECTRA: What shall I do? Who can I call upon for help?
　No hope, since we have made the gods our enemies!
ORESTES: Bring me my horn-tipped bow – Apollo gave it me
　And told me it would keep at bay these goddesses
　When they unnerved me with this raving lunacy.
　　[ELECTRA hands him the bow.]
　A goddess will be wounded by a mortal's aim
　If she won't move herself and get out of my sight!
　You can hear me, can't you? Don't you see this powerful bow,
　These feathered arrows coming at you – there! and there!
　　[He shoots two arrows into the air.]
　Ha, ha! Well, move, then! Spread your wings and scale the sky!
　And tell Apollo the blame is on his oracles!
　Ah!
　Why am I raving, panting, gasping? Where am I?

I was in bed . . . The storm's blown over. Now there's calm.

    [ELECTRA *is sitting on the ground with her head wrapped*
    in her gown.]

Sister, uncover your head; don't weep. I am ashamed
To think I make you share my troubles, and inflict
My horrible sickness on a woman. Do not be
Shattered by what I suffer. You, I know, consented
In word, but it was I who shed our mother's blood.
I blame Apollo; he urged me to this hideous act,
Encouraged me with promises – and did nothing.
I believe my father, had I asked him face to face
Whether I ought to kill her, would have gripped my hand
And begged, implored me not to lift a sword against
My mother, since that could not bring him back to life,
While it doomed me to the agonies I now endure.

    Come, then, dear sister, uncover your head, and don't
Cry any more, however desperate things are.
And when you see me losing heart, support me and
Comfort me in the horror of my insanity;
And when you weep, I will be at your side, and speak
Loving encouragement. This is the kind of help
We ought to give in time of need to those we love.

    So come, Electra, go indoors now and lie down
And give your weary eyes the sleep they sadly need,
And take something to eat and drink, and have a bath.
If you collapse, exhausted by your care of me,
Or catch some sickness, I am lost; since, as you see,
I have no other friend or helper, only you.

ELECTRA: I won't collapse, or fail you. I will die or live
With you. Indeed I have no choice; for if you die –
What can I do, a woman? Alone, without friend,
Father, or brother, how can I survive? I'll go,
And do as you advise. Now lie down on your bed,
And if these terrors come to scare you from your rest,
Try to ignore them; just stay there and keep quite still.

Such sickness, even when more imaginary than real,
Still racks the sufferer with anguish and despair.

> [ELECTRA *goes in*; ORESTES *lies on the bed.*]

CHORUS: Hear us, have pity!
               Hound-swift, wing-borne
               Sovereign divinities, ruling
               Your kingdom of tears and groans
               Where dance and song are joyless;
               Black-visaged Benevolences
               Brandished across the taut sky,
               Exacting justice, exacting the price of blood:
               We implore, we beseech you
               For the son of Agamemnon.
               Release him, let him forget
               The fury and frenzy of madness!
               O unhappy Orestes,
               For the hideous task appointed you,
               For the obedience that destroyed you,
               When in the Delphic temple
               You heard the voice of Apollo
               Chanted from the tripod throne,
               Echoed from deep caverns in the womb of
                   earth!

               O Zeus, listen!
               What mercy is there?
               Pitiful son, what is this agony,
               This blood-hunt, this persecution?
               There is a fiend of vengeance
               That drowns your life in tears,
               Sinks your house in your mother's blood,
               Destroys your mind with madness.
               I mourn, I groan, I grieve.
               The greatest happiness is not permanent
               In the world of men;

But the storms of God rise against it,
Like a light sailing-ship they shatter it,
Terrors and disasters roll around it,
Till crashing waves close over death.
And this was the house of Tantalus,
Born from the marriage of gods —
A house that claimed my reverence
More than any house I have known.

Look! Here comes King Menelaus, adorned
With magnificent robes
Which proclaim him a son of this glorious
     house,
Of the line which Tantalus fathered.
Hail! you who commanded the thousand ships
That sailed against Troy!
With the favour of gods and of Fortune, you
Have achieved the desire that you prayed for.

[*Enter* MENELAUS.]

MENELAUS: My father's house! To see you now on my return
From Troy brings pleasure, yet no less is cause for grief.
Is there another home so miserably enmeshed
In crime and anguish, as this house? I know of none.
I learnt of Agamemnon's fate, and how he died
Slaughtered by his wife, when I put in to Malea.
There Glaucus, son of Nereus, who speaks prophecies
To sailors, an infallible divinity,
Stood visible before me, and pronounced these words:
'Menelaus, your brother lies dead, struck by his own wife
As he stood naked in the purifying bath.'
This news filled me and all my men with tears of grief.
When we reached Nauplia, and my wife had started out
Already for this house, and I was looking forward
To embracing Agamemnon's son Orestes, and
His mother, thinking all was well with them — I heard

From one of the fishermen about this atrocious murder
Of Tyndareos' daughter. So, young women, if you know
Where Orestes is, the perpetrator of this act,
Tell me. When I left Sparta for the voyage to Troy,
Orestes was a baby in Clytemnestra's arms.
Even face to face, I would not recognize him now.

ORESTES: Menelaus, I am the man you're asking for, Orestes.
I'll tell you my whole wretched story willingly;
But first I kneel and clasp your knees, a suppliant.
My prayers must serve for holy wreaths and claim your ear:
Save me! You come in my last moment of despair.

MENELAUS: Ye gods! What am I looking at? Some ghost from
hell?

ORESTES: You are right; terror and pain make me a living
corpse.

MENELAUS: This savage look, this matted hair – I'm sorry for
you.

ORESTES: What you describe is outward; my torments are
real.

MENELAUS: Your eyes are glazed with horror; your look
frightens me.

ORESTES: I no longer exist; only my name is left.

MENELAUS: Words could not picture such ghastly disfigure-
ment.

ORESTES: This is myself – my unhappy mother's murderer.

MENELAUS: I heard. Don't harp on horror – be sparing in
your speech.

ORESTES: The gods have not spared me; I sink in agonies.

MENELAUS: What agonies? What is the disease that ravages
you?

ORESTES: Conscience. I recognize the horror of what I did.

MENELAUS: I advise you to be clear, not clever. What do you
mean?

ORESTES: This: what destroys me more than anything is
grief –

MENELAUS: A formidable divinity; yet curable.

ORESTES: And insane fits, which punish me for my mother's death.

MENELAUS: When did this madness first attack you – on what day?

ORESTES: The day I raised the mound over my mother's grave.
  I waited for the pyre to cool; and in the night,
  When I went to take up her bones, this madness came.

MENELAUS: Was anyone at hand to help you?

ORESTES: Pylades,
  Who shared with me the bloody work of killing her.

MENELAUS: And in your fits what kind of sights appear to you?

ORESTES: I seemed to see three women; they were black as night.

MENELAUS: I will not name them; but I know what Powers you mean.

ORESTES: They are to be feared; you're wise to shrink from naming them.

MENELAUS: And these drive you to madness with your mother's blood?

ORESTES: They drive me, hound me, lash me – it is agony!

MENELAUS: This is not strange; such deeds must earn such suffering.

ORESTES: Well, I can still unload this guilt and misery –

MENELAUS: Don't talk of suicide. That would be a fool's way out.

ORESTES: No – on Apollo. My revenge was his command.

MENELAUS: A command showing some ignorance of law and right.

ORESTES: What are the gods? We don't know – but we are their slaves.

MENELAUS: Well, you obeyed him; doesn't he now come to your help?

ORESTES [*sarcastically*]: Oh yes — he's *going* to help me. That's
    the way of gods.

MENELAUS: And how long is it since your mother — breathed
    her last?

ORESTES: Only six days. Her funeral embers are still warm.

MENELAUS: Those goddesses lost no time in pursuing you.

ORESTES: I can't argue about gods; but I'm a loyal son.

MENELAUS: And what advantage has it brought — this loyalty?

ORESTES: None yet; and, as I see it, that means none at all.

MENELAUS: What is the city's attitude towards your crime?

ORESTES: They all hate me. No citizen will speak to me.

MENELAUS: Have you not cleansed your hands from blood in
    form of law?

ORESTES: How can I, when they lock me out from every
    house?

MENELAUS: Which of the citizens demand your banishment?

ORESTES: Oeax. At Troy he was my father's enemy.

MENELAUS: Of course; he avenges Palamedes' blood on you.

ORESTES: I had no part in it. And destruction crushes me
  From a third source.

MENELAUS: Who's that? Aegisthus' friends, per-
    haps?

ORESTES: Yes, they insult me. They now have the city's ear.

MENELAUS: Does Argos now let you possess your father's
    throne?

ORESTES: Is it likely, when with one voice they demand my
    death?

MENELAUS: What are they actually doing? Try to keep to
    facts.

ORESTES: The vote that finds us guilty will be taken today.

MENELAUS: Will it be banishment? Or death? Or less than
    death?

ORESTES: The citizens of Argos will stone us to death.

MENELAUS: Why don't you get across the frontier, if that's
    so?

ORESTES: We are in a trap; there are armed men on guard all round.

MENELAUS: Your private enemies, or the regular Argive force?

ORESTES: Every Argive is on duty, to make sure I die.
As simple as that.

MENELAUS: A desperate predicament.

ORESTES: Menelaus, all my hope rests upon you alone.
Look: here am I, in the lowest depth. You have come home
Successful. I am your brother's son. Give me a share
Of your well-being. Don't keep for yourself alone
The happiness you've won, but take your turn in griefs
And pay where it is due the debt you owe my father.
Friends who in times of trouble are no longer friends
Mock the true force of friendship with an empty name.

CHORUS: Why, see! Here comes the royal Spartan, Tyndareos,
Hurrying in spite of all his years. His robe is black,
And his head shorn, in mourning for his daughter's death.

ORESTES: This seals my fate, Menelaus. Tyndareos is coming,
The man whom, more than any other, I would avoid.
After what I did, how can I meet him face to face?
When I was a small child he brought me up; and often
Kissed me, and carried me on his shoulder, calling me
Agamemnon's boy; both he and Leda, and the two
Dioscori, always made much of me. And now –
O wretched, reckless wickedness! What a return
I have made them! Where is darkness fit to hide my face?
What veil of cloud can save me from Tyndareos' eye?
    [Enter TYNDAREOS.]

TYNDAREOS: Tell me, where can I find Menelaus my son-in-law?
I heard just now, standing by Clytemnestra's grave
To pour libations, that after all these years he had come
Safe home to Nauplia with his wife. Take me to him.

It's good to see an old friend after many years;
I want to welcome him, and clasp him by the hand.

MENELAUS: Greeting, Tyndareos, marriage-partner with
    great Zeus!

TYNDAREOS: Menelaus! Greeting, my dear son-in-law. – Ah,
    look!

The curse of life is never knowing what you'll meet.
Here he is – the abominable mother-murderer,
With poisoned lightning flashing from his adder's eye!
Menelaus, you don't speak to this polluted wretch?

MENELAUS: Why not? I loved my brother, and this is his son.

TYNDAREOS: Was this unnatural monster Agamemnon's son?

MENELAUS: Yes. I must honour kinship, even in distress.

TYNDAREOS: Ten years in Asia made you a barbarian.

MENELAUS: To honour kinship at all times is a Greek law.

TYNDAREOS: It's also Greek law not to override the laws.

MENELAUS: To a sober view, compulsion makes a man a
    slave.

TYNDAREOS: All right – you hold that principle. I never will.

MENELAUS: Quite so: anger combined with old age is unwise.

TYNDAREOS: In this man's case, to ask what's wise or what's
    unwise

Is not the point. Since right and wrong are clear as day
To us all, what man was ever born more void of sense,
Conscience, or decency, than he? He never glanced
At processes of justice; he made no appeal
To the common standards of Hellenic law. Clearly,
When Agamemnon gasped his life out, with his skull
Split by my daughter's weapon – an outrageous act
Which I'll never defend – his duty was to take
Lawful proceedings, prosecute for murder, and
Expel his mother from the palace. In that way
From his misfortune he would have won a name for wise
Behaviour, would have preserved both law and piety.
But now, his life bears the same curse his mother bore.

Rightly regarding her as criminal, he made
Himself, by killing his mother, a worse criminal.

　　I'll ask you this one question, Menelaus. Suppose
Orestes here were murdered by his wedded wife,
And in revenge his son then shed his mother's blood,
And after that his son again requited murder
With murder – where will you set a bound to misery?
Our ancestors established a sound principle:
The man guilty of murder they forbade to intrude
On sight or presence of the citizens; his crime
Must be atoned by exile, not by blood for blood;
Otherwise always one man's lot is to be involved
With murder, taking on his hands the last blood-guilt.

　　I, for one, hate a wicked woman; most of all
My daughter, who killed her husband. And your wife Helen
Will get no praise from me, nor will I speak to her.
You went to Troy to fetch home a bad wife: and I
Don't envy you. I'll back the law with all my power,
To check this bestial, bloodthirsty rage, which still
Destroys our cities, and brings Hellas near to death.

　　– You pitiful wretch! What did you feel, that moment
　　　when
Your mother knelt before you, bared her breast, and begged
For mercy? I did not see that horror; but the thought
Still scalds my eyes with grievous tears. Clearly the gods
Hate you, and with these raving lunacies and terrors
Punish you for your mother's death; this witnesses
To all I have said. With such a sight before my eyes,
What other proof is needed of your wickedness?

　　– Be warned, then, Menelaus; and don't let your wish
To help this man lead you to side against the gods.
The death my daughter suffered was her just desert;
But it was not for him to execute sentence.

　　In all other respects I have had a happy life –
But for my daughters. There I have not been fortunate.

CHORUS: The man is to be envied who has been fortunate
In his children, and has avoided dire calamity.

ORESTES: Tyndareos, I am afraid to plead my cause with you,
Since what I say inevitably will give offence.
Yet I will speak, and in my speech try to forget
Your old age, which unnerves my tongue; and let my words
March on a clear path. But at this moment I am trembling
At your white hair. I know I'm a polluted man –
I killed my mother. But that is not the sole truth.
I avenged my father; and for that act I am pure.

    What was my duty? To your double charge I make
A double answer. First, my father planted me,
Your daughter bore me – a field sown with another's seed.
Without the father there can be no child; therefore,
I reasoned, the prime author of my life must have
My loyalty, more than she who supplied care and food.
Secondly, this daughter of yours – I blush to say 'my
    mother' –
Indulged in lecherous and unlawful intercourse
In a lover's bed. In naming her disgrace I name
My own; yet I will speak. Aegisthus was the man,
The secret husband. Him I killed; and to complete
The sacrifice, my mother too. It was a crime –
But I avenged my father.

               As for your demand
That I be stoned to death, my answer is that I
Am a benefactor of all Hellas. For if wives
Grow bold enough to kill their husbands, and then fly
For refuge to their children, snaring their soft hearts
With bared breasts, husband-murder will become a sport,
Excused by any trifle. What you loudly call
My 'crime' at least has made that ploy improbable.
I killed my mother because I justly hated her.
She, when her husband, in the service of all Hellas,
Far from his home, led our armed forces, then forsook

Chastity, and betrayed him. Aware of her own guilt,
She laid no sentence on herself, but, to avoid
Her husband's sentence, laid the punishment on him
And killed my father! In the gods' name – and I know
It's not the time, when I am justifying murder,
To call on gods – yet, suppose, now, I had approved
My mother's act by silence, what would my dead father
Have done to me? Would he not loathe me, haunt my life
With raging Furies? Or do you think those goddesses
Rally to help my mother, but when my father falls
By a worse outrage, take no notice? It was you
Ruined my life, when you begot your vile daughter.
Her shameless action made me fatherless, made me
A matricide. Look at Telemachus: he did not
Murder Odysseus' wife Penelope, since she
Welcomed no second husband to her husband's bed,
But in her home chastity is honoured. Look at Apollo:
There from his shrine at the earth's centre he dispenses
Words of pure truth; what he commands, that we obey –
I killed my mother in obedience to him!
Call *him* polluted, then; stone *him* to death! The sin
Is his, not mine. What ought I to have done? Is God,
Then, powerless to absolve the guilt I lay on him?
He gave command; if he can't rescue me from death,
What refuge is left now for any man? My action
Was a right action; and don't tell me otherwise –
Though it proved ruinous to me. When marriage stands
Stable and pure, its harvest is a happy life;
Corrupted, it gives birth to unmixed misery.

CHORUS: It's always women who prove natural obstacles
    Placed in the path of men, to spoil their happiness.

TYNDAREOS: Since you are brazen in speech, and practise no
        restraint,
    But aim your answers to offend me, my resolve
    To see you dead shall burn the hotter for your words;

I'll happily add this task to that for which I came,
Namely, to pay last honours to my daughter's grave.
I'll come before the assembly of Argive citizens
And urge them – they'll not need much urging – to condemn
To death by stoning you and your sister. Indeed, she
Deserves death more than you, since she inflamed your rage
Against your mother, sending constant messages
Secretly to you, full of venom; telling you
Of dreams that Agamemnon sent, and how the Powers
Below the earth, no less than mortals here, condemned
Her adultery with Aegisthus, till she had ignited
The whole palace in one conflagration of hate.

   Menelaus, I warn you – and what I say I'll carry out:
Reckon the cost of having me for an enemy,
Reckon the value of our kinship; and refuse
To save this man's life in defiance of the gods.
Leave him to suffer death by public stoning – or
Never hope to set foot again on Spartan soil.
You have heard me; now remember: don't reject your friends
Who reverence God and honour right, to choose instead
An impious criminal. Servants, conduct me home.

   [*Exit* TYNDAREOS.]

ORESTES: Go! Let what I must say now to your son-in-law
   Reach him uninterrupted by your sour old age.
   Menelaus, why are you pensive, pacing back and forth,
   Your mind distracted between two anxieties?

MENELAUS: Let me alone; I'm worried, and I want to think.
   I ask myself which way to turn, and find no answer.

ORESTES: Don't bring your pondering to a conclusion yet;
   Listen to what I have to say, and then decide.

MENELAUS: That is fair; have your say, then. Silence is
      sometimes
   Better than speech; and sometimes speech is preferable.

ORESTES: Then I will speak now. Many words carry more
      weight

Than few words, and are easier to understand.
   Menelaus, give me – not something that is your own;
But what my father gave to you, repay to me.
I don't mean wealth, possessions; if you save my life,
My life is the one dearest thing that I possess.
To ask your help is unjust; in return for this
You should help me – unjustly; as my father too
Unjustly gathered the Hellenes and marched off to Troy.
In this, Agamemnon did no wrong himself, but tried
To heal the unjust wrong committed by your wife.
You, then, should help me, and repay like with like. My
    father,
In the sweat of battle, as a true friend to his friends,
To help you get your wife back, sold his life for you.
So now, repay me that same debt you incurred then;
Labour one day for me, not ten long years; stand up
And save my life. That further debt, which Aulis owes
For Iphigenia's blood offered in sacrifice,
I make no claim for – I'm not asking you to kill
Hermione. In my present trouble, naturally
You have the advantage, and I am willing that you should.
But my life, and my sister's life so long deprived
Of marriage – grant this, for our unhappy father's sake.
If I die, I leave desolate my father's house.
'Nothing can be done,' you'll say. Is it not at such a time,
When nothing can be done, that friends should give their
    help?
When everything goes well, there is no need of friends;
If Fortune's in a helpful mood, that is enough.
   Menelaus, you love your wife – all Hellas thinks you do;
And that's not flattery to cajole you: in her name,
For Helen's sake, I kneel to you! – O miserable!
What have I sunk to? Yet I must, and swallow shame;
I'm begging for deliverance for our whole house.
My father's brother! Think that he from his dark home

Hears me; that his ghost hovers about your head, and speaks
My words, pleading my tears, my groans, my sufferings!
    I have spoken. I have entreated for my life, in hope
Of gaining that which all men crave, not I alone.
CHORUS: We too, though we are women, join our prayers
        with his
That you will help him in his need. You have the power.
MENELAUS: Orestes, I have a personal respect for you,
    And I would gladly share your burden of distress;
    Indeed it is our duty to lend a helping hand
    To relatives in time of trouble – if heaven grants
    The power to do so – to destroy their enemies
    And risk one's own life. How I wish the gods would grant
    This power! But I have come here worn with voyaging
    And hardship, carrying my single spear, with no
    Fighting-men at my back – a feeble company
    Of my surviving friends. In battle, certainly,
    We could not overpower the Argives; if we could
    Carry our point by tactful speech – well, that is now
    All we can hope for. Great things cannot be achieved
    Without great effort; only a fool would dream of it.
    When citizens are stirred to anger and violence,
    A raging fire is easier to control. But if
    You approach them gently, slack sail to the storm, and watch
    Your opportunity, calm will probably return;
    And when the sky clears, you can ask for what you please
    And get it. Citizens can be tender-hearted, can
    Be indignant. Choose your moment, and this quality
    Is invaluable. I'll go now to Tyndareos
    And try to induce him, and the city, to moderate
    Their fury. A ship with mainsheet drawn too taut will find
    Her deck awash; but slack the sheet – she rights herself.
    Gods hate extremists; so, in fact, do citizens.
    One thing I know: if I'm to save you, it must be
    By shrewdness, not defiance of superior strength.

You may imagine I could save you by main force:
Impossible. What can one man's sword avail against
The threatening facts you're faced with? I would not attempt
To beg Argos for mercy in any other case;
But as things are, we must; there's no alternative.

    [*Exit* MENELAUS.]

ORESTES: You coward! Did you once command an army?
    Yes —
To win a woman; not to help your friends. Traitor!
Do you run away? Do you turn your back on me? Have you
Forgotten Agamemnon? Then, father, you have
No friend to turn to in your need. I am betrayed;
There is no hope now. Argos will put me to death;
For my one hope of safety lay with Menelaus.
   — Who's that? Oh, it's my best of friends, Pylades, come
From Phocis! What a welcome sight! More welcome than
Calm sea to sailors is a trusty friend in need.

    [*Enter* PYLADES.]

PYLADES: I've been hurrying through the streets to find you,
    since I heard about
This assembly — yes, I saw them gathering — summoned to
    condemn
Both you and your sister; and they say the sentence will be
    death.
What is this? How are things with you? Dearest to me of my
    friends
Young or old, or of my family — yes, you are! Now, what's
    the news?

ORESTES: Here's my whole disastrous story in one word: I'm
    a dead man.

PYLADES: Then you'll dig a grave for me too. Friends share
    everything alike.

ORESTES: Menelaus has proved a traitor to my sister and to me.

PYLADES: No surprise, that a false woman's husband should
    turn false himself.

ORESTES: He came; but, for all the help he gave me, might
  have stayed away.

PYLADES: Menelaus really has come back at last, then?

ORESTES: Yes,
  at last;

  And, once back, he lost no time in openly betraying me.

PYLADES: That abominable wife of his – has he brought Helen
  home?

ORESTES: No, it wasn't he who brought her home to Argos.
  She brought him.

PYLADES: That one woman sent Achaeans to death by thousands. Where is she?

ORESTES: In my house here – if indeed I can any longer call it
  mine.

PYLADES: Tell me, Orestes – what did you ask Menelaus to
  do for you?

ORESTES: Not to stand aside and see me and my sister stoned
  to death.

PYLADES: Well, by all the gods! What did he say to that, I'd
  like to know?

ORESTES: He was very cautious – treacherous friends all do
  this to their friends.

PYLADES: What excuse did he put forward? I want the whole
  story clear.

ORESTES: Someone else came – the begetter of two daughters
  fair and chaste.

PYLADES: You mean Tyndareos? He must be furious at his
  daughter's death.

ORESTES: You are right. Menelaus slights my father for his
  father-in-law.

PYLADES: So he dares not stand by you in trouble and support
  your cause?

ORESTES: Not he. He'll be bold with women; he's no man to
  hold a spear.

PYLADES: Then you're in great danger. Are you sure your
  sentence will be death?

ORESTES: I am charged with murder; and the citizens will cast their votes.

PYLADES: Tell me, what point will their vote determine? That's what I fear most.

ORESTES: Life, or death. That's a short answer with a long corollary.

PYLADES: Well, escape, then! Take your sister with you and get away from here.

ORESTES: Haven't you noticed? We're surrounded by armed guards on every side.

PYLADES: Yes, I saw the streets were posted – ranks of armour everywhere.

ORESTES: We two are besieged like any city ringed with hostile troops.

PYLADES: Well, now ask for *my* news. Like you, I don't know which way to turn.

ORESTES: One disaster heaped upon another! Who's your enemy?

PYLADES: Strophius my father banished me in anger from his home.

ORESTES: Privately? Or on some charge against you that concerned the state?

PYLADES: I helped you to kill your mother; I am polluted, so he says.

ORESTES: Oh! Then my pollution promises to wound your life as well.

PYLADES: I'm no coward like Menelaus; this is something I must bear.

ORESTES: Aren't you afraid Argos may want to take your life as well as mine?

PYLADES: I'm a Phocian subject; Argos has no power to punish me.

ORESTES: With unscrupulous leadership, the rabble is a dangerous thing.

PYLADES: Yes; but under honest leaders they'll make honest policies.

ORESTES: True. Well, I'll go and address the people.

PYLADES: What
    will you say to them?

ORESTES: Now, suppose I tell them –

PYLADES: That your act was fully
    justified?

ORESTES: I avenged my father!

PYLADES: They might seize the chance
    and set on you.

ORESTES: Well, must I lurk here in silence and die like a
    coward?

PYLADES: No!

ORESTES: What then shall I do?

PYLADES: Suppose you stay here, is
    there any hope?

ORESTES: None at all.

PYLADES: But there's at least a hope of safety if
    you go?

ORESTES: With luck, it could happen.

PYLADES: Then to go is better than
    to stay.

ORESTES: Right; I'll go.

PYLADES: Even if the people kill you, you'll
    die honourably.

ORESTES: True; this way I avoid the name of coward –

PYLADES: More
    than by staying here.

ORESTES: And my cause is just.

PYLADES: At least it can appear so;
    cling to that.

ORESTES: There's a chance, too, they may pity me –

PYLADES: You're
    royal; that's a help.

ORESTES: Outraged by my father's murder.

PYLADES: All that's plain
   to everyone.

ORESTES: I must go; an ignominious death is cowardly.

PYLADES: I agree.

ORESTES: Should we tell my sister what I'm doing?

PYLADES: For the
   gods' sake, no!

ORESTES: Probably there'd be a scene, and tears.

PYLADES: And that
   would bring bad luck.

ORESTES: Clearly better to say nothing.

PYLADES: Better, and saves time
   as well.

ORESTES: There's one thing that could upset the plan.

PYLADES: What
   have you thought of now?

ORESTES: This: suppose the Furies drive me mad?

PYLADES: Then I'll
   look after you.

ORESTES: When my sickness comes, to touch me is revolting.

PYLADES: Not to me.

ORESTES: Take care you get no infection from me.

PYLADES: Think no
   more of it.

ORESTES: You won't shrink, then?

PYLADES: Why should I? I'm not a
   coward; I'm your friend.

ORESTES: Come, lead on, then; be my pilot.

PYLADES: Willingly; I'll
   see you through.

ORESTES: And first take me to my father's grave.

PYLADES: Why – what's
   the point of that?

ORESTES: I must beg him to protect me.

PYLADES: True; it's only right
    he should.

ORESTES: I'll not go within sight of my mother's.

PYLADES: She was your
    enemy.

  Come on, now, in case the Argive vote condemns you first,
      unheard.

  Put your arm around my shoulder. How this fever saps your
      strength!

  I care nothing what the rabble thinks; I'm not ashamed of
      you!

  We'll march straight through Argos! Why, how should I
      show myself a friend,

  If when you're so deep in danger I don't help you all I
      can?

ORESTES: Pylades, you prove the proverb, *Get you friends, not
    merely kin.*

  One man, of a different blood, whose temper's welded with
      your own,

  Makes a trustier friend in need than thousands of your
      family.

    [ORESTES *and* PYLADES *go out together.*]

CHORUS: That splendour of prosperity, that warlike
                  prowess
              Which flaunted its pride over Hellas
              And by the banks of Simois
              Has deserted the descendants of Atreus.
              The ebb of their full fortune began long ago
              When the house was cursed with a quarrel over
                  a golden lamb,
              And there followed that most piteous feasting
              And the slaughter of princes;
              Whence murder succeeding murder
              Found bloody fulfilment
              In the fate of the sons of Atreus.

That noble deed was not noble –
To pierce a parent's flesh with a fire-born
    blade,
And show to the radiant sun
The sword black-laced with gore.
'Crime in a just cause' is an impious sophistry,
An insanity breeding in evil hearts.
The unhappy daughter of Tyndareos
Screamed in terror of death: 'My son,
You outrage all sanctity if you kill your mother;
In honouring your debt to your father
You fetter your life to eternal infamy!'

What sickness, what weeping, what anguish
Is sharper than the sin that stains
A hand guilty of a mother's murder?
Such, such is the act whose accomplishment
Has destroyed the son of Agamemnon
With frenzied lunacy,
With Furies hounding to the death,
With fugitive eyes rolling in terror.
O wretched sinner, who saw
Her breast burst from her gold-embroidered
    gown,
And seeing, struck and slew his mother
To avenge the death his father suffered.

[*Enter* ELECTRA.]

ELECTRA: Women, where is Orestes? Have the pitiless gods
  Driven him helpless and insane out of the palace?

CHORUS: No, no; he has gone to face the assembly of citizens,
  And stand the appointed trial which will decree your life
  Or death.

ELECTRA: Oh, no! What has he done? Who made him do it?

CHORUS: Pylades. – Look! Here comes someone to bring us
  news

About your brother, and tell us all that happened there.
    [*Enter a* MESSENGER.]
MESSENGER: O doomed, unhappy son of great King Agamem-
    non!
Princess Electra, listen to my terrible news.
ELECTRA: This means our death; your words already make
    that clear.
Tell us at once the bad news that you have to tell.
MESSENGER: The full court of the Pelasgian people by their
    vote
Today condemned your brother and yourself to die.
ELECTRA: To die! I knew it. This heart-chilling certainty
Has gnawed at me for many dreadful days. Tell me,
What happened at the trial? What arguments led to
Our condemnation, and ensured the death-sentence?
Tell me, old friend: are we appointed, he and I,
To share one fate? And what death? Are we to be stoned?
Or must I take a dagger and cut my own throat?
MESSENGER: Well, as it happened, I was coming from the
    farm
Into the town, anxious to find out how things were
With you and Orestes. All my life, you know, I've been
Loyal to your father. Your house fostered me. I'm poor
But faithful to my friends. Well now, I saw a stream
Of people going to take their seats on that hill, where,
They say, Danaus first called a council of citizens
When brought to trial by Aegyptus. So, seeing this crowd,
I asked someone, 'What news in Argos? What has put
The city of Danaus in this flutter? Is there a war?'
'Look,' said he, 'don't you see Orestes there, coming
To stand on trial for his life?' I looked, and saw
A sight as heart-rending as it was unexpected:
Pylades and Orestes walking side by side,
Your brother's head bowed, his frame shattered by disease,
Pylades like a brother sharing all his pain,

Tending his sickness, guiding and supporting him.
    When the full roll of citizens was present, a herald
Stood up and said, 'Who wishes to address the court,
To say whether or not Orestes ought to die
For matricide?' At this Talthybius rose, who was
Your father's colleague in the victory over Troy.
Always subservient to those in power, he made
An ambiguous speech, with fulsome praise of Agamemnon
And cold words for your brother, twisting eulogy
And censure both together – laying down a law
Useless to parents; and with every sentence gave
Ingratiating glances towards Aegisthus' friends.
Heralds are like that – their whole race have learnt to jump
To the winning side; their friend is anyone who has power
Or a government office. Prince Diomedes spoke up next.
He urged them not to sentence either you or your brother
To death, but satisfy piety by banishing you.
Some shouted in approval; others disagreed.
    Next there stood up a man with a mouth like a running
        spring,
A giant in impudence, an enrolled citizen, yet
No Argive; a mere cat's-paw; putting his confidence
In bluster and ignorant outspokenness, and still
Persuasive enough to lead his hearers into trouble.
(For when a pleasing speaker, of evil principles,
Persuades the people, then disaster's on the way;
While honourable, intelligent advice will lead,
Sooner or later, to a profitable end.
And when we judge our leaders we should take the same
View; for a speaker is not more responsible
For the decision taken, than his hearers are.)
He said you and Orestes should be killed with stones;
Yet, as he argued for your death, the words he used
Were not his own, but all prompted by Tyndareos.
    Another rose, and spoke against him – one endowed

With little beauty, but a courageous man; the sort
Not often found mixing in street or market-place,
A manual labourer – the sole backbone of the land;
Shrewd, when he chose, to come to grips in argument;
A man of blameless principle and integrity.
He said, Orestes son of Agamemnon should be
Honoured with crowns for daring to avenge his father
By taking a depraved and godless woman's life –
One who corrupted custom; since no man would leave
His home, and arm himself, and march to war, if wives
Left there in trust could be seduced by stay-at-homes,
And brave men cuckolded. His words seemed sensible
To honest judges; and there were no more speeches.
    Then
Your brother rose. 'Inheritors of Inachus,'
He said, 'Pelasgians once, and later Danaids,
In your defence, no less than in my father's cause,
I killed my mother. For if wives may kill husbands
And not be guilty, you had all best lose no time,
But die today, before your wives make slaves of you.
To vindicate her would be a preposterous act.
As things stand now, the traitress to my father's bed
Has paid for it with her life; but if you now kill me
The law is void; the sooner a man dies the better,
Since wives lack but encouragement, not enterprise.'
    Yet he did not convince the assembly, though his words
Seemed plausible. That wretch who held the people's ear,
Demanding your death and your brother's, won the day.
Orestes barely gained this favour for you both,
To escape stoning; and he promised that his own hand
Would this day make an end of his life, and of yours.
Now Pylades, in tears, is bringing him from the court,
And many pitying friends come with him, weeping too –
A sight full of distress, a sight to break your heart.
    Prepare your dagger, then, or noose your rope; for you

Must leave this light. No help to you was royal birth;
And Phoebus on his throne of prophecy has proved
Not saviour, but destroyer.

CHORUS: Veiled, with eyes downcast,
Speechless you stand, ill-starred Electra, while your flood
Of anguished lamentation waits to overflow.

ELECTRA: Land of Pelasgus, I begin the dirge of death.
                White fingers trace their ruin
                Crimson across my cheek;
                My head sinks under blows
                Which pay the tribute due
                To Persephone, fair princess
                Of the dead below the earth.
                Shout and wail aloud, Cyclopian land,
                Lay the sharp knife to the hair,
                Mourn the griefs of the house.
                Here is pity, here is indignation
                For the fate of those who will die,
                Who once were leaders of the armies of Hellas.

                Lost, lost and vanished,
                Gone is the race of Pelops, root and branch,
                The prosperous home that was the world's
                    envy,
                Destroyed by divine jealousy,
                By the malice of citizens and the sentence of
                    blood.
                Weep and lament, mortals who live for a day,
                Generations rife with tears and rich in suffer-
                    ing;
                See how destiny denies your hopes!
                Over slow centuries sorrow succeeds to sor-
                    row;
                In the length of mortal life there is no perma-
                    nence.

I wish I could reach that rock
Slung on swinging golden chains
Mid-way between sky and earth,
That turning mass blown by winds from
     Olympus;
Then I would shout in grief and reproach
Against Tantalus our aged ancestor.
He it was – he begot them,
The fathers of my house
Who saw those fatal crimes performed:
First, the rival running of wing'd horses,
When Pelops behind his yoke of four
Thundered his chariot between the two seas;
And then the murder of Myrtilus
Whom Pelops hurled into the roaring waves
When he had won his race by the shore of
     Geraestus
White with foam of the salt swell.

From these two crimes began
The curse which drowned our house in tears,
When Hermes the son of Maia placed among
     Atreus' flocks
A new-born lamb with a golden fleece –
A prodigy that sent ruin and death
Upon Atreus rich in horses,
And brought to birth the deadly feud
Which turned the sun's wing'd chariot round
Changing his course towards the dawn;
While Zeus guided to a different path
The seven tracks of the running Pleiads,
And caused old deaths to be avenged with new
Through the banquet that bears Thyestes' name
And the adultery of Aërope,
The Cretan wife who betrayed her husband.

Now last of all on me and on my father
The curse of the house falls cruel and irresistible.

[*Enter* ORESTES *and* PYLADES.]

CHORUS: See! Orestes comes, your brother, assigned
To death by the court, and his faithful friend
Supporting his steps and his weakened frame
With a steadfast care
And the gentle concern of a brother.

ELECTRA: Oh, brother, this sight breaks my heart. I see the
grave
Open, I see you stand before the pyre of death.
How can I bear it? This is the last time that I
Shall ever see you! I am lost! Oh, what shall I do?

ORESTES: Now stop this female wailing; learn to keep quiet,
and
Accept hard facts. Our situation is pitiable;
But this is how things are; we must endure what comes.

ELECTRA: Keep quiet – how can I? You and I never again
Shall see the sun's immortal light. We are condemned.

ORESTES: Isn't it enough that Argive hands should kill me?
Must
You kill me too? Stop harping on our miseries.

ELECTRA: I weep, Orestes, for your youth, your destiny,
And death before your time. You ought to live, not die.

ORESTES: For the gods' sake! This miserable talk can lead
Only to tears. Don't wrap me round with cowardice!

ELECTRA: We're going to die. It is impossible not to weep.
For everyone, life's precious, and death pitiful.

ORESTES: Today is our day. We must either fix a rope
And hang ourselves, or learn to handle a sharp sword.

ELECTRA: Then *you* must kill Agamemnon's daughter, and
save me
The indignity of being killed by some commoner.

ORESTES: My mother's blood is curse enough; I won't kill
　　you.
End your own life – and do it any way you please.
ELECTRA: I will. My courage shall not lag behind your sword.
But oh, brother! Let me first take you in my arms!
ORESTES: Embrace me, if it gives you pleasure. An embrace
Is little help to those within one step of death.
ELECTRA: My dearest! Oh, my darling brother! How I love
To call you my own brother! Our two hearts are one.
ORESTES: Oh, you will melt my firmness. Yes, I must hold
　　you
In my most loving arms – come! Why should I feel shame?
Body to body – thus, let us be close in love.
Say 'brother', sister! These dear words can take the place
Of children, marriage – to console our misery.
ELECTRA: If it were right, I wish one sword might kill us, one
Memorial carved in cedar-wood receive us both.
ORESTES: I share your wish. But think – where are the friends
　　who might
Have buried us together? We have lost them all.
ELECTRA: But Menelaus – that cowardly traitor to my father –
Did he not speak one word, not one plea for your life?
ORESTES: He did not show his face. Succession to the throne
Was his one thought. He took care not to save his friends.
　　Come, sister, let the manner of our dying show
That we are royal and worthy of Agamemnon's line.
I'll show all Argos what nobility is, driving
My sword home to the heart; with equal courage you
Must do the same. Be umpire of our rival deaths,
Pylades, and wrap our dead bodies decently;
And take us both and bury us in our father's grave.
Good-bye. I'm going now to do what must be done.
PYLADES: No, wait. Did you think I would care to live when
　　you
Were dead? That is the first thing I reproach you with.

ORESTES: What obligation rests on you to die with me?

PYLADES: Do you ask? What is life worth when I have lost my
friend?

ORESTES: *You* did not kill your mother; you don't share my
curse.

PYLADES: I shared your deed, and I must share its consequence.

ORESTES: Go back and be your father's son. Don't die with
me.

You have a city, which I have not now. You have
Your father's home – all the resources of his wealth.
I pledged Electra to you, loving you as a friend;
Her evil fortune robs you of your marriage-hopes.
But find another bride; beget sons, Pylades.
We thought we would be brothers; that won't happen
now.
Dearest of friends, whose friendship meant so much to me,
Good-bye! Good luck – *we*'ve missed it, but it may be yours.
For us, the dead, good luck is a forgotten hope.

PYLADES: You've little notion of the way my mind's made up.
Listen: may neither fruitful earth receive my blood,
Nor sunlit air my dying breath, if ever I
Save my own life by leaving or betraying you.
I shared the killing with you, and I'll not retract;
All you now suffer for was my deliberate choice;
Therefore my duty is to perish with you both.
I meant to marry Electra; therefore in my eyes
She is my wife. How could I gloss my own conduct,
Going home to Delphi and the Phocian citadel,
If I, who was your close friend while your fortune held,
Now you're in trouble, show myself no more your friend?
Out of the question; I am as much involved as you.
So let's put heads together, since we're going to die,
To ensure a share of suffering for Menelaus.

ORESTES: Friend! I could die contented, if I saw that done.

PYLADES: Listen to me; and let your sword's edge wait a
　　　while.

ORESTES: I'll wait. If I can once pay out my enemy —

PYLADES: Speak quietly. I've no faith in women — who are
　　　these?

ORESTES: Don't be afraid of anyone here. They are all our
　　　friends.

PYLADES: Let's kill Helen — and send Menelaus raving mad.

ORESTES: How can we do it? I'm ready, if the plan will work.

PYLADES: Why, with a sword. She's here now, hiding in your
　　　house.

ORESTES: She is, yes — making a list of all the valuables.

PYLADES: When she gets Hades for a lover, she'll stop that.

ORESTES: How shall we manage? She has a Phrygian body-
　　　guard.

PYLADES: What bodyguard? I'm not afraid of Phrygians.

ORESTES: True — chaps who polish her mirrors and set out her
　　　scents.

PYLADES: Has she brought all her Trojan frills and trinkets
　　　here?

ORESTES: Hellas falls far below her standard for a home.

PYLADES: Well, slaves will have no chance against *us*.

ORESTES:　　　　　　　　　　　　　　　　　　　　True;
　　　and if
　We could bring *this* off, I'd be ready to die twice.

PYLADES: And so would I, to strike a blow for your revenge.

ORESTES: Explain your plan; tell me just what you have in
　　　mind.

PYLADES: We'll go indoors — ostensibly to kill ourselves.

ORESTES: That much is clear, but I don't see what happens
　　　next.

PYLADES: We both start moaning to her about our piteous
　　　fate —

ORESTES: While she weeps loudly, to conceal her secret joy —

PYLADES: And we practise the same deception upon her.

ORESTES: Right. What's the next move in the game?

PYLADES: We have
    our swords
  Hidden in our clothes.

ORESTES: How can we make our kill before
  Her servants?

PYLADES: We'll shut them all up in various rooms.

ORESTES: Any that doesn't hold his tongue we'll have to
    kill.

PYLADES: And after that, our task itself will point the way.

ORESTES: Our watchword for today: 'Kill Helen' – there it
    is.

PYLADES: You have it. – And my plan is honourable. Listen:
  Suppose we used our swords against some chaster wife,
  Our action would be criticized; but Helen's death
  Brings satisfaction to all Hellas – to everyone
  Whose son, or father, she destroyed, and every wife
  She made a widow. There'll be cheering in the streets,
  Bonfires will blaze to all the gods, and prayers rise up
  For blessings on us both, because we justly shed
  The blood of a bad woman. Kill her, and your name
  Of 'matricide' will be forgotten, giving place
  To a more glorious title: you'll be called 'the man
  Who killed the killer of thousands, Helen'. Gods forbid
  That ever Menelaus should thrive, while your father,
  And you, and your sister, all die, and your mother too –
  Well, it's perhaps more suitable to leave her out –

  Only that Menelaus, who owes his safe return,
  And his wife's, to Agamemnon, should possess your house!
  I'd rather die at once than not draw sword against
  That woman. And if we fail to bring off Helen's death,
  We'll burn this house about our ears and so perish.
  One glory or the other we can't fail to win –
  A noble death, or else escape and victory!

CHORUS: The daughter of Tyndareos, who has disgraced her
    sex,
  Deserves the loathing of all women everywhere.

ORESTES: I am moved. Nothing's more precious than a
    loyal friend,
  Not wealth, not kingship. A whole city to command
  Is worthless, weighed against one honourable friend.
  It was you planned the downfall of Aegisthus; you
  Stood at my side in danger; you now, yet again,
  Point to the path of vengeance on my enemies,
  And shirk nothing. But I'll stop praising you; excess
  In praise may, as in other things, be burdensome.
  Since I am now at my last gasp in any case,
  I want to hurt my enemies before I die,
  To pay back those who have betrayed me in their own coin,
  And hear them howling who brought misery on me.
  I am the son of Agamemnon, whom Hellas
  Chose for command by merit – no despot, but one
  Who had a god's strength in him; whom I will not shame
  By a slave's death, but breathe my last like a free man,
  Getting revenge on Menelaus. There's yet one thing
  Which good fortune might give us – if by some strange
    chance
  Deliverance came; if we could kill and not be killed.
  So this I pray for; words are wing'd and cost nothing;
  Wishes are sweet upon the tongue, and warm the heart.

ELECTRA: Brother, I think I see this very wish come true –
  A way to save us all, you, Pylades, and me.

ORESTES: Some god must have inspired you. Tell us, what's
    the plan?
  I know you have an active brain; you always had.

ELECTRA: Listen, then; you too, Pylades, come here. Now,
    look –

ORESTES: Well, what, then? Any ray of hope is worth the
    pleasure.

ELECTRA: You know Helen's daughter Hermione? Of course
     you do.

ORESTES: I know – she lived here, and my mother brought
     her up.

ELECTRA: Hermione has gone to Clytemnestra's grave.

ORESTES: What will she do there? – What hope are you hint-
     ing at?

ELECTRA: When she comes back, seize her and hold her as a
     hostage.

ORESTES: And what malady will that cure for us three friends?

ELECTRA: When Helen's dead, if Menelaus makes any threat
     Against you, or him, or me – we're all in this together –
     Tell him you'll kill Hermione. You must draw your sword
     And hold it tight against her throat. If Menelaus,
     With Helen's body lying in blood before his eyes,
     Will promise you your life to save Hermione's,
     Then hand her over to her father; but if he
     Attempts to kill you in his uncontrollable rage,
     Then cut Hermione's throat. I think, even if at first
     He's very fierce, he'll cool down in good time. He's not
     In fact a bold or warlike man. Well, there's my scheme –
     I hope, a bulwark that may save our lives. That's all.

ORESTES: Oh, what a manly spirit and resolve shines out
     From your weak woman's body! You deserve to live,
     Not die! Pylades, this is the wife you'll die to lose,
     Or live to win as a rich blessing on your house.

PYLADES: God grant it! May I bring her to my Phocian home,
     Where wedding song and dance and feast shall do her
          honour!

ORESTES: But how soon will Hermione come back to the
     house?
     We have first to capture this atrocious father's cub;
     If we succeed in that, the rest should work out well.

ELECTRA: By now, I think, she must be very near the house;
     She has been gone long enough to do what she had to do.

ORESTES: Good. Now, Electra, you stay here outside the house
  To meet Hermione when she comes. Keep watch in case
  Anyone comes indoors before the killing's done,
  Whether some friend of ours, or Menelaus; if so,
  Give warning – knock on the door, or shout into the hall.
  Pylades, we'll go in now; for this last ordeal
  Let's take our swords in hand; you share this task with me.
    My father, dwelling in the shadowy halls of night,
  Your son Orestes calls on you. We need your help;
  Come now and save us! For your sake I am condemned
  Unjustly. Though my act was righteous, I am deserted
  By Menelaus; now I intend to take his wife
  And kill her. Be our helper in this enterprise!

ELECTRA: Father, your children call on you. If from your grave
  You hear us, come! We die for our loyalty to you.

PYLADES: My father's kinsman, Agamemnon, lend your ear
  To my entreaties too, and save your children's lives.

ORESTES: I killed my mother –

ELECTRA: My hand too was on the sword.

PYLADES: I counselled them, and when they shrank dispelled their fears.

ORESTES: – In your cause, father!

ELECTRA: I too proved my loyalty.

PYLADES: Let not their fate reproach you; save your children; come!

ORESTES: For offerings, receive my tears –

ELECTRA: My cries of grief.

PYLADES: Cease now; let's to the work at once. If prayers can thrust,
  Like javelins, through the deep earth, Agamemnon hears.
  – Grant, Zeus, our ancestor, and holy Justice, grant
  To Orestes, and his sister, and to me, success!

One perilous struggle, one just cause, unites three friends:
We all must either live, or pay our debt and die.

[ORESTES *and* PYLADES *enter the palace.*]

ELECTRA:　　Friends, women of Mycenae,
　　　　　　　Noble ladies of ancient Argos —

CHORUS:　　 What do you say, Princess Electra? — this is
　　　　　　　　　still
　　　　　　　Your title in the city of Danaus.

ELECTRA:　　Stand here to guard the house; some of you
　　　　　　　　post yourselves
　　　　　　　There on the highway, others here along
　　　　　　　　this path.

CHORUS:　　 Tell us, why do you ask us to do this for
　　　　　　　　you?

ELECTRA:　　I am afraid that someone standing to watch
　　　　　　　　the palace
　　　　　　　Might discover this murder,
　　　　　　　And make disaster even more disastrous.

SEMI-CH. 1:　Come on, let's be quick;
　　　　　　　I'll go here and watch the highway,
　　　　　　　Looking towards the sunrise.

SEMI-CH. 2:　And I'll watch westward along this path.

ELECTRA:　　Turn your eyes to this side and that.

SEMI-CH. 1:　We are looking from left to right,
　　　　　　　Then behind us, as you ask.

ELECTRA:　　Turn round now, look round;
　　　　　　　Peer through your hair, search every direc-
　　　　　　　　tion.

SEMI-CH. 2:　Who is that on the road? Look hard; who is
　　　　　　　　it?
　　　　　　　Some countryman prowling round your
　　　　　　　　palace.

ELECTRA:　　Friends, this will destroy us!
　　　　　　　At any moment he will betray to our
　　　　　　　　enemies

Those two lurking lions, with swords in
their hands!

SEMI-CH. 2: Don't be afraid; you were mistaken, the
road is empty.

ELECTRA: What of your side? Is all safe still?
Give us a welcome report
If all's clear over there, facing the court-
yard.

SEMI-CH. 1: All's clear on our side; keep a watch on
yours.
No one from Argos anywhere visible here!

SEMI-CH. 2: The same all round; nothing stirring this
way either.

ELECTRA: Wait, now — I am going to listen at the
door. [*She waits, listening; then shouts*]
You in the house there!
Why do you take so long? The coast's
clear!
When will you blood the sacrifice?
— They aren't listening. O gods, what
misery!
Are their swords blunted at the sight of
beauty?
Any moment, some Argive, fully armed,
Will burst in to the rescue,
And meet them in the palace!
Watch more carefully — this is no time for
sitting down;
Keep moving around, this way and that.

CHORUS: I'll move over there, and look every way.

HELEN [*from inside the palace*]: Help, help, ancient Argos! I am
murdered!

SEMI-CH. 1: Hear that? The men are at their bloody
work.

SEMI-CH. 2: That scream was Helen's voice, I am sure.

ELECTRA: O Zeus immortal, Zeus almighty,
                 Come to the help of my friends with all
                    your power!

HELEN [within]:   Menelaus, I am dying; and you're not here
                    to help me!

ELECTRA: Kill, stab, destroy her, both of you!
                 Aim your swords – *in!* – *in!*
                 Two hungry blades flashing in your hands!
                 Kill her!
                 She deserted her father, she deserted her
                    husband;
                 Countless Hellenes died in battle by the
                    riverside –
                 And she killed them!
                 Tears flooded upon tears
                 There, where iron spears flew
                 Beside the seething Scamander.

CHORUS: Hush, all of you, be quiet! I heard footsteps.
     Someone
   Is on the road, quite near the house.

ELECTRA: Oh, dearest friends!
   Hermione is here within the circle of blood.
   Let's all be quiet; she's coming now, and she will fall
   Into the netted snare – a fine catch, if she's caught!
   Stand where you stood before, compose your faces; give
   No sign of knowing what is done. I will put on
   A bitter, fierce expression, as if unaware
   Of what we have accomplished.
       [*Enter* HERMIONE.]

                         Oh, Hermione,
   You're back! Have you hung Clytemnestra's grave with
         wreaths
   Of flowers, and poured wine-offerings to the gods of earth?

HERMIONE: I have, and I have won her favour. But while I
   Was still some distance from the house, I heard a cry

From indoors. What was that? It filled me with alarm.

ELECTRA: Does not our present fortune call for cries of
   pain?

HERMIONE: Don't tell me any worse news! What has happened, then?

ELECTRA: Argos condemns Orestes and myself to death.

HERMIONE: Oh, no! Not you, my own cousins!

ELECTRA: That is decreed.
   We stand under the yoke of hard necessity.

HERMIONE: So that explains the cry I heard?

ELECTRA: A suppliant
   Was falling at Helen's knees and pleading for his life.

HERMIONE: Well, who? Unless you tell me, I'm still in the
   dark.

ELECTRA: Orestes – trying to save my life as well as his.

HERMIONE: No wonder, then, the palace echoes with despair.

ELECTRA: What better cause is there for crying? But now
   come,
   Join your entreaties with your friends'; fall on your knees
   And beg your mother, whom the gods so richly bless,
   That Menelaus may not stand by and see us killed.
   Hermione, my own mother brought you up herself:
   Take pity on us, help us in our misery!
   Come, this is where the crisis lies – I'll lead the way;
   For you hold in your single hand his life and mine.

HERMIONE: Of course I'll come as quickly as I can; and you
   Shall be saved if it's in my power.

   [HERMIONE *enters the palace*; ELECTRA *stays by the
   door. The voices of* HERMIONE *and* ORESTES *are heard
   from inside.*]

ELECTRA: You in the palace!
   Are your swords ready? Your prey's coming: capture her!

HERMIONE: Oh, oh! What's this? Who are these men?

ORESTES: Now you keep quiet.
   You're coming in here for *our* safety, not your own.
ELECTRA: Now hold her, hold her! Set a sword across her throat
   And hold it there; let Menelaus see for himself
   He has to deal with men, not fumbling Phrygians.
   He'll find he's cornered as a coward deserves to be!
     [ELECTRA *enters the palace.*]
CHORUS: Now, everyone, a noise!
         Raise a din, stamp and shout
         Here in the palace court, lest the murder done
         Breed panic and dread, and bring too soon
         The Argive citizens rushing to the rescue
         Before we've seen with our own eyes
         The dead body of Helen bleeding on the palace
            floor,
         Or heard a clear account from one of the ser-
            vants.
         We know part of what's happened, but not
            everything.
         How justly divine vengeance
         Has fallen upon Helen!
         For she filled Hellas full of tears
         For the sake of her damnable lover
         Paris of Ida, Paris the accursed,
         Who dragged Hellas to Troy.

         Hush, listen! I hear the bolts being drawn.
           Who is coming out?
   It's one of those Phrygians in the palace, Helen's servants.
   We'll ask him what has happened there; he's sure to know.
     [*Enter by the palace door, a* PHRYGIAN SLAVE.]
PHRYGIAN: That Argive with a sword come after me –
   I escape from death!
   I climb over the cedar-beams of the portico
   In my Persian slippers; through the Doric triglyphs –

Away, away — oh, heaven and earth!
Persian man run away, why not?
I tremble! Ladies, how can I escape?
Can I fly up to the hoary sky?
Or jump into the circling sea, which Oceanus,
With his head of a bull,
Cradles in his arms on the round rim of the world?

CHORUS: What is happening, slave of Helen, native of Ida?

PHRYGIAN: O fields of Phrygia, beautiful town of Ilion —
Weep, weep for unhappy Ilion! —
Holy Mount Ida, I mourn your overthrow,
I sing for you a Persian tune,
The dirge of the chariot. You were destroyed
By the bird-begotten, swan-winged beauty
Of the bright eyes of Leda's chick,
Who laid the curse on Apollo's polished fortress,
Hell-Helen! Misery and mourning, tears and wailing!
Unhappy land of Dardanus,
Your happiness lost for the horseman Ganymede
Who shared the bed of Zeus!

CHORUS: Do tell us plainly what has been happening indoors.
Speak! I can make no sense of what you have just said.

PHRYGIAN: *Ailinon, ailinon* — the first word of death;
The *barbaroi* say it — Oh, misery! —
In their Asiatic speech,
When by murderous iron swords
The blood of kings is poured on the ground.
   Now, into the house came —
Yes, I tell you everything exactly —
Two twin Hellenic lions.
One was the son of the famous general;
The other was a bad-hearted man,
The son of Strophius,
A man like Odysseus, who deceive you and say nothing,
A bold fighter, loyal to his friends,

A shrewd soldier and a bloodthirsty monster.
Curse him for his smooth treachery −
He was up to no good!
    Well, they come in, they come where Helen was sitting −
The woman Paris the archer married.
Their eyes were dirty with tears;
They crouch low and humble,
One on this side, one on that side;
The two close her in, left and right.
Then both fell suppliant before her,
Threw their arms round Helen's knees.
So all her Phrygian servants came running up,
Running at full speed.
And we said to each other, suddenly afraid,
I hope this is not treachery.
And some thought everything was all right;
Others thought that the child of Tyndareos
Was being snared in a treacherous trap
By that monster who murdered his mother.

CHORUS: Where were you then? Already fled in panic, yes?
PHRYGIAN: As it happened, I was standing near to Helen
Stirring the air, as we Phrygians do,
With a round fan of feathers
To make a breeze for Helen's hair
And to cool her cheek − it's a custom in Phrygia;
We always do this in the East.
And she was spinning a linen thread,
Twisting it in her fingers,
And the spun thread trailed on the floor;
For she meant to use this thread
To embroider a purple robe from the Phrygian spoils
As a gift for Clytemnestra, to adorn her tomb.
    Then Orestes spoke to Spartan Helen:
'Daughter of Zeus, leave your couch,
Stand on your feet and come with me

To the ancient altar-hearth of Pelops, our ancestor,
To hear what I have to say to you.'
So he draw her, draw her on;
She follow him, with no foreboding of his purpose.
Meanwhile his accomplice, that Phocian thug,
Was off on another errand:
'Clear out, you wretched Phrygian bastards!'
And he locked us all in different rooms,
Some in the stables and outhouses, some here, some there,
Making sure we were all well away from our mistress.

CHORUS: Yes – what happened next?

PHRYGIAN: Goddess of Ida, holy Mother!
  What horrible wickedness I saw!
  I saw it all, there in the royal palace,
  A wicked, dreadful outrage, bloody murder!
  From under the shadows of their purple cloaks
  They pull their swords and hold them;
  Orestes look this way, Pylades that way,
  To see no one was there.

Like mountain boars they stand facing a woman;
And they say, 'You shall die, you're going to die,
And your death will be due to your treacherous husband,
Who in the Assembly of Argos
Betrayed his brother's son to death.'
    Then Helen screamed aloud,
'What shall I do?' she screamed.
Her white arms beat upon her breast, her hands
Battered her head with pitiful blows.
Then she try to escape;
Her gold sandals clattered as she ran.
Orestes in his hunting-boots darted at her;
He twist his fingers in her hair;
He bent her neck down to her left shoulder;
He held his black sword ready
To drive into her throat.

CHORUS: What of the other Phrygians in the palace?
   Could they not help? Where were they?
PHRYGIAN: We raised a great shout; we got crowbars
   And wrenched out the doors and door-posts
   Of the rooms where we were shut in;
   Then from every corner of the house
   We ran to the rescue; some carried stones,
   Others had javelins, others a drawn sword.
   And that curs'd Pylades advanced on us
   With a terrible look – he looked like Phrygian Hector
   Or Aias of the triple plume – I saw them once –
   What a sight they were! fighting in Priam's gate.
   Then we clashed sword-blades; and immediately
   It was clear how far we Phrygians
   Fall below the fighting valour of Hellas.
   One ran away and vanished, another lay dead,
   Another wounded, another kneeling in terror
   To beg for his life.
   So in the darkness we were escaping;
   But some fell lifeless, some reeled and crumpled,
   Some lay still.
      Then Hermione, unsuspecting, came indoors
   As her mother, drenched with blood, lay on the ground.
   Those two ran at the girl, like unholy Bacchants
   Pouncing on a mountain cub, and caught her;
   Then turned back to the child of Zeus, to their kill.
   Helen was gone!
   Vanished from the room, from the whole house!
   Earth and sky, where is she hidden?
   Day and night! was it miracle, or magic,
   Or did the gods steal her away?
      I don't know any more; I crept out of the palace
   And ran for my life.
   Poor Menelaus! All his misery and hardship
   All endured for nothing, nothing! His wife,

Home from Troy after all these years — for nothing!

CHORUS: An incredible story! And yet more's to come — see
now!

Orestes, with his sword drawn, bounding out of the palace
And looking like a madman.

[*Enter* ORESTES.]

ORESTES: Where's that Phrygian I was chasing with my
sword? He dodged out here!

PHRYGIAN: Kneeling prostrate at your feet, my lord — as any
Phrygian would.

ORESTES [*lifting him by his clothes*]: Get up, you! You're not in
Troy now. This is Argos — just learn that! [ORESTES *throws
him down again.*]

PHRYGIAN: Troy or Argos — everywhere a wise man wants to
live, not die.

ORESTES: You weren't shouting to Menelaus to come to the
rescue, were you, now?

PHRYGIAN: No! I shouted, Come and help Orestes! — You're
the better man.

ORESTES: Answer my question now: was Helen justly or unjustly killed?

PHRYGIAN: Very justly. If she had three throats, they should
all three be cut.

ORESTES: That's not what you're thinking. You pick words
to please me, like a coward.

PHRYGIAN: Didn't she plunge Greeks and Trojans all in one
calamity?

ORESTES: Swear you didn't say that just to please me — or I'll
kill you. Swear!

PHRYGIAN: By my life I swear I didn't — that's the holiest
oath I know.

ORESTES: Tell me, did sharp steel make all the Phrygians
quake like this at Troy?

PHRYGIAN: Take your sword away; it glints like murder —
it's too near my neck.

ORESTES: Is this a Gorgon's head? Are you afraid your body'll turn to stone?

PHRYGIAN: Turn to dead meat — that's what I'm afraid of, not your Gorgon's head.

ORESTES: You're afraid of death — and you a slave? Why, death will set you free!

PHRYGIAN: Every man loves living. Sunlight's precious even for a slave.

ORESTES: That's well said; your mother-wit has saved you. Go on, get indoors.

PHRYGIAN: You won't kill me?

ORESTES: You're let off.

PHRYGIAN: Oh, that's a welcome word to hear!

ORESTES: Any moment now I'll change my mind.

PHRYGIAN: Oh, no, no! Don't do that!

ORESTES: What a fool! — to think I'd bring myself to blood your wretched throat!

Well, what sort of creature are you? Neither a woman nor a man!

It was time to stop your shouting; that was why I came out here.

[*The* PHRYGIAN *escapes.*]

Once a clamour starts, this city's all too quick to take the alarm.

I've no fear of meeting Menelaus within one sword's length;

Flaunting copper-coloured curls down to his shoulders — let him come!

If he brings a force of Argives to attack the palace and

Get revenge for his dead Helen — if he still won't guarantee

Safety for me, and my sister, and my ally Pylades,

Then he'll see his daughter, like his wife, lie dead before his eyes.

[*Exit* ORESTES *into the house.*]

CHORUS: Oh, what is happening?
  Yet once again terror engulfs the palace,
  And Atreus' sons are locked in conflict.
  – What shall we do? Shall we run to rouse the city?
  Or say nothing? It is safer to keep quiet.
  – Look there, look now! Smoke coming from the house,
  Leaping skyward, tells what is happening.
  – They are lighting pine-wood faggots
  To fire the palace of Tantalus;
  And they won't stop short of murder!
  – God guides mortal man to his end;
  And his end is as God appoints;
  For the power that guides is great.
  – Since Myrtilus fell to death from his chariot,
  A haunting curse has plunged this house
  Deep in a welter of its own blood.
  Look there, friends! Menelaus is coming. I see him hot-foot
    on his way.
  He has been told what's happening here. – Electra, Orestes,
    bar the gates,
  Lose not a moment! Barricade the house! A man proud in
    success
  Has no mercy, Orestes, for the defeated and the desperate!
  [*Enter* MENELAUS.]
MENELAUS: They tell me frightful news of violence perpe-
    trated
  By those two savage animals – I won't call them men.
  What is the truth? My wife, they tell me, is not dead,
  But has vanished out of sight – an absurd story which
  Some frightened idiot brought me, a clownish rigmarole
  Concocted by the mother-murderer. – Open, there!
  Slaves, open the doors! At least I may be in time to save
  My daughter from their bloody hands. As for my wife –
  Sad, pitiable Helen! – let me but find her, and this hand
  Shall stretch my poor wife's murderers dead at her side.

[ORESTES *appears above with* PYLADES *and* HER-
    MIONE.]

ORESTES: You there — yes, you, Menelaus, you tower of
    arrogance!
  Keep your hands off those doors, or I shall smash your skull
  With this stone coping torn from the old masonry
  Of Atreus' ramparts! Every door is bolted fast.
  Racing to the rescue's no use: you'll not get inside.

MENELAUS: God help us, what's this? Lighted torches, and
    those two
  At bay, manning the battlements — and Hermione,
  My child, held prisoner, with a sword's edge at her throat!

ORESTES: Do you want to question me, or hear what I have to
    say?

MENELAUS: Neither; but I am forced, it seems, to hear you
    speak.

ORESTES: I intend to kill your daughter — if you want to know.

MENELAUS: You murdered Helen — now you'll kill Her-
    mione?

ORESTES: I wish I had achieved that. The gods baffled me.

MENELAUS: You deny killing Helen? Then are you mocking
    me?

ORESTES: I deny it — with extreme regret. I only wish —

MENELAUS: Only wish what? You frighten me.

ORESTES: I wish I had
  Sent down to hell this country's evil genius.

MENELAUS: Restore me my wife's body. I must bury her.

ORESTES: Ask the gods for her; but I'm going to kill your
    child.

MENELAUS: The mother-murderer now adds blood to blood!

ORESTES: The son
  Who avenged his father — whom you then betrayed to death.

MENELAUS: Was your first crime, your mother's murder, not
    enough?

ORESTES: I'll not grow weary taking wicked women's lives.

MENELAUS: Pylades, in this murder do you claim a share?

ORESTES: His silence claims it. Let my word suffice for him.

MENELAUS: You'll pay for it; unless you have wings you'll
not escape.

ORESTES: We shall not try to escape; we'll set fire to this
palace.

MENELAUS: You mean that? You'll destroy your own ances-
tral home?

ORESTES: Yes, to prevent *you* having it; and I'll cut her
throat
Over the flames.

MENELAUS: Do it – I'll have your blood for this.

ORESTES: I'll do it, then. [*He raises the sword.*]

MENELAUS: No, no, no! Stop! Do no such
thing!

ORESTES: You deserve all you've got; so endure it silently.

MENELAUS: Do *you* deserve to live?

ORESTES: Yes, and to rule the land.

MENELAUS: What land?

ORESTES: Pelasgian Argos and these territor-
ies.

MENELAUS: *You* would perform the sacred cleansing – ?

ORESTES: And
why not?

MENELAUS: Sacrifice victims before battle?

ORESTES: And would *you*
Be worthier?

MENELAUS: Yes; my hands are clean.

ORESTES: Your heart's corrupt.

MENELAUS: What man would speak to you?

ORESTES: Every man who
loves his father.

MENELAUS: What of one who respects his mother?

ORESTES: A lucky
man!

MENELAUS: Unlike you!

ORESTES: True; I abhor female depravity.

MENELAUS: Take your sword from Hermione's neck.

ORESTES: You're a born liar.

MENELAUS: Then — you will kill my daughter?

ORESTES: Now you speak the truth.

MENELAUS: What shall I do?

ORESTES: Go to the Assembly and persuade —

MENELAUS: Yes?

ORESTES: Beg the citizens to spare our lives.

MENELAUS: Or else You'll kill my daughter?

ORESTES: Yes.

MENELAUS: Oh, Helen, your cruel fate!

ORESTES: And what of mine?

MENELAUS: I brought her home for *you* to kill!

ORESTES: I wish I had!

MENELAUS: After all the hardship I went through!

ORESTES: For me you undertook nothing.

MENELAUS: This is outrage!

ORESTES: You failed me in my time of need.

MENELAUS: You have me trapped.

ORESTES: It was your native wickedness that laid the trap.
— Electra! Now's the moment! Set this house on fire!
And you, my most faithful of all friends, Pylades,
Now make a bonfire of these walls and battlements!

MENELAUS: O land of Danaus, charioteers of Argos, help!
To arms, to arms! To the rescue, all you citizens!
This murderer, stained with his mother's blood, threatens
Violence and death against you all, to save his life!

[*Enter* APOLLO, *above.*]

APOLLO: Menelaus, curb the whetted anger of your heart;
  I am Apollo, Leto's son, who speak to you.
    — You too, with your drawn sword on guard at this girl's
        throat —
  Orestes, calm your fury and listen to my words.

    First, as to Helen, whom you meant to kill, and move
  Menelaus to rage — your purpose failed; for this is she,
  Whom you see here, enfolded in the sparkling sky;
  Not dead at your hands, but preserved. I snatched her up
  At Zeus her father's bidding, and saved her from your sword.
  From Zeus immortal born, immortal she must live,
  Reverenced as the goddess who saves seamen's lives,
  Enthroned beside her brothers in the folds of heaven.

    So, Menelaus, choose for your home another wife;
  For Helen's beauty was to the gods their instrument
  For setting Greeks and Trojans face to face in war
  And multiplying deaths, to purge the bloated earth
  Of its superfluous welter of mortality.

    So much for Helen. You, Orestes, must depart
  From Argos, and for one whole year your home shall be
  Parrhasia; and in memory of your exile there
  The Arcadians shall call the place Oresteion.
  Thence make your way to Athens, and there stand your
        trial
  Arraigned by the three Furies for your mother's blood.
  On Ares' Hill gods shall dispute your case, and cast
  Most righteous votes; and you shall leave their court ab-
        solved.

    Hermione, at whose throat, Orestes, you now hold
  Your sword, Fate gives you for your wife: Neoptolemus,
  Who fancies he is going to marry her, is not.
  Destiny appoints him death by Delphian swords, when he
  Demands from me a blood-price for his father's death.
  Bestow on Pylades the wife you promised him,

Your sister; for the years to come a life of bliss
Awaits him.

    Menelaus, yield the throne of Argos to Orestes;
Go back yourself to Sparta, be king there, and keep
It as your lost wife's dowry — compensation for
The griefs and cares she never ceased to plague you with.
Lastly, for the bad odour in which Orestes stands
With the Argive citizens, I will take steps to deal
With that, since I forced him to shed his mother's blood.

ORESTES: Loxias, god of Prophecy! Your oracles
Were not deceptive after all, but sound and true.
Yet, I confess, I felt uneasy, lest the voice
I heard, and took for your voice, was in truth the voice
Of some accursed fiend. But all ends well; and now
I obey you, and release Hermione from my sword;
And when her father gives consent, I'll marry her.

MENELAUS: Helen, daughter of Zeus, farewell! What happiness
For you, to find a home among the blessed gods!
Orestes, at Apollo's bidding I betroth
My daughter to you, a bride as noble as yourself.
Heaven bless you in receiving, me in giving her.

APOLLO: So now depart, each as I have appointed you;
And bring your hatreds to an end.

MENELAUS: We must obey.

ORESTES: I agree with you. I call a truce now with events,
Menelaus; — and likewise, Loxias, with your oracles.

APOLLO: So depart on your way; and to holiest Peace,
The most noble and lovely of goddesses, give
The desire of your hearts.

Now, soaring aloft to the star-bright sphere,
Helen I will conduct to the mansion of Zeus;
There men shall adore her, a goddess enthroned
Beside Hera and Hebe and great Heracles.
There she, with her brothers, Tyndareos' sons,

Shall be worshipped for ever with wine out-
        poured
As the seamen's Queen of the Ocean.

CHORUS: Great and holy Victory,
            Guide my ways and keep my life,
            Give me still the poet's crown!

IPHIGENIA IN AULIS

CHARACTERS

AGAMEMNON, *king of Argos*
OLD MAN, *slave of Agamemnon*
CHORUS *of young women from Chalcis in Euboea*
MENELAUS, *king of Sparta, brother of Agamemnon*
CLYTEMNESTRA, *wife of Agamemnon*
IPHIGENIA, *daughter of Agamemnon and Clytemnestra*
ACHILLES, *one of the Greek leaders*
MESSENGER

*

The Scene is outside Agamemnon's tent in the camp at Aulis.

It is a little before dawn. AGAMEMNON *is pacing to and fro.*

AGAMEMNON: Old man, come here. Come out here.
OLD MAN [*from inside*]:   I'm
                    coming.
                    What strange business are you up to now,
                    King Agamemnon?
AGAMEMNON: Come, hurry, will you?
OLD MAN [*appearing*]: So I do. I don't sleep much, you know.
                    I'm getting old; and that keeps your eyes
                    On the alert.
AGAMEMNON: What is that star
                    Sailing along there?
OLD MAN: Sirius, that is –
                    At the zenith still, and shooting close
                    To the sevenfold tracks of the Pleiades.
AGAMEMNON: No cry of a bird, no sound from the sea,
                    The winds are silent, Euripus hushed.
OLD MAN: Then why should *you* be shooting about
                    Outside your tent, Agamemnon my lord?
                    Everything's still quiet here in Aulis;
                    The guards on the ramparts make no stir.
                    Let us both go in.
AGAMEMNON: I envy you, friend;
                    And I envy any man who has reached
                    The end of his life safe, humble, obscure.
                    The great, the famous, I envy less.
OLD MAN: But greatness and fame are the glory of
                    life.
AGAMEMNON: Is it so? This glory's a snare. High place
                    Is desirable, but, when attained, a disease.
                    When our life's not baulked and be-
                    devilled by gods,
                    It's torn into shreds

By the peevish scheming of mortals.

OLD MAN: Agamemnon, these are no words for a
                 king.

When your father begot you, did he stip-
ulate
For a life of unbroken good luck? No.
Being mortal flesh, you have to accept
Both joy and pain.
This is the gods' decision, whether
You like it or not. Yet here you sit
By the spreading light of a lamp, and
     write
That letter you still have there in your
     hand;
Then you cross it all out;
You seal it up, and then break the seal;
You throw it all to the ground, while hot
Tears pour from your eyes. You're in
     despair,
Half-way to madness. What troubles you?
Something has happened, King. What is
     it?
Look – why not tell the whole thing to
     me?
I'm an honest man, one you can trust.
I was given to your wife,
As part of her dowry, by Tyndareos,
To attend her when you were married.

AGAMEMNON: Leda, Thestius' daughter, was mother of
     three girls,
Phoebe, and my wife Clytemnestra, and Helen.
Many of the most splendid princes of Greece gathered
As suitors to win Helen; and each man swore that if
He did not win her, he would kill the man who did.
At this, her father Tyndareos, at his wits' end

To know how best to deal with the situation – whether
To give her in marriage or not give her – finally
Hit on this plan: he made the suitors swear an oath,
Pledge their right hands, offer burnt sacrifice, and pour
Libations, to confirm this solemn undertaking:
Whoever of them should win Helen for his wife
Should have the united help of all, if any man
Usurped her husband's bed, or stole her from his home;
All would take arms and march against him, be he Greek
Or Asiatic, and level his city with the ground.
In this way wily old Tyndareos cornered them –
Quite cleverly; then, their word once pledged, he told his
    daughter
To let sweet Aphrodite's wind blow where it would,
And from the suitors name the husband of her own choice.
She chose – I curse the day he won his wish – Menelaus.

    So then this Paris, the man – you know the tale – who
        judged
The three goddesses, left Troy for Sparta. His gown gleamed
With flowers; gold sparkled in barbaric luxury.
He loved Helen, and she him. He chose a moment when
Menelaus was out of Sparta, seized his prize, and took her
Off to the farmlands of Mount Ida. Then Menelaus
Went like a raging fury round the Hellene states
To invoke that oath the suitors swore to Tyndareos,
And as the injured husband claim their armed support.
The Hellenes seized their weapons, leapt at the call to war,
And came here to the land-locked shore of Aulis Bay
With ships, shields, horses, chariots – the whole array of
    battle.

    Because I was Menelaus' brother, they chose me
As commander-in-chief; and I wish to God that someone
    else
Had been given this honour instead of me. Well, when the
    army

Was all gathered and organized, the weather changed.
We could not sail. We waited on, at our wits' end.
At last Calchas the prophet said that we must offer
To Artemis, in her temple here, Iphigenia,
My own child, as a sacrifice; if we did so,
We'd get a fair wind and sack Troy; not otherwise.
     When I heard this, I told Talthybius to make
A general proclamation dismissing the whole army,
Since I would never consent to kill my own daughter.
And then my brother, with every kind of argument,
At last made me agree to this atrocious crime.
I wrote a letter and sent it to my wife; I told her
To send our daughter here to be married to Achilles.
I made much of Achilles' reputation; said
That he refused to sail with us, unless a bride
Out of our family should return with him to Phthia.
I had to find a way to persuade my wife, and so
Patched up this lie about a marriage for the girl.
No one else knows all this, except Calchas, Odysseus,
And Menelaus. I made a wrong decision then;
Now I'm reversing it. You saw me, friend, under
Shelter of darkness, unseal and then seal again
This letter. This carries my right decision. Come,
Take it, and get to Argos. I'll repeat to you
In words what I have written – the secret hidden here;
You're faithful to my wife and to our family.

OLD MAN: Yes, tell me, so that my spoken word
                  Will tally with what you've written here.

AGAMEMNON: 'To follow my former letter,
                  I write this, daughter of Leda.
                  Do not send forth your child to where
                  The Euboean cape like a wing enfolds
                  The unruffled harbour of Aulis.
                  Our daughter's wedding-banquet
                  Must wait for another season.'

OLD MAN: And if Achilles loses his bride,
             Will his indignation not blow high
             Against you and your wife?
             There is danger here; so tell me your
                mind.

AGAMEMNON: Achilles lends us his name, no more.
             This marriage, and all our scheming, he
                knows
             Nothing of; doesn't know that I've
                promised to give
             My daughter to his embrace and bed
             As his wedded wife.

OLD MAN: It was rash, it was wrong, King Agamem-
                non,
             To assign your child
             As a bride to the son of the goddess, and
                then
             Bring her here for the Greeks
             To cut her throat at an altar.

AGAMEMNON: I am out of my mind, God help me!
             I sink in ruin and madness.
             — Go, fast as your feet can take you!
                Forget
             That you're an old man.

OLD MAN: I'll hurry, my lord.

AGAMEMNON: No resting, remember, by shady springs!
             Don't soften in sleep.

OLD MAN: What a thing to say!

AGAMEMNON: When you come to the point where the
                road divides,
             Look in every direction; take great care
             That you let no carriage speed by un-
                awares
             Bringing Iphigenia
             Down here to the ships of the Hellenes.

OLD MAN: Trust me.

AGAMEMNON: If you meet her escort flying
                   From the safety of home, send them fly-
                       ing back,
                   Drive hard, loosen rein, and get them
                       home
                   To our giant-built walls.

OLD MAN: But will they believe my message? What
                       proof
                   Shall I show to your child and your
                       wife?

AGAMEMNON [*giving his ring*]: This seal
                   Is the seal on the letter. Keep it. Now go.
                   There's a glimmer of dawn as the fiery
                       team
                   Of the sun drives up, and the sky turns
                       pale.
                   So, help and save me!

[*The* OLD MAN *sets off.*]

                                        No mortal man
                   Can ever hold on
                   To success and luck till the end of his
                       life.
                   So sure as you're born you will suffer.

[AGAMEMNON *goes into the tent. Enter the* CHORUS.]

                                            [*Strophe*

CHORUS: We have sailed through the running tide
              Of Euripus, and beached here on the sandy shore
              Near the sea-port of Aulis.
              Our city is Chalcis, across the narrow channel,
              Nurse of the streams that flow
              From the clear spring close to the brine,
              Far-famed Arethusa. And we have come
              To see the Achaeans, heroes descended from
                  gods;

To see the Achaean army and their fleet of
    oared ships.
With a thousand keels of pine, our husbands
    tell us,
They are sailing to Troy, led by tawny Menelaus
And noble Agamemnon, to bring back Helen,
Whom Paris the shepherd-prince
Stole from her home by the reedy banks of
    Eurotas,
Claiming the gift that Aphrodite gave him
When beside the cool-flowing fountain
The goddess of love matched jealousy against
    jealousy
With Hera and Pallas for the prize of beauty.

We ran quickly up past the altar   [*Antistrophe*
In the grove of Artemis; and like a shy girl
I blushed crimson as I came,
For what I wanted to see was the wall of
    shields,
The tents, the men in full armour,
And the throngs of horses.
And I saw, sitting side by side,
Aias the son of Oileus
And the other Aias, son of Telamon,
The pride of the island of Salamis.
And I saw Protesilaus sitting
With Palamedes, grandson of the sea-god,
Enjoying the complications of a game of
    draughts;
And Diomedes lustily throwing the discus;
Near him Meriones, descended from the god
    of war –
He is a sight to gaze at ! –
And Laertes' son, from the isle of mountains,

And with him Nireus, most handsome of the
    Achaeans.

And I saw the runner Achilles   [*Epode*
Whose feet are like the wind,
Whom Thetis bore and Cheiron trained –
As he ran along the shingle in full armour,
Matching his strength and speed against a four-
    horse chariot,
Rounding the post to win.
The charioteer was Eumelos, grandson of
    Pheres;
As he shouted to his splendid horses
And goaded them on, I saw
Their bridles flashing with fine-wrought gold.
The yoke-horses in the centre
Were dappled, with flecks of white;
The trace-horses, right and left,
Pulling opposite at the turning-points,
Were bays with spotted fetlocks;
And beside them, level with the rail and the
    singing hubs,
Achilles in his armour sped along.

Then we began counting the ships –   [*Strophe*
What a sight beyond description!
And how women's eyes love looking!
We looked and looked, gorging on honey.
The right wing of the fleet
Was the Myrmidon force from Phthia,
With fifty fast vessels; high on their sterns
Rose golden effigies of the immortal Nereids,
A battle-standard for Achilles' men.

Next to them the Argive warships [*Antistrophe*
Were ranged, equal in number;

Their commander was the son of Mecisteus
And grandson of Talaos; and with him
Was Sthenelos son of Capaneus.
Leading sixty ships of Attica
The son of Theseus held the next place,
And his banner was the divine Pallas
Set in a winged chariot drawn by horses,
A cheering symbol for the crews.

I saw the Boeotian squadron,   [Strophe
Fifty sea-going ships rigged with ensigns;
Theirs was Cadmus, a golden snake in his hand,
High above every poop;
Their commander was the earth-born Leitos.
There was a force from Phocis,
And an equal number of Locrian vessels
Led by Aias son of Oileus,
From the famous town of Thronion.

From giant-built Mycenae   [Antistrophe
The son of Atreus leads a contingent
That crowds his hundred galleys.
Sharing his command, Adrastos,
As bound in love, comes to ensure
That Hellas metes out justice
On the wife who fled from her home
And gave herself to an eastern prince.
From Pylos comes Nestor of Gerena;
And I saw, as a symbol on his stern,
The bull-figure of the god Alpheios,
River of his birthplace.

                                  [Epode
The Ainians have twelve ships in commission,
And their king Gouneus commands them.
Next to them are the dominant tribe of Elis,

Whom the army call Epeians,
Commanded by Eurytos, who also leads
The white-oared warships of the Taphians
Under their king Meges son of Phyleus;
He comes from the Echinian islands,
Which sailors avoid.
Aias (the one born in Salamis)
Keeps his right wing in touch
With the left of those stationed nearest;
He has twelve ships, very light to handle,
Knitting the end of the line.
So we were told, and sight of the fleet confirm-
    ed it.
No enemy, I am sure,
Attacking with Asian craft,
Could ever win safe home, so powerful
Is the fleet we have seen in the bay;
And besides what we have seen, there are
    many facts
About the assembled armament
Which I heard at home, and store in memory.

[*Enter* MENELAUS, *holding in one hand Agamemnon's
letter, and with the other grasping the* OLD MAN.]

OLD MAN: Menelaus, this is an outrage! You have no
              right at all —

MENELAUS: Get out! You're overdoing your duty to
              your master.

OLD MAN: If you call that a fault, then it's a fault I'm
              proud of.

MENELAUS: If you meddle in what doesn't concern you,
              you'll be sorry.

OLD MAN: You had no business to open a letter I was
              carrying.

MENELAUS: Nor you to be carrying a letter which betrays
              all Greece.

OLD MAN:	You can argue that with others. Give me back the letter.
MENELAUS:	I'll never give it back.
OLD MAN:	And I'll never let go.
MENELAUS:	You'll feel my stick – you want a bloody head, do you?
OLD MAN:	Go on, then; it's an honour to die for my master.
MENELAUS:	Let go; you talk too much for a slave.
OLD MAN:	Help, master, help!
	He's got your letter – taken it out of my hands by force!
	He doesn't know what right is. Agamemnon! Help!

[*Enter* AGAMEMNON.]

AGAMEMNON:	Here – what's all this? Violence, shouting, brawling – at my very door?

[*The* OLD MAN *begins to speak, but* MENELAUS *breaks in.*]

MENELAUS:	You'll attend to *me* first; my reply takes precedence over his.
AGAMEMNON:	Well, Menelaus – and what's the quarrel? Why must you lay hands on him?
MENELAUS:	As a start for this discussion, look me in the eyes.
AGAMEMNON:	Atreus
	The fearless was my father: do you think I'm afraid of facing you?
MENELAUS:	Do you see this letter? – courier of the most disgraceful –
AGAMEMNON:	Yes.
	And first, hand that letter to me.
MENELAUS:	Never, till I've shown the whole Army of Hellas what is written there.

AGAMEMNON: Did
          you dare to break my seal,
     Read what you'd no right to?

MENELAUS: Yes, I did.
          Unfortunate for you.
     I know all your secret treachery.

AGAMEMNON: Where
          did you find him? Oh, the gods!
     Have you no shame?

MENELAUS: I was on the road
          from Argos, looking out
     For your child's arrival.

AGAMEMNON: Barefaced impudence!
          That's *my* concern.
     Why must you go spying – ?

MENELAUS: I had an itch
          to. And I'm not your slave.

AGAMEMNON: This is intolerable. May I not manage my
             own family affairs?

MENELAUS: No! You're crooked; always changing –
             this way, that way, back again.

AGAMEMNON: You are plausible – a black heart, a glib
             tongue. What more odious?

MENELAUS: Maybe; but your shiftiness is a doubtful asset to
     your friends.
   Let me ask you a few questions; don't just fly into a rage
   Or deny what's undeniable – and I won't be hard on you.
   Cast your mind back to the time when you were hoping for
     the command –
   You pretended to be indifferent, but your heart was set on
     it.
   Your politeness then, your universal handshake, open house
   For the common soldier, ready audience to all without
   Favour, whether sought or unsought – then, by such be-
     haviour, you

Tried to buy votes in the open market, for the generalship.

Afterwards, once you held power, your manner changed.
  Your former friends

Found your friendship less forthcoming; you were busy;
  your door shut,

Your time precious. A man of principle should not change
  character

As he grows great. When good fortune gives him power to
  help his friends,

That's the time when most of all he ought to prove reliable.

There's my first criticism, the point where I first found you
  treacherous.

Then, when you and the whole Greek army came to Aulis –
  suddenly

You were no one – shattered by the shift of chance sent by
  the gods:

No fair wind for Troy, the Greeks impatient to disband the
  fleet

And waste no more sweat at Aulis. What a dismal figure you

Cut then, how crestfallen, at the thought that you might
  never fill

Priam's plain with armed men, as commander of a thousand
  ships!

  So you came to me. 'What shall I do! How can I find a way

To avoid losing my command and all the glory attached to it?'

Then, when Calchas bade you offer sacrifice to Artemis

With your daughter's life, and promised us fair winds, then
  you were pleased,

Gladly undertook to kill her; sent a letter to your wife,

Willingly – you can't say you were forced to it – command-
  ing her,

'Send the girl here, to be married to Achilles' – so you said;

And this very sky above you then was witness to your words.

Now you change your mind. We catch you sending a different letter, saying

You're no longer willing to be your daughter's murderer.
    Quite so.
Thousands like you go the same way – struggle steadily up to
    power,
Then – they fall with ignominy, sometimes condemned by a
    stupid vote,
Sometimes justly, being themselves incapable of sound
    statesmanship.
Oh, it's Hellas I feel sorry for, hapless Hellas! After these
Lofty ambitions, she'll sit by and let effete barbarians
Jeer at her, and all for you and your daughter. As in politics,
So in an army, noble blood doesn't make a leader. Any man
With some sense can lead a city; an army chief must have a
    mind.

CHORUS: When brothers fall to quarrelling, it is terrible
              And strange to watch the battle of their angry
                 words.

AGAMEMNON: I have harsh words to speak to you in turn;
    not many, nor will I
Throw too sharp a glance on your shameless conduct, but
    moderate
What I say, since you're my brother. Nobleness respects such
    bonds.
Tell me, why this bursting indignation? Why these blood-
    shot eyes?
Who has wronged you? What are you wanting – lusting for?
    A virtuous wife?
That I can't provide; the one you got, you governed fool-
    ishly.
Then must I, who made no error, pay the price of your mis-
    chance?
Or does my position sting you? No! You want one thing: to
    hold
In your arms a handsome woman; and for that you'll throw
    away

Reason, honour! True, a vicious man's pleasures are like
    himself.
 I made an unwise decision; if I reverse it now, and act
Wisely, is that madness? You're the one who's mad: you
    lost a bad
Wife, and now you throw away the good luck the gods sent
    you, and
Want her back! Her suitors, in their misguided zeal to marry
    her,
Swore the oath Tyndareos asked for; but it was no fear of you
Made them keep it; they were lured by Hope – a goddess
    without doubt.
Take *them*, then; they're willing, poor fools; go and fight
    your war with *them*.
Gods aren't blind; they're well aware when oaths are taken
    foolishly
Or upon compulsion. But, for me – I will not kill my child;
Nor shall you flout decency to punish your disgraceful wife
And console your pride, while I pass nights and days in
    anguished tears,
Guilty of unnamed wickedness towards the child of my own
    blood.
So, I've told you, in few words, and clear, and easy. If you
    won't
Choose a wise course, I'll arrange my own affairs as best I
    may.

CHORUS: What you say now is contrary to what you said
             Before; but your resolve to spare your child is
             right.

MENELAUS: All's over, then. I'm in despair. I have no
             friends.

AGAMEMNON: You have – if you'll stop trying to ruin your
             friend's lives.

MENELAUS: Did one father beget us both? Will you
             prove that?

AGAMEMNON: I'll be your brother in fair dealing, not in
             crime.

MENELAUS: As a true friend, you ought to feel for my
             distress.

AGAMEMNON: Use kindness, drop your malice; and then
             call on me.

MENELAUS: You mean, then, you won't help your
             country in her need?

AGAMEMNON: Some god has struck my country, and you,
             with lunacy.

MENELAUS: Well, then: boast of your generalship;
             betray your brother.

I have other resources, and I have other friends.
I'll go to them.

          [*Enter a* MESSENGER *hurriedly*.]

MESSENGER: Agamemnon, lord of all the Hellenes!
We have brought your daughter to you, whom you named
    at home
Iphigenia. Her mother, your noble Clytemnestra,
Is with her; and, to delight your heart, since you have been
So long away from home, your son Orestes too.
After a long and weary journey, they are now
Cooling their feet beside a flowing spring – both they
And the horses, which we turned loose in a green meadow
To graze. I've run ahead, to bid you be prepared.
The whole camp knows your daughter has arrived; the
    news
Spread quickly. Thousands are hurrying for a sight of her;
For people love to talk about and gaze at those
Fortune has blessed! 'Is there a wedding afoot?' they ask,
'Or what is it? Has the king brought his daughter here
Through longing to see her?' Others suggest, 'They are
    offering
A marriage-sacrifice to Artemis, Queen of Aulis;
Who is the bridegroom?' Come, prepare the holy rites;

And you, and Lord Menelaus, put garlands on your heads!
Set all in order for a wedding, and in your tents
Let music of flutes peal out, and the sound of dancing feet;
For sunrise brings a day of blessing for Iphigenia.

AGAMEMNON: I commend you. Go inside now. Fate will
take its course,
And what's to come shall be well.
[*Exit* MESSENGER.]

Gods! What shall I say?
Where can I begin? What a man-trap of compulsive Fate
I have fallen into! Some divine power, cleverer
Than all my cleverness, has tricked and defeated me.
To be low-born, I see, has its advantages:
A man can weep, and tell his sorrows to the world.
A king endures sorrows no less; but the demand
For dignity governs our life, and we are slaves
To the masses. I am ashamed to weep; and equally
I am ashamed not to weep, in such a depth of grief.
And what, for pity's sake, can I say to my wife?
How can I receive her, meet her look? I did not tell
Her to come – this, on top of all the agony
I had already, is the last blow! Yet, naturally,
She must come to her daughter's wedding, to fulfil
A mother's loving part – where she shall find *my* part
The opposite! And then – poor maid! – Is she a maid?
It seems Death will soon lie with her. Poor girl, poor girl!
I hear her begging me: 'Father, will you take my life?
Is this my marriage? May you, and all you love, find such
A marriage yours!' And little Orestes will be there –
He can't talk yet; but his unwitting cries will speak
Clear to my heart. The first cause of all this, O Paris,
Paris, your love for Helen, has destroyed my life!

CHORUS: As far as a woman from another city may
Mourn a king's anguish, my heart too is filled with grief.

MENELAUS: Brother, your hand – give me your hand.

AGAMEMNON [*giving it*]:   You've
    won; I'm lost.

MENELAUS: I swear by Pelops, famous father of your father
  And mine, and by our begetter Atreus, I will speak
  My heart's truth, with no hidden purpose, laying bare
  My whole mind. When I see the tears fall from your eyes,
  My own heart melts, my tears join yours; now I unsay
  The words I said before. I am not your enemy;
  I'll stand where you stand; and I urge you not to kill
  Your child, nor put my interest before yours. Why should
  You weep, and I be happy, your child die, and mine
  Live? It's not just. What after all, do I desire?
  If it's a wife I'm longing for, can I not get
  Another, of rare choice? Am I to cast away –
  Of all men – my own brother, to possess Helen,
  Lose what is good, to keep what's evil? I behaved
  Just now as a fool, a boy, until I looked closer
  And saw what kind of act it is to kill one's child.

    Besides, compassion moves me for the unhappy girl,
  Remembering she is of one blood with me, and faces
  Death at an altar for the sake of my false wife.
  What, after all, is Helen to her? Let the expedition
  Break up now, and leave Aulis. Brother, dry your tears,
  Which make my own eyes flow. If *you* are under duress
  By oracles about your daughter, let *me* have
  No part in it; my share I give to you. You'll think
  I've made a quick change from my hostile tone. Why not?
  The change is natural; we are sons of the same father.
  I'm not a bad man; and I prove it by being ready
  Still, as events move on, to follow the best course.

CHORUS: Your noble sentiments are worthy of Tantalus,
  Son of Zeus; you have brought honour on your ancestors.

AGAMEMNON: Menelaus, I thank you. Your words took me
    by surprise.
  The course you urge is right, and worthy of yourself.

Brothers will quarrel – over a woman, or a throne;
Their very kinship has this hateful quality,
That it embitters one against the other. Yet,
Your kind words can lead nowhere. We are in Fate's grip,
We are forced to go on; we must shed my daughter's blood.

MENELAUS: Why? She's your own child. Who is going to
force your hand?

AGAMEMNON: The whole assembly of the Achaean armament.

MENELAUS: Not if you send your daughter back again to
Argos.

AGAMEMNON: This I might manage secretly; but something
else
Would foil me.

MENELAUS: What? Don't be too nervous of the rabble.

AGAMEMNON: Calchas will publish the oracle to the whole
army.

MENELAUS: Not if he dies first; which can easily be arranged.

AGAMEMNON: Prophets – their whole power-thirsty breed –
are damnable.

MENELAUS: They are: no good, and good for nothing – while
they live.

AGAMEMNON: There is another thing I fear – no doubt you
too.

MENELAUS: If you don't speak your meaning, how can I
understand?

AGAMEMNON: The son of Sisyphos knows this whole predicament.

MENELAUS: And what harm can Odysseus do to you and me?

AGAMEMNON: He's sly by nature; and loves popularity.

MENELAUS: Ambition, yes – it rules him; and that's dangerous.

AGAMEMNON: Well, do you think Odysseus won't stand up
before
The assembled Argives, and inform them what oracle

Calchas pronounced? – how I first undertook to make
This sacrifice to Artemis, and now retract?
He'll whip the men up into a rage, urge them to kill
Both you and me, and sacrifice Iphigenia.
Even if I escape to Argos, they'll come after me,
Capture the town, Cyclopian walls and all, and make
The land a ruin. Such is my pit of misery,
The blind despair in which the gods now have me trapped.
  Menelaus, mind one thing: as you go through the camp
Make certain Clytemnestra hears no word of this,
Before I take my daughter and deliver her
To death, that I may drown in crime with fewest tears.
– And you, women of Chalcis: not one word of this.

      [*Exit* AGAMEMNON *to his tent,* MENELAUS *to the camp.*]

                                                      [*Strophe*

CHORUS: Happy are those on whom divine Aphrodite
               Comes in seemly measure, in moderate power,
               Who sail in calm seas, untroubled
               By the stings that madden the heart
               Where Eros of the golden hair aims from his
                    bent bow
               The twin arrows of his charms –
               One to bestow lifelong content,
               The other, ruin and confusion.
               Lovely Cyprian, I entreat you,
               Avert such ruin from my marriage-bed!
               Let sweet delight be mine in due measure,
               And my desires lawful;
               Let me share in Aphrodite's gifts,
               But be saved from the fulness of her power.

               Men's natures are diverse,   [*Antistrophe*
               Diverse too are their ways;
               But real goodness is always seen.
               A childhood nurtured by sound training

Imparts a strong tendency to virtue;
For scrupulousness is wisdom,
And, further, possesses this transforming
      grace –
The vision of duty revealed by reflection;
In which pursuit, recognition
Crowns a man's life with ageless glory.
The quest of virtue is a wonderful thing;
Whether in women, to avoid unchastity,
Or in men, whose manifold devotion to disci-
      pline
Exalts a city to greatness.

You returned, Paris, to the place   [*Epode*
Where you grew up as a herdsman among
The gleaming-white heifers of Mount Ida,
Piping tunes of the East, blowing on reeds
Music like that which Olympus
Drew from his Phrygian flute.
Deep-uddered herds were grazing
Where goddesses awaited your judgement;
And your choice sent you to Hellas,
To stand before a palace of ivory,
And pour your love in Helen's gazing eyes,
And be love-shattered in return.
So that day's strife on Ida
Brought strife to Hellas, and led
Spearmen and ships against the walls of Troy.

Look now! See now! and welcome the great
In their greatness of fortune! See Iphigenia,
Agamemnon's royal daughter, and
Clytemnestra, daughter of Tyndareos!
The splendour of their origin matches
In fortune the glory of their destiny.

Indeed, the possessors of wealth and power,
To the unprivileged, appear as gods.

[CLYTEMNESTRA and IPHIGENIA *enter in a chariot,
with women in attendance.*]

CLYTEMNESTRA: I take your kind words and your friendly
welcome as
A happy omen; and indeed I have good hope
That I am here as a mother to present this bride
To a noble marriage. [*To Attendants*] Come, lift down the
gifts I've brought
For my daughter's dowry, and carry them indoors* care-
fully.
Come now, dear child, step down; it's a rough place for
you
To walk on, and you're tired as well. – Girls, help her down;
Give her your arms, now – hold her. Someone help me too;
I need a steadying hand, to get up from this seat
With dignity. – And, some of you, go and stand in front
Of the horses' heads; horses are nervous at the sight
Of strange surroundings, unless someone talks to them.
And here is Orestes, Agamemnon's little son;
Take him, he's still only a baby. – Little one,
Are you asleep? Did the jolting make you tired? Wake up,
And wish your sister happiness for her wedding-day.

[AGAMEMNON *has entered unobtrusively.*]

You're going to have a hero as noble as yourself
For your brother-in-law, the godlike son of the sea-nymph.
– Come, Iphigenia, stand here, as a daughter should,
Next to her mother – there now, so that these ladies may
Call me a fortunate woman, when they see you here
Standing beside me. Come now, give your father a kiss.

IPHIGENIA: Oh, mother, don't be angry if I go before you;
I want to put my arms round him and hug him close.

* There are two doors to Agamemnon's tent, one used by the men, the
other by the women.

CLYTEMNESTRA: Great Agamemnon, my most honoured lord and king,
We have come, in due obedience to your commands.

IPHIGENIA: Oh, but I want to be the first, father, to hold you
In my arms, after such a long time! I've been longing
Just to look at you. Don't be angry with me, mother.

CLYTEMNESTRA: Why, child, it's only right. Of all our children, you
Were always the one to show your father most affection.

IPHIGENIA: I am so happy to see you after so long, father.

AGAMEMNON: And I to see you. That is equally true for both.

IPHIGENIA: You did a good thing, father, bringing me here to you.

AGAMEMNON: A good thing – or not good? I don't know what to say.

IPHIGENIA: But, if you're glad to see me, why this worried look?

AGAMEMNON: A king and a general bears responsibilities.

IPHIGENIA: Don't turn your mind to them now; spend this time with me.

AGAMEMNON: Well – now my mind is all with you and nowhere else.

IPHIGENIA: You look so anxious; now, smooth out your brow and smile.

AGAMEMNON: There then – I am happy, as I should be when I see you, my dear.

IPHIGENIA: And yet the tears are falling from your eyes, father.

AGAMEMNON: Yes; a long time of separation faces us.

IPHIGENIA: My dearest father, I don't know why you're saying this.

AGAMEMNON: You speak so understandingly, I weep still more.

IPHIGENIA: Then I'll speak foolishly, if that will comfort you.

AGAMEMNON: I can't help weeping. Thank you for your loving words.

IPHIGENIA: Father, stay with your children, at home.

AGAMEMNON: That is my wish.

   To have lost the power even to wish – that is my pain.

IPHIGENIA: This war, and Menelaus' troubles – my curse on them!

AGAMEMNON: Before they end, the curse which has cursed me will fall

   Elsewhere.

IPHIGENIA: You have been so long boxed up in Aulis here.

AGAMEMNON: And one thing still lies between me and setting sail.

IPHIGENIA: Father, where is this famous town of the Phrygians?

AGAMEMNON: Where Priam's son Paris lives – I curse the day he was born!

IPHIGENIA: After you've left me, father, will your voyage be long?

AGAMEMNON: When both our voyages end, my dear, I'll see you again.

IPHIGENIA: If only we both had to make this voyage together!

AGAMEMNON: You must sail too; and as you go you'll think of me.

IPHIGENIA: Will my mother sail with me, or must I go alone?

AGAMEMNON: You will go alone, far from your mother and from me.

IPHIGENIA: But you have found another home for me, father?

AGAMEMNON: Enough now; such things are not for young girls to know.

IPHIGENIA: Come quickly back from Troy, father – victorious!

AGAMEMNON: But first I have a sacrifice to offer here.

IPHIGENIA: Of course, what is pious must be performed with holy gifts.

AGAMEMNON: You will have a place by the altar. All will be made clear.

IPHIGENIA: By the altar! Shall I lead the dancing there, father?

AGAMEMNON: If only I could be like you, and know nothing!
But go indoors; you should be with your women now.
Give me your hand, my dear, and give me a sad kiss;
Your home from now on will be far away from me.
Dear bosom, soft cheeks, and bright hair, what cruelty
Helen and Troy have brought upon you! No more words;
Your hand's touch brings the swift tears flooding from my eyes.
Go indoors now.

    [*Exit* IPHIGENIA.]

               I beg you will forgive me this,
Daughter of Leda, if I am too deeply moved with grief
At this prospect of giving my daughter to Achilles.
Such partings may be happy occasions; none the less
They are hard for parents, when the child of so much care
Is sent off by her father to another home.

CLYTEMNESTRA: I am myself not heartless; you may be sure that I,
So far from blaming you, shall suffer the same pangs
When I lead forth your daughter at her wedding-rite.
But custom, joined with time, will ease our sadness. — Now,
This man to whom you've promised her: I know his name,
But I must learn his family too, and where he lives.

AGAMEMNON: Asopus' daughter Aegina was his ancestress.

CLYTEMNESTRA: And she — what mortal or what god was joined to her?

AGAMEMNON: Zeus; and she bore him Aeacus, prince of Oenone.

CLYTEMNESTRA: What son of Aeacus then inherited his house?

AGAMEMNON: Peleus; he married the sea-god Nereus' daughter, Thetis.

CLYTEMNESTRA: Did the god bestow her, or did he take her in defiance?

AGAMEMNON: She was betrothed and given by Zeus her guardian.

CLYTEMNESTRA: Where did he wed her? Deep among the salt sea waves?

AGAMEMNON: Where Cheiron lives, on the stern slopes of Pelion.

CLYTEMNESTRA: Where, as the old tale says, the centaurs had their home?

AGAMEMNON: There the gods celebrated Peleus' wedding-feast.

CLYTEMNESTRA: And who brought up Achilles – Thetis, or his father?

AGAMEMNON: Cheiron – that he might not learn the ways of evil men.

CLYTEMNESTRA: Indeed? A wise teacher, chosen by a parent wiser still.

AGAMEMNON: Such, then, is the man who will be husband to your child.

CLYTEMNESTRA: No fault to find there. What Greek city is his home?

AGAMEMNON: A highland town in Phthia, on the Apidanos.

CLYTEMNESTRA: And that's where you will take your little girl and mine?

AGAMEMNON: I? No, he'll take her, as her husband.

CLYTEMNESTRA: Bless them both!
   Which day is the wedding?

AGAMEMNON: At the full moon – for good luck.

CLYTEMNESTRA: Have you already offered preliminary rites
   To the goddess?

AGAMEMNON: I am about to. That's what keeps us here.

CLYTEMNESTRA: And after that you'll celebrate the wedding-feast?

AGAMEMNON: When I've first made a sacrifice I owe to the gods.

CLYTEMNESTRA: And where can I prepare to hold the women's feast?

AGAMEMNON: Here, by the high sterns of the Argive ships.

CLYTEMNESTRA: Well, if I must, I suppose I can. I hope all will go well.

AGAMEMNON: Now this is what you have to do – be ruled by me.

CLYTEMNESTRA: What must I do? Of course I'm always ruled by you.

AGAMEMNON: I shall stay here in Aulis, where the bride-groom is –

CLYTEMNESTRA: Without the bride's mother – to do what I should do?

AGAMEMNON: I and the other Greeks will give away your daughter.

CLYTEMNESTRA: And what of me, pray? Where must I be all this time?

AGAMEMNON: Go back to Argos and look after the little girls.

CLYTEMNESTRA: Leave Iphigenia here? Then who will raise the torch?

AGAMEMNON: I will attend to the traditional marriage-torch.

CLYTEMNESTRA: This is not right. Do you think such matters unimportant?

AGAMEMNON: It is not right for you to stay in a crowded camp.

CLYTEMNESTRA: It is right for a mother to give away her child.

AGAMEMNON: The little girls ought not to be left at home alone.

CLYTEMNESTRA: The house is well protected; they are per-
 fectly safe.

AGAMEMNON: Do as I tell you.

CLYTEMNESTRA: No, by Hera goddess of
 Argos!
 You manage war and politics: I'll run home affairs.
        [*Exit* CLYTEMNESTRA.]

AGAMEMNON: Oh, gods! What a defeat, a feeble, flat col-
 lapse
 Of hopes and schemes to get my wife out of the way!
 I tell lies, I plot tricks against my own dear child,
 And after all I'm beaten out of hand! I'll go
 And talk to Calchas the soothsayer, and get from him,
 If I can, the truth about what pleases Artemis,
 Tortures me, and must plunge Hellas in shame and blood.
    A man of sense should have a wife whom he can trust,
 A wife who knows her duty – or else get rid of her.
        [*Exit* AGAMEMNON.]

CHORUS: Soon, to the silver swirl   [*Strophe*
             Where Simois meets the sea
             Will come the massed soldiers of Hellas,
             Ranged in their ships and weaponed,
             To Ilion, and the ground where Phoebus
                 founded Troy;
             Where, as I hear, Cassandra
             Adorned with a garland of green laurel
             Tosses her bright locks, when the god
             Breathes on her the compulsions of prophecy.

             The people of Troy will stand   [*Antistrophe*
             On Troy's battlements and along her walls
             When an army of bronze shields advances over
                 the sea
             Riding on proud prows and rhythmic oars
             Towards the quays of Simois,

Eager to bring back from Priam's city
Helen, sister of the Celestial Twins,
Won with shield and spear as the prize of
    battle.

And what of Pergamus, city and home of
    Phrygians?
Around its battlements of stone
The Achaean army will close in a circle of
    blood;
There will be heads forced back, throats cut;
Streets stripped, every building gutted and
    crashed;
Screams and sobs from young women,
And from Priam's wife;
And Helen daughter of Zeus
Shall learn what it is to leave a husband.
God grant that neither I nor my children's
    children
Ever face such a prospect
As Lydian and Phrygian wives will see awaiting
    them
When they sit, glittering in gold, before their
    looms
And ask each other, 'Who will be the man
Who twists his hard hand in my silken hair
And like a plucked flower drags me away
While my tears flow hot and my home burns?'
— And all this for your sake, Helen,
Daughter of the long-necked swan;
If indeed the tale may be trusted
That Zeus, changed to the form of a winged
    bird,
Got you upon Leda;
Or, maybe, imagined myths

Purveyed to men this false and foolish fancy
In the pages of poets.

[*Enter* ACHILLES.]

ACHILLES: Where's the Commander-in-Chief Agamemnon?
    Anywhere here?
One of you servants, tell him Achilles son of Peleus
Is here in front of his tent door looking for him.

[*He turns to address the audience.*]

This loitering by the Euripus falls more heavily
On some than on others. Those of us who are unmarried
Have left their fathers' homes defenceless, and sit here
Idle on the shore; others have wives and families –
Astonishing how the craze to join this expedition
Has gripped men's minds; there's something supernatural
    in it.
However, I'd better explain what my own grievance is;
If any of the others wants to, he can speak for himself.
You see, I've left Pharsalus, and my old father;
And now, stuck here, with barely a breeze over the strait,
I have to keep the Myrmidons quiet. They're always at
    me:
'What are we waiting for, Achilles? How much longer
Must we keep counting the days till we set sail for Troy?
Have you got plans? If so, tell us; if not, let's all go home.
Why waste time waiting for those two to make up their
    minds?'

[*Enter* CLYTEMNESTRA.]

CLYTEMNESTRA: I heard your voice from indoors, son of the
    sea-goddess,
And came out quickly.

ACHILLES: Goddess of blushes! Who is this?
I see a lady richly endowed with comeliness.

CLYTEMNESTRA: We have not met before, so it is no sur-
    prise
That you don't know me. I approve your shyness, though.

ACHILLES: Who are you? Why have you come here to the
       Danaan camp,
  A woman alone before a wall of soldiers' shields?

CLYTEMNESTRA: I'll tell you. I am a daughter of Leda, and
       my name
  Is Clytemnestra. I am King Agamemnon's wife.

ACHILLES: I'm glad you told me straight out; just as well to
       know.
  But I'd rather not be seen here talking to a woman.

CLYTEMNESTRA: Don't run away! Stay here. Come, give me
       your right hand,
  And take mine, as a pledge of happiness in your marriage.

ACHILLES: I – take your hand? Why, what do you mean? It's
       not my place
  To be holding your hand. What will Agamemnon say?

CLYTEMNESTRA: Dear boy, of course it's your place, since
       you're going to marry
  My own dear daughter – you, the immortal sea-nymph's son.

ACHILLES: Marry? You strike me speechless. What is all this
       about?
  Why this absurd talk? Are you mentally deranged?

CLYTEMNESTRA: Well, it's quite natural, this embarrass-
       ment, when you meet
  Your new relations, and they talk of weddings.

ACHILLES: Madam:
  I never was a suitor for your daughter, nor
  Have I heard mention of marriage from any son of Atreus.

CLYTEMNESTRA: What can this mean? No wonder, then, you
       found my words
  Astonishing; and so, indeed, are yours to me.

ACHILLES: Think, now; it's in both our interests to think.
       Perhaps
  Neither of us is talking nonsense after all.

CLYTEMNESTRA: Have I been practised on? I've come here,
       it now seems,

For a wedding that's a mere fiction. I die with shame.

ACHILLES: Some one, no doubt, has made a fool of you – and me.
Well, now, don't worry; give it not another thought.

CLYTEMNESTRA: Good-bye. How can I look you in the face? I have
Been made a liar. This outrage was not deserved.

ACHILLES: Good-bye to you too. I'm going in to find your
husband.

[*As* ACHILLES *approaches* AGAMEMNON's *door the*
OLD MAN *looks out furtively.*]

OLD MAN: Sir! Grandson of Aeacus, wait a moment – yes, it's
you I mean,
You, Achilles son of Thetis, and you, Clytemnestra, too.

ACHILLES: Who's this calling from the doorway? He sounds
like a frightened man.

OLD MAN: I'm a slave; but this is urgent – we can't stand on
ceremony.

ACHILLES: Whose slave? Not mine. I and Agamemnon don't
share property.

OLD MAN: That's my mistress there; her father gave me to
her, Tyndareos.

ACHILLES: Well, I'm waiting. Speak if you want to; tell me
what you stopped me for.

OLD MAN: Are you sure there's no one else about here, only
she and you?

ACHILLES: We're alone; you may speak freely. Shut the door
and come out here.

OLD MAN: Now may Fortune, and my foresight, save the life
I hope to save!

ACHILLES: Your preamble will take time to save a life; it's
overweight.

CLYTEMNESTRA: Don't waste time in kneeling to me, if you
want to say something.

OLD MAN: You know well I'm faithful to you and your
children – always was.

CLYTEMNESTRA: I know you're an old-established servant of
    the royal house.

OLD MAN: I came with you when you married; Agamemnon
    took me then.

CLYTEMNESTRA: Yes, you came to Argos with me, and you
    always have been mine.

OLD MAN: That's the truth. *You* have my deepest loyalty;
    your husband – less.

CLYTEMNESTRA: Get it out, man; tell me quickly what it is
    you have to say.

OLD MAN: Iphigenia – her father – with his own hand – means
    to murder her.

CLYTEMNESTRA: What? Oh, what a filthy thing to say! You
    must be raving mad.

OLD MAN: With his sword he'll cut through her white throat
    – poor, miserable child!

CLYTEMNESTRA: Oh, what shall I do? Can it, then, be my
    husband who is mad?

OLD MAN: Yes, he's mad – towards you and your daughter;
    otherwise he's sane enough.

CLYTEMNESTRA: What's his reason for it? What destroying
    Fury drives him on?

OLD MAN: Some god's bidding – so says Calchas – so that the
    Greek fleet can sail.

CLYTEMNESTRA: Sail where? Oh, heaven help me, and help
    the child her father wants to kill!

OLD MAN: Why, to Troy, to help Menelaus get his lost wife
    Helen back.

CLYTEMNESTRA: So, Fate's price for Helen's homecoming is
    Iphigenia's life?

OLD MAN: That's the truth. Her father means to sacrifice her
    to Artemis.

CLYTEMNESTRA: And this marriage made the pretext which
    brought us from Argos here?

OLD MAN: Yes, so that you'd gladly bring your daughter, as Achilles' bride.

CLYTEMNESTRA: Oh, my child, it's death we have come to meet here, you and I alike.

OLD MAN: It's a pitiful crime against you both – yes, Agamemnon's crime.

CLYTEMNESTRA: Oh, what shall I do? I'm in despair. I can't hold back my tears.

OLD MAN: Of all griefs that call for weeping, this is worst, to lose a child.

CLYTEMNESTRA: Old man, tell me how you know this; what disclosed the truth to you?

OLD MAN: I was bringing a second letter to you, following the first.

CLYTEMNESTRA: Cancelling, or confirming his command to bring my child to die?

OLD MAN: Bidding you not come; your husband had by then regained his wits.

CLYTEMNESTRA: Then, if you were bringing a letter, why did you not give it me?

OLD MAN: Menelaus, the cause of all our troubles, snatched it from my hand.

CLYTEMNESTRA: Son of Peleus, of the sea-nymph Thetis, have you heard all this?

ACHILLES: Yes. You suffer cruelly; and I can't ignore the insult to me.

CLYTEMNESTRA: They are going to kill my daughter – they used your name as a trap!

ACHILLES: I too call your husband's act an outrage. I won't let it pass.

CLYTEMNESTRA: See, I throw away all pride and fall before you. Since my blood

Is but mortal, yours immortal, why should I disdain to kneel?

What else should I strive and plead for, more than for my own child's life?

Son of Thetis, help! Have pity, first, on my despair, and then

On her who was named, albeit falsely, yet was named your
　　bride.
For your sake I made her wedding-veil; for your sake brought
　　her here
Hoping for a husband, finding in his place a slaughterer's
　　knife.
You will be dishonoured, if you give no help; married or not,
You at least were called the unhappy girl's dear husband. By
　　your beard
I implore you, by your strong right hand, and by your
　　mother's name,
Help and save us! Vindicate your own name, which has been
　　our death.
There's no holy altar I can cling to, other than your knee;
I've no friend within reach; you have heard how Agamemnon
　　plots
Wicked cruelty. I've come here, a helpless woman, as you
　　see,
Into a naval camp, where men are bold in every lawless
　　crime –
Though goodwill may prompt their kindness. If you dare to
　　raise your hand
In my cause, we'll live to thank you; if not, then we have no
　　hope.

CHORUS: Being a mother holds a potent charm, and fires
　　This universal passion, to protect one's child.

ACHILLES: I feel my proud heart stirred to noble action; yet
　　I have learnt, whether in misfortune or in high success,
　　To keep both sorrow and rejoicing within bounds.
　　Those who observe this rule may reasonably hope
　　To live a well-governed life based on intelligence.
　　True, there are times when recklessness may be indulged;
　　And others when the advantage lies in sound judgement.
　　I was brought up by Cheiron, a good man; from him
　　I learnt simple, straightforward ways. If Atreus' sons
　　Act like good generals, I'll obey them; when they don't

I won't obey them. Both here and in Troy, I mean
To show myself a free man, and to do my best
To win some fame in battle. As for you, lady,
Your pitiful plight claims my protection; and I will,
In view of the disgraceful treatment you've received
From your own husband, do all that a young man can
To set things right. Your daughter is engaged to me:
Therefore she shall not die under her father's knife,
Nor will I lend myself to be your husband's tool
For subtle scheming. If I should, my very name,
With no sword drawn, becomes your daughter's murderer.
The fault would be your husband's — true; but I should feel
My very flesh tainted, if this girl, so abused,
Dishonoured past belief or bearing, were to die
Because of me, for a marriage promised in my name.
Why, I become the greatest coward in the camp,
An empty nobody (and Menelaus a man!)
Bred not from Peleus, but from some malevolent fiend,
If my name should spill blood to serve your husband's ends.
I swear by Nereus, fostered in the ocean depths,
My mother Thetis' father, Agamemnon shall not
So much as lay a finger on your daughter's dress;
Or Sipylos, on the fringe of barbarism, the place
Where our great generals' family had its origin,
Shall be a city, Phthia a village never named!
If ever Calchas plays the seer with his barley-meal
And hand-washing, he shall be sorry. What is a seer?
A man who, if he's lucky, tells a little truth
And a lot of lies; and if he's unlucky, vanishes.

   I've said all this, not out of eagerness to marry
Your daughter — thousands of girls pursue me all the time;
But King Agamemnon has insulted me. [*He is now addressing
      the audience*] To use
My name as a bait for the girl — he ought to have asked my
      leave.

It was chiefly my reputation that induced
Clytemnestra to give her daughter to me in marriage.
I would have granted the Greeks permission to use my name,
If that was the one obstacle to their setting sail;
I wouldn't refuse to help the cause of those who were
My colleagues in this expedition. But, as it is,
These generals treat me with contempt; to honour me
Or shame me is all one to them. If any man
Is going to take your daughter from my hands, this sword
Will know the reason; for I'll stain this iron with blood
Before I land at Troy. Rest easy; I have come
For your deliverance like a powerful god. In truth
I am not a god; no matter – for I shall be one.

CHORUS: Son of Peleus, your words are worthy of yourself
And of the immortal goddess, daughter of the sea.

CLYTEMNESTRA: How shall I answer?
What words can praise you fully without fulsomeness,
Yet not, by mean expression, nullify my thanks?
A brave man, being praised, will sometimes find himself
Hating his praiser for extravagance of speech.
I blush to obtrude my pitiful story on your ears,
Since my grief's private; why should my wrongs wring your
    heart?
Yet it shows nobly, if ever from his distant ease
The good man stoops to rescue those less fortunate.
Feel pity for me; for my plight is pitiful.
First, I had hoped to gain you for my son-in-law;
This hope proved false. Then, if my child should die, her
    death
Would surely curse your future marriage; you should guard
Against such an omen. What you said first was well said,
And what you said last. Grant but your goodwill, my child
Shall live. If you wish, she shall come and kneel to you.
This is not proper; but, if you desire it so,
She'll come, and in her look nobility will shine

Through modesty. But if without her presence I
Can win your kindness equally, let her stay indoors;
She is proud. Yet a great need may overbear reserve.

ACHILLES: Don't bring your daughter out to see me; let us
    avoid,
Madam, all risk of earning the reproach of fools.
A mass of men, set free from home with all its ties,
Loves nothing more than scandal and foul, vicious talk.
Anyway, kneeling or not kneeling makes no odds;
Here's my one supreme task: I have to save you both.
One thing I've said, be sure of: I won't tell you lies.
If I do — if I trifle with you, may I die;
And may I not die, only if I save the girl.

CLYTEMNESTRA: Heaven bless you, the unfailing friend of
    those in need!

ACHILLES: Now listen: to ensure success in what we plan —

CLYTEMNESTRA: What do you propose? I'll listen to any-
    thing you say.

ACHILLES: Let us first urge her father to a better mind.

CLYTEMNESTRA: He's cowardly; too apprehensive of the
    army's power.

ACHILLES: Well, our strong arguments will fight down his.

CLYTEMNESTRA: That's a cold hope; still, what do you think
    I ought to do?

ACHILLES: First, kneel and beg him not to kill his child; and
    then,
If he resists you, you must come to me. Suppose
You have won him over: then I need not stir; your cause
Is saved; I'll be in better standing with a friend;
And the army won't accuse me, if I've won my point
By reason, not by force. If this works, everything
Will turn out well, without me, both for you and her.

CLYTEMNESTRA: How wise you are. I'd better do what you
    suggest.
Suppose, though, my appeal to him should fail; what then?

Where shall I see you? I shall be in desperate need
Of your strong arm to save our lives. Where shall I come?

ACHILLES: I'll be on the look-out for you, in the right place;
You had better not be seen rushing distracted through
The soldiers' quarters. Family dignity must be
Preserved; you wouldn't wish the name of Tyndareos
To lose respect; he's highly thought of throughout Greece.

CLYTEMNESTRA: Very well. You shall rule, and I must be
your slave.

[*Exit* ACHILLES.]

If gods exist, you, being an upright man, will taste
Their kindness; if not, nothing further's to be done.

[*Exit* CLYTEMNESTRA *to the tent.*]

CHORUS: Full of joy was the wedding-chorus   [*Strophe*
Which, led by the Libyan flute
With dancing zither and reedy pipes,
Mingled music and voices,
When up the slopes of Pelion, to the feasting
of gods,
Their golden sandals pulsing the ground,
The fair-haired Muses came for the marriage of
Peleus,
And filled the hills of the Centaurs
And Pelion's echoing woods
With the sweetness of their chanting
In praise of Thetis and the son of Aeacus;
And Dardanus' child, Ganymede, prince of
Phrygia,
The dear delight of Zeus's bed,
Dipped deep in the bowl of gold,
Filling the cups for wine-offerings;
While over the white-gleaming sand
The fifty daughters of Nereus,
Honouring the rite of marriage,
Wove and turned in the whirling dance.

Crowned with young leaves, carrying pine-
    wood spears,   [Antistrophe
Came riding the roystering Centaurs
To the table of gods and the bowl of Bacchus.
Loudly they shouted, 'Daughter of Nereus,
    listen:
The son that you bear will shine as the glory of
    Thessaly;
This is the word of Cheiron,
A prophet skilled in Apollo's arts.
Your son will lead his Myrmidons armed with
    spears and shields
To destroy with fire the famous city of Priam,
His body clad and equipped
With the golden armour that Hephaestus
    toiled at,
Which Thetis, the mother who bore him,
Gave him as a gift.' That was a happy day,
When the gods blessed the marriage of Thetis
The great sea-god's daughter,
And sang the wedding-song for Peleus.

Your wedding-day, Iphigenia, will be different.
On your lovely flowing hair
Argive soldiers will place a wreath of flowers
Like the wreath men place on an unblemished
    victim,
A mountain heifer gleaming red and white,
Coming down from the rocky caves;
But the blood they draw from the throat – who
    will give it?
Not an animal grazing to the farm-boy's pipe
Or the herdsman's whistle;
But a girl reared at her mother's side
To be bride to an Argive prince.

Where now can the clear face of goodness,
Where can virtue itself live by its own
    strength? —
When ruthless disregard holds power,
When men, forgetting they are mortal,
Tread down goodness and ignore it,
When lawlessness overrules law,
When the terror of God no longer draws men
    together
Trembling at the reward of wickedness?

[*Enter* CLYTEMNESTRA.]

CLYTEMNESTRA: It is a long time since my husband left his
    tent.
Where can he be? I have come to watch for his return.
My poor Iphigenia is drowned in tears, crying
The music of despair in every piteous key,
Hearing the scheme her father plotted for her death.
— But look! While I've been talking of him, here he comes —
Agamemnon, this father who now shall be exposed,
Guilty of monstrous wickedness against his child.

[*Enter* AGAMEMNON.]

AGAMEMNON: I am glad to find you, daughter of Leda, out
    here alone.
I have things to say while Iphigenia is indoors,
Which it is better for a young bride not to hear.

CLYTEMNESTRA: And for what business is this moment
    opportune?

AGAMEMNON: The girl must come away with me; so send
    her out.
Everything is prepared; water for purifying,
Barley for sprinkling on the sacrificial fire,
And victims which, before the marriage-rite, must fall
And yield their pulsing blood to immortal Artemis.

CLYTEMNESTRA: The words you speak are seemly; but I do
    not know

Such seemly words as could describe the things you do.
– Come out here, Iphigenia; you know everything
Your father's plotting. Wrap Orestes in your gown,
Bring your young brother with you, child.

> [*Enter* IPHIGENIA *carrying* ORESTES.]

                            See, here she comes

Obedient to you. Now I'll speak for both of us.

AGAMEMNON: My dear, why are you crying? Where's your cheerful face?

Why are your eyes downcast and hidden in your dress?

CLYTEMNESTRA: Oh!
Of all my wrongs, which shall I take for starting-point?
There is not one that does not claim first place.

AGAMEMNON: What's this?
You match each other in tears and anger and wild looks.

CLYTEMNESTRA: I'll ask you a question, husband; answer like a man.

AGAMEMNON: You've no need to command me. What do you wish to ask?

CLYTEMNESTRA: Your daughter here, and mine – do you intend to kill her?

AGAMEMNON: To *what*?
A dreadful thing to say, an unworthy suspicion.

CLYTEMNESTRA: You may leave out all that. First answer what I asked.

AGAMEMNON: Ask a fair question, and you'll get a fair reply.

CLYTEMNESTRA: I ask no other question. Give me no other answer.

AGAMEMNON: O divine Destiny, Chance, and my evil fate!

CLYTEMNESTRA: Mine too, and Iphigenia's: one fate, three victims.

AGAMEMNON: Whom have I wronged?

CLYTEMNESTRA: Whom have you wronged? You ask *me* that?

What are you thinking of? Or have you thought at all?

AGAMEMNON [*aside*]: No hope now. Someone has betrayed
    me; it's all known.

CLYTEMNESTRA: Yes, I know. I've heard all you plan to do
    to me.

Your very silence, all these mutterings of despair,

Are your guilty confession. Save yourself the words.

AGAMEMNON: See, I am dumb. Why should I, by a string of
    lies,

Add to my anguish the reproach of shamelessness?

CLYTEMNESTRA: Listen, then. I will use plain terms, waste
    no more time

In hints and riddles. First − to make this the first shame

I charge you with − you married me against my will,

Took me by force, killing my first husband Tantalus;

You grabbed my baby from my breast, and broke its head

On the hard ground. My brothers, the two sons of Zeus,

Mounted their gleaming horses and made war on you.

You knelt as suppliant to my old father Tyndareos;

He saved your life, and you became my next husband.

I was reconciled to you; and you will testify

That I was, both to you and to your family,

A perfect wife; chaste in my person, prosperous

In ordering your household; joy attended you

On entering, and good fortune blessed your going out.

A man with such a wife is the possessor of

A rarity; bad wives are plentiful enough.

I bore you three girls first, and then this boy, your son;

Now you are taking one girl from me heartlessly.

    Tell me: if someone asks you why you are killing her,

What will you say? Or must I speak your words for you?

'So that Menelaus may get back Helen.' A splendid act,

To pay a child's life as the ransom for a slut!

To buy what we most hate with what we dearly love!

Suppose, now, you're with the army, leaving me at home,

And the slow months drag on, and you're still there at Troy,
What thoughts do you imagine will occupy my heart,
When every chair I see will be empty of her,
Her bedroom empty; and I sit alone in tears
Mourning for her, day in, day out? 'Dear child,' I'll say,
'Your father, who begot you, took away your life;
Killed you himself, no other, nor by others' hands.'
And yet it needed but some quickly-framed excuse,
And I, and the three daughters that you left behind,
Shall welcome you as a father should be welcomed home.
In the gods' name, my husband, don't force me to be
A disloyal wife to you; nor be disloyal yourself.

     Well? If you sacrifice her, what prayers will you pray?
What favour will you ask for as you lift the knife?
A homecoming as shameful as your starting out?
Or I, perhaps, should beg some blessing on your head?
This, surely, is to account the gods senseless and blind,
If we should pray for blessing on the blood-guilty!
When you come back to Argos, what then? Will you take
Your children in your arms? You will have no such right.
Which of them will so much as look you in the face
If you've betrayed and killed one of them? Have you yet
Thought all this out? Or is your sole imperative
Your secure sceptre and your military command?
I'll tell you the just answer you should have given the
     Greeks:
'You wish, Greeks, to set sail against Troy? Then cast lots
To choose whose child must die.' That would be fair; but
     not
That you should choose out your child as a sacrifice
And give her to the Greeks to kill. Or Menelaus,
The cause of the whole war, should kill Hermione
To pay for her mother. I am your chaste and faithful wife;
Yet I must lose my daughter, while the whore Helen
Can keep her daughter and live safe and flourishing

At home in Sparta. Now, if anything I've said
Is untrue or irrelevant, tell me; but if I
Have spoken to the point, then change your purpose; do not
    kill
Your child and mine. This is the way of sanity.

CHORUS: Agamemnon, be persuaded; for to save a child
Beyond all contradiction is a noble act.

IPHIGENIA: Father, had I the voice of Orpheus, and could
    charm
Rocks to obey me, and with magic words persuade
Men's hearts at will, then I would use it; but my tears
Are my one magic; I'll use them, for I can weep.
The suppliant garland which I twine about your knees
Is my own body, which my mother bore to you.
Don't kill me, so young! It is good to see the light;
Don't make me gaze at darkness in the world below.
I was the first that called you father, and the first
That you called child; the first who sat upon your knee,
Caressed you lovingly, and was caressed in turn.
This is what you once said to me: 'Shall I, dear child,
See you one day a proud wife in your husband's house,
Living and flourishing, and worthy of your father?'
And then I wove my fingers in your beard, which now
My hand clutches in supplication, and I said:
'And shall I too, dear father, greet you when you are old
And give you warm and loving welcome in my house,
Repaying with comfort all you gave me as a child?'
I well remember what we said; but you forget;
You want to kill me. I implore you, in the name
Of Pelops, and your father Atreus, don't do this! —
And in my mother's name, whose pains when I was born
Are now redoubled in this second agony.
Paris and Helen's love — why, what have I to do
With that? Father, why should his coming mean my death?
Turn your face to me, look at me, give me one kiss —

So that, when I am dead, I may have this at least
To remember, if you will not listen to my words.

   Brother, the help that you can give your friends is small;
Yet join your tears with mine; beg and implore our father
To save your dear sister from death. Even before
A child can speak, he has some sense of grief and wrong.
See, father, how in silence he beseeches you.
Oh, do not spurn me! Have compassion on my life!
Yes, by your beard we plead with you – you love us both;
One is your baby son, and one your grown daughter.
My whole plea in one sentence – and I'll win your heart:
To see this sunlight is for us all our dearest love!
Below is nothing; and to wish for death, madness.
Better a life of wretchedness than a noble death.

CHORUS: Miserable Helen! From you and your guilty love
   This bitter stress and trouble rose for Atreus' sons.

AGAMEMNON: I am well aware what's pitiable and what is
      not.
   I love my children; and I'm not an insane brute.
   I shrink in dread from carrying out this act, my wife;
   Yet if I do not, dread remains. I must do this.
   Look at this fleet of war-ships marshalled here, this huge
   Army of bronze-mailed warriors from the Hellene states,
   Who cannot sail against the walls of Troy, or raze
   That famous city to its foundations, unless I
   First sacrifice you, as the prophet Calchas commands.
   A strange lust rages with demonic power throughout
   The Hellene army, to set sail immediately
   And stop barbarians from raping Hellene wives.
   If I refuse to obey the oracle, they'll come
   To Argos, and kill me, you, the whole family.
   Menelaus has not made a slave of me, my child;
   I came to Aulis not to serve his purposes;
   I am slave to Hellas; for her, whether I will or not,
   I am bound to kill you. Against this I have no power.

So far as lies in you, child, and in me, to ensure,
Hellas must be free, and her citizens must not
Have their wives stolen forcibly by Phrygians.

    [*Exit* AGAMEMNON.]

CLYTEMNESTRA: My friends, what shall I do?
                  My child, why must you die?
                  Your father betrays you to death,
                  And runs away.

IPHIGENIA: Oh, mother, mother! Fate has given
                  . both
                  The same sad song to sing.
                  Daylight and dazzling sun are mine no
                      more,
                  No more!

                  Snow-covered Phrygian valley, I curse
                      you,
                  And you, wooded slopes of Mount Ida,
                  Where long ago Priam exposed a help-
                      less babe,
                  Taking him from his mother's arms to
                      die.
                  Paris of Ida,
                  That was the name they gave him in
                      Troy,
                  The prince brought up as a keeper of
                      cattle.
                  I curse the day when Priam
                  Set him down by the gleaming water,
                  Naming him 'Defender of Men'.
                  By fountains of the Nymphs,
                  In a meadow lush with fresh flowers,
                  Where roses and bluebells are for
                      goddesses to pick –
                  There one day came Pallas

And treacherous Aphrodite,
And Hera, and Hermes, Zeus's mes-
    senger;
The Cyprian priding herself on the
    force of desire,
Pallas on the power of her spear,
Hera on the royal bed she shares with
    Zeus.
They came to a judgement heavy with
    hate,
To compete for a prize of beauty,
And to doom me to death
For the glory of Greek soldiers;
This is the offering Artemis must re-
    ceive
Before the fleet can sail for Troy.

Mother, dearest mother, what shall I
    do?
My father betrays and abandons me!
My curse, my curse on Helen,
And on the fate that linked us!
I am slaughtered and done to death by a
    murderous ritual
And by a murderous father.
A curse on the hour when Aulis wel-
    comed
In this sheltering bay
The oars of pine and the bronze bows
    bound for Troy;
When Zeus breathed over Euripus an
    adverse wind.
For Zeus sends now to one man, now
    to another,
Soft breezes, pleasure in sailing;

> Dispenses grief or disaster,
> Spreading of sail or furling;
> And for some, waiting.
>
> Men who live for a day
> Are a race doomed to suffering, end-
> less suffering.
> Fate we know to be inevitable;
> And when we meet it, it is evil.
> Oh, what misery, what anguish
> The daughter of Tyndareos brought on
> Hellas!

CHORUS: A cruel fate has fallen to you; and for this
I pity you. Such suffering is undeserved.

IPHIGENIA: Mother, mother! Look, a crowd of men is
coming.

CLYTEMNESTRA: It is he,
Child, the son of Thetis, for whose sake today you travelled
here.

IPHIGENIA: I must go in, I must hide. Slaves, open!

CLYTEMNESTRA:　　　　　　　　　　　　Where
are you going, child?

IPHIGENIA: I should blush to meet Achilles.

CLYTEMNESTRA:　　　　　　　　Why?

IPHIGENIA:　　　　　　　　　　　　Because of
that pretence
About marriage; I'm embarrassed.

CLYTEMNESTRA:　　　　　　　We can't stand on cere-
mony;
This is life or death. Stay here—no time for blushing, if we can—
[Enter ACHILLES.]

ACHILLES: Oh, unhappy daughter of Leda—

CLYTEMNESTRA:　　　　　　　　　You have spoken
my true name.

ACHILLES: The whole army's in an uproar, shouting—

CLYTEMNESTRA: Shouting what — say what?

ACHILLES: Shouting for your daughter.

CLYTEMNESTRA: That sounds ominous; I fear the worst.

ACHILLES: They demand her for a victim.

CLYTEMNESTRA: Does no one stand
up to them?

ACHILLES: Yes, I did; and then the rabble threatened me.

CLYTEMNESTRA: What
did they do?

ACHILLES: Picked up rocks to stone me.

CLYTEMNESTRA: What — because you
tried to save my child?

ACHILLES: Yes, just that.

CLYTEMNESTRA: Why, where's the man who would
have dared lay hands on you?

ACHILLES: All the Hellenes would.

CLYTEMNESTRA: Surely your Myrmidons
were there to help?

ACHILLES: It was they who first attacked me.

CLYTEMNESTRA: Then we're lost.
Iphigenia!

ACHILLES: They all shouted, 'You're a woman's man!'

CLYTEMNESTRA: What
did you say to that?

ACHILLES: Told them they should not have my intended
bride to kill.

CLYTEMNESTRA: Well done.

ACHILLES: Said her father gave her to me.

CLYTEMNESTRA: Sent for her from
Argos too.

ACHILLES: Everything I said was shouted down.

CLYTEMNESTRA: A crowd is
mad for crime.

ACHILLES: None the less I'll help you.

CLYTEMNESTRA: You alone against a
    thousand men?

ACHILLES These men here who bear my armour –

CLYTEMNESTRA: Oh, I bless
    your fearless heart!

ACHILLES: I shall get my blessing.

CLYTEMNESTRA: So my daughter won't be
    sacrificed?

ACHILLES: No, not while I can prevent it.

CLYTEMNESTRA: Will they come to
    take her?

ACHILLES [*meanwhile hurriedly fitting on his helmet*]:   Yes,
    Thousands – and Odysseus leading them.

CLYTEMNESTRA: The son of Sisy-
    phus?

ACHILLES: That's the man.

CLYTEMNESTRA: Is he acting under orders, or on
    his own account?

ACHILLES: Chosen, yes; and choosing.

CLYTEMNESTRA: What a choice – to be
    a murderer!

ACHILLES: But I'll stop him.

CLYTEMNESTRA: Will Odysseus drag her away by
    violence?

ACHILLES: He will – by her golden hair, you'll see.

CLYTEMNESTRA: And what
    should I do then?

ACHILLES: Cling fast to your daughter.

CLYTEMNESTRA: If that will save her,
    she shall not be killed.

ACHILLES: It will come to that, I warn you.

IPHIGENIA: Mother, listen
    now to me.

    Anger against your husband is beside the point. For all of us

It's no easy matter to resist what's irresistible.

We should thank Achilles for his zeal in our behalf; but you,

In return, must see he does not lose his good name with the
    Greeks,

Lose his fortune, even his life, maybe – and with no gain to
    us.

Mother, I have thought this over; I know now what I must
    do.

I am resolved to die. Above all things, I want to act nobly

And renounce all cowardly feelings. Mother, look at this
    with me,

And you'll see I am right. The power of all Hellas now looks
    to me;

All lies in my hand – the sailing of the fleet, capture of Troy,

And the future safety of Greek wives from barbarous attacks;

No more forcible abductions from our happy homes, when
    once

Paris has been made to pay the price of death for Helen's
    rape.

All this great deliverance I shall win by dying, and my name

Will be blessed and celebrated as one who set Hellas free.

And indeed I have no right to cling to life so passionately,

Since it was for Greece you gave me birth, not for yourself
    alone.

Why, ten thousand men face battle holding shields, ten
    thousand more

Rowing warships; they're all ready, when their country has
    been wronged,

To attack our enemies for the sake of Hellas, and to die.

And shall my one life now prove the obstacle to their re-
    solve?

Is this fair and just? How could I answer them? And one
    thing more.

Why should Achilles here, to save a woman's life, engage the
    whole

Argive army, and be slaughtered? One man is of more
    value
Than a host of women. And if Artemis has laid a claim
On my body, who am I, a mortal, to oppose a god?
This I cannot do. To Hellas, then, I dedicate myself.
Sacrifice me; take and plunder Troy. For me, your victory
Shall be children, marriage – for all time my glorious monu-
    ment.
Greeks were born to rule barbarians, mother, not barbarians
To rule Greeks. They are slaves by nature; we have freedom
    in our blood.

CHORUS: Your nature, princess, is indeed noble and true;
    But events fester, and divinity is sick.

ACHILLES: Daughter of Agamemnon, some god would have
    given
Me a rare gift, if I had won you for my wife.
Hellas is fortunate in you, and you in Hellas.
Your words were true, courageous, worthy of our land;
You have quit fighting against gods, which proves too hard
For you; and made a virtue of necessity.
Now that I see your true nobility of heart,
My love grows, and I would most gladly marry you.
Think of this; for I want to serve you, and to take
You to my home. I swear by Thetis, I am grieved
If now I am not to cross swords with the men of Argos
To save your life. Consider: death is formidable.

IPHIGENIA: I have considered, and abide by what I said.
It is enough that Helen by her beauty stirs
Battles and bloodshed among men. So, Achilles,
Don't either die for me or kill anyone else;
But go, and leave me to save Hellas if I can.

ACHILLES: Heroic spirit! Since your resolve is firm, I have
No more to say. Your heart is royal – why should the truth
Be left unspoken? None the less, it is possible
Your mind may change; so hear now what I undertake.

I am going to place my weapons at the altar-side,
Ready to forbid, and to prevent, the stroke of death;
And even you will then, it may be, call upon
My promise, when you see the knife near to your throat.
You shall not, for a hasty impulse, lose your life.
So, I will go now with these weapons to the temple
Of Artemis; and I'll wait there until you come.
        [*Exit* ACHILLES.]

IPHIGENIA: Mother, why are your eyes flowing with silent tears?

CLYTEMNESTRA: I have the bitterest reason for a broken heart.

IPHIGENIA: Stop; do not make me weaken now. Do what I ask –

CLYTEMNESTRA: Tell me, dear child. I will do everything you wish.

IPHIGENIA: Do not cut off a mourning lock of hair for me.

CLYTEMNESTRA: But why do you say that? When I have lost my child –

IPHIGENIA: Not lost. I am saved; I shall make your name glorious.

CLYTEMNESTRA: What do you mean? Must I not grieve for your lost life?

IPHIGENIA: No grief at all; and no grave shall be heaped for me.

CLYTEMNESTRA: But you will die. May I not mourn as custom bids?

IPHIGENIA: The altar of Artemis, daughter of Zeus, will be my tomb.

CLYTEMNESTRA: Dear child, I will do all you wish. Yes, you are right.

IPHIGENIA: Think of me as fortunate; I have served Hellas well.

CLYTEMNESTRA: Your two sisters – what message shall I take to them?

IPHIGENIA: See that they too wear no black mourning dress
for me.

CLYTEMNESTRA: And shall I say to them some loving word
from you?

IPHIGENIA: 'Good-bye'. Bring my Orestes up to be a
man.

CLYTEMNESTRA: Hold him close now, and look at him for
the last time.

IPHIGENIA: Orestes dear, you gave us all the help you
could.

CLYTEMNESTRA: Is there some wish I could fulfil for you at
home?

IPHIGENIA: Yes. Do not hate Agamemnon. He is mine, and
yours.

CLYTEMNESTRA: It is a hard course he must run because of
you.

IPHIGENIA: He did not want to take my life. It was for
Greece.

CLYTEMNESTRA: By trickery! It was ignoble; he shamed his
father's house.

[*Some armed guards appear.*]

IPHIGENIA: Who comes as escort, before they drag me by the
hair?

CLYTEMNESTRA: I'm coming with you –

IPHIGENIA: No, mother, this is
not right.

CLYTEMNESTRA: I'll cling to you, I won't let go.

IPHIGENIA: Listen,
mother:

Stay here. That will be better far for both of us.
I see my father's guards have come. Let one of them
Lead me to the field of Artemis, to meet my death.

CLYTEMNESTRA: You are going, my daughter?

IPHIGENIA: Yes, and I
shall not come back.

CLYTEMNESTRA: Leaving your mother?

IPHIGENIA: Yes. This we did not
    deserve.

CLYTEMNESTRA: Wait, now, don't leave me!

IPHIGENIA: You must not
        let one tear fall.

        [CLYTEMNESTRA *goes into the tent.*]

Women of Chalcis, chant a hymn to Artemis,
Daughter of Zeus, a paean for my sacrifice.
Let holy silence be proclaimed throughout the camp.
Prepare the holy vessels; let the pure flame blaze
With sprinkled barley; let my father pace around
The altar, following the sun. I come to give
To all Hellenes deliverance and victory!

    Lead me, a maiden born to overthrow
        Great Troy and all her people;
    Bring flowers, hang garlands round me; take this lock
        Of hair, to grace the altar;
    Bring jars of holy water for my hands.
        Praise Artemis with dances,
    Queen Artemis the blessed; circle round
        Her altar and her temple.
        For with my blood so offered
        I shall, since Fate requires it,
    Cancel and purge the word that spoke from heaven.
        My mother, royal mother,
        For you my eyes are flowing;
    Since at the altar is no place for tears.
        Come, women, join me, singing
        To Artemis, whose temple
    Looks toward Chalcis eastward over the strait,
        Where now impatient spearmen,
        Bound in the narrow waters
    Of Aulis, hear my name and burn for war.

Farewell, Pelasgia, land that gave me birth!
Farewell, dear home, Mycenae!

CHORUS: You call on Perseus' city,
               Built by the labour of Cyclopian hands?

IPHIGENIA: O home that bore me as a light of hope
               For Hellas, I die freely.

CHORUS: Your name will live for ever.

IPHIGENIA: Farewell, <u>bright day</u>, torch-bearer to this
                   <u>world</u>,
                   And farewell, sky and sunlight!
               Another world, another time and place,
                   Shall be my home for ever.
               Farewell, dear light, farewell, farewell, fare-
                   well!

[*Exit* IPHIGENIA *with guards.*]

CHORUS: See her, a maiden born to overthrow
                   Great Troy and all her people,
               Going, with flowers and garlands on her head,
               With purifying fountains for her hands,
                   To stain the holy altar
                   Of this bloodthirsty goddess
               With young life streaming from her tender
                   throat.
                   Your father there awaits you,
               Maiden, with pouring-out of holy wine
                   And ritual of cleansing –
                   And all the Achaean fighters
               Chafing to reach the town of Ilion.
               Come, then, praise the queen-goddess Artemis,
                   Assuming kindly Fortune
                   Has filled this day with blessing.
               You who rejoice in human sacrifice,
                   Dread goddess, bring our army
                   Safe to the plain of Phrygia,
               Bring them to Troy, the home of treachery;

       And grant that Agamemnon,
       With Hellene spears to aid him,
       May crown his head with glory
      And by his victory win undying fame.

[*Enter a* MESSENGER.]

MESSENGER: Come out here, Clytemnestra, daughter of
    Tyndareos;
  Come out, I have news for you.

[*Enter* CLYTEMNESTRA.]

CLYTEMNESTRA: When I heard your voice
  I was beside myself with terror; and I fear
  You have come to tell me of some other misery
  To add to what I know already.

MESSENGER: I must tell you
  About your daughter – something strange and wonderful.

CLYTEMNESTRA: Tell me, then, quickly, waste no time.

MESSENGER: My
    dear mistress,
  I'll start at the beginning and tell you everything;
  Though, as my mind's bewildered, what I have to say
  May sound confused. Well, we went with your child, and
    reached
  The grove sacred to Artemis, and the flowery fields
  Where the Greek forces have their meeting-place. At once
  The army gathered. Then, when Agamemnon saw
  His daughter entering the grove to meet her death,
  He sobbed aloud; the tears streamed down his face; he
    turned
  His head away, and held his robe before his eyes.
  She took her place next to him, and said: 'At your bidding,
  Father, I come, I give my body willingly
  For my home, Argos, and for the whole land of Hellas.
  Lead me to Artemis' altar and there sacrifice me,
  If this is what the god commands. May good fortune
  Prosper you all, so far as lies in me; and may

Heaven give you victory, and bring you safely home.
See to it that no Argive here lays hand on me;
Silent, with steadfast heart, I will present my throat.'
   Those were her words. Each man who heard her stood
     amazed
At her brave spirit and fearless will. Talthybius,
Who was entrusted with the ritual, then stood forth,
And called for holy silence. Next, Calchas, the seer,
Drew from its sheath a keen-edged knife, which he then laid
On a gold vessel; and placed a wreath on the girl's head.
The son of Peleus took the vessel, and the jar
Of holy water; holding them, he ran right round
The altar of the goddess; then he made this prayer:
'Huntress, daughter of Zeus, encircling the night sky
With brilliant beams, receive this sacrifice which we,
The whole Achaean army, and King Agamemnon,
Present to you, the pure blood of a lovely maid.
Grant to our fleet safe voyaging, and to our swords
Victory and the sack of Troy.'
                    Atreus' two sons,
And the whole army, stood with eyes fixed on the ground.
The priest took up the knife, and said the prayer. His eye
Scanned her throat for the place to strike. I bowed my head,
My heart shuddered, I shrank with pain; when suddenly
To our astonished eyes – for every man present
Had clearly heard the blow fall – Iphigenia was
Nowhere to be seen; where she had vanished no one knows.
The priest cried out; and from the whole assembly rose
An echoing cry, at the unexpected miracle
That met their eyes – beyond belief, though plainly seen.
There on the ground, convulsed in death, lay a large deer;
The whole altar was sprinkled with its blood. At this
Calchas – in glad relief, as you may guess – exclaimed:
'Leaders of the Greek army, see this sacrifice,
This mountain deer, which Artemis herself has laid

Upon her altar! This she graciously accepts
In the maiden's place, so that her altar may not be
Defiled by the destruction of a noble life.
In token of acceptance, Artemis grants us
Fair winds to bring our army to the attack on Troy.
So now take courage, every man, and get on board;
This very day we leave the sheltered anchorage
Of Aulis and set sail across the Aegean Sea.'

    Then, when the entire sacrifice had been consumed
In the altar-flames, he offered the appropriate prayer
For the army's safe home-coming. I was sent to you
By Agamemnon, to report all this, and tell you
What kind of fortune he has been given by the gods,
And how he has won immortal glory throughout Greece.
I was there myself; I tell you what my own eyes saw;
Clearly your daughter has been wafted to the gods.
So lay aside your grief, your anger against your husband;
The ways of gods are never such as men expect;
They save those who are dear to them. For this same day
Has looked upon your daughter dead, and living too.

CHORUS: How glad I am to hear this messenger's report;
    He tells us your child lives, and dwells among the gods.

CLYTEMNESTRA: My child, which of the gods has stolen
    you?
       What shall I say to you? Surely I must think that this is a
       false story which has been told to comfort me, so that I
       should cease from my bitter mourning for you?

CHORUS: See, here comes Agamemnon, with the same story
    to tell you.

[*Enter* AGAMEMNON.]

AGAMEMNON: My wife, we may be counted fortunate so far
    as our daughter is concerned; for she has in truth a
    place in the company of gods. Now you must take this
    royal son of mine and travel homewards; for the exped-
    ition is preparing to sail. So farewell; for it will be a

long time before I greet you again, when I return from Troy. May all go well with you.

CHORUS: Son of Atreus, go with good fortune to the land of Phrygia, and with good fortune return. I hope you will capture splendid spoils from Troy.

NOTES

THE CHILDREN OF HERACLES

Page 107. *the people of the Four Towns*: this refers to a group of small towns in Northern Attica, of which Marathon was one.

Page 108. *when good counsel's given, to follow it*: probably a line or two is missing after this.

Page 110. *you get bogged down in war* . . .: literally, 'you put your foot into the bilge-water'.

Page 114. *in all the peopled breadth of Hellas*: this phrase is quoted from A. S. Way's translation.

Page 117. *chanters of oracles* . . . *ancient predictions* . . .: for the distinction between proper consultation of gods and superstitious attention to obscure oracles, see *The Suppliant Women*, especially the censure of Adrastus for his superstition and want of judgement. For contemporary examples of the same issue, consider the panic in Athens at the mutilation of the Hermae in 416, and the fatal result of Nicias' delay in retreating from Syracuse in 413.

Page 119. *do not lay the blame upon this city*: surely the Elders of Marathon mean: 'Not the city, but Demophon is to blame; it was he who gave undue heed to ancient prophecies.' The next two lines, though ostensibly addressed to Iolaus, seem to hint at strong disapproval of Demophon.

Page 120. *provided all the rest goes well*: he means: 'Even after the required sacrifice, we still have to see whether Demophon can defeat Eurystheus in battle.'

Page 122. *Honour Alcmene!* the Greek has, in apposition to 'Alcmene', 'the old woman inside the temple'. This seems to defeat translation, though A. S. Way offers 'the grey queen therewithin'.

Page 131. *and spare the blood* . . .: several lines have been lost here; the words printed in brackets give the probable sense.
from victims' throats: the Greek has 'human throats'; but it

is most unlikely that Macaria's death would be alluded to in a single word. This could well have got into the text from a misguided marginal note which then replaced the original word.

Page 132. *gives warning to all men* . . . : a rather facile sermon on a worn text delivered by an unimpressive preacher; and on a none too appropriate occasion, since we have not been given the opportunity of developing any personal interest in Eurystheus; so the lesson drawn from his fate cannot be more than conventional. (Compare Polymestor in *Hecabe*.)

Page 133. *Now I know this is true*: compare the comfort which Peleus takes from Thetis at the end of *Andromache*.

Page 137. *Alcmene, I would offer* . . . : the MSS do not show who is speaking with Alcmene at this point: it is probably the Servant.

Page 138. *the Pallenian Virgin's shrine*: Pallene was a district of Attica a few miles from Marathon, with a temple of Athene.

a guest, your friend: here Eurystheus addresses the Chorus.

ANDROMACHE

Page 149. *concoct some remedy*: the Greek word means 'to cut up herbs' for making medicine.

Page 150. *to know that I am your friend*: Hermione's arrival is unannounced. Line 154, 'That is answer enough for you', indicates that she heard the last two lines spoken by the Chorus.

you oriental women: the Greek word is 'continental'; but probably 'oriental' better conveys the intended feeling.

Page 152. *belittling Scyros*: Scyros was an island off the east coast of Greece, where Neoptolemus was brought up.

When Aphrodite snared your heart . . . : she means that, if ever Hector fell in love with another woman, she (Andromache) not only did not hate her rival, but was even willing to nurse Hector's bastard child herself, out of love for her husband.

Page 156. *Troy deserved a different conqueror*: after this the MSS give the
following three lines, which are of doubtful genuineness:

> A glittering surface passes for intelligence;
> Below the surface all men are alike – except
> That some are rich; and wealth exerts a mighty power.

Page 159. *an eye for an eye*: literally, 'that those who have suffered
should act in revenge'.

But will you take . . . literally, 'But [will you kill] this
nestling too, tearing him from my wings?'

Page 163. *I've nothing for you*: literally, 'I have no love-potion for
you'. This word *philtron* came to be used for a 'remedy' or
'way to help'.

What is all this?: Peleus has come from Pharsalia (see the
Prologue), and enters through the Orchestra. His first four
lines are shouted from a considerable distance; then for
three lines he is ascending the steps to the stage and
approaching Andromache.

Page 167. After the words *and are you sensible* come ten lines which
there is some reason to regard as interpolated. Their
meaning is

> Look at this further point: if you had given your daughter
> To one of your citizens, and she then found herself
> In Hermione's position, would you do nothing,
> Say nothing at all? I think not; yet now, in defence
> Of a foreigner, you scream abuse at your nearest kin!
> The case of a woman wronged by her husband is as valid
> As that of a man who suffers from a wanton wife.
> But while the man has all the resources that he needs,
> The woman must rely on her family for redress.
> Am I not right, then, to support my own daughter?

Phocus was Peleus' step-brother, whom Peleus murdered
through jealousy of his athletic prowess.

Page 168. *I'll untie these knots*: since Peleus first told the Attendants
to untie them, 140 lines of dialogue have passed, while
Andromache has remained kneeling and bound. This is
another ironical comment on the attitude of men to
women.

Page 169. *the direction from which* PELEUS *arrived*: Andromache's
words, 'lying in wait to attack us on some lonely path',

suggest that Peleus is about to escort them back to his own house in Pharsalia.

Page 176. *I repeat, never*: this expression seems to take us momentarily right out of the play into a sociological argument. See the Introduction, page 27.

Page 177. *the special reasons*: Orestes alludes, of course, to his matricide, as the next sentence makes clear. It is also clear that some years have passed since then. See Introduction, page 39.

Page 178. *Apollo, whose . . .*: Apollo and Poseidon originally built the walls of Troy.
And this was a god's command: at this point four lines in the MSS seem to be corrupt, and the version given is partly conjectural.

Page 181. *Clytemnestra's son*: Clytemnestra too had waited with a hidden sword for her enemy.

Page 182. *a ghastly Pyrrhic dance*: Neoptolemus' other name was Pyrrhus; but the Pyrrhic war-dance seems not to have been named after him.

Page 184. *May I not cry my grief . . .*: the literal meaning is: Shall I not tear my hair, lay upon my head a destructive beating of the hand? English demands less foreign imagery.

THE SUPPLIANT WOMEN

Page 197. *Give your daughters to . . .*: this obscure oracle is referred to again in *The Phoenician Women*, where the symbolism of fighting beasts is further elaborated.

Page 199. *For gods are cruel . . .*: lines 180–83 ('as a poet should take joy . . .') are intelligible only if we assume that four or five lines have been lost before them. The lines here printed in brackets follow the sense suggested by the words which Murray prints below his Oxford Text as a reasonable conjecture.

Page 209. *dying from war-mania*: if Euripides in 421 had already reached this point in perceiving the folly of the war, how can we doubt the irony, or the application, of his comment in plays produced in 409, 408, and 405?

Page 217. *O fools, who strive* . . .: literally, 'O fools, who aim your arrow past the proper target'.

Surely not Theseus . . .: a conjectural line supplying a lacuna in the MSS.

Page 218. *this is a day unlooked for*: the words 'unlooked for' seem to bear two opposite meanings: (1) the women 'had not hoped' to see their sons' bodies brought home for burial; for this reason 'the sight is welcome'; (2) they 'had not expected' to see the death of their sons; for this reason it is a day bringing 'the sharpest pain'.

Page 221. *The praise of Tydeus* . . .: after these three lines come six lines which appear to be alternative versions repeating twice over the same general sense.

Page 225. *But I shall not see them* . . .: after this come three lines of corrupt text; the words as they stand mean something like: 'And may a faithful husband, welded to his noble wife by the genuine impulses of love . . .'

Page 228. *and make way for the young*: the crowning irony of the play.

THE PHOENICIAN WOMEN

Page 239. *so come, climb up*: this rendering deliberately shirks the Greek line, which means literally, 'Ascend with your foot this ancient stairway of cedar-wood'.

Page 240. *an earth-born giant*: after this comes a phrase meaning 'star-faced in pictures', the reference of which is obscure.

Page 243. *From the Tyrian sea-coast* . . .: see Introduction, page 57.

Page 244. *descended . . . from Io*: inevitably the Greek attaches to Io the epithet 'horn-bearing', which seems out of place in an English version. See Aeschylus, *Prometheus and Other Plays*, Introduction (Penguin Classics).

Ares shall soon learn: the reason for this threat against Ares is obscure; but there is no other way of translating the phrase.

Page 245. *By a Theban army*: literally, 'Agenor's grandsons'. Agenor was king of Phoenicia and father of Cadmus.

Page 247. *You have yoked yourself with a wife* . . .: Iocasta's role in the drama places her above the other characters in moral authority; but Euripides' anti-heroic realism balances this by the plain failure of tact and judgement shown in these lines, on which the Chorus (355–6) make an ambiguous comment.

Page 253. *absolute power*: the Greek word is *tyrannis* (see Introduction page 61) both here and in 549 where it is rendered 'sovreignty'.

Page 254. *Nature gave to men the law . . .*: this phrase is quoted from A. S. Way's translation. More literally: 'equity is by nature something permanent in human life'.

Page 256. *the white-horsed riders*: probably not Castor and Polydeuces, who were connected with Sparta rather than Thebes. The builders of Thebes, Amphion and Zethus, seem to be intended, though their interest in white horses is less well documented.

Page 262. *To name each one . . .*: In Aeschylus, *Seven Against Thebes*, one third of the play is occupied with descriptions of the seven champions on each side. It is hard to feel sure what Euripides meant to convey by this line; but it may be considered in connection with 1104 ff., where the Messenger wastes time in just this way, with the result that Iocasta arrives too late to save her sons.

Page 263. *Justice, my ally . . . victory*: compare 501, 'there's no such thing as . . . justice'.

Page 264. *To exhaust with anguish . . .*: the word *polymochthos* used in the first line of this Ode is used again here.

Page 266. *Against Eumolpus*: Eumolpus, with a band of Thracians, helped the Eleusinians in a war against Athens, and was killed by Erechtheus.

Page 269. *insist on fair reply*: literally, 'enter into a contest of words'. It is interesting to compare with this speech the speech Teiresias makes to Cadmus and Pentheus in *The Bacchae*, explaining to them the importance of Dionysus. The same ironical treatment of the prophetic figure can be observed.

Page 274. *When Creon's son, who died . . .*: the matter-of-fact banality of this opening can hardly be other than deliberate and ironical.

Page 276. *and from the ladder . . .*: after this the MSS give three lines
generally thought to be a later insertion; their meaning is:

> Like a spun sling his limbs went, some this way, some
> that,
> His hair up toward Olympus, to the earth his blood,
> His arms, his legs, revolving like Ixion's wheel
> Until his whirling corpse, fire-blackened, crashed to
> earth.

Page 280. *Or for my city, wrapped now in . . .*: Creon knows that his
son is dead; he knows too (1356–7) that the Argive army
has withdrawn from the attack. Since he has no word of
thanksgiving for victory, Euripides must intend to show
him as entirely absorbed in his personal loss.

Page 281. *due piety to the gods of earth*: this statement is to prepare
us for Creon's edict about the body of Polyneices, 1628 ff.

Page 282. *At this, many shed tears . . .*: Some editors consider this
sentence spurious.

Page 290. *Cithaeron did not kill me*: after this a line is missing in the
MSS.

Page 293. *Now, daughter, comes the truth . . .*: these five lines may
well be a later addition to the text.

Page 294. *Do you hear me, Creon . . .*: the Greek is merely the repeated exclamation Io, used often by a person wishing to
claim attention.

Far from protection or comfort: the Greek consists of two
words which may be rendered, 'wandering in conditions
unsuitable for a maiden'.

The MSS conclude the play with six lines modelled on
the closing lines (themselves spurious) of Sophocles, *Oedipus
Tyrannus*, followed by a three-line tag also found at the end
of *Iphigenia in Tauris* and *Orestes*: here is a literal version:

> O citizens of a famous city, look at me: I am Oedipus, who
> understood the famous riddle and was a very great man. I alone
> subdued the power of the murderous Sphinx. Now in pitiful dis-
> honour I am driven from my land. But why do I make these
> lamentations and useless complaints? Being mortal, one must
> endure the fate which the gods impose.
>
> O holy, mighty Victory, guard my life and do not cease to
> award me the crown.

ORESTES

Page 301. *Tantalus*: when Euripides refers to the Atreid family as being descended from Tantalus, he usually seems to be thinking of their heritage of crime and disaster.

Page 302. *built on shifting sand*: the Greek means 'we are riding on weak strength', and the reference is perhaps to 'riding at anchor'. In English we need a more familiar metaphor, and a complete one.

Page 304. *Then why do you not send . . .*: apparently Electra, uneasy at having refused to go herself, is anxious for respect to be paid to Clytemnestra's grave.

Page 314. *I waited for the pyre to cool . . .*: in the Greek the *sticho-mythia* is unbroken; a literal version is:

> Menelaus: Was it at home, or while you sat beside the pyre?
> Orestes: At night, while I was waiting to take up her bones.

Page 317. *more void of sense, conscience, or decency*: this phrase trans-lates a single Greek word, a comparative compound adjective.

Page 318. *Be warned, then . . . side against the gods*: after this the MSS have two lines,

> Leave him to suffer death by public stoning, or
> Never hope to set foot again on Spartan soil.

These two lines recur near the end of Tyndareos' second speech; and it is unlikely that Euripides made him repeat himself in this way. Since in each case the paragraph begins a few lines earlier with a warning to Menelaus, it would be natural for actors to confuse the two passages and insert these lines where they did not belong. Tyndareos in his first speech advocates exile as the proper punishment for murder. In his second speech he has been angered by Orestes' foolish arguments and is now resolved on the death-sentence. It is likely, then, that these two lines belong to the second speech and not to the first.

Page 319. *and in my speech try to forget . . .*: the literal meaning is: 'Let your old age, which frightens me from speech, move aside out of the way of my words, and I will go along the road; but now I fear your (white) hair.'

I avenged my father . . .: four 'arguments' are discernible in this speech: (1) revenge is obligatory; (2) a mother is of inferior importance; (3) my act will be a deterrent; (4) the blame rests with you, with my mother, with Apollo. Compare the 'deterrent' argument as used in *Iphigenia in Aulis*.

Page 320. *my resolve to see you dead* . . .: Tyndareos ignores his own principle, 'by exile, not by blood for blood'.

Page 322. *To ask your help is unjust* . . .: Wedd in his edition rightly calls this passage 'peculiarly frigid'. No doubt logic-chopping arguments may sometimes have bemused Athenian jurymen into giving the desired vote. Euripides certainly did not think this argument had any value or meaning. Just as in *Iphigenia in Aulis* both Agamemnon and Clytemnestra forfeit, rather than gain, our respect by certain speeches, so here Orestes makes us forget whatever sympathy we may have felt earlier.

Page 329. '*Get you friends, not merely kin*': Orestes seems to have forgotten his sister's devotion – possibly because he has just agreed with Pylades to take the usual male attitude and deny her his confidence.

Page 332. *For when a pleasing speaker* . . . *than his hearers are*: this passage reads like genuine Euripides, but it is seriously out of place here. Possibly it was borrowed from one of his lost plays and inserted here for a particular occasion.

Pages *one endowed with little beauty, but* . . .: another character-
332-3. istic irony. 'A man of blameless principle and integrity' is described; and his arguments are mere popular foolishness. The Messenger too is here doing what he accuses heralds of doing – speaking to please his immediate audience. The whole narrative is no doubt a mirror of the contemporary Athenian Assembly, where foolish honest men, unscrupulous schemers, and average men with a bad conscience, all alike offer and accept foolish arguments.

Page 335. *that rock* . . . : this phrase refers to the sun.
Which turned the sun's wing'd chariot round . . . the legend

of the sun changing its direction is told also in Euripides'
Electra 726 ff.; but there it is said that the sun changed to
its present westward course, whereas here it is said to have
changed (temporarily, one assumes) to an eastward course.

Page 336. *For everyone, life's precious* . . .: including e.g. Hermione.

Page 337. *I wish one sword might kill us* . . .: this neurotic, morbid
utterance is made ironical by the pious 'if it were right' – a
strange scruple in the woman who speaks 1199.

Page 339. *making a list of all the valuables*: literally, 'sealing up everything'. Helen, Orestes implies, is sure that her husband
is going to inherit the palace of Argos, and is putting his
seal on cupboards and chests so that nothing will be stolen.

Page 340. *everyone whose son, or father* . . .: for the irony here see
Introduction, page 10.

Page 341. *I am the son of Agamemnon* . . .: compare the contrast between Demophon and Theseus in *The Children of Heracles*.
Athens in 408 is the son of Athens in 433 under the godlike Pericles. See Introduction, page 12.

Page 343. *Now, Electra, you stay here* . . .: this line echoes Aeschylus,
Choephori 554, as the triple invocation a little later echoes,
more closely, the invocation in *Choephori*.

Page 345. *I am going to listen* . . .: Editors are divided as to whether
this line means 'I am going to listen' or 'I am going to
shout'. Probably the former; the point of this passage is
Electra's nervous agitation, almost hysteria; and that after
listening and hearing nothing she should be unable to
resist shouting, is realistic.

Page 346. *O Zeus immortal* . . .: if Tyndareos was upset by the murder
of his daughter Clytemnestra, what does Electra think
will be Zeus' attitude to the murder of his daughter
Helen?

Page 348. *I hear the bolts being drawn*: an ancient commentator con-
cluded from 1371 ('climbing over the cedar-beams') that
the Phrygian made his entry by dropping down from the
triglyphs of the porch; and that later directors of the play,
finding this dangerous, inserted this line so that he could
suitably enter by the door. Some editors therefore regard
1366–8 as spurious.

Page 349. *Ailinon, ailinon*: a cry of mourning, which is used as a refrain in the opening Chorus of Aeschylus' *Agamemnon*.

IPHIGENIA IN AULIS

Page 367. The Oxford Text (ed. G. Murray) transposes lines 49–114 to form the opening of the play. See Introduction.

Lines 1–48, 115 ff. The rhythm of these lines roughly corresponds to that of the Greek anapaests in which these parts of the scene are written.

The winds are silent: a notable difference from the traditional story of stormy north-east winds.

Page 368. *Half-way to madness*: insanity is a recurring theme in this play, as in *Orestes*.

Page 381. *Take them, then*: again it is implied that there is no real difficulty in getting ships to Troy.

Page 383. *we are slaves to the masses*: another recurring theme is the question, Who is a free man, and who a slave?

O Paris, Paris: a variant on the regularity with which Euripidean characters blame Helen for the results of their own folly.

Page 384. *Your noble sentiments are worthy of Tantalus*: the crime for which Tantalus suffered his famous punishment was sometimes said to be infanticide, sometimes perjury. If the Chorus does not know this, the audience does.

Page 413. *'Defender of Men'*: this is the meaning of Paris' other name, Alexander.

Page 419. *I have considered . . .*: This line is missing in the MSS, and is conjecturally supplied.

MORE ABOUT PENGUINS
AND PELICANS

For further information about books available from Penguins
please write to Dept EP, Penguin Books Ltd, Harmondsworth, Middlesex UB7 0DA.

In the U.S.A.: For a complete list of books available from
Penguins in the United States write to Dept CS, Penguin
Books, 625 Madison Avenue, New York, New York 10022.

In Canada: For a complete list of books available from
Penguins in Canada write to Penguin Books Canada Ltd,
2801 John Street, Markham, Ontario L3R 1B4.

In Australia: For a complete list of books available from
Penguins in Australia write to the Marketing Department,
Penguin Books Australia Ltd, P.O. Box 257, Ringwood,
Victoria 3134.

AESCHYLUS
THE ORESTEIAN TRILOGY

Translated by Philip Vellacott

What is justice? How is it related to vengeance? Can justice be reconciled with the demands of religion, the violence of human feeling, the forces of Fate?

These questions, which puzzled thoughtful Athenians in the decades after the battle of Marathon, provided the theme for the *Agamemnon*, *The Choephori*, and *The Eumenides*, those grim tragedies that make up the Oresteian Trilogy. In these plays Aeschylus (525–456 B.C.) takes as his subject the bloody character of murder and revenge within the royal family of Argos – a chain finally broken only by the inter-vention of the goddess Athene. Philip Vellacott's verse translation makes available to the modern reader a mile-stone in the history of drama.

AESCHYLUS

PROMETHEUS BOUND
AND OTHER PLAYS

Translated by Philip Vellacott

Aeschylus (525–456 B.C.) was the first of the great Greek
tragedians. The four plays presented in this volume – together with the Oresteian Trilogy – are all that survive of
his work. *The Persians* is set against the Athenian victory at
Salamis, which took place only eight years before the play
was written. In *Seven Against Thebes* the two sons of Oedipus
are relentlessly pursued to their death by a family curse. But
in *The Suppliants* and *Prometheus* conflict of principle is resolved by rational compromise.

EURIPIDES
THE BACCHAE AND OTHER PLAYS

Translated by Philip Vellacott

Euripides (480–406 B.C.) is the most modern of the great Greek tragedians, as the four plays in this volume demonstrate. *Ion* is concerned with the problem of reconciling religious faith with the facts of human life, whilst *The Women of Troy* is a plain denunciation of the ruthlessness of war. In *Helen* Euripides light-heartedly parodied himself, and finally, in his last and probably greatest tragedy, *The Bacchae*, he dealt with mob violence and mass hysteria. Philip Vellacott's fluent translation and valuable introduction make it easier than ever for the modern reader to bridge the two thousand years between himself and these plays.

EURIPIDES
MEDEA AND OTHER PLAYS

Translated by Philip Vellacott

Four more plays by Euripides (484–406 B.C.) are presented in this volume in modern English by Philip Vellacott, who has already translated many of the great Greek dramas for the Penguin Classics.

Medea, the story of that princess's horrible revenge for the infidelity of Jason, the hero of the Argonauts, is Euripides' earliest surviving tragedy, whilst *Heracles* is among his latest plays. In *Hecabe* and *Electra* he again underlines the wickedness of revenge. An outspoken critic of society and the gods, Euripides was at his most eloquent on the theme of human suffering, and among the most lyrical of all poets.

EURIPIDES
ALCESTIS AND OTHER PLAYS

Translated by Philip Vellacott

Euripides (484–406 B.C.) is seen in the three plays in this
volume as the sceptical questioner of his age. *Alcestis*, an
early play in which a queen agrees to die to save her husband's life, is cast in a tragic vein, although it contains
passages of satire and even comedy, whilst *Iphigeneia in
Tauris*, with its apparently happy ending, melodramatically
re-unites the ill-fated children of Agamemnon. *Hippolytus*,
however, is pure tragedy – the fatal result of Phaedra's un-
reasoning passion for her chaste stepson. Philip Vellacott's
translations, in a blend of prose and verse, are designed for
the modern stage.

*Philip Vellacott has also translated
for the Penguin Classics*

Menander
PLAYS AND FRAGMENTS

Theophrastus
THE CHARACTERS

THE PENGUIN CLASSICS

Each year we are glad to add a few more titles to our ever-expanding list of Classics. This does not just mean works by Latin and Greek writers, but the most comprehensive collection ever of classic works from all countries – China, Japan, India and Iceland as well as Europe – all in new translations.

Here are some of the titles we are publishing in the next few months.

OVID

The Erotic Poems   *Translated by Peter Green*

The Orkneying Saga   *Translated by Hermann Palsson and Paul Edwards*

ZOLA

The Earth   *Translated by Douglas Parmée*

MARIVAUX

Up from the Country/Infidelities
The Game of Love and Chance
Translated by Leonard Tancock and David Cohen

Three Sanskrit Plays   *Translated by Michael Coulson*

SHIKIBU

The Tale of Genji
Volumes I and II
Translated by Edward Seidensticker